ST. LOUIS PLANS

The Ideal and the Real St. Louis

ST. LOUIS PLANS

The Ideal and the Real St. Louis

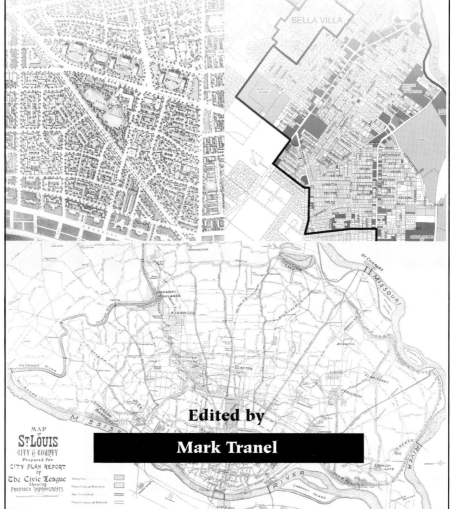

Edited by

Mark Tranel

Dedicated to the memory of Henry J. Schmandt
For his wisdom and goodwill

© 2007 by the Missouri Historical Society Press
All rights reserved 11 10 09 08 07 1 2 3 4 5

Library of Congress Cataloging-in-Publication Data

St. Louis plans : the ideal and the real St. Louis / edited by Mark Tranel.
    p. cm. -- (St. Louis metromorphosis series)
  Summary: "Reviews the history of various aspects of planning in St. Louis
City and County and provides insight into planning successes and challenges"--
Provided by publisher.
  Includes bibliographical references and index.
  ISBN 978-1-883982-61-4 (pbk. : alk. paper)
  1. City planning--Missouri--Saint Louis--History. 2. Regional planning--
Missouri--Saint Louis Metropolitan Area--History. 3. Regional planning--
Missouri--Saint Louis County--History. 4. Planning--Missouri--Saint Louis
Metropolitan Area--History. 5. Saint Louis Metropolitan Area (Mo.)--History.
6. Saint Louis County (Mo.)--History. I. Tranel, Mark, 1950- II. Missouri
Historical Society. III. Title: Saint Louis plans.
  HT168.S79S38 2007
  307.1'2160977866--dc22
                                    2007026838

Distributed by University of Missouri Press
Printed and bound by Thomson-Shore, Inc.

Table of Contents

Foreword

My work as a historian has often carried me into the realm of city planning and public policy. Projects with the Public Policy Research Center, Citizens for Modern Transit, the Urban League, and other organizations have heightened my interest in the processes that have made our city and our region the way it is. Having participated in the creation of the Forest Park Master Plan, I gained a new respect for the way St. Louis and its environs have developed. With everything I learn about this place, I feel my roots going deeper into this soil, making this place more deeply felt as "home."

To truly call a place "home" is to accept responsibility for the place. To be home is to be rooted, to have our very beings entangled with this place, and to finally understand that we cannot escape either the legacies or the burdens of the place. We cannot avoid the past of this place, and why would we if we could? It is the past of this place that makes it worth saving for the future, that sets it apart from all others and makes it special. Without the past, this place would just be a bluff at the confluence of great rivers.

"Home" is a set of reciprocal relationships with a place. Places sustain us; they anchor our memories, create continuity, and produce a special sense of belonging. We make our places, and they make us. They become reflections of us as we pour our lives into them, and we take on the habits, accents, behaviors, and values of our places. My body is more than ninety percent water, so because I live in St. Louis and drink its water, I am the Mississippi River. I am this place.

St. Louis Plans: The Ideal and the Real St. Louis takes us through a century of what St. Louisans thought was good for our community. We have the opportunity, with this array of articulate and knowledgeable authors, to see what worked, what never came to fruition, and what effects for good or ill the plans had on our city and, more important, on our community. Did they help or hinder St. Louis in becoming a good place for its people? How can we reconsider those choices and decisions and build on the legacies that St. Louis plans have left us?

The perusal of the wealth of planning devices that built, or proposed to build, our physical story is a fascinating exercise in the history of our place. It is another example of how the past has created the present. Taken further, it is clear that what we do with our own plans and choices will have a profound effect on what happens a hundred years down the road. Our job is to make that road as straight and smooth and durable as we possibly can.

ROBERT R. ARCHIBALD, PH.D.
PRESIDENT, MISSOURI HISTORICAL SOCIETY

Introduction

From Dreams to Reality: The Arch as Metaphor for St. Louis Plans[1]

Mark Tranel

> In our profession, a plan that everyone likes for different reasons is a success. A plan everyone dislikes for the same reason is a failure. And a plan everyone likes for the same reason is an act of God.—Richard Carson

This third volume in the *St. Louis Metromorphosis* series continues to tell the story, from an urban planning perspective, of how metropolitan St. Louis has changed and is changing. There are many factors that shape the St. Louis area. Relative to planning there are physical plans that determine the built environment, and there are plans by numerous organizations that determine what happens within the built environment. St. Louis has a rich history of both forms of planning that heretofore have not been documented collectively. Planning occurs at the regional, subregional, and neighborhood levels, as well as within specific sectors such as education, health care, and workforce development. One of the most dramatic planned changes ever to occur in St. Louis is the Jefferson National Expansion Memorial—the Gateway Arch and the parkland that surrounds it, including the Old Courthouse. The Gateway Arch is commonly acknowledged as a symbol for St. Louis, but it is more than that (Artibise 2000). It is also a metaphor for the process of planning.

The eighty-five-acre waterfront green space from which the Gateway Arch rises underwent a problematic transformation from its days as a bustling warehouse district to a national symbol of westward expansion. That

---

[1] "From Dreams to Reality" was the headline of an editorial in the *St. Louis Globe-Democrat,* February 8, 1935, a copy of which is in the 1935 report *Jefferson National Expansion Memorial* by the United States Territorial Expansion Memorial Commission.

1

same physical space was from the 1820s to the 1860s the literal heart not only of St. Louis but also of the western territory of the United States. Goods from the eastern United States arrived on steamboats and were prepared for overland shipment to the developing western territories. After a fire in 1849 that destroyed most of the commercial structures that served the steamboat traffic at the port of St. Louis, more than four hundred three- to four-story brick buildings were built in the area bounded by Third Street on the west, Mill Creek (present-day Chouteau Avenue) on the south, and Washington Avenue on the north. This commercial center also included housing, business services, and governmental institutions.

Change is, however, a fundamental characteristic of the urban environment. Two changes profoundly affected the riverfront commercial district of St. Louis. First, like the territory it served, St. Louis began to expand westward. Banks, hotels, housing, and a growing manufacturing industry began to expand well beyond the riverfront. And second, by 1870 a rapid transformation in transportation technology, from riverboats to railroads, left the built environment of the St. Louis waterfront an economic anachronism. While the riverfront languished, St. Louis experienced growth and change in the era of the railroad and manufacturing. The population nearly doubled between 1860 and 1870. After a pause in the 1870s, it grew from 350,000 in 1880 to over 575,000 by 1900. St. Louis, like other large cities, had become densely populated, unhealthful, and, some argued, ugly. While it had fashionable residential locations such as Lucas Place and Vandeventer Place, many residents lived in abject poverty in areas known as Clabber Alley and Castle Thunder (Primm 1990).

Nationally, the response to wretched urban conditions from the professions of architecture, engineering, and landscape architecture was to spearhead park development, housing reform, the City Beautiful movement, and the Garden City movement (Lubove 1970). What these movements shared was a belief in public intervention: The public sector should develop open space in cities; the public sector should regulate housing conditions; the public sector should develop grand boulevards and civic infrastructure. A theme of these movements was the democratization of urban life. It was their professional argument that everyone should have access to environmental amenities and safe housing, not just the few who lived in mansions.

These were not idle belief systems. These professionals acted to change the built environment and improve the quality of urban life. As shown in Figure 1, the various professions that responded to these problems coalesced to become the American planning profession in the first decade of the twentieth century.

Figure 1. Antecedents of Contemporary Planning

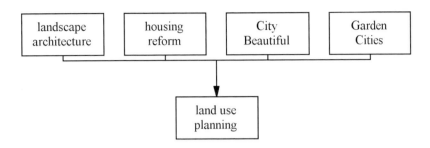

Planner Alexander Garvin defines three forms of twentieth century planning: project by project; comprehensive city strategies; and process—proposals changed in response to public demand and financial reality (Garvin 2006). Garvin prefers the project-based accomplishments of Robert Moses or Daniel Burnham to the utopian high-density Radiant City concept of Le Corbusier or low-density Garden City philosophy of Ebenezer Howard. "However much planning was inspired by imaginary dream cities, public action to improve cities throughout the twentieth century has consisted of projects, plans, and processes that grew out of the requirements of implementation rather than the images of an ideal future" (Garvin 2006, xii).

The story of urban planning can be told in biographies. Planning traces its lineage back as far as the Egyptian Imhotep in 2600 B.C., a great project planner, and Vitruvius in first century B.C. Rome, one of the earliest proponents of the radial form of the ideal city (Hugo-Brunt 1972). Imhotep is not, however, much of a role model for planning today. He was the architect/planner for a centralized powerful theocracy. American urban planning evolved from the work of landscape architects like George E. Kessler and Frederick Law Olmstead, architects like Daniel Burnham and Julius F. Harder, and social reformers such as Charles Mulford Robinson (Scott 1969).

The Gateway Arch is a project-based plan that can be related through the biographies of two men, Bernard Dickmann and Luther Ely Smith, encapsulated in the history of the plan for the Jefferson National Expansion Memorial, site of the Gateway Arch. While there are many people who played a significant role in what happened and how it happened, Dickmann and Smith started the project, shaped it, and sustained it.

In defining the planning process, Garvin stipulates six ingredients that "must be intelligently dealt with for any project to succeed." The ingredients are time, location, entrepreneurship, financing, market, and design. These were all critical factors in the planning and implementation of the Gateway Arch and its grounds.

Time

Garvin identifies three time sequences that affect the success of a project—first, the time during which a person passes through an area; second, what will occur in an area twenty-four hours a day, seven days a week; and, third, what occurs over the long term. It is this third dimension, the most extended time sequence, that must be considered regarding not just the success of the Gateway Arch but even its existence. This was a project literally decades in the making.

Aerial View of St. Louis Riverfront before Clearance.
Photograph, 1932. MHS Photographs and Prints.

The process started with a meeting of civic leaders in the office of St. Louis mayor Bernard Dickmann on December 15, 1933, to discuss creating a national memorial to Thomas Jefferson and his role in acquiring and leading to the settlement of the American West. They quickly embraced the idea, and in April 1934 the State of Missouri incorporated the Jefferson National Expansion Memorial Association (JNEMA). With the supportive action of the Missouri congressional delegation, federal legislation was adopted and on June 15, 1934, President Roosevelt signed the bill establishing the United States Territorial Expansion Memorial Commission (USTEMC). In January 1935, St. Louis architect Louis LaBeaume proposed the concept of an architectural competition to select a design for the memorial. On April 13, 1935, the USTEMC executive committee approved plans for the memorial—its boundaries, the historical significance, the architectural competition, and a cost estimate of $30 million. The full commission approved the plans on May 1, 1935. It had taken less than eighteen months to produce a plan and an organizational structure responsible for implementing it.

The keystone section of the Arch was installed on October 28, 1965, more than thirty years later. What happened over those thirty years shows the importance of Garvin's other five elements of a successful plan and, although somewhat extreme, is representative of public planning processes in metropolitan St. Louis.

Location

The two key factors of location for Garvin are a site's inherent characteristics and its proximity to other locations. The parkland that is now the Jefferson National Expansion Memorial was a naturally bounded area when, in 1763, Pierre Laclede Liguest chose it as the site for a fur trading post because of its innate characteristics that readily supported river-based economic activity. A limestone bluff rose along the Mississippi River's bank, providing both direct access to the river and a substantial land area that would never flood. There was a forested area that extended west to approximately today's Fourth Street and south to Mill Creek.

From the very beginning, this area was laid out with a grid system of north-south and east-west streets. It developed slowly over the next eighty years, a mixture of commercial and residential buildings. The genesis of the warehouse district that occupied the land when the Jefferson National Expansion Memorial first was proposed was several multistory stone warehouses in 1829, a dozen years after the first steamboat landed on the shore of the Mississippi River (St. Louis City Plan Commission 1969). The commercial buildings obliterated residential development close to the riverfront, as by 1850 St. Louis became the second-largest port in the country, as measured by tonnage. Some of this volume of cargo was due to the growth of St. Louis itself, but most of it was goods transported overland for destinations in the developing western territories of the Louisiana Purchase.

Virtually the exact site of what would become the Jefferson National Expansion Memorial was leveled by a fire in 1849. Brick buildings of three to four stories were built after the fire (St. Louis City Plan Commission 1969). Even after this disaster, the commercial buildings were rebuilt without sprinkler systems. This proved to be an enormous liability affecting occupancy fifty years later.

A precipitous decline in commercial riverboat traffic began with the westward expansion of rail service after the Civil War. It didn't take long after the completion of the transcontinental railroad for the commercial district close by the port of St. Louis to become the city's first urban problem. The forty blocks of mid-nineteenth-century structures were physically obsolete, and the active market in real estate development had moved out to Jefferson Avenue by this time.

Interest in redevelopment of the waterfront dated to at least 1880, but for decades amounted to nothing more than an expression of hope. This was based on the negative side of Garvin's proximity measure of location. The deteriorating warehouse district on the riverfront was becoming a liability for the rest of the downtown area surrounding it. A combination of civic pride and concern about adjacent property values led to expressions of concern about such a large area of decay in such a prominent area of St. Louis. In 1898, it was proposed that the site be used to commemorate the one hundredth anniversary of the Louisiana Purchase with the reconstruction of the original fur trading village. This idea evolved into the 1904 World's Fair, which was held entirely in Forest Park and made no use of the riverfront.

In the early twentieth century, there were a number of formal plans, none of which were implemented. The 1928 City Plan Commission's *A Plan for the Central Riverfront—St. Louis* included a project to acquire all the property from Third Street to the river from Spruce Street to Franklin Avenue for a riverfront plaza (Duffy 1995). The 1933 *A Plan for the Central Riverfront* expanded the property acquisition area to Morgan Street and Clark Avenue, largely for the purpose of parking for six thousand "or more" automobiles. The plan found this to be an improved use for the property given its deterioration due to the city's westward growth, decline of early forms of river traffic, inaccessibility due to narrow streets and steep grades, and obsolescence of large numbers of buildings.

It was not until the 1930s that there was not only a plan, but also action.

Entrepreneurship

As stated earlier, the dream and the reality of a national memorial on the St. Louis riverfront can be traced in the biographies of two men: a civic leader named Bernard F. Dickmann, mayor of the City of St. Louis from 1933 to 1941, and a civic entrepreneur, Luther Ely Smith, by profession a lawyer and by politics an independent Republican in a city of Democrats. On some aspects of the riverfront memorial the two men worked together and on others they divided the labor.

Garvin notes that it is the "extra drive" of entrepreneurs that turns urban plans into successful projects. Of the two key players in the redevelopment of the St. Louis riverfront as a site with worldwide recognition, Smith was the more extraordinary. As mayor, Dickmann was elected to take action on behalf of the city. Smith, however, was a citizen volunteer.

Smith had prior experience as a commissioner for a national memorial located outside of Washington, D.C. He served as a member of a commission that developed the national memorial to Revolutionary War hero George Rogers Clark in Vincennes, Indiana. He had previous experience in open-space development, having organized an Open-Air Playground Committee. This committee developed the first municipal playgrounds in St. Louis (National Park Service 2001). He was not just a tireless civic volunteer; he was most often in the leadership position, including his service as chairman of the Citizen's City Plan Commission.

Smith took the initiative to contact Dickmann about redeveloping the riverfront after viewing the largely abandoned warehouse district while returning to St. Louis by train. The original plan he proposed was a City Beautiful park centering a Washington Mall–type monument in a large open space. Dickmann called a meeting of civic leaders, and agreement was quickly reached to organize. Dickmann and Smith provided the leadership that incorporated the JNEMA to be responsible for St. Louis–based efforts and secured the commitment of federal legislators to establish the USTEMC to be responsible for efforts at the federal level. Although the association and the commission had dozens of members between them and a host of elected officials and agency staff worked on the project, Dickmann and Smith provided the extra drive.

An entrepreneur is "one who organizes, manages, and assumes the risks of a business or enterprise" (Webster's 1965). The risks organizing and managing a public project to redevelop eighty-five acres of private land on the St. Louis riverfront as a national memorial were enormous. The scale of the project was beyond the capacity of the City of St. Louis to finance, implement, and maintain. It involved securing local and national funding; acquiring hundreds of parcels of property; relocating an arterial rail line; and selecting a design for the memorial. There were multiple obstacles involved with each of these project components. Through it all, Dickmann and Smith assumed the responsibility to sustain the project.

The story of the incredible challenges faced by Dickmann and Smith has been told in exceptional detail by Sharon Brown in "Jefferson National Expansion Memorial Administrative History, 1935–1981" (1984). While they did not face the physical trials of Lewis and Clark, the crises faced by Dickmann and Smith in building a memorial to westward expansion were every bit as great as the Corps of Discovery in first exploring the territory.

Dickmann's efforts were critical in maintaining congressional support for the project. Smith was pivotal in negotiating funding through a federal bureaucratic maze, in securing funding for the association, and ultimately in raising the local funds for the design competition. The detail of the processes of securing funding described in the next section is indicative of not only these two men's efforts, but also their entrepreneurial skills.

Financing

St. Louis architect Louis LaBeaume, working with Smith on the JNEMA, developed a budget of $20 million to create Smith's vision for the memorial. With another $10 million for land acquisition and demolition, the project faced an early estimated cost of $30 million. Local funding toward this cost came fairly quickly. On April 15, 1935, the Missouri legislature authorized the City of St. Louis to vote on $7.5 million in bonds, on the condition that federal funds match the bond proceeds at a three-to-one ratio. St. Louis voters approved the bonds on September 10, 1935. Bonds were sold in May 1936, just twenty-nine months after the first meeting in Mayor Dickmann's office.

Federal funding was much more complicated. In 1934, Missouri representatives and senators unsuccessfully attempted to secure the funding directly from Congress. The USTEMC approved the plans for the memorial on May 1, 1935, including the budget. The Commission, however, had no resources to commit to the project. At this point, the project would have lapsed had not Smith's "extra drive" kicked in. "All through June [1935], Smith kept the memorial alive by having Association and Commission members write to government officials" (Brown 1984).

Dickmann and Smith thus began a long and circuitous path to securing the federal funding. One of the challenges was that they were seeking two types of funding—not only the immediate $2.25 million needed to match the money approved by St. Louis voters for the monument, but also a long-term commitment to operate and maintain the memorial.

The most viable federal funding source for construction of the memorial turned out to be Depression relief funds. The obvious choice for operation and maintenance was the National Park Service (NPS). Relief funds were administered through several federal agencies. At the time that local interest in securing funds for the Jefferson National Expansion Memorial was at a peak, the federal agencies were just being set up. Dickmann and Smith spent considerable time determining how Works Progress Administration (WPA) funds could be disbursed and by whom.

The most detrimental issue at this point was an opinion from the U.S. attorney general. A project of the scope of the Jefferson National Expansion Memorial would take years to complete. Congress budgets money one year at a time, and it was the attorney general's opinion that the president could not authorize a project dependent on future funding from Congress. This problem required Dickmann's political finesse. He appealed to the attorney general in his role not as counsel to the government, but as a Democratic national committeeman. He advised the attorney general that if President Roosevelt did not provide the funds for this critical St. Louis project, as mayor of St. Louis he could not guarantee that he could deliver enough votes for Roosevelt to carry St. Louis in the upcoming 1936 election. Using authority granted in the Historic Sites Act that Congress had just approved, on December 21, 1935, Roosevelt signed Executive Order 7253, allocating $3.3 million in WPA funds and $3.45 million in PWA funds for site acquisition. With the $2.25 million from City bonds, the project had $9 million, which technically became available in February 1936.

This proved to be sufficient for acquisition of the land and demolition of the buildings, which was accomplished over the next several years despite a number of local lawsuits. A standstill followed the initial momentum; for a number of reasons there was no action on developing the memorial for the next two decades. World War II suspended any federal attention and resources. But perhaps more important, the project lost its two champions. Bernard Dickmann's last year as mayor was 1941. And ten years later, Luther Ely Smith died of a heart attack while walking to his office. Other civic and political leaders labored to complete the project.

In 1958, city and federal officials negotiated a $23 million total budget for the project: $17.25 million in federal funds and the balance from the

City of St. Louis. It took four federal funding appropriations over a period of several years, but by 1961 all of the federal funding was committed to the project.

Market

Garvin defines market as "a specific population's desire for something and its ability and willingness to pay for it in the face of available alternatives." In the case of a publicly planned and managed project, the willingness to pay means willingness to pay taxes. As just described in the financing of the Jefferson National Expansion Memorial, the initial market for the site was public.

Although there was controversy over its outcome, to the degree that supporting taxes is a measure of a public market for a planned project, the results of the 1935 bond issue election document a local public market for redevelopment of the riverfront as a national memorial.

As the site was being cleared, and particularly once all the structures except the Old Cathedral and the Old Courthouse were removed, a number of alternative uses were proposed. A proposal was made to construct a

St. Louis Riverfront after Clearance.
Photograph by Ted McCrea, 1948. MHS Photographs and Prints.

temporary landing strip for experimental aircraft, but no formal action ever was taken. It was suggested in the 1950s that the site was the only open area large enough to accommodate the bomb shelter needs for downtown St. Louis. There were proposals for housing development and a sports stadium. It was used for over a decade as a parking lot for over 3,500 cars.

On every occasion that an alternative use was proposed, the memorial project retained enough support among both local and national leaders to deflect serious consideration of anything other than the national expansion memorial.

Design

It is Garvin's expressed belief that design is the most misunderstood element of successful planning. Design is not just the physical manifestation of any project, integral to its success or failure from the time of inception, but also the arrangement of the project components, and the relative character and size of those components.

The Jefferson National Expansion Memorial was a particularly complex project because it involved seven design elements:

- an architectural monument
- preservation of the site of Old St. Louis
- creation of a living memorial to Thomas Jefferson
- encouragement of active use of the open space
- provision of on-site parking
- relocation of railroad tracks
- accessibility of the site given the pending construction of an interstate highway through the western edge of the site.

The design had to incorporate the two purposes that had evolved in the development of the project. Congress created the USTEMC and authorized it to create a national expansion memorial. The Historic Sites Act, authorizing the NPS to create a national historic site, provided the funding for the project. These two purposes were not inherently in conflict but they were subject to potentially different interpretations in design.

John Nagle was the site manager for the NPS, in effect the federal administrative director for the project. His design concepts became the planning principles for the ultimate memorial project. His first principle was that preservation of any structures within the eighty-five acres would be determined by their significance to national events, not to St. Louis history. Second, there would be as little development on the site as possible, creating a memorial that was primarily open space. Third, there had to be a physical connection of the memorial with the Mississippi River. Fourth, the monument would symbolize St. Louis's role as "Gateway to the West." And, fifth, there should be a national competition for the architectural design of the monument.

Indicative of the problems faced by this complex project, the NPS, as administrator of the project, had the authority to determine the design but it didn't select the architect. Due to the slow action on the part of the federal agencies in the mid-1940s, Smith had encouraged the St. Louis-based JNEMA to proceed with selecting a design for the memorial. Not without difficulties, the Association proceeded to raise $225,000 to fund a competition.

In September 1947, the competition was launched, and 172 entries were submitted. The competition's jurors selected five finalists after four days of deliberations. The jury then chose a winner.

Unanimously, the jury selected the design of Eero Saarinen. He had proposed a stainless steel arch, located on an axis with the Old Courthouse, rising from a tree-lined mall, connected to the Mississippi River by a grand staircase.

Although the design incorporated a plan for the entire eighty-five-acre site, it was this structure, the basic geometric shape of a catenary curve applied to the central monument, that has come to symbolize the project. Although it would be almost two decades before construction of the monument would be completed, Luther Ely Smith wrote to Eero Saarinen in 1948, "It was your design, your marvelous conception, your brilliant forecast into the future, that has made the realization of the dream possible" (National Park Service 2001).

The Plan of the Volume

The chapters that follow tell many more stories about land use plans and organizational plans that have been significant in shaping the present St. Louis. They are organized into two groups. The first traces the history of planning in the City of St. Louis and St. Louis County, and to some extent the metropolitan region, through most of the twentieth century. The second examines planning for specific sectors including economic development, education, social services, transportation, and workforce.

The publication of this volume purposefully coincides with the one hundredth anniversary of the 1907 Civic League plan. In Chapter 1, "A Document That Changed America," Mark Abbott asserts the national importance of *A City Plan for St. Louis* as a democratic comprehensive plan. The plan is distinguished as an urban constitution, developed not by the city government but rather by a group of citizen committees and by its comprehensive structure, consolidating in one planning document what previously had always been dealt with as separate planning components.

The City's comprehensive plan would next be updated four decades later. In Chapter 4, titled "The 1947 *Comprehensive City Plan* and Harland Bartholomew's St. Louis," Abbott details the far-reaching effects of this plan and something of the man who wrote it. In Chapter 3, Joseph Heathcott provides more insight into Harland Bartholomew and how St. Louis shaped him as much as he shaped St. Louis. Charles Kindleberger brings the story up to date in Chapter 5, "Planning Since the 1970s in the City of St. Louis." He highlights the influence of both the chief elected officer and the professional planner, played out against the backdrop of changing regulations and funding from the federal government.

"Ahead of the Curve?: Planning in St. Louis County, 1930–2000," Chapter 6, by E. Terrence Jones recounts not only the changes in St. Louis County as it grew and then stabilized, but also the changes in the planning profession as it shifted its attention from land to people. Jones details the experience of a suburban county attempting to adopt principles for growth in a market environment expanding and changing at a very fast pace.

Don Phares chronicles, in Chapter 2's "Planning for Regional Governance in the St. Louis Area," the initiatives to plan governmental reorganization for St. Louis City and St. Louis County. The chapter describes that planning is not just about land use and physical infrastructure. Phares emphasizes that the form of government is key to distribution of resources to fund public services.

William E. Winter describes another planning process with a regional focus initiated in the mid-1990s by St. Louis civic and corporate leaders in Chapter 7, "Civic Planning in St. Louis: The Case of St. Louis 2004." Organized by a deliberately temporary nonprofit organization with a goal of civic transformation to mark the centenary of the 1904 St. Louis World's Fair, this planning process included extensive citizen engagement in developing goals in eleven key areas. Winter identifies how the plans in these areas succeeded or failed along the lines of existing government and governance structures.

In the first of the chapters on sectoral plans, Robert M. Lewis's "Economic Development Planning in Metropolitan St. Louis," Chapter 8, elucidates the difference between proactive and reactive planning. In the area of economic development, planning in St. Louis often responded to changes caused either by economic cycles or the evolution of the national economy from a manufacturing to a service base. Lewis traces the growth of networking among economic development professionals that evolved in response to the challenges posed by these changes.

The four authors (Carole Murphy, Helene Sherman, Chris Wright, and Diana Bourisaw) of Chapter 9, "Aspects of Educational Planning for Public Schools in St. Louis County," detail the differing planning approaches to training superintendents and teachers and to planning in St. Louis County districts compared to St. Louis Public Schools.

Richard Patton's Chapter 10 "Social Planning in the St. Louis Region" shows both the challenges to planning for social services compared to the more robust land use planning and to planning for social services in the St. Louis community.

"Pursuing an Elusive End: Highway and Transit Planning in St. Louis," Chapter 11, by Jerry Blair, shows the persistent problem of planning for transportation in the absence of a regional land use plan. St. Louis's lack of such a plan leaves transportation planners at the beginning of the twenty-first century responding to congestion and ineffective transit, as did their predecessors at the beginning of the twentieth century.

David Laslo focuses on the latter half of the twentieth century in Chapter 12, "The Challenges to Workforce Development Planning in Postwar St. Louis." Similar to Blair's discussion of the impact of not having a regional land use plan, Laslo cites the significance of not having a workforce goal, a gap for which he suggests global competitiveness.

Several themes run through the independent work of these authors. The most notable is the persistent discussion of the level of citizen participation in St. Louis plans. From the 1907 Civic League plan to St. Louis 2004, St. Louis has a tradition of civic-initiated and -produced plans, a number of which incorporate some level of regional issues. In addition to citizen initiative, many of the formal planning processes by City or County agencies include outreach to the community.

Planning processes that incorporate citizen participation do not, however, guarantee equity in access to the process, or influence in the adoption of a plan. Disadvantaged populations on several demographic dimensions have been, for a number of reasons, at best underrepresented, if represented at all, in both land use and organizational planning processes. Those citizens who do participate often find they have had little or no impact on adoption of plans.

As these chapters detail, planners often experience the same frustration. The authors identify a number of issues, governmental structure most prominent among them, that limit not only the effectiveness of citizen input but also that of the planning professionals. Despite evidence of the technical proficiency of the planners at projecting community change and needs (although they are not flawless), their policy recommendations are not accepted in many cases.

Planning scholar Susan Fainstein observes that planning theory has achieved a level of optimism at the beginning of the twenty-first century. Partially in reaction to the frustration cited above, planners had in the latter decades of the twentieth century expressed more critique of the policy process than practice of directed intervention. Fainstein notes a return to the roots of the activism of Burnham, Kessler, and Robinson in the late nineteenth century (Fainstein 2000).

The cry often is heard that St. Louis lacks leadership. To the degree that they meet Reubin Askew's definition that "a leader is someone who cares enough to tell the people not merely what they want to hear, but what they need to know," professional planners provided leadership throughout the twentieth century. From Harland Bartholomew and his small staff in the 1940s to the current substantial staffs in a number of city, county, and nonprofit agencies, planners have made a practice of telling the St. Louis community what it needs to know. Perhaps a goal for St. Louis for the twenty-first century is for the community to listen to the planners, in response.

References

Artibise, Alan. *The Arch as Symbol: Reflections on the Meaning and Value of a Monument*. St. Louis: University of Missouri–St. Louis Public Policy Research Center, 2000.

Brown, Sharon. "Jefferson National Expansion Memorial Administrative History, 1935–1981." 1984. http://www.cr.nps.gov/history/online_books/jeff/adhit.htm (accessed June 1, 2007).

City of St. Louis. "A Preservation Plan for St. Louis." 1996. http://stlouis.missouri.org/government/heritage/ (accessed June 1, 2007).

Duffy, Robert. "Riverfront Plans." 1995. http://stlouis.missouri.org/government/duffy/riverfront.html.

Fainstein, Susan S. "New Directions in Planning Theory." *Urban Affairs Review* 34 (2000): 451–478.

Garvin, Alexander. *The American City: What Works, What Doesn't*. New York: McGraw-Hill, 2002.

———. "Planning Now for the Twenty-first Century." In *Urban Planning Today*, edited by William S. Saunders. Minneapolis: University of Minnesota Press, 2006.

Houghton-Evans, William. *Planning Cities: Legacy and Portent*. London: Lawrence and Wishart, 1975.

Hugo-Brunt, Michael. *This History of City Planning*. Montreal: Harvest House, 1972.

Jefferson National Expansion Memorial Association. *Progress Report of the Jefferson National Expansion Memorial*. St. Louis: Author, 1940.

Lubove, Roy. "The Roots of Urban Planning." In *The Urbanization of America: An Historical Anthology*, edited by Allen Wakstein. Boston: Houghton Mifflin, 1970.

McElroy, Paul Simpson. *The Story of the Gateway Arch*. St. Louis: B. Herder, 1968.

National Park Service. "Luther Ely Smith, Founder of a Memorial." *Museum Gazette*, March 31, 2001. http://www.nps.gov/jeff/historyculture/upload/luther_ely_smith.pdf (accessed June 1, 2007).

National Park Service. Map of the Jefferson National Expansion Memorial Showing Various Historic Sites and Buildings. 4th ed. 1939.

Primm, James Neal. *Lion of the Valley*. Boulder, CO: Pruett, 1990.

Scott, Mel. *American City Planning Since 1890*. Berkeley: University of California Press, 1969.

St. Louis City Plan Commission. *Physical Growth of the City of St. Louis*. 1969. http://stlouis.missouri.org/heritage/History69/index.html.

United States Territorial Expansion Memorial Commission. *Jefferson National Expansion Memorial*. St. Louis: Author, 1935.

Webster's Seventh New Collegiate Dictionary. Springfield, MA: G. & C. Merriam, 1965.

Chapter 1
A Document That Changed America: The 1907 *A City Plan for St. Louis*

Mark Abbott

Ideals are like stars: you will not succeed in touching them with your hands, but choosing them as your guides and following them you will reach your destiny.—Carl Schurz (St. Louis Civic League 1907, 2)[1]

On the opening page of the 1907 *A City Plan for St. Louis*, Henry Kent, president of the Executive Board of the St. Louis Civic League, told his fellow St. Louisans that the League had decided in November 1905 to appoint a committee that would "consider the feasibility and scope of a *comprehensive* city plan" (author's italics) and that the committee had reported back that "a city plan for St. Louis was not only feasible but most essential and desirable" (St. Louis Civic League 1907, 7). Just as the shots fired at Lexington on April 19, 1775, started a revolution, these lines were the opening salvo of a revolution that would not only transform city planning in the United States, but would fundamentally alter American political culture in ways that are reverberating yet today.

Up until 1907, planning in the United States had been done in a piecemeal fashion. There had been park plans and street plans, as well as civic center plans. But *A City Plan for St. Louis* was the first master or comprehensive plan. For Kent and the other members of the Executive Board, bundling the various reports that composed the plan into a bound volume was not merely an act of efficiency. It was a deliberate strategy to treat

---

[1]St. Louis Civic League, *A City Plan for Saint Louis: Reports of the Several Committees Appointed by the Executive Board of the Civic League to Draft a City Plan* (St. Louis: Woodward and Tiernan, 1907).

the city as a coherent, integrated whole. Just like a living organism, the functions of one component of the city affected all others. As a result, the elements of the city had to be planned in a comprehensive fashion. However, the master plan did more than imply that the physical elements had to be treated as an integrated whole. It was a tacit argument that the people of the city not only lived next to one another, but their lives were intimately intertwined as an integrated whole, as well. In short, the city existed as "a" community that functioned as a single entity with a discernible identity and set of interests. The plan, therefore, was more than a blueprint for how to lay out the city's streets or where to place public buildings. It existed as the voice of the people. This idea would influence planning and American politics for the next century.

"For Your Consideration": Statement of the Executive Board

After the title page, *A City Plan for St. Louis* listed the committees created by the St. Louis Civic League and their members who worked on the plan. It read as a "who's who in St. Louis." The St. Louis Civic League was formed by Louis Marion McCall in 1901 as the St. Louis Improvement Association and quickly attracted a variety of professionals who were interested in an array of Progressive Movement causes such as model tenements, health and sanitation ordinances, charter revision, public bathhouses, and city playgrounds.[2] City planning was something that many members had become interested in through various initiatives leading up to the 1904 World's Fair.[3] The League was intimately involved in the city cleanup campaign for the Fair, as well as being supportive of the construction of a temporary viaduct on Kingshighway to improve Fair access from the southern half of the city. In addition, the majority of the League was undoubtedly impressed—as most Fairgoers were—by the model future street at the Fair. Featuring a wide curvilinear street, with uniform building setbacks and neoclassical structures, the model was intended as a way of demonstrating the most current planning ideas. It was not surprising, then, that the League was the body that spearheaded the movement to write a plan in 1907.

---

[2]For more background on the Civic League, see James Neal Primm, *Lion of the Valley: St. Louis, Missouri* (2nd ed., Boulder, CO: Pruett, 1990), 402–434.

[3]For an overview of the historical background of city planning in the United States, see Mel Scott, *American City Planning Since 1890: A History Commemorating the Fiftieth Anniversary of the American Institute of Planners* (Berkeley: University of California Press, 1971) and Daniel Schaffer, ed., *Two Centuries of American Planning* (Baltimore: Johns Hopkins University Press, 1988).

The plan was prepared by six committees. The General Committee that was to oversee the coordination of the reports had six members and was chaired by William Trelease, who was the director of the Missouri Botanical Garden. The other members were also quite prominent, such as John Davis, who was a vice president at the Mississippi Valley Trust Company, a large banking and real estate interest in St. Louis. Another well-known committee member was Dwight Davis, who was on the Library and Public Bath Commission.

Apart from Trelease, each of the General Committee members chaired one of the five other committees. The most star-studded committee was Inner and Outer Parks. It was chaired by John Davis, but also included Robert Brookings, the chairman of the board at Washington University, and Enos Clarke, the president of the League itself. In addition, it included the nationally recognized landscape architect George Kessler, who had designed park and boulevard systems throughout the Midwest.

The committee on Civic Centers was also impressive. Besides Dwight Davis, the chair, the committee included Mrs. Philip N. Moore, the former president of Wednesday Club, a prominent middle-class reform group in St. Louis. Like the Parks committee, it included a nationally known landscape architect, Henry Wright. Though he was still very interested in urban design, Wright was becoming more interested in the social aspects of city planning and was spearheading a national effort to have planning encompass social issues, as the Civic Centers report reflected.

While the other committees were not made up of such recognizable names, they were still represented by some of the most prominent St. Louisans. The Street Improvements Committee was chaired by J. Charless Cabanne, a local businessman, and included Theodore Link, a well-known local architect, and James C. Travilla, the superintendent of the Street Department. John Lawrence Mauran, a local architect and chair of the Public Buildings Commission, chaired the Municipal Art Committee. The final committee was the Legislation Committee, chaired by John Lee, president of the St. Louis Bar Association. The other members of this committee were four local lawyers, one of whom was Luther Ely Smith, who would later become famous for his work leading to the creation of the Jefferson National Expansion Memorial and the Gateway Arch.

There was no Public Buildings Committee, even though there was a Public Buildings report. The report had been prepared in 1904 by the Public Buildings Commission, which had been established by the mayor, as one of the many initiatives that emerged out of the Fair. While the League did not technically author the report, John Lawrence Mauran, the chair of the Municipal Art Committee, was the chair of the report and was seen from the beginning as fundamental to the plan. Like the Parks and Civic Centers committee, the Public Buildings reports had involved a nationally known figure, the local architect William S. Eames, who became famous for the design of many St. Louis public schools.

Even though the committees included some of the most important people in St. Louis, the Executive Board announced that whether or not the plan would ever be implemented was up to the citizens of St. Louis. The plan had been published and bound, the Executive Board told their fellow citizens, in order that they could "present [it] for your consideration" (St. Louis Civic League 1907, 7). As Kent and the members of the Board made clear, they were able to speak for the citizens because they were of them. As they explained, the plan had been prepared by "forty-two citizens representing almost every profession and interest in the city" (St. Louis Civic League 1907, 7).

They were writing the plan now, the Board argued, for fiscal expediency and out of concern for the future direction of the city. "While the report is issued at this particular time with the hope it will furnish suggestions for the public improvements contemplated in the recent $1,200,000 bond issue, its primary object is to supply this city with a plan which will to some extent, direct its future development along right lines" (St. Louis Civic League 1907, 8). They were not some group of wide-eyed Pollyannas. They knew that the plan could not guarantee that the city would be a perfect place. For Kent and the Board, the plan did not even have the power to make the city a better place. As the Board inferred, the plan was nothing more—but nothing less—than an overall strategy to deal with the challenges and opportunities that industrialization and growth had presented to St. Louis. Just as with a general directing an army, a strategy—a plan—did not win a war. Only the soldiers—the citizens—could do that. But like winning a war, building a city that reflected their desires demanded a strategy—a plan—that would coordinate resources to maximize their impact.

To continue the military analogy, the Board felt that a city the size of St. Louis could not hold its position as the fourth-largest city in the United States by fighting one battle at a time and neglecting to see the big picture. As the Board noted, "the piecemeal policy which has characterized [St. Louis's] past growth can no longer be permitted if this city is to retain her position as one of the great American municipalities" (St. Louis Civic League 1907, 8). Like other cities, industrialization had necessarily made St. Louis much more interdependent. It was not like a bunch of grapes, made up of disparate, self-contained parts. The industrial city was a big machine where all of the components needed to work together. To plan the city required that all of the pieces of this great machine fit together in a precise, harmonious fashion.

Trying to convince their fellow St. Louisans that a comprehensive plan was critical, the Board insisted that time was of the essence. If St. Louis's population was extrapolated a half generation into the future, Kent and the Board noted, St. Louis would double its population to 1.25 million and would physically expand to Clayton or Kirkwood within twenty-five years (a very accurate prediction if suburban annexation had occurred). As a result the Board concluded, "a fundamental plan to meet the needs of this growth is necessary" (St. Louis Civic League 1907, 8).

For the Board, possessing a plan to direct the future was a question of survival. "The industrial future of the city demands it," they declared (St. Louis Civic League 1907, 8). Maybe in an earlier day, cities could prosper by chance and the public and private realms could be considered two separate worlds. But that day was over, the Board maintained. "A city can not, in the modern sense of the word," they made clear, "maintain a high commercial standing unless it maintains, at the same time, a high civic life" (St. Louis Civic League 1907, 8). An orderly public buildings group, ample open space, an integrated transportation network, an attractive and accessible riverfront, and ordinances to prevent unsightly signage were not frivolous amenities. In the minds of Kent and his fellow Board members, St. Louis was in a fight to the death with its rivals and "if one city makes itself more inviting than its neighbor it is bound to attract more people" (St. Louis Civic League 1907, 9). It was a fight St. Louis had to win at whatever cost. "If St. Louis doesn't plan now," Kent explained, "it will have to later at higher cost." While what they were proposing was expensive—$25,000,000 or roughly three quarters of a billion in 2007 dollars—such a plan would actually save the citizens money because it would "furnish a guide" so that this money would be spent wisely and effectively to win this war (St. Louis Civic League 1907, 9).

As we celebrate the hundredth anniversary of this amazing document, it is apparent that the arguments the Civic League made in 1907 in support of the plan are the same arguments that are being made in 2007, in St. Louis and in cities across America. That planning is the will of the people, that the city is an organic whole, that planning enables one city to dominate over its rivals, that planning is cost effective—these are arguments that have shaped not only how Americans think about their cities, but also how Americans have come to think about the function of government. The rest of this chapter will explore the designs of the Civic League and how their ideas manifest themselves in *A City Plan for St. Louis*.

"The Practical and the Attainable": The Need of a City Plan for St. Louis—Statement of the General Committee to the Executive Board

"We hope," William Trelease and his fellow chairs told the League's Executive Board in the plan's preface, "that the plan as outlined will at least aid in arousing the public sentiment of St. Louis to the need of civic improvements on a comprehensive scale" (St. Louis Civic League 1907, 10). While this statement by the General Committee was addressed to the League's Executive Board, there is no doubt whom the real audience was. Presumably written before the Executive Board's statement, the General Committee's remarks were supposed to be a cover letter to the Board informing them that their work was complete. But there was no question that the Executive Board would accept the General Committee's reports and publish them together as a whole. Trelease and the Committee knew that the Board would include their letter in the plan and that they were really writing, in effect, to the citizens of St. Louis.

If Kent and the Executive Board had tried to gently persuade the citizens of the city of the need for a comprehensive plan, Trelease and the plan's General Committee were making the "hard sell." Almost like the sermon "Sinners in the Hands of an Angry God" by Jonathan Edwards, the opening of the statement of the General Committee described a St. Louis of wasted possibilities and one facing ruin and destruction for wont of a master plan. But by the end of the statement, Trelease and the Committee were appealing strictly to the self-interest of their readers, trying to convince them that a plan would result in "civic orderliness and beauty."

For Trelease, nature had given St. Louis unparalleled advantages. Its location at a bend on one of the world's most magnificent rivers combined with its undulating surface "might have made it one of the most beautiful cities in America" (St. Louis Civic League 1907, 10). It could have had wide, beautiful boulevards that would have been part of a fan-shaped street system that was convenient and comfortable. Instead, according to Trelease and the Committee, the city had turned its back on the river and wasted most of its natural assets. As they concluded, "its growth has been haphazard and has followed the lines of least resistance" (St. Louis Civic League 1907, 10). Rather than being a beautiful setting, for example, the riverfront had "been given over without reservation to smoking factories and railroad tracks" (St. Louis Civic League 1907, 11). The bluffs along the river could have been the site of beautiful homes and parks. But as Trelease noted, they were "being scooped off for brick" (St. Louis Civic League 1907, 11).

This last point would seemingly indicate that Trelease and the rest of the General Committee saw the plan as necessary for protecting the wealthy and the professional class—people like themselves—from the ravages of industrial growth. What is interesting though is that immediately after this comment, Trelease and the committee remarked that "only the 'Places' [the private streets] are protected from the encroachment of street cars, switch tracks, and objectionable buildings" (St. Louis Civic League 1907, 11). The rich could take care of themselves. With their money, they could "plan" their world in any way they wanted. On the other hand, the committee argued, "the average citizen who is seeking a quiet home away from the noise and discomfort of traffic, is helpless in the face of this riot of conflicting and selfish interests—the direct results of a lack of plan and insufficient regulations" (St. Louis Civic League 1907, 11). A plan was necessary, therefore, for Trelease and the League because "real estate speculators and property owners have been permitted to follow their own caprices and self interest" (St. Louis Civic League 1907, 10).

It was not that Trelease and his colleagues were altruistic saints, willing to act counter to their own class interests in the name of the public good. They realized that some beautiful residential streets—which were not "places"—had been lessened by the intrusion of incompatible uses and by property owners doing whatever they wanted with their property. They also knew that even among the rich there were differing interests. Building a factory or a railroad at some location might be beneficial for the factory owner or the railroad, but would totally conflict with the interests of other well-off members of the community. For Trelease and the rest of the General Committee, industrialization and the resultant urban growth had to be controlled. Unless the citizens had the power to impose order on the city, no one would benefit. Even the factory owner or the railroad stockholders would eventually see their interests "unplanned" by another factory or railroad blocking their path and undermining their interests. What a comprehensive plan would do, in Trelease's mind, would be to even out the interests of the citizens and make them one.

According to the Committee, this was already being done by other cities. Citing street system improvements in New York, a public buildings mall off Lake Erie in Cleveland, Ohio, the completion of the Washington, D.C., mall, and a comprehensive public building and street system plan drafted before the earthquake in San Francisco, the Committee called upon its readers to follow suit. Just like Kent and the Executive Committee, Trelease and the General Committee noted that it was a matter of competition. Other cities were moving ahead because of their willingness to plan. If St. Louis did not keep pace, it would be left behind. Chicago (St. Louis's arch-nemesis), for example, not only had laid out an integrated park system and provided public baths throughout the city, but also "the [Chicago] Commercial Club [had] employed the services of D. H. Burnham, the well-known architect, to draft a city plan for Chicago as broad and comprehensive as the Washington Plan" (St. Louis Civic League 1907, 12). Trelease and the General Committee warned St. Louisans.

The committee was not calling St. Louisans "rubes" for not planning like Boston, Cleveland, or Chicago. The point that Trelease and the rest of the committee wanted to make was that St. Louis needed to do it better and could do it better. "While St. Louis has not been so far behind in this movement, as is seen in the report of the Public Buildings Commission and the Kingshighway Commission," Trelease noted, "the time has come when these reports should be incorporated into a more complete city plan which is essential to any systematic development of this rapidly growing city" (St. Louis Civic League 1907, 13).

In short, what Trelease and the committee were calling for was a game plan that would enable St. Louis to continue the growth that had made it the fourth-largest city in America. The reports contained in the plan were not the work of wild-eyed visionaries, Trelease assured his readers. As he told them, the reports represented "the practical and the attainable" that would be accomplished over many years. In a way, the plan would pay for itself (St. Louis Civic League 1907, 14). The economic and social advantages of a citywide plan would more than compensate for the costs associated with implementing the plan.

In their minds, the General Plan Committee believed that the master plan would bestow four primary benefits on St. Louis. The first was balance. By treating city needs as a piece, St. Louisans could rationally allocate resources as part of an overall strategy. It would give "due importance to each field of municipal improvements," the committee stressed. Situations and needs might spring up unexpectedly or unplanned (St. Louis Civic League 1907, 14). Just as with a family budget, the purpose of a plan was not to anticipate every thing, but to articulate a rationale for how resources were being spent.

For Trelease and the other committee members, though, the plan was not just fiscally expedient, it allowed for public debate and for public decision-making. As Trelease noted when listing the second advantage of a city plan, "it will furnish a nucleus around which public sentiment can crystallize" (St. Louis Civic League 1907, 14). By articulating what the city would act on, the rationale behind it, and how much it would cost, the plan forced public debate on the direction that the city would take. More important, though, by having debated the plan, the plan became that of the citizens; it would become theirs and not just the Civic League's.

However, the real magic of the plan, the committee exclaimed, was that the plan was more than just an expression of the city being a community. It made St. Louis into a community. While the city might be divided by racial, ethnic, and class divisions, implementing the plan would give all St. Louisans a common identity and sense of purpose. As the committee argued in its third rationale for why St. Louis needed to adopt a city plan, "it will help to realize the unity of our civic life by bringing together the different sections of the city" (St. Louis Civic League 1907, 14). Trelease and his fellow General Committee members were serious people. They did not think for a moment that the plan would make St. Louis into some kind of utopian community where everyone loved one another. The rough and tumble of everyday industrial city life made that impossible. What it could do, though, was impress upon St. Louisans that they confronted many of the same problems and shared a common interest.

For Trelease and the General Committee, that common interest was what they declared, in their fourth rationale for a city plan, as a desire and a need for "civic orderliness and beauty" (St. Louis Civic League 1907, 14). It was in no one's interest—rich or poor, Italian or Irish—to live in a congested, inconvenient, ugly city. Even if a citizen never went to one of the parks proposed in the plan, or utilized the public buildings center, or took advantage of the improved riverfront, it would benefit him or her in bringing these things about because they would contribute to the grandeur of the city, which reflects back on the citizen.

It was an argument that would be the foundation of American urban planning for fifty years.

"It Is Not Yet Too Late": Historical Sketch: The Physical Growth of St. Louis

The next section of the 1907 plan would become a staple component of master plans until today—the historical sketch. For the Civic League, as well as for planners today, the purpose was to explain how the lack of a plan had caused problems and how having a plan would solve them.

Unlike the other parts of the plan, it is unclear who the primary author of the historical sketch was. But there is no doubt why the League included the chapter. From the opening paragraph, the League's intent was to convince St. Louisans that the city did not develop according to any preconceived plan and that most of its problems were the result of this fact. While the League noted that Pierre Laclede and his stepson, Auguste Chouteau, had laid out the initial street plan according to a plan or strategy, they argued that the city had refused to plan for the most part since then, even though the citizens had been presented with several opportunities since 1764 to do so. One opportunity, according to them, would have been 1822, when St. Louis became a city. Another would have been 1841, when the city had made a major annexation. But these early opportunities were ignored and the city unconsciously made a number of errors that could never be rectified.

One of the errors that the League pointed to, curiously, was the riverfront. From its perspective, St. Louis had wasted the opportunity to fully utilize the riverfront as early as the time of Lewis and Clark. While most planners today would argue, when looking at Laclede's street plan, that he had done a very good job of laying out the city with his limited knowledge of urban design, the League implied that the city had forever foregone the possibilities of the riverfront. Laclede had provided for a public square in the middle of the city, as well as making the grid plan longer along the river instead of the usual square, thus allowing wider access to the river. However, the League presented an 1804 map of the St. Louis street plan with the caption "Map Showing How St. Louis Early Turned Her Back on a Beautiful River Front" (St. Louis Civic League 1907, Map of St. Louis, 1804).

While the League really did not comment on the map, the probable reason they felt that Laclede had made a mistake was that Laclede's plan did not contain street radials or vistas; these were quite popular at the turn of the century because of the 1893 Chicago World's Fair and the nostalgia that it created for baroque design.

In continuing their litany of missed planning opportunities, the League next pointed to the City's appointment of a street committee right after St. Louis had been incorporated as a city. Their main criticism of the committee was that it had failed to generate a comprehensive street plan that would have anticipated future growth. They did praise the committee, though, for pushing an ordinance through the Board of Aldermen that provided for small amount of street paving and for requiring property owners to pave sidewalks abutting their property. What is interesting about the League's comments on this matter is not that they chose to praise the

committee, but what they said about the period before the city's incorporation in 1822. What struck them was that before 1822, street platting and
building lines were left up to developers, and they could do whatever they
wanted without municipal supervision. According to the League, there
had been attempts by St. Louis to gain more control over the streets, but
the "unprogressive portion of the inhabitants had been able to defeat those
measures" (St. Louis Civic League 1907, 23).

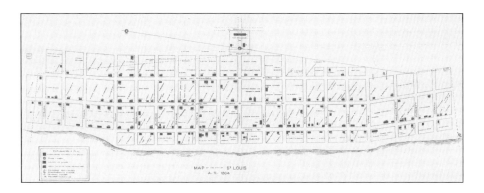

Map of the City of St. Louis, 1804.
A City Plan for St. Louis, 18a.

This was the whole crux of the League's arguments for planning and
for having a plan. They did not deny that property owners had rights. But
for them, the city as a whole had rights as well, and they felt those rights
superseded those of individuals. Even if it was their land, property owners
could not do whatever they wanted to do with it, if it negatively—or potentially negatively—impacted the interests of the citizens. But the League
went further than this. Being heirs of English common law, Americans
could trace their acceptance of the state's right to police powers back to
the Middle Ages. All citizens had the right not to be adversely affected by
the actions or property of another. What was different about the argument
of the League was that they were arguing that the state—the city—had a
right to proscribe what property owners had to do with their property.

This argument was as controversial in 1907 as it is in 2007. Just like with
police powers, cities had a well-established right to take private property
with compensation if it was needed for the public good. This right—which
is legally known as eminent domain—entitled cities, for example, to take
someone's property to build a highway, a public school, or a park. As long
as it could be argued that this "taking" was in the public interest and that
the property owner was compensated through due process, this exercise

of eminent domain was not only grounded in centuries of precedent in English common law, but in the Fifth Amendment of the United States Constitution. However, what the League was implying—and what two generations of American planners have argued since—was that dictating what a private property owner did with his or her property was technically not a taking of property without compensation if it could be demonstrated that a particular use of that property compromised the rights, not of other citizens, but of the city itself. One of the least appreciated uses of the Fourteenth Amendment of the Constitution is its application with regard to corporate entities such as public companies or governmental bodies, like cities. What the courts have generally maintained over the last century is that corporate entities are entitled to the same rights of citizenship as individual citizens, such as the rights to be protected from adverse harm.

However, it was one thing then—and one thing now—to be protected from adverse harm and quite another for the city to act in such a way as to project its interests so that it required property owners to act in a particular way. For the Civic League, though, if St. Louis and its citizens were not allowed to exercise their right to become what they had the potential of becoming, they were the ones who were denied "due process" and "fair compensation." Pointing to a map of St. Louis's early street plan and implying that the haphazard development of the city by private developers had wasted a chance to make St. Louis a truly spectacular metropolis, the Civic League noted in a caption that it "illustrates in a slight degree the absence throughout its history of a well-considered plan to guide the growth of this city." In short, if only St. Louis had had a L'Enfant and a comprehensive plan, it "might have been far more attractive" (St. Louis Civic League 1907, 29).

But for the Civic League not all was lost. While St. Louis had been robbed of what it could have been, the Civic League told St. Louisans that "it is not yet too late to profit from past experience and plan wisely for a future Greater St. Louis" (St. Louis Civic League 1907, 29). The historical sketch was meant not so much to inform but to agitate and arouse. In the minds of the Civic League, their plan was more than a blueprint for what the city could look like. It was a call for St. Louisans to reclaim their city and make it their own. Although not quite as dramatic a gesture as the proletariat storming the Bastille during the French Revolution, the Civic League viewed implementing the plan as a declaration that St. Louis belonged to St. Louisans and not just to the powerful who had been able to thwart the rights of the people in the past.

From the vantage point of a half generation of controversies over TIFs and public financing of sports facilities, present-day St. Louisans may be a little skeptical of such arguments and see them as nothing more than propaganda to get the public to support a private agenda. Members of the League were not unaware of public suspicions even in their time. There had even been discussion about the Business Club sponsoring the plan and not the Civic League, since there was a lot of carryover between the two groups. But the League decided that the public would be more likely to accept proposals by the Civic League than the Business Club because it would be assumed that the Business Club would only be acting in the interests of St. Louis business. Yet this was merely a tactical decision. According to the League, just because something aided business did not make it wrong. Pushing a particular business agenda was only wrong or tyrannical if the people did not have a chance to examine the agenda and decide its merits for themselves. For the Civic League, this is what the plan did. It made public decisions public and enabled the citizens to make known their desires about how they wanted the city to develop.

Plan 1 and Plan 2: Report on the Public Buildings Group

A third of the way through the report, which was just over one hundred pages, the Civic League turned its attention to the actual proposals that it wanted to recommend to the citizenry. Having dispensed with the preliminaries and the polemics, the League was ready to lay out its case for how it felt St. Louis should be physically reconfigured and give the five major reports on the public buildings group, neighborhood civic centers, inner and outer park systems, street (and riverfront) improvements, and the need for a municipal arts commission.

It was not surprising that the Public Buildings report was placed first. For members of the Civic League, Public Buildings Group was the most important proposal of the plan. Like for similar associations in other cities, public buildings groupings symbolized what this new movement called city planning was all about. It was the use of government power to make the city a more attractive and a more prosperous place for the benefit of all citizens that would be a model for private action. Just like with Cleveland and Washington, D.C., the grouping of major public buildings would not only have a major architectural impact, but also facilitate business by making the center a place for "one-stop shopping." With a public buildings group, a St. Louisan could visit several city departments in city hall, do research in the public library, and conduct business with the courts. All the while, the citizen would feel an incredible sense of pride that he or she was a citizen of such a magnificent city to have built such an edifice. Yet pride was not the only emotion that the Civic League wanted the citizen to feel about the municipal center. They wanted the Public Buildings Group with its classical architecture and orderly design, to instill within the citizenry the desire to replicate the beauty and order of the center throughout the city, with their own property.

The Public Buildings Group report had actually been in the works for some time. John Mauran and William Eames had been appointed by Mayor Rolla Wells to the Public Buildings Commission in 1904. The report that became part of the 1907 plan was a modification of an earlier report that had been prepared for the commission. What had prompted the report was a bond issue that authorized the construction of a new courthouse, jail, police station, and a building to house the health department. For the Civic League and for most St. Louisans, the roughly simultaneous construction of all of these significant public buildings, including a potential new public library, presented a unique opportunity to improve the St. Louis landscape.

The plan that Mauran and Eames proposed was not one plan, but two—aptly called Plan No. 1 and Plan No. 2. Both plans were oriented to the new city hall located at Market and Twelfth Street (now Tucker Avenue) and were, according to Mauran and Eames, "two schemes of apparently equal merit" (St. Louis Civic League 1907, 31). The new city hall was an imposing Gothic structure, built with the intention that it would be the focal point of a complex of municipal buildings. It would serve to pull the central business district farther to the west and would be the catalyst for redeveloping an area of the city that had become antiquated and dilapidated.

The axis of Plan No. 1 was Twelfth Street. It would be the focus of a center that would run from Pine Avenue to Spruce Street. The basic premise was that City Hall, to be situated on the western side of the avenue, would balance the placement of new court buildings that would be placed on the eastern side. To the north and south of this cluster on Twelfth, there would be other public buildings such as the police station and jail, and a possible "city archives." To add to the monumentality of the site, Mauran and Eames also provided for fountains and other street improvements down the middle of the boulevard.

Although Mauran and Eames had told their readers that the two schemes were of equal merit, it was clear that Plan No. 2 was their favorite, even though they said its projected cost was "a trifle less" (St. Louis Civic League 1907, 34). More like the Cleveland and Washington, D.C., public buildings plans, Plan No. 2 would carve out a mall that would be surrounded by municipal buildings by removing Thirteenth Street. As with Plan No. 1, Plan No. 2 used city hall as an anchor, but this time it was on the eastern side of the axial, with the Civil Courts building on the west. The jail and the other municipal buildings provided by the bond issue would be south of city hall along Twelfth Street. But unlike Plan No. 1, Plan No. 2 made the new Municipal Court building the southern anchor of the mall at the end of the Thirteenth Street closure, with the proposed new public library at the opposite end to the north.

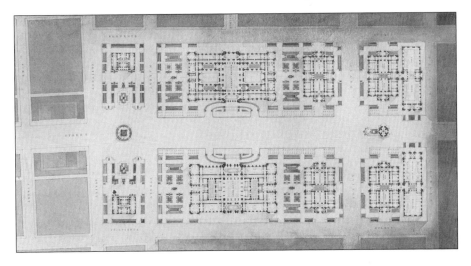

Plan No. 1—Showing a Possible Grouping along Twelfth Street.
A City Plan for St. Louis, 32a.

Plan No. 2 was clearly the bolder initiative of the two and was given the greatest amount of coverage in the report, both verbally and graphically. It was also the one for which Mauran and Eames made the strongest case. As they argued, Twelfth Street already had an established commercial character. Placing the axial of the civic center on Twelfth would upset that identity and use. Making Thirteenth Street the axial would have the advantage of pulling the central business district farther to the west, while also drawing it more to the south. While Plan No. 2 had the difficulty that the jail and the municipal court building would not be adjacent to one another, the value of the land offset this difficulty.

However, as Mauran and Eames made clear, the main goal of the report was not to persuade St. Louisans of a particular plan for the public buildings group, but merely to decide to have one. "St. Louis," Mauran and Eames explained to their readers, "has the opportunity, at a little more than the cost of the buildings, which are an immediate necessity, of securing breathing space, a beauty spot and a scheme for present grouping and future development, of which we may all be proud" (St. Louis Civic League 1907, 33). To ease the apprehension that St. Louisans might have about the potential cost of such bold undertakings, they reminded their fellow citizens that the plan—like any plan—was not meant to be implemented in one swoop, but over a long period of time. In fact, that was the purpose of a plan. It was supposed to direct action over a long period of time so that policy decisions would have coherence. The plans were offered, Mauran and Eames noted, "not with the expectation that the whole project should be undertaken under one administration," but over succeeding administrations (St. Louis Civic League 1907, 34).

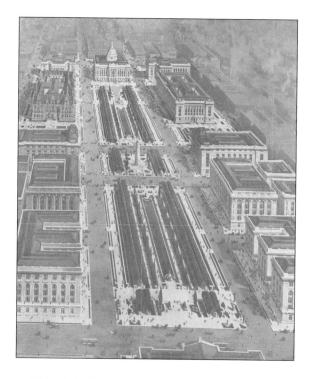

Proposed Municipal Court and Public Parkway—Looking South.
A City Plan for St. Louis, facing p. 37.

It has become commonplace to mock city planners for never implementing their plans. Maybe this is no truer than in St. Louis. St. Louisans almost seem to delight in pointing out which plans do not come to fruition. For planners such as Mauran and Eames, this kind of attitude would have seemed incredibly naïve. No planner expects every aspect of a plan to be realized. Things happen. The purpose of the plan, for them and for

St. Louis Plans

most planners today, is not to assure every component of a plan comes to be, but to lay out a strategy that will make future actions consistent and the most effective. Similar to a family budget, no plan—no matter how comprehensive—can predict or control the future. But it can lay out a strategy for addressing different contingencies.

Having said that, it is amazing how much of the Public Buildings Group plan was realized and how much of an impact that it has had on the city. For the most part, Plan No. 2 was the scheme that was adopted. The Thirteenth Street mall was created and has served as the axial for the Civic Center. A new public library was built at the northern end of the mall. While the Municipal Courts building was not built at the southern end of the mall, it was placed on the mall across from city hall. This was done to place the criminal courts next to the jail, which was built on the western side of the mall instead of the eastern side, as Plan No. 2 had specified. The headquarters of the St. Louis Metropolitan Police Department was also built on the mall, south of city hall on the eastern side. Interestingly, though, no public building has ever been built at the southern end of the mall. It would be virtually impossible, now, with the ramp to the elevated section of I-64 located there.

Perhaps the most significant impact of the Public Buildings report was not one of its recommendations, but an entire other scheme that it set up. This was the Central Parkway that was proposed by the St. Louis City Plan Association in 1911.[4] The Association was a splinter group of the League that was created to push for the implementation of the 1907 plan and the creation of an official City Planning Commission for St. Louis. While the Association report for 1911 made a number of other recommendations (one was extending Natural Bridge and Gravois into the city), the main proposal was a second public buildings mall that would intersect with the Thirteenth Street Mall. This mall was intended to extend from Twelfth to Grand between Market and Chestnut. The western focal point for this new mall was supposed to be a new symphony hall. This second mall never was extended all the way to Grand, but it was built essentially as planned from Aloe Plaza across from Union Station to Twelfth Street, where the magnificent Civil Courts Building was constructed in the 1920s as the eastern anchor. Of course, the concept of the Central Parkway became the foundation of the Gateway Mall that was intended to provide a vista from the Civil Courts Building to the Old Courthouse and eventually the Gateway Arch.

---

[4] St. Louis City Plan Association, *1910–1911 Report* (St. Louis, 1911), 14.

In short, while Mauran and Eames did not realize everything that they planned, their Plan No. 2 had an impact that city planners today only dream about.

"Develop a Neighborhood Feeling": Civic Centers for St. Louis

While the proposals of Mauran and Eames contained the physical aspects of the 1907 plan with which most St. Louisans are familiar, it was the next section of the plan that made this creation of the Civic League different from any other planning document in America before it. It was Henry Wright's report on neighborhood civic centers that made the plan "comprehensive" or, as Frederick Law Olmsted Jr. would later say of the whole comprehensive planning movement, "a new sort of thing."[5] What Wright had done with the Civic Center report was to make planning truly comprehensive by incorporating social as well as physical elements of the city. By addressing both social and physical elements of a neighborhood, Wright was acknowledging that a city was more than just the built environment. It was the whole web of relationships that bound the citizens together at many different levels. But the real significance of Wright's scheme was the message that planners had the power to alter that social reality and make it what they willed.

Wright, who was a landscape architect and who would later gain national acclaim for his work on new towns with Clarence Stein, knew that he was suggesting something unique with his set of proposals for a collection of neighborhood civic centers strategically placed around the city. "The term 'Civic Center,' as understood by this committee," he told his readers, "refers not, as is often the case, to any one institution which may supply some of the needs of a neighborhood, but rather to a grouping of the various public, semi-public, and private institutions which have for their object and aim the mental, moral or physical improvement of the neighborhood in which they are located" (St. Louis Civic League 1907, 37). Wright's statement was revolutionary on two accounts. First, he was ready to plan public and private property—and say so openly. Elements of his civic centers included parochial schools, churches, social and athletic

---

[5] See F. L. Olmsted Jr., Introductory Address on City Planning from "Proceedings of the Second National Conference on City Planning," in *The Urban Community: Housing and Planning in the Progressive Era,* ed. Roy Lubove (Englewood Cliffs, NJ: Prentice-Hall, 1967), 81–94.

organizations, model tenements, and settlement houses—all private institutions—as well as public uses such as police and fire stations, city parks
and playgrounds, public baths, branches of the public library, and public
schools. Second, he clearly intended to mold the social and cultural life
of the neighborhood. As he said, the object of his civic centers was "the
mental, moral, or physical improvement of the neighborhood"—itself, a
social construct.

For Wright, his civic centers would have a number of important advantages. One, according to Wright, was that the center would centrally locate
most of the everyday interests of the residents and would allow the different
institutions to supplement one another. This would be where they would go
to worship, to attend school or adult education classes, to obtain recreation
or entertainment, to conduct public business—or even to take a bath.

The one activity that Wright did not list for neighborhood centers was
retail and/or services.[6] Perhaps he assumed its presence. But Wright had
a bigger goal in mind than taking care of the residents' need for groceries
or a haircut. He wanted to change their lives. So while another advantage
that he listed was that the civic center would improve the visual aesthetic
of the neighborhood, the point was not to create beauty for beauty's sake.
The point was to use the aesthetics of the center to instill civic pride. They
were to be a "model" that would be an "influence . . . to every home in the
district" (St. Louis Civic League 1907, 37).

In Wright's mind, this "influence" would operate on two levels. On
one hand, it would better connect the residents of the neighborhood to
the larger city and to municipal government. According to Wright, many
neighborhood residents, especially recent immigrants, distrusted and were
fearful of government located in the centralized municipal centers. Taking the government to the people, rather than forcing them to come to
the government, Wright argued, would reduce the antagonism that many
immigrants felt toward the government. This would not only strengthen
the connection between the residents and municipal government, it would
strengthen the bond between the residents and the city as a whole. For
Wright, seeing the neighborhood police station on the way to church or
to the synagogue would make the residents feel that they were truly a
part of the whole city and instill within them a sense of their identity as
St. Louisans.

Wright also aimed through his civic centers to instill a "neighborhood
feeling" in the residents (St. Louis Civic League 1907, 37). Realizing that

---

[6] For a discussion on New Urbanism, see Peter Katz, *The New Urbanism: Toward an Architecture
of Community* (New York: McGraw-Hill, 1993).

St. Louis neighborhoods, like neighborhoods across the country around the turn of the century, were not true ghettoes with strictly defined boundaries between ethnic groups, Wright sought to bring Italians, Jews, Germans, and so on, together through common activities. What he believed and what later became a basic planning premise throughout much of the twentieth century was that a common identity could be infused in these different groups of people by bringing them physically together on a daily basis to do things that were mutually enjoyable and beneficial.

These were certainly ambitious goals considering the budget that Wright and the committee were given. As Wright explained, the committee was obligated to working within the $670,000 (approximately $20 million in today's dollars) that was allocated in the recent bond issue for perhaps a dozen centers. Consequently, the centers had to be located where the city would realize the greatest benefit for its investment. As Wright noted, density of population, social conditions, and the location of pre-existing conditions would determine where the centers would be situated.

For Wright, it was both the fairest policy and the most financially expedient policy to place the centers in the poorest neighborhoods. Examining the benefits of small parks and playgrounds, Wright noted that the older, poorer sections of St. Louis east of Jefferson were drastically underserved by the city's parks. Not only were they "not receiving a fair share of the public benefits," Wright argued, the higher rates for disease, juvenile crime, and fires that resulted from this lack of park facilities actually entailed higher costs for the citizens. "When the vital importance to the city of the proper development of the health and morals of its citizens—and especially of its poorer citizens—is considered, it will readily be seen that merely as a provision for the social welfare, if for no other reason, a large increase in the park area east of Jefferson Avenue must be made" (St. Louis Civic League 1907, 41).

But for Wright, it was not just a matter of dollars and cents. Again, anticipating a theme that would be uttered repeatedly in twentieth-century master plans, Wright maintained that addressing the social ills of one part of the city was crucial in preserving the health not only of that community, but also of the whole city. "Schools, parks and playgrounds, public baths and like institutions are necessary to the physical, moral, and mental development of the people living in the congested districts," Wright declared (St. Louis Civic League 1907, 42). While contemporary social critics would accuse Wright of having a naïve belief that better physical conditions could create better people, his main point was that slums and congestion would ultimately undermine the whole city. "To deprive 48 percent of its citizens of the full benefit of these institutions," Wright went on to say, "is social suicide to a community" (St. Louis Civic League 1907, 42).

Wright singled out two near north side communities to demonstrate how the neighborhood civic centers would work. One was located at Tenth and Carr. The other was situated around Carr Square, approximately a half mile to the west. Both communities were in some of the oldest parts of the city. Both had populations consisting predominantly of recently immigrated Italians and Russian Jews. Both were very dense and very poor.

In describing these two neighborhoods, Wright generated a litany of urban ills. Their streets were dark and unpaved. They had poor sanitation and a high rate of tuberculosis (TB). Unlike many urban reformers of the period, though, Wright generally did not blame the residents. Instead, he placed the fault for the conditions of the neighborhood at the foot of the property owners and the city. He noted that the poor sanitation of the tenements and the resultant high rate of TB were due to the plumbing not being inspected. In like manner, Wright argued that enforcement of the city's housing regulations was "left to the tender mercies of the rapacious landlord" (St. Louis Civic League 1907, 42). And while the neighborhood had a high crime rate, he pointed out that "crime [was] punished but not prevented" (St. Louis Civic League 1907, 42). Similar to a present-day criminologist, Wright maintained juvenile delinquency and gang behavior were caused by a "lack of privacy" in the tenements and the "corrupting influences of factory life" that had "weakened the moral fiber of the children" (St. Louis Civic League 1907, 44).

What was needed, Wright implied, was for the city to take responsibility for addressing the needs of the residents and the neighborhood. Not only did the city need to enforce the regulations already on the books, it needed to proactively provide those facilities that would make the neighborhood healthy and thriving. So while the city had just built a new school in the neighborhood, it needed a playground and a public bath. It also needed a model tenement that would be an "example in cleanliness and decency." (St. Louis Civic League 1907, 43).

Although the first generation of master planners is often criticized for believing that all urban problems could be solved by physical solutions, a noteworthy aspect of Wright's discussion is how much emphasis he placed on the need for social and educational programs. The types of needs he identified and the types of programs he proposed are basically the same ones that reformers today suggest. He called for recreation activities for seniors. He wanted a summer school program for the children that would address their educational deficiencies. He proposed English classes and acculturation programs for so that parents would have "a chance to develop with their children" (St. Louis Civic League 1907, 44). "In short," Wright said, the civic center would provide "every institution which would tend to promote the mental, moral, and physical up building of the people of the district" (St. Louis Civic League 1907, 42).

Wright's goal was nothing less than transforming the neighborhood into a community. Although some of his racial and ethnic stereotypes may shock contemporary readers, what is clear in Wright's discussion is that he saw the clustering of neighborhood facilities as more than a means of creating physical expediency. He believed that binding neighborhood institutions together would bind the people together. Speaking of the civic center proposed for Tenth and Carr and the need for a playground and a public bath, Wright noted that a "belt of negroes" had kept the residents from using Carr Park because of their "different customs and social conditions" (St. Louis Civic League 1907, 43). Nonetheless, he argued, "the park should be so located as to bind together the institutions now established or in the course of construction" (St. Louis Civic League 1907, 43). As Wright envisioned the plan, it and the civic centers that it generated would make the people of the neighborhood one. By placing a swimming pool adjacent to the neighborhood school and offering summer school, for example, Wright believed that the civic center would "make school attractive to the Italian child, who lacks the desire for learning which possesses his Jewish neighbor" (St. Louis Civic League 1907, 43).

In Wright's mind, the plan was the tool that would democratize the city by pulling the citizens together in achieving a common set of goals and objectives. Teaching the Italian child not only brought Italian and Jewish residents together in improving the neighborhood schools, it tightened the bonds that connected St. Louis's poor neighborhoods with the city at large. However, as Wright reminded his more affluent readers, not to address the social ills of those neighborhoods placed those residents at risk, as well as themselves. "These are dangers," Wright noted of the poor education and sanitation facilities of the neighborhoods where he wanted to place the civic centers, "which strike at the very roots of society" (St. Louis Civic League 1907, 53). For Wright, the city was a community of communities. Like a human body, they all contributed to the functioning and to the health of the whole. Even if a small portion of the city was dysfunctional—"diseased"—the whole city would become infected and dysfunctional.

Because Wright's civic centers were conceived in terms of pre-existing facilities and institutions, remnants of neighborhood civic centers that the 1907 plan proposed are strewn across St. Louis today. While none of the civic centers was developed totally as planned, an amazing number were partially built during the teens and twenties.

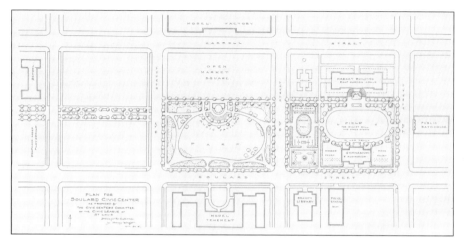

Soulard Civic Center.
A City Plan for St. Louis, 46a.

One center which is still fairly well intact is located in the Soulard neighborhood at Broadway and Lafayette avenues. The center was constructed at a major intersection near a number of neighborhood churches. At the heart of the center was a large public library. The center also included an extensive playground and an expanded farmers' market. It did not have a swimming pool, but it did have a large wading pool for infants and toddlers.

Although the Kosciusko Redevelopment Project and the building of I-55 in the late 1950s and early 1960s destroyed much of the neighborhood that the Soulard Civic Center was intended to serve, the plight of the center is indicative of the strengths and weaknesses of Wright's civic centers. Even today, the architecture and design of the center is impressive. All of the facilities utilized a classical motif and continue to visually work well with the rest of the neighborhood. However, neither the buildings nor the services provided in the buildings were able to make Soulard a sustainable community. What Wright and the first generation of master planners did not realize and what planners since then have had to learn over and over again is that neither physical nor social plans can make a neighborhood a community. Only the residents can make themselves into a community. Libraries and swimming pools do not transform people into a community.

Reading and swimming together is not enough. They have to consciously strive together to achieve a common project. In short, community building needed to be the goal of the residents and not just Wright. Simply placing people side by side—no matter how nice the venue—would not make them see each other as one.

"Parks and Boulevards Pay": Inner and Outer Parks and Boulevards—A Complete System Connecting Existing Parks and Forest Reservations in the County

While the next section of the plan was not as innovative or imaginative as Wright's proposal for neighborhood community centers, the parks plan was the section of the master plan that has had the greatest long-term impact on the St. Louis region. Modeled after similar proposals that had been prepared for Boston and Chicago, the purpose of the plan was not so much to lay out new parks and recreational areas as to pull together what was already present into a citywide and regional system. By connecting all of the pieces, the committee believed that it could create a network of open spaces that would be greater than the sum of its parts.

Although the parks committee was chaired by John Davis, a vice president at the powerful Mercantile Trust, and had such notable members as William Trelease, the director of the Missouri Botanical Garden, and Robert Brookings, the chairman of the board of directors at Washington University, the noted landscape architect George Kessler was undoubtedly the driving force behind the underlying goals of the parks plan. Kessler, who had gained his fame by designing a system of boulevards for Kansas City, had been working extensively in St. Louis since 1902 on projects related to the 1904 World's Fair. Because of his continued involvement with the parks plan after the 1907 plan was published, Kessler would locate his office in St. Louis by 1910.

Kessler began his report just like park planners had been beginning their reports for the last eighty years. He told St. Louisans that parks were not only important in beautifying the city and the surrounding region, but for the "proper physical and moral development of a city's population" (St. Louis Civic League 1907, 54). Like his mentor, Frederick Law Olmsted Sr., and the last generation of landscape architects, Kessler believed that parks were necessary in molding "future citizenship" by providing a "healthful," "refreshing," and "uplifting" environment. "While parks are of inestimable value in making a city inviting to desirable residents and visitors," Kessler noted, he went on to argue that "these are matters of small consideration when compared to the imperative necessity of supplying the great mass of the people with some means of recreation to relieve the unnatural surroundings in crowded cities" (St. Louis Civic League 1907, 54).

But after genuflecting to these truisms of the profession, Kessler got down to the real rationale for the report, which was aesthetics and money. In Kessler's mind, St. Louis would be a more attractive place for a relatively small expenditure if the city would simply join existing parks together and anticipate the recreational needs of what he, the committee, and the whole Civic League assumed would be an eventually greatly enlarged city. For Kessler, making St. Louis attractive by design was crucially important since, as he lamented (as St. Louisans are always lamenting), the city did not abut mountains or an ocean. However, as he pointed out, St. Louis already had the makings of an excellent system. It possessed 2,286 acres of parkland and had three major parks—Carondelet, Forest, and O'Fallon. The problem, according to Kessler, was not that St. Louis's parks were insufficient. If anything, Kessler maintained, the city's parks were underutilized. Many St. Louisans were unaware that excellent parks like Carondelet or Benton even existed. What was "seriously lacking," Kessler told St. Louisans, was "a well-defined and well-connected system" (St. Louis Civic League 1907, 54).

Kessler's "system" was actually four systems roughly connected to one another. The first was making Kingshighway a boulevard that would connect most of the major parks in the city. The second was creating a scenic vista along the Mississippi River to the southern point of Kingshighway. The third was improving the River Des Peres from Forest Park (which was on Kingshighway Boulevard) to the Mississippi. The fourth was a boulevard connecting a number of suburban communities that originated at the northern point of Kingshighway Boulevard.

As Kessler noted, the first system was almost complete. In fact, Kingshighway Boulevard was what brought Kessler to St. Louis in the first place. Conceived as a both a means of enhancing the northern and southern approaches to Forest Park and the World's Fair, as well as an opportunity to improve access to the city's central corridor from the south, Kingshighway Boulevard was well under way when the 1907 plan was published. The reason it was included in the plan was to demonstrate how it fit with the overall park scheme for the city. "The Kingshighway," Kessler explained to St. Louisans, "was outlined some four years ago, the money has been appropriated and the plans for its construction, which have followed closely the original report of the Kingshighway Commission, are practically completed" (St. Louis Civic League 1907, 55).

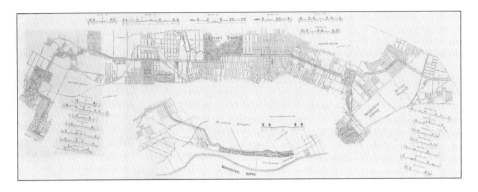

Kingshighway Plan.
A City Plan for St. Louis, facing p. 56.

What Kessler and the Parks Committee wanted to do by including the Kingshighway report in the plan was set up the rationale for the other proposals. According to Kessler, the Kingshighway and by implication the whole park system had three functions. The first was economic. "The completion of this magnificent parkway," Kessler said of the Kingshighway, "will return to the city and the abutting land owners many times its cost in the increase of property values" (St. Louis Civic League 1907, 59). But that was not all. According to Kessler, the Kingshighway would repay the city "in the pleasure of the citizens in its use" (St. Louis Civic League 1907, 59). Finally, Kessler argued that the Kingshighway—and presumably the planned park system—would "become an enduring monument to the energy and civic pride of St. Louis" (St. Louis Civic League 1907, 59).

The second component of Kessler's park system was a scenic river drive south of St. Louis's downtown. "We believe," Kessler wrote, "that no comprehensive plan for park development should fail to include some portion of the ten miles of water-front particularly in the southern portion of the city" (St. Louis Civic League 1907, 59). While Kessler's plan was compromised in its implementation, his proposal was for the city to "condemn and purchase" a strip of property two hundred to three hundred feet wide, from President Street (just north of the Marine Hospital in what is now the Marine-Villa neighborhood) to Bellerive Park at the southern terminus of the Kingshighway. Kessler's intention was to place a thoroughfare inside the strip with a promenade on the river side and a manicured tree line on the opposing side. In Kessler's mind, the site offered a "range of bluffs which are susceptible of almost unlimited improvement as a beautiful drive and parkway" (St. Louis Civic League 1907, 59–60). Kessler's goal was to create a boulevard similar to Riverside Drive in New York City. "The tops of these bluffs," Kessler maintained, "afford a superb view of the Cahokia Bottoms, the distant hills on the Illinois side, and a sweep of the river both north and south" (St. Louis Civic League 1907, 60). Kessler pointed to cities in the United States and Europe in an effort to convince St. Louisans of the impact that riverfront treatments had for other cities. Providing photographs of riverfronts of Paris and Frankfurt, Kessler tried to persuade St. Louisans that the Mississippi could be more spectacular than either the Seine or the Rhine.

Kessler was aware that the obstacle of realizing such a vision was money. The city did not own the land, and there were already competing uses. But Kessler maintained that the city could secure the property "for a comparatively reasonable sum" (St. Louis Civic League 1907, 61). The institutions that were already there could be induced to sell or relocate. However, Kessler explained, the longer that the city waited to secure the land, the more likely that residences would be built on the bluffs or that they would be "ruined by brick-makers or stone quarries" (St. Louis Civic League 1907, 61). Unfortunately, Kessler proved to be quite prophetic. New institutions and homes were built on the bluffs, and the city never was able to build what could have been one of the most spectacular riverfronts in the world.

The third leg of Kessler's park system was a series of improvements of the River Des Peres that Kessler claimed had an "aesthetic and utilitarian motive" (St. Louis Civic League 1907, 62). As he explained, the large stream that flowed from the city's central corridor to the Mississippi in a southwestwardly fashion repeatedly flooded during periods of heavy rain. The problem was the excessive winding of the river. According to his design, the length of the river would be reduced from 16.5 miles to 9.5 miles by straightening. In addition to being straightened, the channel would be deepened to further facilitate the handling of excessive rainwater.

Besides reducing flooding in the southern part of the city, Kessler argued that an improved River Des Peres, which had been essentially a cesspool or a dry creek bed during non-rainy periods, could be an opportunity for creating new open space. Not only could the city create recreational areas adjacent to the new riverbed, but a new parkway could be created from Forest Park to the Mississippi. But in his mind, it would be fruitless to spend money on aesthetic improvements if the river were not straightened. However, Kessler told St. Louisans, the River Des Peres had the potential of increasing the value of real estate in the area fivefold and the "increase in taxes received from that portion of the city will have paid for the entire improvement" (St. Louis Civic League 1907, 64).

For Kessler, though, the crucial part of the proposed River Des Peres Parkway was not the section between Forest Park and southwest to the Mississippi, but a parkway that would run between the park and the river to the north. Tacking its way in a northeasterly direction, Kessler's plan would eventually double back to the Kingshighway, thereby connecting the two park systems. For Kessler, connecting these two systems would "give to this city a parkway system unsurpassed in variety and beauty of scenery by any city in the Union, with the possible exception of Boston" (St. Louis Civic League 1907, 64). As he pointed out, the two parkways combined would have a total length of thirty-five miles—longer than both Chicago's and Boston's famed parkways. It would be a major undertaking, Kessler noted, but "this comprehensive plan for St. Louis does not appear too ambitious," considering that at least twenty other cities were also planning "extensive systems" (St. Louis Civic League 1907, 64).

What was ambitious, though, was Kessler's scheme to create a parkway that would circle what he assumed would eventually be the City of St. Louis. Like many St. Louisans, Kessler was aware of how fast St. Louis would continue to grow and how its political size was already being constricted by the artificial boundaries imposed on St. Louis in the city/county "divorce" of 1875. Yet, like most St. Louisans, Kessler assumed that the city would be allowed to grow to its natural size and that many of the nearby suburbs would eventually be annexed. "If the same rate of increase in population continues for thirty years to come," Kessler remarked, "this city will contain a population of a million and three quarter inhabitants"—in other words, it would double in size—"and the limits of the city will no doubt include Webster, Kirkwood, Clayton, University City and a number of other suburban towns" (St. Louis Civic League 1907, 65). While St. Louis would never be allowed to grow beyond its 1875 borders, the parkway that he envisioned closely anticipated the paths of both Lindbergh Road and the I-270 beltway. The parkway that Kessler mapped out was to originate at the Chain of Rocks Bridge north of the city on the Mississippi and extend westward to Florissant—a suburb dating back to colonial days. At that point, it would continue westward until reaching Woodson Road, where it would meander southward toward Rock Hill, Webster, and Kirkwood. The final leg of the parkway would circle back to the Mississippi south of the city. Unlike the northern leg, Kessler aimed for the southern terminus to be much farther south than the southern tip of Kingshighway. The southern leg of the proposed parkway was supposed to extend from Kirkwood to Grant's Farm and on to Jefferson Barracks and the Mississippi.

In addition to the parkway, Kessler also recommended a number of reservations along the route of the parkway. One was to be on the bluffs overlooking the Chain of Rocks on the Mississippi. Another was to be situated at the St. Ferdinand Common Fields overlooking the Missouri River, north of St. Louis. A third was to be located around Creve Coeur Lake, almost due west of the city. The fourth reservation was to be near Kirkwood at the Meramec Highlands. The fifth reservation was to be an expansion of Jefferson Barracks, the military installation south of St. Louis on the Mississippi. All of the reservations would eventually be tied to the parkway and, as Kessler noted, all of the reservations except the one at the St. Ferdinand Common Fields could already be reached from the city by railroad, streetcar, or rock road.

It was a masterful plan. In one broad stroke it combined all of the region's somewhat unassuming natural assets into a stunning system. Taken by themselves, the region's natural resources—the Mississippi, Missouri, and Meramec rivers, the foothills of the Ozarks, the gently rolling terrain—were not especially noteworthy. But taken together they were almost spectacular. But more important, it made a logical outline of what should have been St. Louis's political boundaries.

However, Kessler's mind was not on metropolitan government, but finances. He knew that the city would eventually grow out to the suburbs and envelop them. By then, though, it would be too late. The land would be too expensive and an opportunity would be lost forever. "Obviously," Kessler explained to St. Louisans, "some provision should be made for connecting the rapidly growing suburbs with a broad, attractive and well-paved thoroughfare, before the territory is so built up as to make the cost of the improvement prohibitive" (St. Louis Civic League 1907, 65).

In the concluding section of the report, entitled "Parks and Boulevards Pay," Kessler and the committee tried to persuade St. Louisans that their expansive plan was fiscally responsible. They admitted, though, that it had an expensive price tag and would be hard to accomplish. Although they did not anticipate the system being completed for at least a quarter century and though it would have to be implemented in pieces, the sixty miles of boulevards would involve "considerable legislation and the expenditure of several millions of public revenues" (St. Louis Civic League 1907, 68). But for them, it would be worth it. "The experience in every other city," Kessler argued, "where an extensive park and boulevard system has been constructed is that the immediate effect is to double or quadruple the valuation of property" (St. Louis Civic League 1907, 68).

Kessler thought "parks and parkways should be classed as an investment to a city." Many of Kessler's arguments sound similar to a developer today trying to secure a TIF. Kessler maintained that a comprehensive park system would increase taxable valuations in both the city and suburbs, "attract a desirable class of citizens," encourage the building of "fine residences," and stimulate tourism. What is significant, though, is that Kessler concludes by saying, "but more than all else they furnish an antidote to the unnatural conditions which must accompany the segregation of large populations in crowded cities" (St. Louis Civic League 1907, 68).

What Kessler was arguing was what Wright and Eames and the whole plan committee were arguing throughout all of the reports: that the plan was both an expression of and a means of making St. Louis into a community. While it has become commonplace a hundred years after the publication of the 1907 plan to interpret such language as nothing more than self-interested propaganda, Kessler and his planning colleagues truly did see the city as an integrated whole, composed of complementary parts whose welfare rested on ensuring the well-being of the entire citizenry. "A future test of civic spirit in American cities," Kessler told St. Louisans, "will be the care which they show for the physical and moral development of their people by supplying them with those elements of nature which city life tends to destroy" (St. Louis Civic League 1907, 68–69). But for Kessler, such sentiments were not some altruistic gesture. St. Louis and St. Louisans would either succeed or fail as one. Kessler's point was clear. "If St. Louis [was] to keep her place among the progressive cities of America," St. Louisans would have to be willing to jointly implement the bold proposals of the park plan and the other initiatives of the 1907 master plan (St. Louis Civic League 1907, 69).

"The city is a great organism": Street Improvements— Suggestions for the Improvement of the Riverfront, Railway Entrance, Triangles, and Street Railway Lines

The last major report of the Civic League master plan dealt with the riverfront and with the street system of the city. In comparison with the Public Buildings report, Wright's plan for neighborhood community centers, and Kessler's plan for a regional system of parks and parkways, the Street Improvements report was not nearly as bold, far ranging, or innovative.

While the rest of the report laid out schemes that were meant to chart a course for at least a quarter of a century, J. Charless Cabanne and the rest of the committee made it quite clear on the first page of their report that they were only considering proposals "which seem possible of accomplishment within the next decade" (St. Louis Civic League 1907, 71). Yet what the report lacked in urban design vision, it more than made up for in clarity of articulation when it came to the underlying social and political assumptions of the Civic League. Nowhere else were the planners as frank about how they viewed the city and how the plan related to it. For Cabanne and the committee, the streets were more than just instruments for facilitating transportation from one point to another. They were the "arteries of communication" that tied together the living social body that was the city. Just like arteries in a body, the streets were the life force that allowed the interdependent parts of the city to function as a whole. As a result, for them "the street plan [was] the element of first and greatest importance in the making or remaking of a city." City planners then, in the minds of Cabanne and the rest of the Civic League, were the doctors of the city. They gave birth to the city by creating the systems that made the city a living body. They were also the ones who could try to restore the body to health if something threatened its smooth functioning.

But unlike planners a generation later in St. Louis and elsewhere, Cabanne and his committee approached this role with trepidation and caution. Although they realized the importance that the street system had for St. Louis, they did not see themselves so much as gods, but as midwives. There were limits to what they could do. Once the streets and the rest of the city's infrastructure were in place, the city took on a life of its own and responded to a whole array of forces.

The riverfront was a case in point. It was not surprising that Cabanne and the committee tackled this problem first. The river in front of the downtown had become unsightly and ugly. Once the pride of the city, the riverfront had become a disgrace. With river travel on the decline with the ever-increasing dominance of the railroad, the city had largely abandoned its reason for being. However, the planners did not have a clean slate to do whatever they wanted with the riverfront. They still had to act within the constraints of business. While the river was not as important as it once was, the city was still dependent to a large degree on river transport, and whatever plan was derived for the riverfront had to provide for the rail tracks that ran parallel to the river.

However, the committee informed St. Louisans, the city was at an "opportune moment" to consider waterfront improvements (St. Louis Civic League 1907, 72). An increase in river transport anticipated with the dredging of the Mississippi, the building of a new free municipal bridge, and the dilapidated conditions of the riverfront all created a moment that gave St. Louis the chance to create a "national entranceway unique among American municipalities" (St. Louis Civic League 1907, 72). What the Street Improvements Committee's plan called for was a comprehensive remaking of the riverfront from the Eads Bridge to the new municipal bridge that was to built at the foot of Poplar Street and that would feed railroads into the Mill Creek Corridor. According to Cabanne and the other committee members, while the rail tracks abutting the river would have to remain, the steep grade from the river made "a dignified treatment of the river-front easy" (St. Louis Civic League 1907, 73). Using the waterfront in Algiers as a model, the plan proposed an esplanade with the rail tracks hidden underneath. Terraced stairs would bring pedestrians to the river's edge if they so desired. The last component of the plan was the creation of a rail station for suburban commuter lines adjacent to the esplanade.

The River Front as It Should Be.
A City Plan for St. Louis, 72b.

While Cabanne and his committee felt constrained by certain business realities when dealing with the riverfront, they felt powerless in addressing the transportation needs of the downtown. As they told St. Louisans, the ideal street plan that the early settlers could have established would have provided a series of radials that would have converged at a common center, reflecting the curvature of the Mississippi, "but they did not" (St. Louis Civic League 1907, 75). Although other cities had carved out such thoroughfares into the heart of the city, the committee argued that "the inconveniences of travel are not yet such as to demand these radical changes," even though later St. Louisans would (St. Louis Civic League 1907, 75).

Consequently, most of the committee's recommendations for the area of the city that was already heavily built out were rather modest. They recommended that streetcars vacate Locust Street from Broadway to the triangle where Olive, Lindell, and Locust converged so that Locust would be treated like a boulevard similar to the treatment of Jackson Street in Chicago. They also recommended that Twelfth Street be widened from Market to Mill Creek Valley—again, a proposal that would not involve large expenditures of funds. In a similar fashion, the committee wanted to expand the area of the city where overhead lines had to be buried and establish guidelines for what types of trees could be planted by property owners along city streets. In addition, they called for the use of ornamental iron poles for the streetcars.

The two most daring proposals of the committee were the creation of a parkway between Union Station and Tucker and a north-south boulevard that would connect a number of small parks east of Jefferson. The first of these proposals became the foundation of the Central Arterial plan that would be issued a few years later and that eventually became the western component of the Gateway Mall. Noting that Union Station (which had been built in the 1890s) was a landmark of which "the city can justly be proud," Cabanne and the committee maintained that the dilapidated business area between city hall and Union Station was "a constant rebuke to the aesthetic ideals of the city" (St. Louis Civic League 1907, 77). What they proposed was buying land in the block between Chestnut and Market from Twelfth Street to Eighteenth Street for the "transformation of this area into a park," similar to the Champs-Elysées in Paris (St. Louis Civic League 1907, 77). The other major Street Improvements Committee proposal was the creation of a series of boulevards east of Jefferson that would form a parkway like Kingshighway. Utilizing existing streets, the committee suggested that a number of streets be restricted to create a scenic route from Bissell Point on the city's north side to a proposed park at Marine Hospital overlooking the Mississippi on St. Louis's south side.

While Cabanne and the Street Improvements Committee demonstrated constraint in giving planners power to transform the city, they had no hesitancy when it came to outlining new construction. Even though they were dealing with private property and individual rights, Cabanne and his colleagues believed that they had every right to dictate how property could be developed, citing not their wishes but the "comfort and convenience of the people" (St. Louis Civic League 1907, 86). This was especially true with respect to how new subdivisions should be platted. The committee recommended that the city street department be given the power "to control the opening of all new additions and compel conformity with the general plan of streets in their direction, width, and names" (St. Louis Civic League 1907, 86).

Though such a recommendation may now seem rather innocuous, this was a major departure in the treatment of private property in American jurisprudence. Although American cities had always had the power to use eminent domain to buy private property and use it for the general welfare, it was always assumed it was a violation of the sovereignty of ownership to tell individuals how to use their property. While building codes had become commonplace in American cities after the Civil War as a means of protecting the health and safety of occupants, they were seen as a limited use of a city's legitimate use of police powers; but this was something different. Cabanne was not talking about preventing something that would be injurious to the citizenry, but of the "comfort and convenience of the people." In the past, developers had generally lined up new streets with existing ones because it was logical, not because they had to. It was their property. They could do whatever they wanted to do with it—as the willy-nilly pattern of many city streets testified. In contemporary language, then, what Cabanne and the committee were suggesting was giving the city the power, in the name of the citizens, to dictate how private property was to be used even if it involved a "taking" of the potential value of that property. But the committee did not stop there. Not only did they want the power to dictate how undeveloped city land was to be platted, they wanted the power to plat surrounding suburbs as well. Assuming that the city would be eventually allowed to annex surrounding land "when the city has doubled its present population," it would need the power to control platting of suburban areas "to prevent the inharmonious arrangement of streets" (St. Louis Civic League 1907, 86).

The implications of this argument by these first master planners were clear. Cabanne believed, just as the whole Civic League planning committee believed, that the city—at least the modern city—had become too interdependent to permit individual citizens to do whatever they wanted with their property. As the Street Improvements Committee emphasized in their report conclusion, "a city can no longer be considered as a mere aggregation of separate buildings erected solely for the convenience of the owner" (St. Louis Civic League 1907, 87). The city was not just a physical entity, but a social one as well. For the committee, "the city is a great organism with closely related parts" (St. Louis Civic League 1907, 87). As a result, the welfare of the city was more important than the interest of any particular citizen. "Consequently," the committee told St. Louisans, "its growth must be directed and shaped" (St. Louis Civic League 1907, 87). What would give St. Louisans that power was the plan.

Toward an Urban Constitution: A Municipal Arts Commission and Legislation

The last two minor reports of the plan addressed implementation. The first of the two called for the creation of a municipal arts commission. The second examined the question of cost and the powers necessary to make the plan a reality.

The report on the municipal arts commission was only six and a quarter pages long and had a limited function. Its only purpose was to propose an arts commission similar to commissions in other cities. Unlike the call for greater control over private property in other reports, the Municipal Arts Committee's report was only interested in greater scrutiny of the design of public works such as bridges, public baths, school buildings, and monuments. The committee chaired by John Lawrence Mauran, a prominent local architect, wanted an advisory commission of city freeholders who would report to the Board of Public Improvements, which would then recommend the design of proposed public projects. The reason the committee was making this suggestion was that they felt public design in St. Louis had lagged behind that found in other cities, and because a municipal arts commission would prevent such cases of the placement of the new city hall "in the midst of unsightly and dilapidated buildings" (St. Louis Civic League 1907, 92).

According to the committee, the proposed commission was needed "not merely for art's sake." Its true function was that by enhancing the "attractiveness of a city . . . it arouses a civic spirit among all the people and creates a pride in the city" (St. Louis Civic League 1907, 92). For Mauran and the rest of the committee, a city was a community not by chance but by design. "A citizen's love of the city is not an abstract sentiment," Mauran told his fellow St. Louisans, but instead "it attaches itself to the beautiful in the city. If we would have our people united for the upbuilding of St. Louis we should surround them with illustrations of the city's greatness" (St. Louis Civic League 1907, 92–93).

But for John Lee and the members of the Legislation Committee, a comprehensive plan was justified in the first place because the city already existed as a community and that plan represented the collective will of the people. As Lee acknowledged, the total proposed improvements would probably cost the citizens in excess of $25 million (approximately $750 million a hundred years later). This expense was justified because the improvements would benefit all St. Louisans, not just a few. That is why Lee and his committee felt the costs and benefits of the improvements should be shared by all St. Louisans. According to the committee, the city could pay for the improvements through two traditional ways—increasing taxes and selling bonds—and both would undoubtedly have to be used. However, this was not the main strategy that the Legislation Committee recommended. While it argued that taxation could raise a substantial amount of money by simply making assessment practices more equitable, and since St. Louis's debt rate was comparatively very low, the Legislation Committee recommended utilizing a new technique called excess condemnation. How excess condemnation worked was a city would condemn—and subsequently purchase—not just the property needed for the improvement but adjacent land as well. The benefit of this approach was that once an improvement was made—such as a street widening—the abutting land would be more desirable, and hence more valuable. By reselling the property, the city would benefit from the new value of the land and not the property owner. From the vantage point of the Legislation Committee and proponents of excess condemnation elsewhere, this was fair because even though the city had "taken" the value of the improvement for itself, it was the city—and hence, the citizens—who had created it in the first place. As Lee explained, "if a municipality expends millions of public revenue for an extensive improvement which greatly enhances the value of contiguous property, then the municipality should reap at least a portion of the benefits" (St. Louis Civic League 1907, 100).

However, what Lee and the Legislation committee did not say, but what they implied, was that the city was not merely being a speculator. It did not perform the improvement and take the new, more valuable property just to turn a profit. It performed the improvement to implement the plan. Excess condemnation was a capricious act. It was justified by the rationale of the plan itself.

The plan then was what reconciled the visions of Mauran and Lee. The plan was both an embodiment of the city as a community as well as an instrument of its creation. This was why the Civic League plan was so revolutionary and why its impact continues to be felt beyond the realm of city planning. By making the plan comprehensive, it made it a set of rules that reflected the will of the people, which shaped and molded the people over and over again. In effect, the plan became an urban constitution where the citizens consciously chose the direction they were going to take as a community. It was and is a powerful idea.

References

Katz, Peter. *The New Urbanism: Toward an Architecture of Community.* New York: McGraw-Hill, 1993.

Olmsted, F. L., Jr. Introductory Address on City Planning, in "Proceedings of the Second National Conference on City Planning." In *The Urban Community: Housing and Planning in the Progressive Era,* edited by Roy Lubove. Englewood Cliffs, NJ: Prentice Hall, 1967.

Primm, James Neal. *Lion of the Valley: St. Louis, Missouri.* 2nd ed. Boulder, CO: Pruett, 1990.

Saint Louis City Plan Association. *1910–1911 Report.* St. Louis, 1911.

Schaffer, Daniel, ed. *Two Centuries of American Planning.* Baltimore: Johns Hopkins University Press, 1988.

Scott, Mel. *American City Planning Since 1890: A History Commemorating the Fiftieth Anniversary of the American Institute of Planners.* Berkeley: University of California Press, 1971.

St. Louis Civic League. *A City Plan for Saint Louis: Reports of the Several Committees Appointed by the Executive Board of the Civic League to Draft a City Plan.* St. Louis: Woodward and Tiernan, 1907.

Chapter 2
Planning for Regional Governance in the St. Louis Area: The Context, the Plans, the Outcomes

Don Phares

The political and fiscal organization of local government in American metropolitan areas has long been a topic of scrutiny ranging from journalistic commentary to well-funded, comprehensive academic analysis, to legislative deliberations.

The focus of this chapter is the St. Louis area, which has a long tradition as a textbook example of a highly fragmented metropolitan area with the associated problems. It also has a history of planning for regional governance that goes back to the "great divorce," the separation of St. Louis city from St. Louis County. This chapter examines what has taken place in regional governance planning in the St. Louis area.

The St. Louis Saga

In a countywide election in 1876, voters approved the separation of the city of St. Louis from St. Louis County (prior to this the city was in the county). At that time, there were five incorporated cities in the county; sixty years later there were twenty-eight. By 1955, the number had expanded to ninety-six and there already had been three dis-incorporations. New municipalities were quite easily incorporated. These new municipalities often began as subdivisions, and the residents incorporated in order to maintain control over planning and zoning, land use, and tax base.

In response to developments since 1876, in 1957 the Metropolitan St. Louis Survey noted the following "continuing problems" for the St. Louis city/county area. Since then, given the passage of almost five decades, the list reflects not only the past but an almost prescient account of the present day status (1957a, 83–85):

- wide disparities in the number and extent of public services provided
- substantial variation in tax base to finance essential services
- some essential area-wide services are inadequate
- some communities have failed to recognize their responsibility to the entire urban area
- competition among municipalities to increase their potential tax resources impedes planning for the entire area
- growth will occur in unincorporated St. Louis County and *ad hoc* annexations and incorporations will not provide an adequate solution
- St. Louis County will have to provide an increasing amount of municipal services to unincorporated county residents

By the 1960s, St. Louis County had reached the haphazard governmental pattern reflected in Figure 1. There is little doubt that such development would have continued, had the Missouri Supreme Court not ruled in 1963 (*City of Olivette v. Graeler*) that the impact of new annexations and incorporations *on all of St. Louis County* must be taken into account. The interest of one group for incorporation would now be viewed in the context of the impact on all county residents. De facto, this decision vested control with the county through its ability to dominate in future annexation and incorporation cases. Its position was to oppose any significant boundary changes.

This situation prevailed for two decades. While it did not stop annexations or incorporations, it dramatically curtailed the earlier trend. In 1983, however, this legal environment changed when the Missouri Supreme Court reversed its 1963 decision (in *City of Town and Country v. St. Louis County, et al.*) concerning the impact on the county. This allowed far greater freedom for existing cities to annex contiguous areas and for new cities to be incorporated.

This new, more lenient environment produced a virtual "land rush" of activity to internalize the resource base from the growth in taxes on sales and utility gross receipts, which were collected in the rapidly developing unincorporated portions of St. Louis County. Annexation proposals manifested often blatant attempts to capture pockets of commercial and industrial tax base. Recent incorporations (Maryland Heights in 1985,

Chesterfield in 1988, and Wildwood in 1995) were driven by the desire to maintain control of the rapidly growing revenue base in their area and to protect it from being annexed by contiguous cities. The haphazard boundary change pattern that had already evolved in the county was reopened.

Figure 1

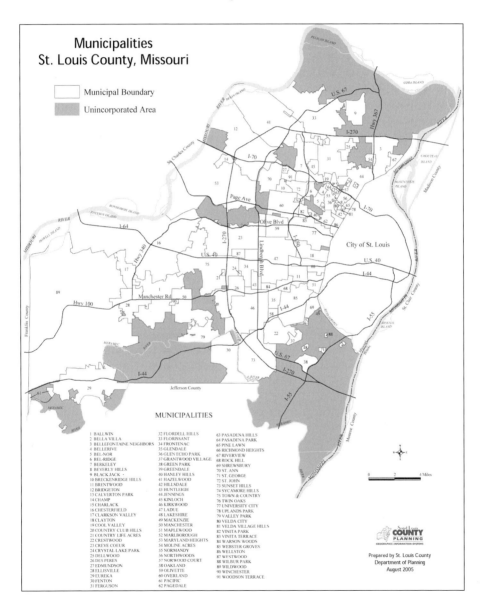

Planning Attempts and the Power of the Fisc

Ninety-one cities now exist in the county (see Figure 1). These cities provide municipal services to 687,753 county residents, more than 67 percent of the county population. Unincorporated St. Louis County contains 328,562 people. They receive their municipal-type services from county government. Several issues emerge from this organization.

First, in addition to providing all county functions, St. Louis County is also the largest single provider of municipal services. This requires a resource base appropriate for this dual responsibility. With the increased pace of attempts and successes for annexations and incorporations, the tax base available to the county is in danger of further deterioration, primarily due to the loss of both the 1 percent general sales and the 5 percent utility gross receipts taxes collected in unincorporated areas. These revenues flow to county coffers until an area becomes part of a municipality through annexation or incorporation.

Second, population for the present 91 municipalities ranges from the Village of Champ with 12 residents to Florissant with 50,497; two have less than 100 people, 22 cities have fewer than 1,000, 21 have more than 10,000, and only 10 have a population in excess of 20,000.

Third, the local resource base available to support municipal services is distributed very unevenly among the existing incorporated areas. This results in vast differences in both the quantity and quality of services and a necessity in many instances to compromise on basic services, without any consideration given to those that enhance the quality of life in a community (Patton 1986) or promote economic development (Ward 1987).

Fourth, resource base disparities are being further exacerbated by the "land grab" annexation/incorporation activity mentioned earlier. The most financially well-endowed areas of unincorporated St. Louis County are being absorbed whenever possible. This leaves those areas, dominantly residential, often poorer, with fewer resources for the county to provide services or for the residents to fend for themselves and get by with less.

A crucial fiscal factor for municipal finance relates to local sales and gross receipts (utility) taxes and how their taxable base is distributed among cities within the county. At present, these two revenue sources account for more than 60 percent of total municipal revenue and over 75 percent of all municipal taxes.

In 1977, the Missouri legislature passed a bill that allowed for a 1 cent countywide sales tax. It was approved by the voters and became available in 1978. As the result of a compromise, the proceeds were distributed to county municipalities in two ways, "point-of-sale" and "pool." Point-of-sale distribution allowed city governments that already had an existing local option sales tax to keep all sales tax revenue generated within their boundaries. Pool allocation provided for a per capita distribution of all revenue from cities without a sales tax in effect prior to 1977 and all funds collected from unincorporated portions of the county.

With the 1983 Town and Country court decision, the possibility of new annexations flared to the surface. Existing cities looked to annex contiguous unincorporated areas that contained pockets of commercial/industrial tax wealth to augment their existing revenue base. The issue of sales tax distribution took on new importance under this court decision since loss of wealth in unincorporated areas due to annexation led directly to a reduced tax base for all pool cities and also for county government.

In March 1983, during an emergency session, the Missouri legislature passed legislation that placed all future annexed and newly incorporated areas in the pool allocation rather than point-of-sale. The annexing or "new" city would receive a per capita allocation but would not be able to retain all sales taxes collected in the newly annexed area. This decision in March avoided the obvious problem that would have arisen with the passage of several annexation proposals on the 1983 April ballot.

Sales tax allocation continued to be a major point of fiscal contention in the county. To help ameliorate this, in 1993 the sales tax allocation formula approved in 1977 was revised to adjust for some of the inequities that had become evident. The new allocation procedure provided for a "progressive, sliding scale" sharing of point-of-sale city revenues with pool cities and unincorporated St. Louis County. It also allowed the county to retain some of the revenues that would be lost with future annexations and incorporations. This compensated in part for some of the wide disparity in municipal sales tax revenue that had evolved.

As of 2005, sales tax allocations continue to differ widely from the pool allocation of about $125 per capita to a large point-of-sale range up to $728.[1] This has been a very powerful fiscal incentive for point-of-sale cities to maintain the fiscal status quo. Because of the 1983 change in state law, any newly incorporated area receives the pool city allocation. From a county government perspective, however, any new annexation or incorporation means a direct sales tax loss.

---

[1] This is stated in revenue per 1 cent of sales tax levied. Localities are allowed by state law to enact, with voter approval, several other local option sales tax levies. Counting these would make the gap even wider.

Another major contributor to municipal coffers, and also to the prevailing overall level of fiscal tension, is the gross receipts tax on utilities (water, gas, electric, and telephone). This applies to commercial and industrial as well as residential activity. A very strong incentive exists to capture this revenue base within an incorporated area since all proceeds are kept by the city. Any new incorporations or annexations represent a direct loss to county government of its 5.0 percent gross receipts tax revenue. Generally, those areas with a high sales tax yield tend also to be those areas in which large utility receipts are generated. Thus, the fiscal problem is further exacerbated.

Per capita utility consumption, as an indication of the gross receipts tax base available for cities, varied from lows in the range of $400–$500 to highs that exceeded ten times this amount. Since cities have the legal option of setting the rate charged (with voter approval), the revenue potential is great and in many cities the yield matches or exceeds the sales tax. Gross receipts rates presently range from zero to as high as 11 percent.

A more recent wrinkle on the county fiscal machinations arose during the 1994 Missouri legislative session. Missouri voters had approved riverboat gaming in a statewide vote in November 1993. As a part of the revenue distribution scheme, any incorporated area in which gaming facilities are located will receive 2 percent of net gaming proceeds plus $1 of a minimum $2 admission charge. This was seen as a potential major new source of funds, and legislation was introduced to place gaming revenues into a countywide pool to be allocated on a per capita basis rather than permit it to accrue to the "home dock" city. The revenue pooling scheme was not implemented but it reappears in the legislature on a regular basis.

The Ongoing Planning Debate—What Scale for Government?

The release of the two Advisory Commission on Intergovernmental Relations (ACIR) reports, in 1988 and 1992, brought once again into national focus the question of government organization in metropolitan areas. What is the appropriate scale of local government operations? These ACIR reports documented in great detail the innovative arrangements undertaken in two highly fragmented metropolitan areas (St. Louis and Allegheny counties) to respond to service needs.

Working within a "public choice" framework, the ACIR reports praised the creativity of "public entrepreneurs" and part-time officials in small cities. Myriad service contracts, cooperative arrangements, informal agreements, shared systems, local associations, and volunteer officials provided the glue that binds together this complexity of local jurisdictions. This has assumed the more recent label of the "new regionalism."

In a planning context, one completes a reading of the ACIR reports with the overpowering sense that:

- local government should operate in this way;
- smaller, and implicitly more, is better; and
- the free market in governmental organization should be allowed to operate, absent concern for the overall areawide implications.

Release of the ACIR report on St. Louis coincided to the month (September) with the formal submission of a plan for a comprehensive governmental and fiscal reorganization within St. Louis County. There is stark contrast between the findings of this ACIR report (1988) and the provisions in the *Plan for Governmental Reorganization in St. Louis & St. Louis County* (Board of Freeholders 1988a) submitted by the board authorized by the Missouri constitution, to be discussed below. The ACIR report praised the existing governmental arrangement, noting in conclusion that "the experience of the St. Louis area in metropolitan organization *has much* to teach the rest of metropolitan America" (emphasis added, ACIR 1988, 168).

In sharp contrast, the Board of Freeholders (1988a) proposed a plan for a major organizational and fiscal restructuring for all county, municipal, and fire and emergency medical services (EMS) in St. Louis County. Establishment of this Board and the underlying premises that guided formation of its complex plan will be discussed in the following sections. Its major provisions will be outlined. They are summarized in Appendix I.

To put events in context, a review of past attempts at "metropolitan reform plans" in the St. Louis area will be discussed. They, de facto, go back to the city/county separation in 1876.

Planning and Reform Using the Missouri Constitution

Specific provisions in the Missouri State constitution have been a major vehicle for "regional reform" since the separation of St. Louis City from St. Louis County in 1876 (see Appendix II). There have been seven attempts at reform over more than one hundred years beginning with the "great divorce" of the city and county in 1876 and most recently with the 1990 Board of Electors. Most of the other significant attempts at reform have used a constitutional amendment route. One major case, the 1962 Borough plan, is discussed below, since it was a direct spinoff of a Freeholder plan.

1876: The "Great Divorce": Separation of the City from the County

By 1876, St. Louis City was a large city contained in a mostly rural county that had very sparse population and limited commercial business activity and tax base. This led to an increasing demand for the city to separate itself from the county and thus avoid the financial burden of supporting the county. The relationship between these two units had been characterized by "uninterrupted controversy" since the early 1860s; much was related to the Civil War and the following decade (Cassella 1959, 87). Increasingly, the complete separation of the city from the county was advanced as a better solution than consolidation or reorganization of the county (Cassella 1959, 91).

When a constitutional convention was called in 1875, the relationship between the city and county was brought to the forefront. By an overwhelming majority, the convention adopted a provision that authorized the separation of the city from the county. The new constitution was approved in late 1875.

Pursuant to this provision, a Board of Freeholders was elected in early 1876 with a specific charge to prepare a scheme for the separation to be submitted for voter approval. After considerable controversy over the actual vote outcome, it was declared passed on October 22, 1876. The city was "emancipated," and in the process its size was increased from about eighteen to sixty-one square miles, an area that was deemed to be more than adequate to accommodate future growth of St. Louis City.

As events evolved, one of problems with the new constitution was that it contained no scheme for any subsequent adjustment of city/county borders; they were absolutely fixed. By the early 1900s, it was increasingly obvious that the city and county were becoming a unified urban area, with interrelated problems, but there was no way to deal with the regional issues due to the formal 1876 separation.

It is in this historical context that the following Board of Freeholders proposals emerged to deal with the shortsightedness of the "great divorce," the complete separation of 1876. Ironically, the planning for regional governance that emerged out of the 1876 plan was its antithesis.

1926: Consolidation of the City and County under City Government

After the city/county separation, the feeling increasingly became more prevalent that this might well have been a mistake and a merger of some sort would be appropriate. However, the city approached the change with a hostile attitude. The 1876 constitution that allowed for the separation had included no way for reunification to occur either statutorily or constitutionally.

To correct this deficiency, deliberations began on a constitutional amendment in 1922 that resulted in an amendment that passed easily in November 1924 in the city, county, and state. The newly passed amendment had three options for "reuniting" the city and county:

- the city would extend its limits to include the entire county

- the county would extend its limits to include the city which could then extend its limits under existing law, and

- the city could annex part of the county under the exclusive jurisdiction of the city.

Thus, de facto, it was a takeover, reentry, or annexation but dominated and controlled by the city.

On June 25, 1925 a Board of Freeholders was convened and held its first meeting. In March 1926, a plan was introduced that:

- made the city charter the governing document for the new area

- eliminated all county offices and placed them under city control

- transferred all county property to the city

- eliminated all municipalities in the county

- put the city police department in control of the entire new area, and

- abolished all county school districts placing them under the city school board's control (Board of Freeholders 1926; Jones 2000).

There were two financial concessions included that were almost trivial in the context of overall city dominance:

- the city would assume financial responsibility for all affected county governments and

- county agricultural land would be taxed at no more that 50 percent of the city rate.

Needless to say, the county representatives on the Board were outraged and presented counterproposals. However, through political maneuvering that obtained the signature of one of the nine County Board members, the plan was adopted and placed on the ballot for October 26, 1926. It passed overwhelmingly in the city by 87 percent but in the county failed by 67 percent.

After fifty years, the regional governance status of the city and county remained the same.

1954: Creation of the Metropolitan Sewer District

The fact that water naturally seeks a lower level, in this case flowing toward the city from the county, led to the formation of another Board of Freeholders in 1953. Beginning in the mid-1800s with a serious cholera epidemic and rapidly gaining momentum from this event, it became obvious by the early 1950s that treatment of sewage in the county was having a serious impact on the city. The county was littered with treatment facilities ranging from fifteen municipal systems to twenty-four sewer districts to seventy-five subdivision systems to thousands of septic tanks (Jones 2000, 105). The county was growing, adding more people, and suffering the severe downside of the associated waste. With population growth it was increasingly imposing this waste problem on the city as well.

In this context, the Bi-State Development Agency conducted an engineering study of sewer needs in the county. The findings indicated the following (Metropolitan St. Louis Survey 1957a, 68):

- there was a serious sewer problem in both the city and county

- the health hazards were area-wide

- the sewer problems could not be handled separately since the urbanized area of the county drained through the city, and

- piecemeal efforts failed because they covered less than an entire watershed and had inadequate resources to address the issue.

The solution was a plan that established a special purpose district, the Metropolitan St. Louis Sewer District (MSD). It would include the city and the more urbanized portion of the county. City residents would not be required to pay for the county since subdistricts would be defined to set fees according to specific needs in areas of the county (Board of Freeholders 1954).

Reception at the polls was overwhelmingly positive: 77 percent in the city and 75 percent in the county (Jones 2000, 107). The MSD was established. Most of the remaining parts of the county were added to the MSD in 1977 by an overwhelming positive vote.

1955: Metropolitan Transit District

In 1949, following deliberations that began in 1948, the Bi-State Development Agency was established to deal with transportation issues in the Missouri/Illinois bi-state region. Bi-State was a "governmental wimp." It had "empowerment" to deal with area transportation issues but no authority to tax or to do much else except "make plans" but not to set policies (Jones 2000, 97).

In 1952, the question of who should own and operate public transit became an issue for the region. The region's ridership was then more than 400,000 and more than fifteen companies provided transit services. Out of this chaotic environment came a proposal for a Board of Freeholders (Metropolitan St. Louis Transit District 1955) to deal with the current and emerging region's transportation problems. A Board was appointed in the spring of 1953. The issue, however, was plagued by a lack of interest by the public or business community either pro or con.

This Board decided to delay the issue of public ownership of transit facilities and focus on the control over the power for the setting of fares being shifted from the state Public Service Commission to a new Metropolitan St. Louis Transit District. This fledgling measure that avoided the crucial issue of public ownership satisfied virtually no one; either it should be done or not. Voter turnout was extremely light with only 54,000 votes being cast out of a total of 576,000 registered voters, 10 percent of city registered voters and 8 percent of county. As a result, the proposal was defeated by a scant 3,099 votes in the city and 2,110 in the county (*St. Louis Globe-Democrat* 1955; Jones 2000, 96–99).

1959: Creation of the Metropolitan St. Louis District

During the more than three decades since the last comprehensive look at the St. Louis area's governmental structure in 1926, the nation had gone through the Great Depression and World War II. Attention now began to shift back to the region and its existing and emerging problems. This began with a large-scale study that examined the needs and problems of the St. Louis region. The Metropolitan St. Louis Survey, as it was called, issued two reports (1957a and 1957b), which discussed metropolitan issues in great depth.

Two proposals, albeit conflicting, were considered. The first was a metropolitan district that would deal with seven major functional areas. The second was a complete merger of city and county into a single entity called the "municipal county." The vote from the board on the plan was heavily discussed and highly disputed but finally emerged as ten for the district and nine for the municipal merger (later called the Borough plan).

The plan proposed by the 1959 Board of Freeholders was called the "Greater St. Louis City-County District." Spelled out for this district was the following set of functions (Metropolitan Board of Freeholders 1959, i–ii):

- establish and maintain a system of arterial roads, expressways, and major streets
- regulate mass transit including fares, routing and schedules, traffic lanes, and other means of encouraging use of such facilities
- take over the Metropolitan Sewer District established in 1954
- organize civil defense under one central administration
- encourage establishment of industrial locations to attract new business
- engage in comprehensive area-wide planning
- coordinate a centralized police communication and reporting sytem.

In addition, the plan could be amended to include "additional services" (not defined in the plan) when approved by a majority of voters in both the city and county. The District's capital and operating expenses would be covered by a property tax levied on all tangible personal property in the District. It would be set annually to produce required revenues (Metropolitan Board of Freeholders 1959, 18).

The plan was put on the ballot on November 3, 1959, and lost by large margins: 67 percent in the city and 75 percent in the county. The closeness of the split on the Board—ten in favor of the district and nine for merger—led quickly to another proposal. However, this time it was decided not to use the Freeholders provision of the state constitution.

1962: The Borough Plan

Out of the consternation surrounding the 1959 District plan, movement began immediately to draft a constitutional amendment to consolidate the city and county. It was essentially the same proposal put forth by the minority in the 1959 District proposal. However, unlike the other proposals discussed here, it was decided to use a constitutional amendment process rather than a Board of Freeholders. It was feared that a Board of Freeholders, once put in place, might decide to adopt a different plan than the borough plan that was defeated by just one Freeholder vote in the 1959 District deliberations. It would require statewide voter approval, not just the approval of voters in the city and county.

The new governmental entity was to be known as the Municipal County of St. Louis and would consolidate *all governmental bodies* in both the city and county. It would fulfill the dual role of city and county. It would include cities, towns, villages, fire protection districts, the Metropolitan Sewer District, all other sewer districts, public water supply districts, and all other municipal corporations. School districts were excluded due to the intense opposition expressed in the past.

The Municipal County would be divided into twenty-two boroughs. Eight would be within the city, seven within the county, and the remaining seven would straddle the city/county border. The purpose here was to give the "assurance" that the city was not just swallowing up the county.

This plan was to become even more heated than the District plan proposed in 1959. Opposition emerged from all sides, and the Borough plan constitutional amendment was defeated by 74 percent statewide, 79 percent in the county, and 55 percent in the city. The results were viewed as a strong statement that consolidation (read merger) was not the way to solve city/county problems (much of this is derived from Sengstock et al. 1964).

A Two-Decade Hiatus in Planning Reform Attempts

At present, Article VI, Section 30, of the Missouri State constitution enables the establishment of a Board of Freeholders (now Electors). Constitutionally, this Board has the authority to address issues pertaining to any and all types of local government subject to voter approval. On September 28, 1987, the first such Board since 1959 was sworn in.

Section 30(a) of the constitution now designates five types of reform that can be considered. The first three relate to reentry or merger between St. Louis City and St. Louis County, which have been legally separated since 1876 and were put in place in 1924 (presently the city is a county as well as a municipality and a school district). The fourth addresses the formation of one or more areawide districts and was put in place in with the new constitution of 1945. The fifth option was added to the constitution by a statewide referendum in 1966. It is extremely broad in scope and allows the Board: "to formulate and adopt *any other* plan for the partial or complete government of all or any part of the city and the county" (emphasis added).

Under the purview of the fifth option this new Board, set up in 1987, delved into the myriad issues pertaining to local government organization and finance within St. Louis County. While this provision vests constitutional authority to propose the restructuring of any and all local governments, including school districts and special districts, the Board made a conscious decision to focus only on county and municipal issues. Such a focus also mandated an examination of fire/EMS services since twenty of the forty-three county providers of fire protection and EMS were municipal departments.

Planning for Reform in St. Louis: Comprehensive or Incremental?

The Board's focus on municipal and county government organization and finance derived directly from the adverse fiscal environment that had been evolving for decades, as was discussed previously. A context for its work was provided by several studies: one of which posed an intriguing question for the title of its final report, *Too Many Governments?* (Confluence St. Louis 1987). After long and careful deliberation, this Board developed several premises that guided its deliberations and the formulation of its plan.

First, the nearly 400,000 residents of unincorporated portions of the county were being inconsistently and, in many instances, inadequately served by the county's provision of municipal services. The complete incorporation of the county was proposed as a solution to this problem.

Second and obviously related, it was proposed that the county government no longer provide any municipal services; this responsibility would vest with newly created cities. This would relieve the county from its responsibility to provide both municipal and county services to the same area. This was significant because, often, the county provided varying levels of municipal services. As a guiding premise for this proposal, a clear delineation of functional service responsibility between city and county was developed (Board of Freeholders 1988b, A1–A2).

Third, a structure was proposed within which all residents of the county would have access to adequate, basic municipal and fire/EMS services. During its lengthy deliberations, the Board determined that the highly fragmented local government structure and associated large revenue base disparities produced an environment in which adequate public services were not available to all county residents. Nothing suggested that the situation would improve over time.

Fourth, it was blatantly obvious that adequate financial resources must be made available to support municipal, county, and fire/EMS services. Documented vast differences in available public resources and service levels mandated a plan that would realign existing resources and also allow for the provision of additional resources as necessary. The existence of disparities, per se, did not dictate this premise. Rather, what prevailed was the need to guarantee adequate basic service provision to all residents of the county, no matter where they lived, and to provide sufficient financing to accomplish this objective.

Fifth, an "end state" plan with clearly defined municipal and fire/EMS boundaries was specified rather than adopting a "process" or more step-by-step, incremental approach. The Board's standing was to provide as much certainty as possible that the new governmental organization would incorporate the entire county and provide an adequate resource base to finance the reformulated county government, the proposed new cities, and the new fire/EMS districts.[2]

In the end, thirty-seven new municipalities (see Figure 2) and four fire/EMS districts covering the entire county were delineated. A detailed fiscal profile for each new city and the reconfigured county government was prepared to document an adequate balance between revenues and expenditure needs (Board of Freeholders, 1988b).

The proposed thirty-seven new cities ranged in population from 6,400 to 78,200 with only five having less than 10,000 residents; the average

---

[2] The Board of Freeholders's plan also provided for two entities that formally link the City and County. This was required in the constitutional mandate under which the Board was created. One is an Economic Development District that deals with the promotion of areawide economic development; the second is a Metropolitan Commission that can be called into existence on an "as needed" basis to deal with areawide problems as they arise in the future. Refer to Articles 3 and 4 of the Board plan (1988a) for full detail.

population size was about 27,000. Per capita assessed valuation (in 1987) ranged from $3,912 to $24,461, with an average of $10,380. Per capita sales taxes ranged from $79 to $138, with an average of $98; the variation here resulted from the 25 percent of sales tax yield that existing point-of-sale cities were allowed to retain outside of the per capita distribution.

The 1987 Board of Freeholders Plan

The Board's plan was to incorporate the entire county into thirty-seven new cities (shown in Figure 2; the then-existing and the proposed new cities are contrasted in Figure 3). Most of the thirty-seven proposed cities were derived using an existing city (or cities) as a core; six new cities, however, were formed primarily from the large unincorporated portions of the county shown clearly in Figure 1 as the dark shaded areas.[3]

As a pivotal component, the fiscal plan realigned municipal finances so that each of the new cities would have a revenue base that would allow it to provide adequate public services. The same procedure was followed for the reformulated county, which would now have the responsibility for providing only county-type service following the clear division of functional service responsibility discussed above (Board of Freeholders 1988b).

The fiscal component of the reorganization plan contained four major elements. First, a newly implemented 1 percent countywide earnings tax on wages, salaries, and business profits, fashioned after the one already long in existence in St. Louis City (and Kansas City), would fund county government and the majority of fire/EMS services. It would also provide funding for a net revenue–sharing pool to be used for municipal resource equalization and infrastructure needs. Since an earnings tax was in place in St. Louis City, the new county earnings tax would be collected only once from any individual or business; no income would be taxed twice.

Second, a new 6 percent gross receipts tax on non-residential utilities (gas, electric, water, and telephone) would provide additional revenue to each of the thirty-seven cities. Third, all general sales tax collections in St. Louis County would be distributed on a 25 percent point-of-sale and 75 percent per capita (pool) basis. No longer would any city government retain all sales taxes generated within its boundaries. Last, reliance on the property tax would be substantially reduced. For the entire current

---

[3] Not shown in Figure 1 in 1987 when this Board was developing its plan is a large unincorporated area which became the City of Wildwood in 1995. It is equal in size to the city of St. Louis and included most of the western unincorporated portion of the County.

operations portion of county government it would be eliminated; only the property tax for debt funding would remain. In addition, an average of 72 percent of total property taxes for fire services would also be eliminated. Replacement funding for both county and fire/EMS services would come from the new earnings tax.

Figure 2

Final Freeholders Proposal

1. Spanish Lake	17. Town and Country	34. Ballwin
2. Florissant	18. Ladue	35. Eureka
3. Hazelwood	19. Clayton	36. Ellisville
4. Bridgeton	20. Richmond Heights	37. Chesterfield
5. Bellefontaine Neighbors	21. Brentwood	
6. Ferguson	22. Maplewood	
7. Berkeley	23. Shrewsbury	
8. St. Ann	24. Webster Groves	
9. Maryland Heights	25. Glendale	
10. Overland	26. Crestwood	
11. St. John	27. Sunset Hills	
12. Normandy	28. Affton	
13. University City	29. Mehlville	
14. Olivette	30. Fenton	
15. Creve Coeur	31. Kirkwood	
16. Jennings	32. Des Peres	
	33. Manchester	

The proposal would divide the county into the 37 municipalities shown here. Only Lambert Field would remain unincorporated. Pacific, most of which is in Franklin County, would retain its sliver of land in southwest St. Louis County.

Source: St. Louis County Planning Department

Tom Borgman/Post-Dispat

MILES
0 2 4 6

Several objectives were accomplished by this plan. All municipal services would be provided by a city not by the county. The fiscal portion of the plan would balance resources with needs and provisions for future revenue growth potential would be enhanced through reliance on a sales and income tax base rather than on property. Each city government and the county government would be fiscally enabled to deliver adequate basic services to its residents. In addition, adequate fire/EMS protection would now be available throughout the county.

Figure 3

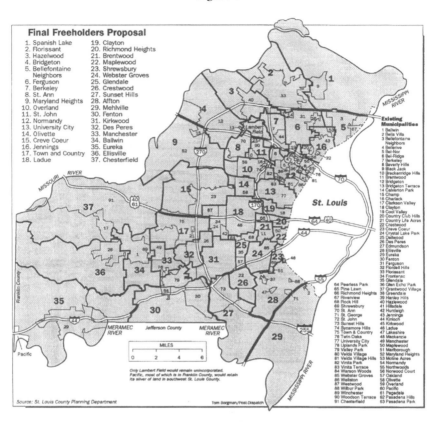

Final Freeholders Proposal

1. Spanish Lake
2. Florissant
3. Hazelwood
4. Bridgeton
5. Bellefontaine Neighbors
6. Ferguson
7. Berkeley
8. St. Ann
9. Maryland Heights
10. Overland
11. St. John
12. Normandy
13. University City
14. Olivette
15. Creve Coeur
16. Jennings
17. Town and Country
18. Ladue
19. Clayton
20. Richmond Heights
21. Brentwood
22. Maplewood
23. Shrewsbury
24. Webster Groves
25. Glendale
26. Crestwood
27. Sunset Hills
28. Affton
29. Mehlville
30. Fenton
31. Kirkwood
32. Des Peres
33. Manchester
34. Ballwin
35. Eureka
36. Ellisville
37. Chesterfield

Existing Municipalities

1 Baldwin
2 Bella Villa
3 Bellefontaine Neighbors
4 Bellerive
5 Bel-Nor
6 Bel-Ridge
7 Berkeley
8 Beverly Hills
9 Black Jack
10 Brackenridge Hills
11 Brentwood
12 Bridgeton
13 Bridgeton Terrace
14 Calverton Park
15 Champ
16 Charlack
17 Clarkson Valley
18 Clayton
19 Cool Valley
20 Country Club Hills
21 Country Life Acres
22 Crestwood
23 Creve Coeur
24 Crystal Lake Park
25 Dellwood
26 Des Peres
27 Edmundson
28 Ellisville
29 Eureka
30 Fenton
31 Ferguson
32 Flordell Hills
33 Florissant
34 Frontenac
35 Glendale
36 Glen Echo Park
37 Grantwood Village
38 Greendale
39 Hanley Hills
40 Hazelwood
41 Hillsdale
42 Huntleigh
43 Jennings
44 Kinloch
45 Kirkwood
46 Ladue
47 Lakeshire
48 Mackanzie
49 Manchester
50 Maplewood
51 Marlborough
52 Maryland Heights
53 Moline Acres
54 Normandy
55 Northwoods
56 Norwood Court
57 Oakland
58 Olivette
59 Overland
60 Pacific
61 Pagedale
62 Pasadena Hills
63 Pasadena Park
64 Peerless Park
65 Pine Lawn
66 Richmond Heights
67 Riverview
68 Rock Hill
69 Shrewsbury
70 St. Ann
71 St. George
72 St. John
73 Sunset Hills
74 Sycamore Hills
75 Town & Country
76 Twin Oaks
77 University City
78 Uplands Park
79 Valley Park
80 Velda Village
81 Velda Village Hills
82 Vinita Park
83 Vinita Terrace
84 Warson Woods
85 Webster Groves
86 Wellston
87 Westwood
88 Wilbur Park
89 Winchester
90 Woodson Terrace
91 Chesterfield

St. Louis

Franklin County

Jefferson County

MERAMEC RIVER

MERAMEC RIVER

Pacific

MILES
0   2   4   6

Only Lambert Field would remain unincorporated. Pacific, most of which is in Franklin County, would retain its sliver of land in southwest St. Louis County.

Source: St. Louis County Planning Department

Tom Borgman/Post-Dispatch

A Legal Challenge to Reorganization

During the process of its work, the legal status of the Board of Freeholders, and eventually of its plan, was considered by a variety of courts. These included the Federal District Court, the State Circuit Trial Court, the United States Court of Appeals for the Eighth Circuit, and the Missouri Supreme Court. Each court considered the interpretation of "freeholder" as requiring property ownership status as a prerequisite for the original appointment as a member of the Board. This had been challenged by a variety of groups as a denial of equal protection under the U.S. Constitution because it excluded those who did not own property. After a long series of legal machinations, the Board's constitutional status was upheld by the Missouri Supreme Court upon referral from the U.S. Court of Appeals.

The legal battle, however, did not stop there. On February 21, 1989, in a one-line order, the U.S. Supreme Court agreed to review the Missouri Supreme Court's decision in its fall session that was to begin *after* the already scheduled vote on the Board of Freeholders' plan. The final outcome of these myriad legal deliberations remained for the highest court of the land to determine.

The Board had completed its work, all nineteen members signed the plan, and it was filed formally with the city and county Boards of Election Commissioners for submission to the voters in each area. The Board of Freeholders went out of existence on September 16, 1988. The voters would have exercised their prerogative on June 20, 1989, with a simple "yes" or "no" on the entire 155-page plan. The U.S. Supreme Court action delayed any vote pending its decision.

For St. Louis County, choice of a dramatically new local government structure would have been an option available at the polls. Contrast between the 1988 ACIR study and the Board plan could not have been much more stark.

Resolution Without Reform

After a lengthy process of legal proceedings, as outlined above, the question of the constitutionality of the Board of Freeholders was granted *certiorari* by the U.S. Supreme Court, on appeal from the Supreme Court of Missouri. The case was argued on April 25, 1989 (*Quinn et al. v. Millsap et al.*), and a decision was delivered on June 25, 1989. The U.S. Supreme Court reversed the Missouri Supreme Court in a unanimous vote. It argued that the land ownership requirement for selection to the Board of Freeholders violated the equal protection clause of the U.S. Constitution.

This decision invalidated the Board of Freeholders and its plan, thus no vote was held. Although the legal status of this Board and its plan was settled, nothing was done to address planning for the ongoing, fundamental issues confronting the area: political fragmentation, revenue disparities, haphazard boundary changes driven by fiscal self-interest, regional economic development, and the provision of adequate public services in the county.

Given the U.S. Supreme Court decision, the option of dealing with these issues through Article VI, Section 30, of the Missouri constitution was now in question. The U.S. Supreme Court did not note any changes, remediation, or removal in its decision. The Missouri Supreme Court heard arguments on January 3, 1990, as to whether this section of the Missouri constitution should remain intact, with "freeholder" clearly interpreted to be qualified elector not property owner, or whether it should be deleted from the constitution as a result of the U.S. Supreme Court decision.

The Missouri court decided to leave this section of the Missouri constitution intact and to interpret "freeholder" to mean qualified elector. As a part of its decision, it also required immediate appointment of a new board, the "Board of Electors," to prepare a new plan. With the legal status of the Missouri constitutional provision now settled by the United States and Missouri Supreme Courts, a new Board could now revisit the plethora of problems and issues that have been discussed over the past one-hundred-plus years.

The 1990 Board of Electors Plan

A Board of Electors was appointed and sworn in. It began its work in July 1990. During its yearlong deliberations, it considered a wide range of plans and ideas including "the formation of a single county government structure for the City and County" (Board of Electors 1991, 2).

Interestingly, it did not make much direct use, if any, of the work completed by the 1987 Board of Freeholders. By this time, the issue of planning for comprehensive local government organization and fiscal reform had become anathema. The objective seemed to be to fulfill the mandate of the court for a new board to be appointed and to prepare a plan and then to cease to exist with as little controversy as possible. It accomplished this!

The Board plan had two proposals. One was to establish a Metropolitan Economic Development Commission and the other to create a Metropolitan Park Commission. The Metropolitan Economic Development Commission would "finance programs which will create, attract, retain, expand, develop, improve and enhance employment opportunities within the City and County" (Board of Electors 1991, 5–6).

This Commission would be financed by a 2 percent tax on non-residential utility service. The powers of the Commission would be vested in an eleven member Board of Commissioners appointed by the mayor of the city and the county executive. Its activities would be carried out primarily by contracting with existing agencies and organizations.

The Metropolitan Park Commission would "govern, administer, repair, maintain, conserve, sustain, protect and improve any and all Commission Parks" (Board of Electors 1991, 24). De facto, only the 1,300-acre Forest Park in the city would be under its purview unless expanded authority and funding were approved by voters.

The Park Commission would be funded by a tax not to exceed 6 cents per $100 assessed value on taxable real and personal property in the city and county. Up to 2 cents of this was an "Operation Tax" and up to 4 cents was a "Capital Improvements Tax." The capital tax would expire after twenty years unless reapproved.

The final Board of Electors plan was placed on the ballot on April 7, 1992. It was defeated by the voters: 54 percent in the county and 53 percent in the city. Given the scope and breadth of governmental and fiscal issues facing the St. Louis area, it seems ironic that the Board of Electors plan avoided virtually all of them. Even so, its modest (albeit not unworthy) proposal was defeated.

Planning for Regionalism: An Incremental Perspective

If one examines the St. Louis area's attempts to govern itself more regionally primarily using comprehensive planning proposals such as governmental consolidation or multifunctional districts, there is failure. The 1954 Board of Freeholders has been the only such post-1876 group to secure approval and it dealt with a single service: sanitary and storm water sewers.

Because St. Louis has high local governmental multiplicity, much of it rooted in self-interest and parochialism, because so many consolidation attempts have been proposed only to fail at the ballot box or in the courts, and because the conventional wisdom among most civic leaders and the local media has been to decry localism and urge consolidation, St. Louis itself and the metropolitan planning reform community more generally have made the area the poster region for fragmentation.

The preoccupation with failed major reform plans has obscured the incremental movement toward regionalism in the St. Louis region over the past half century. Starting with the establishment of the Metropolitan Sewer District in 1954, there has been increasing intercounty cooperation. Until recently, almost all of it occurred between the area's two largest jurisdictions: St. Louis County and the City of St. Louis. Over the last decade, however, efforts have involved a broader geographical area.

Cooperation has involved many service areas and taken on many forms. The services include sanitary and solid waste, education, cultural institutions and the arts, transportation, public safety, tourism, parks and open space, sports venues, economic development, and health care for the indigent. The forms include various types of public authorities, special purpose districts, intergovernmental agreements, cooperative arrangements, and umbrella organizations.

Planning for Reform in St. Louis—What's Next?

Given the more than 130-year history of planning attempts to restructure governmental and fiscal arrangements in the St. Louis metropolitan area, one can legitimately pose the question, what's next? Clearly the situation outlined above shows some progress incrementally toward dealing with specific issues. Problems remain, however, and may well worsen. In addition to the intra-St. Louis County issues that have been discussed, there remain concerns over effectively dealing with areawide problems such as environmental quality, transportation, economic development, solid waste disposal, and sewage and wastewater treatment. Many attempts to date have focused on the city/county area but not the entire metropolitan area, which it should be noted includes two states and now sixteen counties in the St. Louis MSA. Also, one could make an argument that there is too little coordination among these entities. Are they moving toward regional governance or just piecemeal responses to regional issues? Also, are they reactive or proactive to areawide problems and issues?

The more comprehensive attempts using the Board of Freeholders (now Electors) approach has failed in every attempt except two. The first was in 1876, which separated the city from the county. In many respects, this set the stage for some of the problems that continue play out more than one hundred years later. The second was the establishment of the Metropolitan Sewer District, which emerged from a major actual, and potentially even worse, health context. All of the other five comprehensive proposals have failed at the ballot box, usually overwhelmingly.

St. Louis's leadership—both governmental and business—generally agree that the St. Louis area still requires more regionalism. The disagreements center around "what does more entail" and in "what form will it be implemented." Some within both sectors continue to argue for merging the City of St. Louis and St. Louis County, with the most frequent option having the city reenter the county as its ninety-second municipality (preserving city identity and political control) and cease performing its county functions. Others propose adding to the now quite long list of cooperative ventures (e.g., a regional airport authority) or expanding existing districts (e.g., the Zoo-Museum District) to additional counties (especially St. Charles County).

In this sense, perhaps regionalism has won the rhetorical war. Even elected officials who are reluctant participants in the move toward metropolitan-wide efforts are sensitive about sounding too parochial. The debate is now much more about how rather than whether.

Over the years, much planning has been proposed and discussed, and many attempts have proven successful, but there is still weight to what remains. St. Louis has long been a textbook example of governmental structure problems. Might it become a textbook example of what can be done to correct them—more narrowly and incrementally rather than globally and all at once?

Appendix I: Major Features of the 1987 and 1990 Board Plans

Board of Freeholders Plan: 1987

On September 28, 1987, the first Board of Freeholders since 1959 was sworn in. It was composed of nineteen members; nine appointed by the mayor of the city, nine appointed by the county executive, and one by the governor.

It is under this fifth provision of Section 30(a) that the 1987 Board of Freeholders delved into the myriad issues pertaining to local governments in St. Louis County. The Board was convened by a petition of 3 percent of the number of voters in the last gubernatorial election in both the city and county.

The Board of Freeholders went out of existence on September 16, 1988 (it had a constitutional existence of one year) after submitting its plan to the Boards of Election Commissioners in St. Louis City and St. Louis County. The plan was scheduled to be on the ballot on June 20, 1989, at a special election held in the city and county. A simple majority was required in both areas for approval. The vote would have been "yes" or "no" on the entire 155-page plan; there was no possibility of it being submitted or voted on in segments.

St. Louis County Issues

ORGANIZATIONAL/ STRUCTURAL

- All of the county incorporated (except Lambert Airport)
- Cities reduced from 90 to 37
- Clear division of responsibility between cities in the county and county government spelled out
- St. Louis County provides no municipal-type services
- Control over all municipal matters remains with cities except in

unusual cases where some gross violation of the municipal/county master plan arises

- Number of fire protection providers is reduced from forty-two (twenty-three districts and nineteen municipal) to four, each with a full array of fire protection and EMS services.

REVENUES/ FUNDING

- A countywide 1 percent earnings tax is imposed on salaries, wages, and business profits (without any double taxation) to fund
- Part of the fire/EMS district cost county government a municipal development fund
- All sales tax revenues distributed:
  - 25 percent point-of-sale
  - 75 percent per capita (pool) distribution
  - A gross receipts tax of 6 percent imposed on non-residential utility usage; earmarked for municipal use only
  - The county property tax rolled back by 56 cents/$100 assessed valuation; only 14 cents for debt service remains
  - Fire property tax rates rolled back from present levels (as high as $ or more) to 13 cents/$100 assessed value. Cities and fire/EMS districts will have the option to change rates once the plan is implemented.

IMPLEMENTATION

- A transition commission (separate for fire and municipal services) provides assistance during the two-year implementation period.
- Residents within each of the newly proposed thirty-seven cities have the power to determine (vote on) the form of government, elected officials, changes in tax rates, municipal name, etc.

City/County Areawide Issues

AREAWIDE ECONOMIC DEVELOPMENT

- A joint city/county economic development district will be established. It will be funded through a 1 percent tax on nonresidential utility usage in the city and county plus all taxes derived from St. Louis International Airport (Lambert Airport).

FUTURE AREAWIDE ISSUES/PROBLEMS

- A Metropolitan Commission will be established with the authority to examine specific issues (e.g., solid/toxic waste disposal) that affect the city/county area. Only one such Commission may be in session at any given time. Funding will be shared equally by the city and county.

Board of Electors Plan: 1990

This board was called into existence in 1990 by a Missouri Supreme Court order after the 1987 Board of Freeholders was declared unconstitutional by the U.S. Supreme Court. The proposals presented to the voters by this Board affect both St. Louis City and St. Louis County.

ECONOMIC DEVELOPMENT

- Establish a Metropolitan Economic Development Commision "to finance programs which will create, attract, retain, expand, develop, improve, and enhance employment opportunities within the City and County" (Board of Electors, 1991, 4)

- This Commission would be financed by a 2 percent gross receipts tax on non-residential utility customers (water, gas, electric, telephone).

REGIONAL PARKS

- Establish a Metropolitan Park Commission "to govern, administer, repair, maintain, conserve, sustain, protect, and improve any and all Commission Parks" (Board of Electors 1991, 16). De facto, only the 1,300-acre Forest Park in St. Louis City would be affected unless expanded authority and funding was approved by voters

- This Commission would be financed by a tax of up to 6 cents per $100 assessed valuation on property in the city and county. Up to 2 cents could be used for operations and up to 4 cents for repairs and capital improvements

- The Board of Electors's plan was presented to city and county voters on April 7, 1992. It was defeated at the polls.

Appendix II: Missouri Constitutional Context for Governmental Reform in the St. Louis Area

The new constitution enacted in 1876 allowed for the separation of the city from the county. It did not, however, contain any provisions for adjustment of city/county borders after separation.

More recently, Article VI, Section 30, of the Missouri State constitution allows for the establishment of a Board of Freeholders (later called Electors) to address local government structure in St. Louis City and St. Louis County.

The constitution Section 30(a) designates five types of reform that the Board can consider. The first three (added in 1924) deal with reentry or merger between St. Louis City and County. The fourth (added in 1945) addresses the formation of one or more area-wide districts; under this provision the Metropolitan Sewer District was approved by voters in 1954. The fifth option allows the Board "to formulate and adopt any other plan for the partial or complete government of all or any part of the city and the county." This much more expansive option was added to the state constitution in 1966.

This provision has always been interpreted to mean that any proposed plan must include some provision that affects both the city and the county. Any proposal must receive voter approval.

Boards Convened Under the Missouri Constitution from 1876 to the Present Article VI, Section 30

Year	Proposal	Status
1876	Separate St. Louis City from St. Louis County	Passed
1926	Merge St. Louis City and County under city government	Failed

Year	Proposal	Status
1954	Metropolitan Sewer District	Passed
1955	Create a transit district	Failed
1959	Create a multipurpose district (Greater St. Louis City-County District)	Failed
1987	Fundamentally restructure St. Louis County government and establish two areawide "districts"	*
1990	Establish a Metropolitan Economic Development and a Metropolitan Park Commission	Failed

*This Board was declared unconstitutional by the U.S. Supreme Court in 1989.

References

Advisory Commission on Intergovernmental Relations (ACIR). *The Organization of Local Public Economies.* Washington, DC: Author, 1987, A-109.

———. *Metropolitan Organization: The St. Louis Case.* Washington, DC: Author, 1988, M-158.

———. *Metropolitan Organization: The Allegheny County Case.* Washington, DC: Author, 1992, M-181.

Barclay, Thomas. *The St. Louis Home Rule Charter of 1876: Its Framing and Adoption.* Columbia: University of Missouri Press, 1962.

Board of Electors: St. Louis City/St. Louis County. *Plan for Metropolitan Economic Development Commission and Metropolitan Park Commission of the City of St. Louis and St. Louis County.* St. Louis: Author, 1991.

Board of Freeholders. *Board of Freeholders Proposal No. 8: Proposal for the Consolidation of the Territories and Governments of the City of St. Louis and the County of St. Louis into One Legal Subdivision Under the Municipal Government of the City of St. Louis.* St. Louis: Author, 1926.

———. "Proposed Plan of the Metropolitan Sewer District." Plan submitted to the St. Louis City and St. Louis County Board of Freeholders at a special election, St. Louis, MO, February 9, 1954.

———. *Plan for Governmental Reorganization in St. Louis & St. Louis County.* St. Louis: Author, September 1988a.

———. *Supplement to the Plan for Governmental Reorganization in St. Louis & St. Louis County.* St. Louis: Author, September 1988b.

Cassella, William. "City-County Separation: The 'Great Divorce' of 1876." *Missouri Historical Society Bulletin* 15 (January 1959): 85–104.

Confluence St. Louis. *Too Many Governments?* St. Louis: Author, 1987.

Jones, E. Terrence. *Fragmented by Design: Why St. Louis Has So Many Governments.* St. Louis: Palmerston & Reed, 2000.

Loeb, Isidor. "Government for the St. Louis Metropolis." *National Municipal Review* 19 (June 1930): 405–410.

Metropolitan Board of Freeholders. "Proposed Plan of the Greater St. Louis City-County District." Plan submitted to the St. Louis City and St. Louis County Board of Freeholders for a special election, St. Louis, MO, November 3, 1959.

Metropolitan St. Louis Survey. *Background for Action.* St. Louis: Author, February 1957a.

_____. *Path of Progress for Metropolitan St. Louis.* St. Louis: Author, August 1957b.

Metropolitan St. Louis Transit District. *Proposed Plan of the Metropolitan St. Louis Transit District.* St. Louis: The St. Louis and St. Louis County Transit Board of Freeholders, 1955.

Patton, R. H. "Local Government Structure and the Quality of Life in Metropolitan St. Louis." *Urban Resources* 3 (Spring 1986): SL1–SL4.

Schmandt, H., P. Steinbicker, and G. Wendel. *Metropolitan Reform in St. Louis: A Case Study.* New York: Holt, Rinehart and Winston, 1961.

Sengstock, Frank, P. Fellin, L. Nicholson, and C. Mundale. *Consolidation: Building a Bridge Between City and Suburb.* St. Louis: Heffernan Press, St. Louis University School of Law, 1964.

St. Louis County. *2002 Fact Book.* St. Louis: St. Louis County Department of Planning, 2002.

St. Louis Globe-Democrat, January 26, 1955, p. 1.

Ward, R. C. "The Impact of Metropolitan Fragmentation on Economic Development." *Urban Resources* 4 (Winter 1987): SL1–SL4.

Chapter 3
Harland Bartholomew, City Engineer[1]

Joseph Heathcott

Harland Bartholomew built his career as a city planner in the laboratory of twentieth-century St. Louis. From the moment he arrived in St. Louis in 1915, Bartholomew cultivated a professional practice through activities of widely varied scope, all culminating in the production of a system of knowledge about the city. This urban knowledge base disciplined the ways in which planning interventions were imagined, organized, and implemented, as well as the very conception of the city itself. For Bartholomew, one of the leading city planners of the twentieth century, the assignment to St. Louis provided the opportunity to imagine both the profession and the forms of knowledge that constituted the profession.

Scholars have taken note of Bartholomew's career, and have identified four arenas where his impact was most profound. First, he emerged very early as a leader in the effort to consolidate planning as a profession, with governing associations and norms of training and development. Second, he developed deep connections to beltway politics through service to a range of national commissions and through frequent appearances to provide expert testimony before congressional bodies (Johnson 1988). Third, he authored influential studies such as *Urban Land Uses* and coauthored major urban plans such as the 1930 *Plan for the Los Angeles Region* that shaped the contours of planning discourse and practice (Hise and Deverell 2000). And fourth, through the auspices of his private firm Harland Bartholomew and Associates, Incorporated, he seeded cities and towns across the country with his trained apprentices, who more often than not would be hired on as a city's first full-time planner (Johnston 1964, 15–19; Lessoff 2003, 197–232; Serda 1996).

---

[1] Excerpted from Joseph Heathcott, "'The Whole City Is Our Laboratory': Harland Bartholomew, Urban Knowledge, and the Rise of Professional City Planning," *Journal of Planning History* 4, no. 3 (November 2005).

Few scholars, however, have examined the development of Bartholomew's ideas and methods within the grain of the urban "laboratory" that was at his constant disposal. Eric Sandweiss and Mark Abbott provide some of the only studies of Bartholomew's work in St. Louis during the formative years of his career. For Sandweiss, Bartholomew and twentieth-century city planning emerge as a weak counterpoise to the far more powerful forces that drive the city building process, such as real estate speculation, small-time home building, and the jumbled regulatory framework. Abbott demonstrates that Bartholomew's concept of the "comprehensive plan" was a dead letter, arriving to prominence at the very moment that cities were abandoning long-term planning approaches in favor of major blockbusting projects such as urban renewal and public housing. In each case, the picture that emerges of Bartholomew's work in St. Louis is one of continual frustration, setback, and disappointment (Sandweiss 2001; Abbott 1985).

This chapter builds on the work done by Sandweiss and Abbott to examine how Bartholomew assembled a national professional practice within and often against the frustrating landscape of St. Louis politics. I examine his career from his arrival in St. Louis through World War II, as he cultivated the profession and formulated many of the methods that would dominate the practice of city planning for decades. In the context of rapid metropolitan growth and expansion, he consolidated the legitimacy and authority to plan, however limited in nature and scope, and delineated arguments about the optimal tools for shaping urban land use. He deployed a nationally influential urban research method based primarily in the systematic inventory of land and physical plant, the organization of this plant into taxonomies of land use, and the discernment of ratios of parts to wholes that he believed would yield the best environmental relationships and thus the common civic good.

As the city reeled from constant cycles of boom and bust, Bartholomew and his staff mobilized the rationale and legal instruments to re-imagine the city as a place of stable, predictable land uses and functions, to define the social parameters of property through zoning, to raise huge capital sums through municipal debt instruments, to knit the region together with road building, to consolidate property into large contiguous parcels of land, and to transform whole neighborhoods through redevelopment projects of unprecedented scale. In the teeming, often inchoate streets of St. Louis, Bartholomew derived a systematic approach to the production of urban knowledge, that is, knowledge about the city that he deemed sufficiently objective to map an urban future. Through the first half of the twentieth century, Harland Bartholomew forged a local culture of planning in the gritty crucible of St. Louis politics, which he then translated into a national professional culture.

Bartholomew and the World of the Professions

Harland Bartholomew began his career in an age of great ferment and change in the nature of work in industrial society. In all fields of enterprise, men and women labored to consolidate control over what constituted knowledge and authority. To do this, practitioners of disparate crafts and pursuits transformed their endeavors into professions, with rigors of training, standards of application, fundamentals of ethics and service, and control over access. The professions, in effect, emerged as a gatekeeping force, a way to introduce scarcity into markets for information through the consolidation of a knowledge core. The more that industrial capitalism expanded and penetrated work and social life, the more demand grew for professionals, who busily carved out new arenas for the application of their expertise. Ultimately, this professional stratum came to occupy a complicated place in the class structure of American society. While clearly indebted to the wealth creation and endowments of capital, professionals also developed their own sets of interests, with the survival of the professions themselves being among the principal objectives.

Bartholomew's career unfolded within these broader developments. Yet as member number 0001 of the American Planning Institute, Bartholomew also shaped and amplified the trend of professionalization in city planning. He was born in 1889 in Stoneham, Massachusetts, to a middling farm family. After the early death of his mother and grandmother, he was raised by his sister first on their grandfather's farm in New Hampshire, then in Gloucester, Massachusetts, and finally in Brooklyn, New York, where he attended Erasmus High School and worked as a drugstore clerk and delivery boy. A teacher at Erasmus took notice of Bartholomew's intellect and sent him to meet with the president of Rutgers University, who offered him a scholarship and part-time work in the library to pursue a degree in civil engineering. However, lack of funds and exhaustion forced Bartholomew to leave Rutgers after only two years, and although he took night classes in engineering at Columbia University, he never completed the degree (Johnson 1988; Lovelace 1993, 21–26).

Upon leaving Rutgers, Bartholomew dove right into entry-level work with the U.S. District Engineers, occupied first as a landsman and later an inspector on various river channel widening, navigation, and dredging contracts. In 1912, he landed a position with the prestigious firm of E.

P. Goodrich, and he commenced immediately on a range of projects in the construction and modification of terminals, docks, channels, bridges, and railroads. Within a very short time, the precocious young engineer had absorbed substantial experience and skills, and he rose quickly in the esteem of the firm's principals.

In the same year that Bartholomew joined Goodrich, the firm landed a joint contract with the firm of George Ford to produce a comprehensive plan for the city of Newark, New Jersey. They placed Bartholomew in charge, and ordered him to reside in Newark for the duration of the project. While Bartholomew regarded the assignment as a disappointing diversion from his chosen career path in civil engineering, it would actually prove transformative. In Newark, Bartholomew oversaw a staff of two dozen fieldworkers to gather data and conduct analysis of population distribution, traffic flow, transportation systems, parks use, and revenue streams. The Newark plan commission terminated Ford's contract in 1913, and Goodrich remained engaged for only one more year, preoccupied with one of the largest civil engineering projects of the moment, the reorganization of the Los Angeles harbor. In 1914, the Newark plan commission retained Bartholomew as the first full-time public sector city planner in America, and by 1915 he had completed the first comprehensive city plan (Johnson 1988).

For Bartholomew, the experience galvanized his career trajectory and his conceptualization of the work of the city planner. From George Ford, he derived his crucial lifelong lesson: "In the science of city planning," Ford wrote in 1915, "the whole city is our laboratory. All its facts and symptoms are more or less under observation, but the expert city planner soon sifts the significant from the less important" (Ford 1913, 551–552). This quest for total, objective data as a means of land use control would define Bartholomew's conceptualization of the planning scope and method. The Newark project resulted in more than a comprehensive city plan; it organized, in its tables, charts, graphs, maps, and prose, a basic argument for the nature of city planning and the quality of urban knowledge itself.

In 1915, on the recommendation of George Ford, architect Henry Wright and prominent urban reform lawyer Luther Ely Smith recruited Bartholomew to St. Louis in order to translate the vision of the 1907 City Plan into a reality.[2] The plan, one of the first of its kind in the nation, grew out of the momentum and administrative networks of the 1904 World's Fair, reconstituted in the Civic League of St. Louis; the majority of committee

---

[2] Notes from a meeting held regarding the status of Mr. Harland Bartholomew, engineer of the City Plan Commission, December 15, 1937, file 1336, Records of the League of Women Voters, Collection Number 530, Western History Manuscript Collection, University of Missouri–St. Louis. Hereafter abbreviated as LWV Records, WHMC 530.

members who worked on the plan had also served on committees for the Louisiana Purchase Company (Sandweiss 2001). The plan unfolded a City Beautiful agenda through a series of sketches for the treatment of urban forms such as public building groupings, civic centers, parkways, and the riverfront (Civic League of St. Louis 1907).

Yet the plan incorporated little in the way of action steps, strategies, finance, or measures to translate sketches into material form. Despite the fact that the Civic League committees brimmed with talented managers capable of organizing the largest World's Fair in history, they faltered before the far more complex task of managing the city itself. Indeed, one of the first major City Beautiful initiatives after the World's Fair, the Central Traffic Parkway bond issue, was soundly defeated in a referendum just two months before Bartholomew arrived (Schmidt 1986).

In Bartholomew, St. Louis advocates for the planned city found an accomplished civil engineer willing to come to work on a half-time basis. Though only twenty-six years old, he was one of the most promising figures in the nascent profession of city planning by the time his train rolled into Union Station. What most League members did not know, however, was that Bartholomew came equipped with his own agenda: a zealous commitment less to the city of St. Louis, than to the broadcasting of a model of city planning that would take root regardless of the particular location. He saw himself less as the benefactor of a particular group's patronage and more as a provider of disinterested expertise. Dedicated to a client model of professional service, the specific identity of the client was less important in the long run than the application of proven principles in service to the client. St. Louis would be his staging ground, his laboratory.

Though Bartholomew deliberately personified the technocratic planner, he also exhibited a Modernist aesthetic sensibility, locating beauty in the elegant, matter-of-fact functionality of urban improvements. Like many young planners of the early twentieth century influenced by R. S. Peabody and Benjamin Marsh, he regarded the end result of his endeavors not solely or even primarily in terms of beauty, but in terms of efficiency, rationality, and practicality in service of a transcendent common good. "I believe the most practical result to be attained," wrote R. S. Peabody of city planning practice, "is not the beauty of the city, but the consequent elevation of the standard of citizenship" (Peabody 1912, 84–104; Marsh 1909). "Beauty," Bartholomew wrote, "should be an inexpensive adjunct to the primary mode of efficiency in an improvement project" (Bartholomew 1914, 380). In this light, the baroque, airy, Beaux Arts aesthetics of the 1907 City Plan, coupled with the lack of implementation strategies, probably amused the no-nonsense Bartholomew, who imported to St. Louis a vision of the city made modern and livable through practical solutions.[3]

Bartholomew's New England Protestant and agrarian origins must surely have placed him at odds with his rich, urbane, patrons—many of whom were Catholic and harbored a living memory of slave owning.[4] As a group, they were dedicated to the most bizarre origin myths to account for their supremacy. The yearly rite of the Veiled Prophet Ball, with its lavish cotillion of sons and daughters of the ruling families, could only have appeared fantastically self-indulgent to the Yankee engineer (Spencer 2000). Bartholomew, moreover, was a lifelong Republican working for an elite dominated by genteel Southern Democrats. His commitments, then, were less to serving the ends and interests of this peculiar elite, than to implementing a program of urban management while advancing his profession. If he was able to realize the interests of this local elite while accomplishing his broader objectives, so much the better for the ambitious young planner (Porter 1990; Sandweiss 2001, 215–216). But for Bartholomew, these "leaders of civic thought and captains of finance" were more often than not a primary obstacle to the realization of his middle-class, managerial approach to planning the ideal, efficient city (Bartholomew 1925, 85).

The Industrial City as a Progressive Laboratory

One area where Bartholomew's professional interests clearly overlapped with the needs of his elite patrons was in their conception of the city itself. At the heart of the 1907 Plan was a conceit for a central planning agenda

---

[3]For example, in his first major study, *The Problems of St. Louis,* Bartholomew devoted nearly half the book to transportation, and the smallest chapter to physical beautification. See Harland Bartholomew, *The Problems of St. Louis, being a description, from the city planning standpoint, of past and present tendencies of growth, with general suggestions for impending issues and necessary future improvements* (St. Louis: Nixon-Jones Printing Co., 1917). For more on Bartholomew's aesthetic sense, see E. F. Porter, *Harland Bartholomew* (Saint Louis: Saint Louis Public Library and Landmarks Association of St. Louis, 1990), 7-8.

[4]The principal study of the St. Louis elite at the turn of the century remains Alexander Scot McConachie, "The Big Cinch: A Business Elite in the Life of a City, Saint Louis, 1895–1915," Ph.D. diss., Washington University, 1976). To view the connection between the city's large business and institutional interests and the push for city planning, see Civic League *Yearbook* yearly volumes for 1903, 1904, and 1906–1917. The Civic League reads like a who's who of major downtown businessmen, including industrialists such as J. Charless Cabanne, Adolphus Busch, and W. K. Bixby; merchants Charles Stix, William Fuller, and Murray Carleton; real estate barons W. P. H. Turner, Frederick Zeibig, and Pierre Chouteau; and professionals such as World's

that would supposedly transcend ward politics and bossism, worker and immigrant agitation, the interests of small-time landlords, and the disarticulated efforts of property speculators. Civic League members conceived the city as a great business establishment—not a collection of liberal, republican shopkeepers, but rather a vast corporate entity that required strong central management of the various public assets and pools of capital (Sandweiss 1991). "The city," wrote Bartholomew in one of his first major reports on St. Louis, "is an organism whose life and health depend on the successful performance by each part of its necessary function" (City Plan Commission 1917). For Bartholomew, many parts with disparate functions composed the whole, which in turn constituted a total, knowable, organic system—a corporate body, a whole.

This reconceptualization of the city mirrored many of the larger transformations of business and the economy in America toward consolidation and the unified resources of the corporate body (Klein 1993, 42–56; Trachtenberg 1982, 82). To be sure, planning advocates saw a common set of interests and destinies for all of the city's neighborhoods; or at least they imagined that the interests of the Central Corridor elite were roughly coterminous with the interests of the city as a whole. The challenge was to link developments throughout the city into a comprehensive endeavor, in order ultimately to discipline diverse social groups and geographies through the extension of the basic Progressive bargain—quiescence in return for public amenities and services.[5] Thus, the attempt to establish a strong civic core through monumental public building projects would unfold in close harmony with linked reform developments in the immigrant neighborhoods. These linkages would not only foster the common good, but in fact would constitute the very physical evidence of the com-

---

Fair landscape architect George Kessler, Washington University chairman of the board Robert Brookings, and engineering chair Calvin Woodward.

[5]St. Louis Progressive reformers were by no means unique, and they shared a common political language both nationally and across the Atlantic. See John D. Beunker, *Urban Liberalism and Progressive Reform* (New York, 1978); Michael Ebner and Eugene M. Tobin, eds., *The Age of Urban Reform: New Perspectives on the Progressive Era* (Port Washington, NY, 1977). On the ambivalence of Progressive reform with respect to race, class, and immigration, see Marilyn Thornton Williams, *Washing the Great Unwashed: Public Baths in Urban America, 1840–1920* (Columbus: Ohio State University, 1991); K. Austin Kerr, *Organized for Prohibition: A New History of the Anti-Saloon League* (New Haven, CT: Yale University Press, 1985); Dominick Cavallo, *Muscles and Morals: Organized Playgrounds and Urban Reform, 1880–1920* (Philadelphia: University of Pennsylvania Press, 1981); Mark Connelly, *The Response to Prostitution in the Progressive Era* (Chapel Hill: University of North Carolina Press, 1980); and Paul Boyer, *Urban Masses and Moral Order in America, 1820–1920* (Cambridge, 1978).

mon good. Not incidentally for Bartholomew, this reimagining of the city required professional expertise to make wholes out of disparate parts (Sandweiss 2001).

Bartholomew's guiding moral commitment was to a healthy and civil city, peopled by literate and educated nuclear families living in stately detached townhouses, conducting themselves along wide, paved, and efficiently organized streets (Bartholomew 1924; Brownell 1975). Planning for Bartholomew was an endeavor to protect and sustain the good community, comprised of law-abiding middle-class families. But for Bartholomew, this moral vision was continually undermined by the vagaries of industrial nuisance, land speculation, property devaluation, and most notably in the context of St. Louis, bossism and municipal corruption. Good communities had to be sheltered from the noise, pollution, and social disintegration of the city, with its tenements, shops, saloons, and factories all jumbled together on an urban terrain run by ward bosses, committeemen, and political operatives.

One strategy for evading this chaos was to relocate at a distance from the densest, most crowded districts into new residential communities. This practice was already under way when Bartholomew arrived in St. Louis, as wealthy and middle-class families steadily relocated westward from the river, first along streetcar lines, and then along newly developed roads, highways, and expressways. Bartholomew noted this westward trend in relocation with great alarm, arguing that the flight to the suburbs only extended the worst aspects of cities while bringing higher infrastructure costs and diminished returns from ratable property. The compactness of the city, he argued, was the precondition for the rational and efficient extension of services across the plat—insofar as these could be managed without graft and corruption (Bartholomew 1925; Bartholomew 1939, 96–97).

To accomplish his aims, then, Bartholomew argued that urban property had to contain use restrictions in order to keep the various functions of land separate, regulated, and predictable. As a reformer and Progressive civil servant, Bartholomew was intellectually prone to view land in anti-liberal terms; that is, to perceive land not as infinitely partible and autonomous, but rather as part of a broader moral system. Thus, Bartholomew translated the corporatist conception of the city that he shared with his elite patrons into a land use practice that sought to challenge the acephalous laissez-faire real estate economy. For Bartholomew and other planners, a landowner was sovereign in the dispensation of his estate, but should not be sovereign in the determination of its uses. Capital investments and physical improvements, Bartholomew felt, had to proceed according to some sense of central management in order to forestall the decay and confusion of the city and to effect the good orderly community. Since cities exist to confer mutual advantages, according to Bartholomew, community interests of health, safety, and general welfare "supercede the rights of the individual" (Bartholomew 1918).

This, in effect, was the principle behind the incipient practice of zoning (Bartholomew 1918). With the application of zoning, no longer would the mansion of a wealthy citizen have to endure the nuisance of a factory, warehouse, or animal depot. No longer would the single family in the detached bungalow have to suffer the proximity of tenements and flophouses. Through zoning, the city could use its police powers to shape and control uses, values, human experience, and presumably the wider social good. Bartholomew soon became one of the chief proponents of zoning, and St. Louis among the earliest cities to enact zoning laws (Purdy et al. 1920)

Yet Bartholomew realized that zoning alone could not pull the fragmented city together. And while the system of public works envisioned by the 1907 Plan promised to renew the downtown, Bartholomew felt that it lacked the coherence necessary to knit the disparate neighborhoods into a corporate city. For Bartholomew, this coherence could only be achieved through systematic applications and improvements; to this end, he set to work on a street plan for St. Louis (City Plan Commission 1917). Indeed, very soon after his arrival in the city, he commenced conducting traffic studies of the sort he had just completed in Newark. This included deriving the volume of traffic along specific routes by counting numbers of vehicles against the vector of time. This produced a particular form of knowledge about urban streets that eschewed concerns for monumental beauty, multimodality, or the vernacular of daily use in favor of the calculus of vehicular movement through space.

The resultant street plan focused less on the signatures of beauty such as circuses, fountains, and promenades (though these were certainly present), and more on the functional-material aspects of road construction and automobile circulation. Its purpose was less about beauty than about a centrally planned and integrative transportation network. His road system would be a template to lie atop the riotous old city, bringing it together through an elegant choreography of motion. If ward politics kept St. Louis fractious and divided, Bartholomew would use his background in transport engineering to knit the city together through professionally planned and expertly delineated motive arteries (Sandweiss 2001, 217–220). Rational circulation would liberate the city of its congestive points, assemble parts into a whole, and, not incidentally, distribute the benefits of city planning to all corners of the city.

The capstone in the development of Progressive planning in St. Louis was the passage of the 1923 Bond Issue, the city's $87 million improvement package and the largest such municipal debt commitment in the nation.[6] In one of the greatest gifts a city ever gave to itself, St. Louis appropriated enormous sums for street improvements, sewer construction, river channeling, parks and playgrounds, public hospitals, firehouses and equipment, rail and auto bridges, public markets, waterworks upgrade, power plant, and the municipal auditorium and downtown plaza and memorial.[7] The line items of the Bond Issue reflected a closely negotiated pact between the elite and activist elements of the Progressive planning coalition, with Bartholomew knitting together the disparate threads. His primary interest was to secure funds for his transportation overhaul. But he realized that his patrons and sponsors—those who effected his employment with the city in the first place—would have to be appeased. To this end, he lent his considerable organizational skill to the Bond Issue campaign, and specifically to the inclusion of line items for grand civic projects downtown (City Plan Commission 1919). To overcome working-class resistance to the enormous levy for Central Corridor improvements, Bartholomew, Gundlach, Luther Ely Smith, an active Mayor Henry Kiel, and others orchestrated a sophisticated public relations campaign, complete with a propaganda reel to play in all of the city's movie houses and nickelodeons (Primm 1998, 421–424; Leckie 2001).

Yet despite the hoopla over the Bond Issue, for most of the 1920s Bartholomew and his staff had their hands full chasing after rapid development in the western rim of the city (Johnson 1988). As early as 1900, white middle-class families began their long dispersal westward through the city, out of old neighborhoods like Soulard and Carr Square. Large numbers of them moved out through the 1910s and 1920s, first settling west of Jefferson Avenue, and then—with more savings or the passing

---

[6] One explanation of the heavy reliance on bonds to capitalize public improvements derives from the peculiar tax structure of St. Louis municipal government. St. Louis received no revenue from St. Louis County, which was an entirely separate entity, and endured antiquated State-imposed limits of property tax rates and deficit spending. The Earnings Tax, approved in 1956, would ease the city's overreliance on long-term bond indebtedness. See Stanley R. Suchat, "Sinking Fund and Bonded Debt of the City of St. Louis," A.M. Thesis, Washington University, 1993.

[7] General Council on Civic Needs, "The St. Louis General Improvement Bond Issue, and Why You Vote for It," pamphlet, February 1923, MHS Collections; "$40,000,000 of City's Bond Issue Funds Spent," *St. Louis Star: Civic and Industrial Progress Edition*, October 31, 1928; St. Louis Politics Clipping File, MHS Collections; City Plan Commission, *Plan Commission Annual Report, 1944–45* (City of St. Louis, 1946), 24; "Bond Issue Election Results, 1923–1955," file 850, LWV Records, WHMC 530.

of a new generation—removing west of Grand Avenue. These families found themselves drawn by the rapidly expanding housing opportunities to the west, even as far out as the edges of the city (City Plan Commission 1936). Meanwhile, inventories conducted by Bartholomew and his staff indicated a rapid rise of multiple family dwellings. The four-family flat, for example, cropped up in every corner of the city, and multiunit apartment buildings proliferated in new developments throughout the 1920s (City Plan Commission 1936). In fact, the number of building permits for the four-family flat rose as sharply as all other permits in the city combined from 1921 to 1925, the period of greatest residential building in the city's history. During that time, some 7,500 permits were issued for four-family flats. Nevertheless, most common were the residential tracts of bungalows and cottages that filled in the city's western margins. In 1921, the city issued 1,500 permits for single-family homes; just four years later, the city issued 8,000, nearly all of which were for developments in western subdivisions (City Plan Commission 1942).

It was an era of feverish growth, as tract after tract of residential and commercial buildings opened up, sometimes to accommodate demand, other times ahead of demand. Bartholomew kept his planners, drafters, and clerks busy day after day monitoring developments, devising service extension schemes, and negotiating the bewildering pace of growth. Whatever heady gains were made over the past decades in establishing the vestiges of city planning in St. Louis, it was clear to Bartholomew that the driving force of development remained the haphazard, uncoordinated, and barely bridled speculative real estate market. "The marvelous urban development witnessed in this country in recent years," Bartholomew noted with a tinge of irony, "has produced serious economic problems." Taking a breather toward the end of 1924 to write a major essay on city planning for the inaugural issue of the *Journal of Land and Public Utility Economics*, Bartholomew declared that "city growth is at once spectacular and amazingly wasteful." Urban planning was the "science and art of properly directing city growth" that would, though its rational application, mediate the chaos of the metropolis (Bartholomew 1925).

Nevertheless, the authority and legitimacy of city planning was clearly established by the time the Great Depression arrived. Moreover, most of the presumptions that would govern the exercise of planning and redevelopment in the city for much of the twentieth century trace their origins to the early phase of Bartholomew's tenure in St. Louis. First and foremost was the presumption of a unitary urban order, a whole that required managed unification of the disparate parts. Planners believed that the city's parts, its neighborhoods, its downtown, its industrial districts and waterfront, could be knitted together by disinterested experts who bargained amenities for industrial and social peace. Of course, this bargain was never complete, and was never able to transcend the particular class and racial biases of the planners and their patrons in executive government and business.[8] Second, planners and other urban reformers evinced a profound ambivalence toward the plight of the urban poor. In casting a gaze over the tenements, planners were acutely aware of the role of small-time slumlords and real estate interests in fostering decline in the housing stock (City Plan Commission 1917, 65–66). At the same time, they harbored suspicions of the alien, heterogeneous social universe of immigrant and Southern black enclaves, and often supported segregation as a method to check blight. Third, in maneuvering for various reforms, professionals and their patrons realized the importance of controlling debate by shaping the contours of public discourse. To that end, they developed sophisticated techniques in public relations in order to foster a shared language of Progress, with varying degrees of success.

Finally, in zoning, planners reconceptualized land as a bundle of rights, shared between owners and the public domain. In practice, however, zoning lacked teeth in many jurisdictions. From Bartholomew's perspective, zoning in St. Louis was nearly a dead-letter ordinance, as planners retained very limited powers of enforcement. Bartholomew joined other planners nationally in a continual koan about the weak and uneven application of the tools available to him, as "parochial" real estate interests continued to govern land use patterns through variances, spot zoning, and other political favors. Zoning, then, was merely a tool, and subject to the graces of the political regime in power. It meant little without a transformation (and strong centralization) of municipal government.

If planners could use the police power to place restrictions on property and to yield homogeneous land uses, it was no large leap to imagine other interventions. Zoning created the context in which planners could begin to view the city as inherently malleable—both spatially and socially. If property was no longer seen in strictly autonomous terms, then property could be assembled into larger contiguities that transcended the speculative plat. Large assemblies of land could be redeveloped to support any number of uses, all in aid of a planned and managed urban landscape.

---

[8] From "Summary of Achievements under WPA Project No. 69," unpublished manuscript transmitted from Bartholomew to Mayor Darst, City Plan Commission file, 1949–1951, Series One—Box 23, Records of the Mayoral Administrations of St. Louis, Raymond Tucker Papers, Washington University Special Collections.

The Great Depression and the Production of Planning Knowledge

Bartholomew and his staff demonstrated that private investment needs the support of public planning to achieve efficiencies and to direct resources in such a way as to overcome cycles of boom and bust. The Depression elegantly underscored this point. In the context of a largely unregulated and speculative economy, dramatic shifts in consumer demand by the growing middle class led to a rapid, uneven, and ill-timed restructuring of investment, production, and employment through the 1920s. Meanwhile, shifts in the distribution of incomes did not occur rapidly enough to absorb the overstimulated output of big-ticket leisure items. At the same time, significant sectors of the American economy had matured, unable to expand without exogenous sources of investment, resources, or markets. When the speculative bubble in high-end consumer durables collapsed with the 1929 stock market crash, vulnerable sectors of the economy were poorly positioned to generate a recovery, and the crisis spread through consumer goods, finance and credit, and finally to basic production (Bernstein 1989, 32–54; McElvaine 1984, 25–54).

In St. Louis, much speculation had occurred in the housing stock, which had expanded rapidly through the 1920s with little coordination, far outstripping the capacities of the small Plan department to determine zoning and infrastructure requirements. The result, at least as Bartholomew and his staff viewed it, was an overproduction of housing in the western periphery of the city, a stagnation of building in the urban core, and a gap-toothed and uneven population spread. As the Depression deepened through the early 1930s, the sight of homeless families and beggars, once confined to skid row, appeared everywhere, and the occupied city lapsed into crisis.[9]

The New Deal and Applied Planning Research

As city planners around the country clamored for funds and tools to keep their cities afloat, the Great Depression and the World War that followed brought federal and city governments into new, problem-solving

---

[9] *Street begging in St. Louis, including a report of a fact-finding survey of street begging made during November and December, 1936* (St. Louis: Bureau for Homeless Men, 1937).

alignments.[10] Prior to the 1930s, and despite the emergence of federal trust-busting and social reform legislation, most areas of economic growth and development proceeded with little national coordination or oversight. Local governments, creatures of conservative state legislatures, held little authority or resources to direct the engines of recovery. The Depression, however, provided the context within which policymakers and planners organized national coordination efforts, as well as innovative experiments in federal-city cooperation. Indeed, the Urbanism Committee of the National Resource Planning Board not only promoted the idea of city planning to municipalities around the country, but authored the first significant study of national urban trends (Urbanism Committee of the National Resource Planning Board 1937). Many future city planners cut their teeth in the alphabet soup of agencies enabled by Title II of the National Industrial Recovery Act of 1933, particularly the Civic Works Administration (CWA), the Public Works Administration (PWA), and the Works Progress Administration (WPA) (Schwartz 1986, 206–208).

While these efforts never amounted to a national urban policy, cities received a number of short-term and long-term benefits from the fiscal largesse of the New Deal state. In the short term, millions of urban workers left the relief rolls for civil works projects launched through federal underwriting and municipal funds. In January of 1940 alone, ongoing relief projects sponsored by the St. Louis city government provided temporary work for 11,000 men and women.[11] In the long run, cities around the country gained enormous benefit from civil engineering and public building projects, such as levees, dams, sewers, bridges, auditoriums, schools, playgrounds, swimming pools, government buildings, libraries, park improvements, and proximate state recreation areas (Leighninger 1996, 226–236). As war loomed in the late 1930s and early 1940s, the need to work with federal, military, and state officials on civil defense and war

---

[10] From Charles H. Trout, "The New Deal and the Cities," in *Fifty Years Later: The New Deal Evaluated*, Harvard Sitkoff, ed., (New York: Knopf, 1985), 133–153; Joseph Arnold, *The New Deal and the Suburbs: A History of the Greenbelt Town Program, 1935–1954* (Columbus: Ohio State University Press, 1971); Mark Gelfand, *A Nation of Cities: The Federal Government and Urban America, 1933–1965* (New York: Oxford Univesity Press, 1975); Raymond Mohl, "Shifting Patterns of American Urban Policy Since 1900," in *Urban Policy in Twentieth Century America*, Arnold Hirsch and Raymond Mohl, eds., (New Brunswick, NJ: Rutgers University Press, 1993), 8–10; Lawrence Friedman, *Government and Slum Housing: A Century of Frustration* (Chicago: Rand McNally, 1968), 88–90, 94–116.

[11] From a letter from Arthur Meyers to Mrs. Ralph Thayer, January 17, 1940, file 752, LWV Records, WHMC 530. Arthur Meyer was the city's budget director at the time. He explained to League of Women Voters member Mrs. Thayer that not only did the city receive funds to pay workers, but also to engage equipment.

production gave city planners still further experience in mobilizing land and personnel into a public purpose (Funigiello 1978; Funigiello 1972, 91-104). Finally, the housing crisis created by the drop in housing production during the Depression, and amplified by overcrowding in war production centers, resulted in the eventual development of a federally backed, locally administered public housing program.

Nationwide recovery programs launched under the New Deal provided money and personnel to the St. Louis Plan department for a variety of projects over the course of a decade. In short order, St. Louis citizens saw the construction of the Kiel Opera House and the Jewel Box in Forest Park, local airport and waterworks projects, and the clearance of the riverfront for the creation of the Jefferson National Expansion Memorial. Between 1932 and 1936 alone, some $68 million flowed into New Deal works projects in St. Louis (Primm 1998).

For Bartholomew, the promise of the New Deal to underwrite infrastructure and public building projects was alluring enough, but the availability of unprecedented sums for basic research and analysis must have seemed a godsend. With newly available time and resources, bolstered by a national mandate to plan and regulate American economic life, Bartholomew converted his small municipal appendage into St. Louis's first great urban research institution. Much of this research was conceived and undertaken in order to establish a baseline system of measurements against which planners could determine the social and physical elements of city neighborhoods and track their fate over time. With WPA funds, the department launched the largest land use research project undertaken in the city's history—an exact accounting of every square foot of land in St. Louis. In so doing, the plan department could document the "total amount of land used for all of the various purposes . . . [affording] the only scientific basis upon which a revision of the zoning ordinance can be predicated (St. Louis Plan Commission 1936).

In 1932, Bartholomew authored the first application from the city of St. Louis for federal research funds, secured in 1933 under the inauspicious title of Federal Emergency Relief Administration (FERA) Project no. 72. Project no. 72 provided eleven employees working through 4,908 "man-hours" to conduct property use surveys and to draft baseline city maps, over which any number of subsequent maps could be traced to represent demographic data. St. Louis Relief Committee Works Division Project no. 128 provided material and travel costs to undertake surveys and mapping throughout the city. Drafters and architects hired under these projects devised both blue-line and black-line maps at a scale of one thousand feet to the inch (St. Louis Plan Commission 1936). For Bartholomew, the graphic representations and the data collected through "the courtesy of the Works Progress Administration" and other agencies would be of "incalculable value in years to come for approaching problems of housing and zoning" (St. Louis Plan Commission 1937). By 1938, St. Louis had received nearly $2 million in WPA funds, ranking seventh among all cities in New Deal expenditures.[12]

Bartholomew's staff increased and shrank with a periodicity related to the length and terms of New Deal funding contracts. When a new contract would commence, the skeletal staff of the planning department would swell with the likes of interviewers, clerical supporters, transcribers, drafters, surveyors, engineers, and architects. Many came from academic units in the metropolitan region, such as the School of Engineering at Washington University, and the Department of Social Service at St. Louis University. The projects that these temporary professionals labored on were large and involved. For example, in 1935 the Plan Commission landed a one-year contract from the WPA (Project no. 1443) to support ongoing projects and to undertake a range of new studies. Project 1443 included: a municipal cost study reckoned by district; city block maps showing base-line land uses; property absorption surveys; fine-grained property-use maps (two hundred feet = one inch); building line maps for future street-widening programs; and miscellaneous drafting and data crunching projects (St. Louis Plan Commission 1936). Project 1443 provided $9,322 for salary costs in support of twenty-six employees working through 14,456 man-hours. In 1935 alone, the Plan Commission was able to authorize and complete fifty-two specific drafting studies, which yielded demographic maps of a wide range of social and economic indicators by district, from juvenile delinquency and city workhouse rates to infant mortality, tuberculosis morbidity, syphilis cases, and asylum admissions (St. Louis Plan Commission 1937).

Perhaps most ambitious of all was the Property Use Survey, conducted from 1931 to 1935 to support the creation of a general urban land policy for St. Louis. Organized under a grant from the Public Works Division, the survey reckoned "the total amount of land used for all of the various urban purposes," providing a baseline for future measurements of change in the city's residential, commercial, and industrial mix. For Bartholomew, the survey had to be exhaustive and total, not statistical; analyses could later derive from the data set created by the survey. The survey began with an inventory sheet to be filled in by the surveyor, the information from which

---

[12] Exhibit B, WPA expenditures in the 15 largest U.S. cities, July 1938, file 752, LWV Records, WHMC 530.

St. Louis Plans

would then be transferred onto 8.5 × 11 inch city block maps. These maps would be bound together according to twenty-six (later fifty-two) statistical districts, to be known as "neighborhood units" after Clarence Perry's work (Perry 1929; Perry 1933; Lovelace 1993). These so-called neighborhoods would in turn provide the basis of data-gathering, analysis, and knowledge production in support of the application of land use controls. Planners could then geocode their conceptions of social pathology, mapping social data into space by calibrating indices such as race, disease, and crime to their distribution across the neighborhood units.

Plan staff would update information for the units periodically through annotations made from Sanborn Fire Insurance Atlases and building permits. The Property Absorption Survey was similar and provided a composite set of figures for total amounts and values of land given over to various preselected purposes: residential (single-family versus multifamily), commercial, industrial, and infrastructure (St. Louis Plan Commission 1936; St. Louis Plan Commission 1937).

This work conducted by Bartholomew's urban research enterprise was not simply basic research for the sake of it; the data served the production of an urban land policy for the city of St. Louis, completed and published in 1936 (St. Louis Plan Commission 1936). The policy drew on the extensive land use information gathered through the property inventories and absorption surveys. To illustrate the need for a policy, Bartholomew spatialized the city's revenue-expenditure data. He directed his staff to gather figures for tax revenues produced by every neighborhood unit of the city, and for the amount of services absorbed by every unit. In so doing, he presented a picture of tax-gobbling slum districts, draining revenues from middle-class and wealthy neighborhoods for the subsidization of the slumlords. He constructed a picture of the whole of the city as an interrelation of fiscally unequal parts, united through a system of credits and debits.

To forestall what Bartholomew concluded would be an inevitable decline, the policy recommended that the city be carved into neighborhood units, roughly contained by bordering major thoroughfares. In each neighborhood unit, planners would bring a concerted program to bear. The tools of this program would include enforcement of zoning laws and codes, smoke abatement, a minimum housing standards ordinance, property rehabilitation, and, where applicable, slum clearance and reconstruction with public housing (St. Louis Plan Commission 1936).

In practical terms, the *Urban Land Policy* achieved little on the ground, at least in the short run. But it did prepare the city for the slum clearance program that would unfold over the next two decades. Toward that end, the St. Louis slum clearance agenda received a boost with two national events that came in close succession. The first boost came with the passage of the 1937 Housing Act. The Act collapsed all federally backed public housing initiatives into the newly created United States Housing Authority (USHA) under prominent New Dealer and city planning advocate Nathan Strauss (Friedman 1978). Though the Act was replete with compromises that weakened its scope as an instrument of social change, it was a boon to city planners in that it required localities to demonstrate that public housing allotments would be integral to an overall master plan. The second major boost came with the dedication of funds to move ahead with the city's first major slum clearance project, the Jefferson National Expansion Memorial (JNEM). Though a federal effort in support of a national park, the clearance of the city's old riverfront blocks provided a dramatic example of Bartholomew's conception of the city as a corporate entity to be planned and manipulated on a grand scale. Most importantly, city planners gained tremendous experience as they worked with federal officials in exercising eminent domain, condemning properties through the courts, planning infrastructure changes, organizing contractors to proceed with demolition, and grading and preparing the land for a new, singular use as a monumental footprint.[13]

The Commencement of War and the Planning Mandate

In 1939, for the first time since the launching of the WPA studies, the Plan Commission received notice from Congress that funds would be temporarily halted. For a period of six weeks, the city was forced to lay off many employees whose salaries depended on the flow of federal money. Even Bartholomew's half-time position as city engineer came under scrutiny as the city faced an ever-deepening fiscal crisis.[14] While congressional

---

[13]PCAR, 1937–1938, 35–36; PCAR, 1939-1940, 29-31; PCAR, 1940–1941, 30-31; on the local purposes and impact of the JNEM and the Gateway Arch, see Joseph Heathcott and Maire Murphy, "Corridors of Flight, Zones of Renewal: Industry, Planning, and Policy in the Making of Metropolitan St. Louis, 1940–1980," *Journal of Urban History* (March 2005); W. Arthur Mehrhoff, *The Gateway Arch: Fact and Symbol* (Bowling Green, OH: Bowling Green University Popular Press, 1992), 65–81.

[14] The move to terminate Bartholomew's half-time position and to retain him in future on a consulting basis provoked something of a minor scandal among reformers, planning advocates, and housing activists in the city. Then Mayor Bernard Dickmann assured opponents of the move that it did not signal the end of the Plan Commission's work, but rather the potential insolvency of the department (and therefore of staff salaries) should relief measures fail citywide referendum. However, Dean of Washington University School of Architecture A. S. Langsford, who had served

wrangling and deal making eventually restored funds to the WPA, the era of free-flowing funds for research was clearly on the wane (St. Louis Plan Commission 1941, 45). Moreover, as the U.S. mobilized for war in 1940–1941, the Plan Commission was forced to compete with defense industries for qualified professional and blue-collar workers. Finally, on July 1, 1942, an Act of Congress eliminated the WPA as a line item in the federal budget. The St. Louis Plan department finished out the last of its WPA contracts on July 20, 1942, at which time Bartholomew terminated the remainder of the WPA staff in the employ of the Commission.

Nevertheless, by 1940, the contours of a modern professional planning practice were fully consolidated in St. Louis. Indeed, much had been done through the Depression to organize the exhaustive inventories of knowledge about St. Louis upon which future plans would depend. Despite the fact that the loss of funding "greatly curtailed" the research and analysis program of the Plan Department, only fifteen residential and eight industrial districts out of ninety-nine total districts remained unsurveyed.[15] By 1940, the planning staff had completed enough work to support the overhaul of the zoning law and the development of a comprehensive plan.[16]

Even as the city mobilized for war, organized people and materials for production, and sent GIs abroad to fight in Europe and the Pacific Rim, reform advocates continued their fight against the slums. In 1944, they received a big public boost for their efforts when the American Planning and Civic Association held its Citizens Conference on Postwar Planning in St. Louis. Organized to commemorate the fortieth anniversary of the founding of the American Civic Association in St. Louis during the 1904 World's Fair, the conference featured two days of exhibits, talks, and panel discussions. Attended by representatives of some fifty agencies and civic groups around the nation, the conference was also open to the general public, and many St. Louisans came specifically to view the sixteen-panel, five hundred square-foot exhibit on "Our Postwar Cities." The conference provided a national forum for planners, architects, engineers, federal officials, and civic interests to discuss a broad range of urban problems and solutions. Topics at the forefront included reconstruction laws, zoning,

---

for twenty years on the Plan Commission from 1915 to 1935, warned in a letter to the League of Women Voters that there had been numerous politically motivated attempts over the years to remove Bartholomew. See series of correspondence in file 1336, LWV Records, WHMC 530.

[15] From "Summary of Achievements under WPA Project No. 69," unpublished manuscript transmitted from Bartholomew to Mayor Darst, City Plan Commission file, 1949–1951, Series One--Box 23, Records of the Mayoral Administrations of St. Louis, Raymond Tucker Papers, Washington University Special Collections.

[16] From "Summary of Achievements under WPA Project No. 69"; *PCAR, 1942–1943*, 28.

housing standards, postwar employment, metropolitan growth policies, highways and mass transportation, and national resource coordination. Bartholomew capped the conference with a large Saturday tour of St. Louis, highlighting many of the major civic improvements undertaken over the previous two decades (St. Louis Plan Commission 1946, 21–23).

Community interest in planning grew substantially during the Depression and World War II, partly as a result of national recovery and mobilization efforts, and partly from intensified local public relations, exhibits, and conferences. "While the war has caused reduction of staff," Bartholomew wrote in his 1944 report to the Plan Commission, "the general tempo of planning has been increased considerably." Moreover, he suggested, "there is now widespread interest in planning as a means of developing worthwhile projects for postwar employment (St. Louis Plan Commission 1945, 5). Requests for information and speakers from the St. Louis Plan Department increased dramatically in the 1930s, lodged both by locally based groups as well as organizations around the nation. By 1940, St. Louis planners were receiving requests from government agencies around the world, including Australia, Brazil, Canada, China, England, Hawaii, Japan, the Philippines, and Uruguay. At home, representatives of the Plan Commission and its department staff addressed organizations as diverse as the Advertising Club, the YMCA, the Junior League, various high schools and colleges, Washington University School of Architecture, and the League of Women Voters. Requests for information rose from 307 in 1935 to 1,100 in 1945, and reached such a peak in 1946 that the city created a new position for the Plan Department in neighborhood organization and public relations. By the end of the war, planning staff met regularly with high-profile civic groups in order to bolster the city's agenda for dramatic intervention to combat the slums.[17]

A decade of New Deal recovery efforts, as well as the more immediate requirements of war mobilization, had normalized planning as a function of both federal and city government. Moreover, the stresses and strains on urban, rail, industrial, and waterway infrastructure led to heightened awareness of planning among ordinary citizens. As St. Louis emerged as a key inland war production center, hundreds of military and civilian planners, engineers, accountants, scientists, and specialists flooded the city and surrounding towns and bases (Burnette 1987, 8–54). Industrial planners oversaw the retooling of factories to produce ordinances and ammunition. The Army Corps of Engineers worked furiously to rechannel rivers for increased shipping, to improve flood protection to protect war

---

[17] See meeting minutes in file 1337, LWV Records, WHMC 530.

St. Louis Plans

production facilities, and to mobilize barge transportation for materials, parts, and fuel resources (Ruddy 1983).

Bartholomew and the Future of City Planning

By the end of the war, St. Louis and the nation had grown accustomed to the value of macroscale coordination and planning bolstered by the technical research of trained professionals. In this context, city planning emerged from the war as an established feature of municipal government in St. Louis, one with broad support among civic groups and organizations (St. Louis Plan Commission 1941; St. Louis Plan Commission 1943; St. Louis Plan Commission 1946). In 1946, for example, a planning exhibit at Famous-Barr department store in downtown St. Louis could draw "many thousands of persons" to view maps, charts, and drawings detailing postwar urban reconstruction (St. Louis Plan Commission 1948). Moreover, the Plan Commission and its staff had become increasingly integrated into a range of city departments and public projects, including the newly formed Metropolitan Planning Association, the Mayor's Reconstruction Committee (later the Anti-Slum Commission, and still later the Land Clearance for Redevelopment Authority), the Inter-Racial Relations Commission, the St. Louis Air Traffic Board, and the Jefferson Memorial Coordinating Committee (St. Louis Plan Commission 1945). While still politically hamstrung by a lack of enabling legislation or funds to undertake large-scale projects, the Plan Commission nevertheless emerged as a high-profile element of municipal government, and Bartholomew's slum-clearance agenda gained important allies. The commencement of the "postwar reconstruction job" he had so carefully described only awaited passage of the 1949 Housing Act. The modern city planner had arrived on the national stage.

But the quality of urban knowledge and the technocratic identity that governed the profession of city planning by the end of World War II contained serious defects. Bartholomew was by no means responsible alone for these shortcomings, but he had played a major role in developing and broadcasting the methods, techniques, and persona of the modern city planner. Though wrapped in the mantle of scientific disinterest, Bartholomew's modernist approach to city planning was rooted in a moral vision, which in turn conditioned the urban knowledge that he deemed valuable for the purposes of city planning. In St. Louis he had found the proving ground he needed to test this vision. For Bartholomew, the city existed to provide for the common good; however, the common good revealed in his plans betrayed a commitment not to a universal mien or pluralist democracy. Rather, Bartholomew's plans envision a world of white, middle-class citizens in single-family detached homes and working-class families beneficently accommodated in mass housing on curvilinear streets. In each case, the civic good obtains through expert-driven physical interventions. The quality of the urban knowledge that he gathered reflected these commitments; he coded social pathologies and environmental decay against the city's political geography, mapping an agenda for large-scale reorganization of the very terms of twentieth century city life.

Like most planners of his day, Bartholomew held as an article of faith that the city was essentially knowable, and that knowledge of the whole would come through a study of the sum of the disparate parts. To this end, he developed a method of "total knowledge" through land taxonomy, inventory, and analysis. This supposedly "total" comprehension would support the derivation of land use ratios that would in turn support a system of land use designations and controls. From this, a view emerged of the city as an amalgam of manipulable parts, to be assembled and disassembled as per the requirements of land use analysis. For Bartholomew, the connecting thread of the knowable city was not some shared value of urbanism, but rather an artifact of civil engineering—the infrastructure, particularly the system of streets and roads that the planner lays atop the landscape as a template. Between these points of connection lay the vast and jumbled residential, industrial, and commercial developments, bounded by major thoroughfares. For Bartholomew, these inchoate districts became intelligible as "neighborhoods," framed by the arbitrary web of roads and imposed atop vernacular associations and understandings of place. Finally, if infrastructure provides the connectivity, then the "neighborhoods" themselves can be assembled and disassembled, erased, cleared, and reorganized.

In St. Louis, much of this planning vision unfolded in the scrape of bulldozers and the billows of plaster dust. St. Louis, long Bartholomew's principal laboratory, would see its fabric rent apart by one of the largest slum clearance programs in the nation. By the time it was over, the city would clear some one thousand acres of tenements, taverns, shops, churches, synagogues, dance halls, cinemas, factories, and warehouses. Replacing these "slums" were regiments of housing projects, expansive industrial parks, a new university campus plant, and modernist middle-class residential towers. The knowable city had become the malleable city, formed and delineated and clarified using the public purse.

In the end, Bartholomew's laboratory was more complex and elusive than he ever imagined. While the modernist planning practice he helped to create gained substantial ground in the postwar decades, the city itself grew ever more politically convoluted, racially divided, and desperate. Bartholomew had labored for decades to develop the concepts, tools, and means to execute plans, but in the end his Plan Department still lacked political power. The Housing Acts of 1937 and 1949 provided stronger authority to carry out plans, but this authority would be vested not in the city's Plan Commission but in the municipal corporations chartered by the State to undertake slum clearance. In a very short time, the center of gravity of planning had shifted from Bartholomew's purview to the Housing Authority and the Redevelopment Authority. Ironically, these authorities consolidated new powers at the very moment that the city began its long decline through population loss and systematic disinvestment. In the end, the quest for total knowledge was an illusory one, and the planning strategies derived from this quest proved mute in the face of the massive transformations that shook postwar St. Louis to the core. Bartholomew had achieved his long-sought power to manipulate the city's parts, but the whole remained beyond his grasp.

References

Abbott, Mark. "The Master Plan: The Life and Death of an Idea." Ph.D. diss., Purdue University, 1985.

Bartholomew, Harland. "Non-Conforming Uses Destroy the Neighborhood." *Journal of Land and Public Utility Economics* (February 1939): 96–97.

———. "The Prevention of Economic Waste by City Planning." *Journal of Land and Pubic Utility Economics* 1, no. 1 (January 1925): 84.

———. "Publicity and the City Plan." *American City* 11, no. 5 (November 1914): 380.

———. "Reduction of Street Traffic Congestion by Proper Street Design: How St. Louis Is Meeting Its Problem." *Annals of the American Academy of Social and Political Science* 116 (November 1924).

———. *Zoning for St. Louis: A Fundamental Part of the City Plan.* St. Louis: City Plan Commission, 1918.

Bernstein, Michael. "Why the Great Depression Was Great: Toward a New Understanding of the Interwar Economic Crisis in the United States." In *The Rise and Fall of the New Deal Order, 1930–1980,* edited by Steve Fraser and Gary Gerstle. Princeton, NJ: Princeton University Press, 1989: 32–54.

Brownell, Blaine. "The Commercial-Civic Elite and City Planning in Atlanta, Memphis, and New Orleans in the 1920s." *Journal of Southern History* 41, no. 3 (August 1975): 339–368.

Burnette, Betty. *St. Louis at War: The Story of a City, 1941–1945.* St. Louis: Patrice Press, 1987.

City Plan Commission. *A Major Street Plan for St. Louis.* St. Louis: Nixon-Jones, 1917.

———. *Problems of St. Louis.* St. Louis: Author, 1917.

———. *A Public Building Group Plan for St. Louis.* St. Louis: Nixon-Jones, 1919.

———. *St. Louis After World War II.* St. Louis: Author, 1942.

———. *Urban Land Policy.* St. Louis: City Plan Commission, 1936.

Civic League of St. Louis. *A City Plan for St. Louis: Reports of the Several Committees Appointed by the Executive Board of the Civic League to Draft a City Plan.* St. Louis: Author, 1907.

Ford, George. "The City Scientific." *Engineering Record* 67 (May 17, 1913): 551–552.

Fox, Kenneth. *Better City Government: Innovation in American Urban Politics, 1850–1937*. Philadelphia: Temple University Press, 1977.

Friedman, Lawrence M. *Government and Slum Housing*. New York: Arno Press, 1978: 104–108.

Funigiello, Philip. *The Challenge to Urban Liberalism: Federal-City Relations During World War II*. Knoxville: University of Tennessee Press, 1978.

———. "City Planning in World War II: The Experience of the National Resources Planning Board." *Social Science Quarterly* 53 (June 1972): 91–104.

Heathcott, Joseph, and Maire Murphy. "Corridors of Flight, Zones of Renewal: Industry, Planning, and Policy in the Making of Metropolitan St. Louis, 1940–1980." *Journal of Urban History* (March 2005).

Hise, Greg, and William Deverell. *Eden by Design: The 1930 Olmsted-Bartholomew Plan for the Los Angeles Region*. Berkeley: University of California Press, 2000.

Johnson, David A. "Regional Planning for the Great American Metropolis: New York Between the World Wars." In *Two Centuries of American Planning*, edited by Daniel Schaffer. Baltimore: Johns Hopkins University Press, 1988.

Johnston, Norman J. "Harland Bartholomew: His Comprehensive Plans and Science of Planning." Ph.D. diss., University of Pennsylvania, 1964.

Kirschner, Don. *The Paradox of Professionalism: Reform and Public Service in Urban America, 1900–1940*. New York: Greenwood Press, 1986.

Klein, Maury. *The Flowering of the Third America: The Making of an Organizational Society, 1850–1920*. Chicago: Ivan Dee, 1993.

Leckie, William. "Moral Reform in the Burckhardtian City." *Journal of Urban History* (March 2001).

Leighninger, Robert D., Jr. "Cultural Infrastructure: The Legacy of New Deal Public Space." *Journal of Architectural Education* 49 (May 1996): 226–236.

Lessoff, Alan. "Harland Bartholomew and Corpus Christi: The Faltering Pursuit of Comprehensive Planning in South Texas." *Planning Perspectives* 18, no. 2 (April 2003).

Lovelace, Eldridge. *Harland Bartholomew: His Contributions to American Urban Planning*. Urbana: Department of Urban and Regional Planning, University of Illinois, 1993, 21–26.

Marsh, Benjamin Clarke. Chapter 8 in *An Introduction to City Planning: Democracy's Challenge to the American City*. N.p., 1909.

McElvaine, Robert S. *The Great Depression: America, 1929–1941*. New York: Random House, 1984: 25–50.

Mehrhoff, W. Arthur. *The Gateway Arch: Fact and Symbol*. Bowling Green, OH: Bowling Green University Popular Press, 1992.

Peabody, R. S. "Notes for Three Lectures on Municipal Improvements." *The Architectural Quarterly of Harvard University* 1 (September 1912).

Perry, Clarence Arthur. *The Neighborhood Unit*. New York: Regional Plan of New York And Its Environs, 1929.

———. *The Rebuilding of Blighted Areas: A Study of the Neighborhood Unit in Replanning and Plot Assemblage*. New York: Regional Plan Association, 1933.

Porter, E. F. *Harland Bartholomew*. St. Louis: Saint Louis Public Library and Landmarks Association of St. Louis, 1990, 7–8.

Primm, James Neil. *Lion of the Valley: St. Louis, Missouri, 1764–1980*. St. Louis: Missouri Historical Society Press, 1998.

Purdy, Lawson, et al. *Zoning as an Element in City Planning, and for Protection of Property Values, Public Safety, and Public Health*. Washington, DC: American Civic Association, 1920.

Ruddy, T. Michael. *Mobilizing for War: St. Louis and the Middle Mississippi during World War II*. St. Louis: U.S. Army Corps of Engineers, 1983.

Sandweiss, Eric. "Construction and Community in South St. Louis, 1850–1910." Ph.D. diss., University of California–Berkeley, 1991.

———. *St. Louis: The Evolution of an American Urban Landscape*. Philadelphia: Temple University Press, 2001.

Schmidt, Elizabeth Noel. "Civic Pride and Prejudice: St. Louis Progressive Reform, 1900–1916." M.A. thesis, University of Missouri–St. Louis, 1986.

Schwartz, Bonnie Fox. *The Civil Works Administration: The Business of Emergency Employment in the New Deal*. Princeton, NJ: Princeton University Press, 1986.

Serda, Daniel. "Planning Community and Renewal: Harland Bartholomew Associates and the 1951 Armordale Redevelopment Plan." MA thesis, MIT, 1996.

Spencer, Thomas. *The St. Louis Veiled Prophet Celebration: Power on Parade, 1877–1995*. Columbia: University of Missouri Press, 2000.

St. Louis Plan Commission. *St. Louis Plan Commission Annual Report, 1934–1935*. St. Louis City Government, 1936.

———. *St. Louis Plan Commission Annual Report 1935–1936*. St. Louis City Government, 1937.

———. *St. Louis Plan Commission Annual Report 1937–1938*. St. Louis City Government, 1939.

———. *St. Louis Plan Commission Annual Report 1939–1940*. St. Louis City Government, 1941.

———. *St. Louis Plan Commission Annual Report 1940–1941*. St. Louis City Government, 1942.

———. *St. Louis Plan Commission Annual Report 1941–1942*. St. Louis City Government, 1943.

———. *St. Louis Plan Commission Annual Report 1943–1944*. St. Louis City Government, 1945.

———. *St. Louis Plan Commission Annual Report 1944–1945*. St. Louis City Government, 1946.

———. *St. Louis Plan Commission Annual Report 1946–1947*. St. Louis City Government, 1948.

Trachtenberg, Alan. *The Incorporation of America: Culture and Society in the Gilded Age*. New York: Hill and Wang, 1982.

Urbanism Committee of the National Resource Planning Board. *Our Cities: Their Role in the National Economy*. Washington, DC: U.S. Government Printing Office, 1937.

Walkowitz, Daniel. *Working with Class: Social Workers and the Politics of Middle-Class Identity*. Chapel Hill: University of North Carolina Press, 1999, 57–85, 115–140.

Chapter 4

The 1947 *Comprehensive City Plan* and Harland Bartholomew's St. Louis

Mark Abbott

This report offers . . . neither a dream of theorists nor a series of pretty but visionary and impractical pictures; rather it is based on sound planning and engineering principles.—Harland Bartholomew (1947, 2)

"St. Louis," Harland Bartholomew explained to his fellow St. Louisans in the opening sentence of his 1947 *Comprehensive City Plan*, "is a generally satisfactory city, with much solid achievement gained in non-spectacular fashion, in keeping with its tradition of conservatism" (Bartholomew 1947, 1). However, what he was about to propose was anything but non-spectacular or conservative. No other event in the last one hundred years has had as large an impact on St. Louis—good or bad—as the release of Bartholomew's 1947 plan. In its pages, the plan foreshadowed how the city would unfold for the next half century. The plan would drive freeway placement, housing policy, urban renewal projects, and virtually every land use issue in St. Louis far longer than its expected life span of twenty-five years. Bartholomew's goal was to transform St. Louis, and he did.

But the plan's impact went far beyond St. Louis. While the 1907 Civic League plan was the first master plan in the United States, Bartholomew's 1947 plan was and is the most important. Though not as flashy in some respects as some other postwar plans that other cities were preparing, the 1947 plan is perhaps the clearest articulation of what a master plan was meant to be at the peak of its influence. After thirty years of being the St. Louis planning director, Bartholomew had come to embody what midcentury city planning was all about. Largely due to his impact, American city planning had come to be seen as a rational exercise based on scientific principles. For Bartholomew and the planners of his generation, the master, or comprehensive, plan was at the heart of scientific or rational planning. Assuming that the city existed as an integrated whole of inter-dependent parts with each playing a specified role, master planners like Bartholomew could use their knowledge of the city to provide a "modern chart for continued progress" (Bartholomew 1947, 1). Not only because of his previous thirty years of work leading the Plan Department in St. Louis and his massive scholarly output as a professor of city planning at the University of Illinois at Champaign, Bartholomew had more to do with the elements of a master plan than anyone else because of the global reach that he and his consulting firm had in preparing master plans in the United States and around the world. Harland Bartholomew and Associ-ates, Incorporated, would eventually create more than six hundred master plans that essentially established a "formula" for all other master planners that is still being used today.[1]

Ironically, this "formula" and the idea of the master plan had largely outlived its usefulness by 1947. Although American cities would produce hundreds of master plans over the next quarter of a century after 1947, most city planners had lost their enthusiasm for the concept by the early 1950s and no longer saw drafting master plans as their raison d'être. They had become too busy dealing with the mounting disintegration of the city or they had lost faith in the vision of an integrated metropolis. While cit-ies continue to churn out versions of master plans—St. Louis released its latest one in 2005—Bartholomew's construct basically died by the end of the 1960s. Written mostly in response to governmental regulations or as part of "boosteristic" promotions, new master plans are no longer viewed as "chart[s] for progress" (Abbott 1985).

Perhaps this is why understanding the 1947 plan is so important. While present-day St. Louisans may laugh at the plan's designs for thirty-five airports or become outraged at the schemes for bulldozing whole neigh-borhoods, the plan's most important legacy is both the promise and peril of the *idea* of a comprehensive plan. Like the 1907 plan, the 1947 master plan was predicated on the concept that St. Louis could be transformed

---

[1]For an alphabetical listing of master plans prepared by Harland Bartholomew and Associates between 1912 and 1985, see Eldridge Lovelace, *Harland Bartholomew: His Contributions to American Urban Planning* (Urbana: University of Illinois, 1992), A15–19. Lovelace also has a discussion of the elements of a Bartholomew comprehensive plan (49–55). For a discussion of Bartholomew's formulaic construct of comprehensive planning, see Norman J. Johnson, "Harland Bartholomew: Precedent for the Profession," in *The American Planner: Biographies and Recollec-tions,* 2nd ed., ed. Donald A. Kruecheberg. (New Brunswick, NJ: The Center for Urban Policy Research, 1994).

into a community, that the citizens could become one in realizing the goals and aspirations of the plan. The problem was, whose goals and aspirations? How can a plan reflect the will and interests of all the citizens? It is a problem that planning is still grappling with.

The Document

"Dear Mayor Kaufmann," E. J. Russell, the chairman of the St. Louis Plan Commission wrote in the cover letter to the plan, "in accordance with your request . . . the Commission has prepared a Comprehensive Plan . . . [it is] submitted for your consideration and such action as you deem to the best interests of the City" (Bartholomew 1947, v). While Aloys Kaufmann may have made the formal request for the plan, it was undoubtedly Harland Bartholomew's idea. Cities across America were preparing similar documents. Planning had been on a fifteen-year hiatus due to the Great Depression and World War II. The country had neither the time nor the money for long-term strategies. But for Bartholomew and his cohorts, this lull in planning activity had been almost catastrophic for the American city. Older residential areas continued to decay. The automobile became less and less compatible with the central business district. New suburbs pulled more and more residents to their enclaves of detached, single-family housing. For Bartholomew, it was imperative that St. Louis begin to respond to these threats.

However, what strikes contemporary readers of the 1947 plan is how few people Bartholomew had to help him with this endeavor. On the page after the cover letter, the members of the Plan Commission and its staff were listed. In addition to Russell, there were eight citizen members, including one woman, Mrs. T. M. Sayman. The Plan Commission also had five ex officio members: the president of the Board of Aldermen, the president of the Board of Public Service, the director of Streets and Sewers, the commissioner of Parks and Recreation, and the building commissioner. Even in this age of budget constraints and reduced municipal personnel, Bartholomew's staff seems puny by present-day standards, especially given that the mayor had submitted his formal request for the plan on April 19, 1946, and that the plan was released on January 14, 1947 (Bartholomew 1947, v). Besides Bartholomew, who is listed simply as "engineer," the Plan Commission staff lists a secretary, an architect and an architect designer, one planning analyst, two draftsmen, an aide to Bartholomew, plus a stenographer (Bartholomew 1947, vi). Today a plan of the scope of the 1947 plan would take a staff of dozens a decade or more to prepare. The fact that it took Bartholomew and his tiny staff less than eight months—without computers—is mind-boggling.

Nonetheless, Bartholomew and Russell were convinced that the document that followed the cover letter to the mayor was the strategy for St. Louis's survival. "When the Plan becomes official," Russell exclaimed, "it will greatly aid in the City's development for the next twenty-five years" (Bartholomew 1947, v). All that was left was for the mayor and citizens to give the plan their "unqualified approval" and put it into operation.

Introduction: Purpose of the City Plan

Bartholomew had been preparing for the plan for thirty years and he knew what he wanted to say from the opening paragraph. He was confident about St. Louis's inherent strengths and its ability to maintain its position as one of America's premier cities. "St. Louis, with a colorful, historic past and a busy, variegated present," Bartholomew told St. Louisans, "is still a city with a future." But as he argued, "to maintain this position, sound, thorough planning of the community's physical future is essential. The City Plan Commission proposes herein to point the way. It offers a comprehensive, modern chart for continued progress" (Bartholomew 1947, 1).

The primary assumption that Bartholomew was making was that St. Louis City proper would have a population of 900,000 by 1970—the end point of the plan. While this represented only 10 percent growth over the 1940 census figures, Bartholomew argued that "such a growth of 84,000 calls for making proper room for the new roofs, adequate traffic ways for the added automobiles, economical plans for all the additional public and semi-public facilities to be required. Furthermore," he went on to say, "there must be a catching-up with all the improvements perforce neglected during the long war period" (Bartholomew 1947, 1). Anticipating the critics of suburban sprawl by a half century, Bartholomew argued that planning for St. Louis and the region went hand-in-hand. The challenge was to maintain the city's density while providing for a projected metropolis of 1,650,000 in 1970—a regional growth rate of 20 percent. While St. Louis was a virtually built-out city, Bartholomew argued that its "general density of population, fortunately, is relatively light. The need here is to keep a rather intensively built-up urban territory up-to-date for the demands of the years ahead. Those demands will arise not only from within the city limits but from the entire metropolitan area" (Bartholomew 1947, 2).

After a plea for the city and state to adopt the Planning Commission Enabling Act so that the plan could become official, Bartholomew laid out his master plan recipe. The plan, Bartholomew told his readers, would contain a land use plan and a "complete revision of the badly outmoded zoning ordinance" (Bartholomew 1947, 3). It would also contain a housing plan that would not only provide "thousands of new family dwelling units . . . but [would] wipe out the obsolescent blighted areas and the costly decayed slums." In addition, the plan would contain a major street plan and an air transportation plan that would provide for a "series of thirty-five fields in five graduated categories" (Bartholomew 1947, 3). There would also be proposals for the "preservation and improvement of the central downtown business district, the indispensable nucleus of the whole metropolitan structure" plus a "revision of public transportation facilities in the interest of the best disposition of service" (Bartholomew 1947, 3–4). Lastly, Bartholomew said the plan would provide for a "citywide system of neighborhood parks, playfields and playgrounds," as well as a "comprehensive system of homogeneous neighborhoods" (Bartholomew 1947, 4). However, Bartholomew warned his readers, the plan was not intended to spell out each and every project for the next twenty-five years. Rather, Bartholomew said, the plan "is expressed through general principles in most instances, rather than any attempt at exact blueprinting" (Bartholomew 1947, 2).

In short, what Bartholomew was presenting to St. Louisans was a vision—his vision—for how St. Louis could adapt to the next quarter century. The core of this vision was his conviction that the city had to be transformed so that it could compete successfully against the suburbs. "We cannot have a city without people," Bartholomew told St. Louisans. In his mind, St. Louis could not hope to thrive if it did not provide those things which were drawing the people away from the city. "Many people prefer single-family detached dwellings even in the large modern city," Bartholomew reminded his readers. But as he told them, "without careful planning and zoning for large single-family dwelling areas . . . we will repel rather than attract people who may wish to live here" (Bartholomew 1947, 5).

But, Bartholomew did not perceive himself as some type of oracle like a Le Corbusier or a Frank Lloyd Wright might. Instead, Bartholomew saw himself as an engineer who applied scientific principles to mold the city into its optimal form. "The plans herein," Bartholomew exclaimed, "are somewhat surprisingly simple in nature, but they are true to the familiar precept against making 'little plans;' they are meant to be broad and inspiring—and humanly workable" (Bartholomew 1947, 2–3). Although he was hardly a charismatic figure, Bartholomew hoped to inspire his fellow St. Louisans in the pages to follow. "We can build a good city with many people . . . but this goal can be achieved only by a well balanced plan" (Bartholomew 1947, 5). The secret, according to Bartholomew, was that St. Louisans had to work together to bring the plan to fruition. "The city," he exclaimed, "is not an area for unrestrained speculation by any single group, for in this direction lies only chaos—and desintegration [*sic*]"(Bartholomew 1947, 5). The plan, in Bartholomew's mind, would remake St. Louis into a community and enable it to face the challenges of the future. "In the Comprehensive City Plan here presented," Bartholomew told his fellow St. Louisans, "this Commission offers an excellent new starting point for a more efficient and attractive city for today and for tomorrow" (Bartholomew 1947, 5).

The Metropolitan Community: St. Louis Is the Center of a Vast Urban Area

Although the 1947 plan was a plan for the City of St. Louis, Bartholomew began his grand strategy for St. Louis's future with a discussion of the St. Louis region. For Bartholomew, as it was for most of his colleagues, the "real" city of the twentieth century was the central city and all of the surrounding area that it influenced. Indeed, it was more than the city and its suburbs. It was a whole region that increasingly operated as a functional whole. As Bartholomew pointed out, the City of St. Louis covered only 62.4 square miles out of the 956 square miles that the U.S. Bureau of the Census defined as the St. Louis Metropolitan District. This district, Bartholomew informed his readers, was composed of five counties plus the City of St. Louis and that the city was "but one of approximately seven hundred taxing districts in the District, including about one hundred incorporated communities, some five hundred school districts, and one hundred other special sewer, drainage, park and other districts" (Bartholomew 1947, 6).

Bartholomew believed that the region and the central city were dependent upon one another. Neither could thrive without each being strong and vital. Although he projected that St. Louis would contain only 54 percent of the metropolitan population in 1979—down from 60 percent in 1940—Bartholomew continued to see the central city as being pivotal for the region. "During the next two decades," Bartholomew told St. Louisans, "St. Louis will continue to be the main commercial, financial and light industrial center of the Metropolitan District although," he warned, "further decentralization of population and commerce can be expected" (Bartholomew 1947, 9). While the City of St. Louis would never again be the population center it once was, the central city in some ways was even more important than it used to be for Bartholomew. Although its size might remain stagnant, it was now the nerve center for a "super city" that extended a thousand square miles and contained upwards of 2 million people.

What was crucial though according to Bartholomew, if this new super city was going to thrive and maintain its place among other super cities, was that St. Louisans and their regional neighbors had to see—and act—as if the region was a system. Cities and towns, agricultural land, and open space all played a central role in the functioning of the whole. For Bartholomew, as for most planners across the country at midcentury, this meant the region needed a plan just like the city if everything was going to mesh together properly. Similar to other regions, St. Louis already had a regional plan association—the Metropolitan Plan Association—which as Bartholomew remarked "feels greatly encouraged in its efforts to develop a comprehensive plan for the entire metropolitan region. Such a plan is as essential as our own Comprehensive Plan" (Bartholomew 1947, 9).

What Bartholomew did not say was that he and his firm were already working on a blueprint of what such a plan would look like, which the Association was going to publish the next year, in 1948. While the 1948 *Guide Plan* has not received as much recognition as the 1947 St. Louis comprehensive plan, in many ways, it is just as remarkable a document (Bartholomew 1948). The structure of *Guide Plan* closely followed Bartholomew's formula. There were sections on Population, Land Use/Zoning, Mass Transportation, Highways, Housing/Neighborhood Redevelopment, and Recreation, just like the 1947 Plan. However, in the regional guide there was much more emphasis on economic development, infrastructure issues, and environmental matters. Although Bartholomew declared that "the economic background of this area is extremely sound," it was clear that Bartholomew felt that St. Louis owed its size and metropolitan rank to its central geographical position (Bartholomew 1948, 6–7). As a result, the Guide placed a great deal of emphasis on maintaining and improving the region's transportation facilities. Bartholomew felt that the region's continued economic strength depended on continuing to have superior rail, river, air, and trucking facilities. What was also interesting was that Bartholomew anticipated the creation of the Metropolitan Sewer District by more than a decade, arguing that the "piecemeal construction of sewerage facilities" was a drain on the area and that the region needed to combine districts and include areas not in sewer districts (Bartholomew 1948, 6–7). It is also of note that Bartholomew had a section on flood control in reaction to the major flood that occurred in 1947 after the publication of the master plan. While the Guide's map of inundated areas is eerily similar to corresponding maps after the 1993 flood, Bartholomew maintained that "flood control programs currently planned will provide good protection by levees for industrial and a large part of the agricultural sections" of the region (Bartholomew 1948).

However, the most important aspect of the Guide was how Bartholomew saw the region as only a big city and what this meant in terms of policy. In a section entitled "Our New Horizon," Bartholomew remarked that "the Missouri-Illinois Metropolitan Area is basically just one big city" (Bartholomew 1948, 9). Like a city, Bartholomew argued "unified, integrated, functioning of both local and major organic parts is as essential to the large urban community as to the human body" (Bartholomew 1948, 9). Consequently, to ensure that this Greater St. Louis functioned the most efficiently, Bartholomew declared that "big plans for the new big city" were required (Bartholomew 1948, 9).

In Bartholomew's mind, what the St. Louis region needed was a metropolitan planning agency. "Plans for a great city cannot be prepared by a convention of communities," he said (Bartholomew 1948, 9). The planning agency he envisioned would have three functions:

- Prepare an areawide plan: This plan would not replace local plans—such as the 1947 comprehensive plan—but would coordinate them so that the region would operate as a system.

- Assist local government agencies to improve and extend facilities and services of metropolitan significance: This would result in "collaborations" like the Metropolitan Sewer District (MSD).

- Acquire, construct, and administer improvements of metropolitan character: The example that Bartholomew gave was the Port of New York Authority. Such an authority would undertake capital projects from everything from housing to mass transit (Bartholomew 1948, 48).

So while Bartholomew was optimistic about the region's long-term vitality, he was adamant in both the 1947 and 1948 plans that the ability of the region to maintain its national rank depended upon its ability to plan as a region. Concluding his 1948 report, Bartholomew declared in the strongest language he was capable of, "the era of haphazard growth—increasing blight in the central areas, helter-skelter expansion in the outlying areas, with their large economic and social losses—must be succeeded by an era of planned development, or orderly building, and the wise use of the area's rich resources" (Bartholomew 1948, 48).

Population: St. Louis Should Have 900,000 Persons in 1970

From the perspective of the early twenty-first century, one of the more interesting aspects of the 1947 plan was the section on population, particularly Bartholomew's projection that the city would have a population of 900,000 by 1970. Considering that the actual population in 1970 was almost a third less than that figure and that the current population is only a little more than a third of what Bartholomew projected, it would appear that Bartholomew had made an egregious error. However, upon closer inspection, Bartholomew's analysis was very insightful and provides a useful tool in looking at both the city's and the region's population woes over the last generation.

"The City of St. Louis can anticipate a population of 900,000 persons by 1970," Bartholomew told his fellow St. Louisans, "based on these assumptions":

- That the population of the St. Louis Metropolitan District continues to maintain its present proportion to total urban population of the United States.

- That an attractive environment for living will be developed throughout the city to counteract current decentralization trends.

- That the city is, nevertheless, a maturing urban center that can never expect to attain the tremendous past growth of certain earlier periods." (Bartholomew 1947, 10).

These were pretty big "ifs" and only one was even partially something that the citizens of St. Louis and Bartholomew could directly control.

Although Bartholomew did not use the word, he was concerned about metropolitan "sprawl." In a map of the St. Louis region, which is amazing since it was prepared in a pre-Geographic Information Systems (GIS) age, Bartholomew graphically illustrated population loss and gain between 1930 and 1940.

While the southwest quadrant of the city had accumulated new population, the map clearly demonstrated that the region's population was

Figure 1. St. Louis City and County Population Change, 1930–1940.
Comprehensive City Plan, Plate 3.

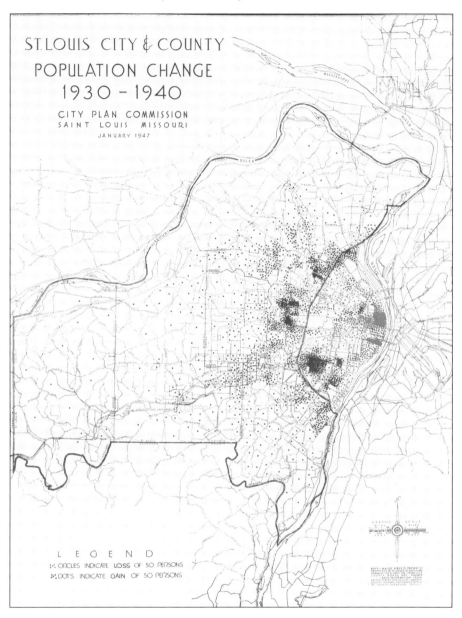

moving west into the county at a faster rate. In accompanying tables, Bartholomew projected that even under the most ideal scenarios, the city's population would become a smaller and smaller proportion of the greater

St. Louis region, as the automobile allowed the region to grow at a faster rate. In 1947, environmental ramifications of unchecked suburban growth had not yet made an impact on the thinking of most planners, but Bartholomew, like most planners who were interested in regional planning, saw unregulated growth as wasteful. It wasted the resources of infrastructure already in place and it wasted resources on developing infrastructure that was not necessary.

The thrust of Bartholomew's strategy to check this undesirable growth was, ironically, to reduce density in the city—or rather more precisely to even it out. In his mind, the primary attraction of the suburbs was the single-family detached house. For the central city to be appealing to St. Louis, it had to provide a range of single-family housing options that would make it competitive with the suburban communities that provided this type of housing. Even in areas that were to remain multifamily, Bartholomew wanted to reduce density and provide more open space. For him, this redistribution of population was a matter of life and death for the city. "If the City of St. Louis," Bartholomew warned, "does not provide through planning an atmosphere for living that will compete favorably with its suburbs it may continue to suffer from decentralization." Indeed, for him, "this population density study is the basis for the Comprehensive Plan" (Bartholomew 1947, 11).

To achieve this goal of more evenly distributing population across the city, Bartholomew had a five-point plan of attack:

1. Reduce the portion of the city allocated for non-residential uses.

2. Increase the percentage of land devoted to single-family housing.

3. Decrease the amount of medium-density (two- and three-family unit) housing.

4. Increase the space set aside for high-density residential uses.

5. Achieve a goal of a maximum density of eighty people/acre.

Although the plan provided for an additional 10 percent population increase and a corresponding increase in overall density to 22.5 people per acre in 1970 as opposed to 20.5 in 1947, it called for a dramatic reshuffling of where those people were to live (Bartholomew 1947, 13–14).

The overall thrust of Bartholomew's density plan was clear. He wanted to increase the amount of land devoted to single-family housing as much as possible while at the same time enlarging the area of the city for multiple-family homes or apartment buildings. From the population section of the plan, we get the first glimpses of Bartholomew's vision of the good city. Perhaps because of his semi-rural background (he spent his early years in Stoneham, Massachusetts—a small town on the outskirts of Boston), Bartholomew never felt comfortable with the high density of the streetcar city. Like most planners of his generation, the automobile had made such densities unnecessary. The automobile had enlarged the city, making it possible for everyone to have more space. For the middle and upper classes, this meant owning a detached, single-family home. But even for the working class and the poor, the automotive city eliminated the space pressures that had led to the unhealthy densities of the turn-of-the-century city. While this meant that some poorer residents might have to give up living in older, smaller structures for the slightly higher densities of two- or three-story garden apartments, this move would actually create more open space by pushing development upward instead of out.

Today, many planners are critical of Bartholomew's aversion to density and his love affair with the single-family house. They maintain that it has led to the "suburbanization" of the central city, stripping it of the character that made it a real alternative to postwar "cookie-cutter" development that was taking place beyond the city limits. Rather than stimulating growth, they argue that it actually resulted in accelerated population loss in the 1950s and 1960s. But few St. Louisans today would feel comfortable with the population densities of the first half of the century. Although the downtown is experiencing an explosion of loft conversions, densities even along Washington Street do not come remotely close to the tenement districts of the early part of the twentieth century. Moreover, in some St. Louis neighborhoods that are undergoing rejuvenation—such as the Shaw neighborhood on the city's south side—the movement is toward reducing density by converting two- and four-unit buildings to single-family dwellings. Looking at the recent success of single-family projects like St. Vincent Place and Botanical Heights—new neighborhoods on the city's south side—and the revamping of superhigh-density public housing complexes like Blumeyer and Darst-Webbe with garden-style townhouses, it is hard not to wonder if Bartholomew's strategy of lower densities might not have allowed the city to retain a higher percentage of the region's population.

On the other hand, one suspects that Bartholomew would have been more appalled not by the drop in the city's population since 1947, but in the region's inability to maintain its metropolitan rank and its percentage of the nation's population. One of Bartholomew's key assumptions was that the city could reach 900,000 if the region grew at the same pace as the rest of the country. It has not. Bartholomew undoubtedly would have to confess to his inability to foresee the demise of manufacturing in the American economy and its impact on a manufacturing region like St. Louis. He also would have been surprised by the rise of technology and its impact on regional alignment. However, if Bartholomew were alive today, he no doubt would place responsibility for much of the region's relative stagnation on metropolitan fragmentation and the inability to plan regionally. Making arguments similar to those he made in the 1948 regional plan, he would point to regions like Portland, Oregon and Indianapolis, Indiana that have experienced rapid growth in recent decades and would contend that their growth can be greatly attributed to their ability to act regionally.

Land Use and Zoning: Imperative Need for Closer Relationship

As it was for all his master plans, the section on land use and zoning was the core of Bartholomew's 1947 plan. "The amount of land used for various purposes in a city, and the amount required for future growth and development" argued Bartholomew, "is a dominant element in the city plan" (Bartholomew 1947, 16). But as he told St. Louisans, "it is not possible or necessary to rebuild the whole city in brief period of time." Yet, in his mind, there were three main land use conflicts in postwar St. Louis. One was that there were a number of neighborhoods that were plagued by scattered small manufacturing firms that would have been better served by their "grouping in well defined areas" (Bartholomew 1947, 17). The second major conflict was the random placement of apartment houses into single-family districts "instead of grouping and creating their own beneficial environment" (Bartholomew 1947, 17). The third major land use conflict for Bartholomew was that "many stores and shops scatter into residence areas instead of grouping into well defined centers" (Bartholomew 1947, 17). But as he remarked, "the broad pattern of land use previously described is logical and sound except for the conflicts noted" (Bartholomew 1947, 19).

Like the section on population and his strategy for evening out the city's density, Bartholomew left no doubt what his ultimate goal was with the land use plan. As he explained to St. Louisans, "the future land use plan should bring about sharper definition of various functional land use areas with ample room for each" (Bartholomew 1947, 19). As the scientific planner extraordinaire, Bartholomew believed that the city performed in the most efficient manner when all of its major "organs" or functions were totally separated from one another. Once this spatial differentiation was perfected, then the rebuilding of the city could commence. As Bartholomew informed his fellow citizens, "within these areas new construction and reconstruction can take place with improved standards of design, arrangement and open space" (Bartholomew 1947, 19).

In a beautiful map, Bartholomew clearly indicated where the primary activities of the city were to take place.

Figure 2. Desirable Ultimate Land Use Plan.
Comprehensive City Plan, **Plate 9.**

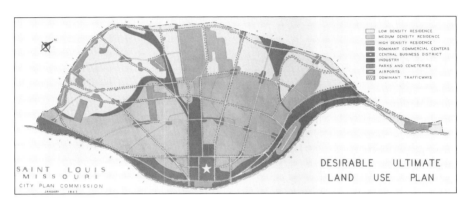

Large chunks of the city in the southwestern and northwestern corners were to be set aside for single-family housing. Most of the medium-density housing was to be located on the city's south side, with the majority of the high-density or apartment districts situated on the city's north side (which at this time was predominantly white). Manufacturing was carefully placed along the riverfront and rail corridors. Commerce was clustered at the intersections of the major thoroughfares. As the caption beneath Plate 9 declared, "an ultimate land use plan should envision the ideal separation of land uses all bound together by a system of major highways" (Bartholomew 1947, Plate 9).

Since the early 1960s, such a stark division of land uses as Bartholomew proposed for St. Louis has come under severe attack. As Jane Jacobs so eloquently argued in her *Death and Life of Great American Cities* (Jacobs 1961), cities depend upon a mixture of activities for their survival. Healthy neighborhoods—even single-family ones—need a variety of services and stores to thrive. For her, a city was not so much like a human body composed of separate organs, but an ecology where life relied on the interplay of a complex web of forces. As she would argue repeatedly, the planning of rational planners like Bartholomew sucked the life out of American cities in the 1950s and 1960s, leaving nothing behind but an empty shell.

In hindsight though, Bartholomew's ideas were not as simplistic as their application by a later generation of planners would imply. For him, the land use plan was not a set of static blueprints, but a plan of action. Its most important function was to provide a rationale for the zoning ordinance which would actually put this rationale into effect shaping land use decisions. The point was to zone or separate functions according to the perceived needs of a neighborhood and the city taken as a whole.

While Bartholomew had been a path-breaker in zoning during the 1910s, he was very frustrated with St. Louis and Missouri's response to it. From his perspective, the tie between its operation and the rationale on which it was based had been lost. While Bartholomew had created the second zoning ordinance in the country in 1919, it had been ruled unconstitutional by the Missouri Supreme Court. But after the U.S. Supreme Court upheld zoning in the 1920s with the *Ambler v. Euclid* decision, St. Louis had settled for, in Bartholomew's mind, "a revised and badly compromised zoning plan" (Bartholomew 1947, 19). Noting that it was still in effect twenty years later, Bartholomew argued that this compromised ordinance had a number of major technical deficiencies. The main one was that it had too few categories with respect to residential areas. For example, the zoning ordinance did not differentiate between single-family and multifamily housing. As a result, Bartholomew pointed out, it was possible to build a high-rise apartment building with hundreds of units inside a neighborhood of mostly single-family houses that would undercut the optimal functioning of each type of housing.

The primary technical change that Bartholomew sought in a proposed new zoning plan was the introduction of additional zoning categories to better spatially differentiate incompatible uses from one another. Instead of five zones, Bartholomew wanted ten. Residential areas would be divided into five separate categories with commercial districts being separated into three different subdistricts or zones. Under Bartholomew's scheme, downtown would be separately zoned as the Central Business District. Bartholomew's proposed new zoning ordinance would also mandate new height limits for residential and commercial areas, off-street parking requirements for certain categories of dwellings, and time limits for non-conforming uses. He also wanted to avoid "spot zoning" by providing certain exceptions in each district. Bartholomew's most innovative provision was for allowing a "Community Unit Plan" that would treat obsolete and blighted districts of twenty acres or more "designated and approved by the Commission" independent of the zoning ordinance (Bartholomew 1947, 22).

But the biggest change that Bartholomew sought was not more categories, but bringing about a better alignment between the land use plan and the zoning ordinance. According to Bartholomew, the existing zoning ordinance was almost a repudiation of the goals and objectives of the land use plan and where the city needed to be. Simply put, in his mind there was not enough land zoned for residential use of any kind and entirely too much space zoned for commercial and industrial. For present-day readers, such a discussion might seem arcane, but what Bartholomew was really getting at was that there was no *reason* for why one area was zoned one way and another was zoned differently. While Bartholomew and his fellow scientific planners are often characterized as being lackeys of real estate interests, he felt that by not firmly grounding the zoning ordinance in the land use plan, the zoning ordinance was vulnerable to whatever political or speculative pressure came along.

To illustrate how he envisioned his zoning ordinance would work, he used a number of neighborhood case studies. One of the case studies was Lafayette Square, a neighborhood located on the edge of the Central Business District and now viewed as one of the true success stories of St. Louis neighborhood rejuvenation. However, in 1947, Bartholomew felt that the neighborhood was beyond saving and saw it as "an obsolete area for the most part" due to "an incongruous inter-mixture of all types of use" (Bartholomew 1947, 24). From the perspective of the early twenty-first century, Bartholomew clearly made a mistake. But from his vantage point, the crucial point was that the proposed zoning plan allowed the Plan Commission to make a choice. Unlike much of the *disjointed incrementalism* of today's development-driven planning model, the Lafayette Square case study illustrated what Bartholomew thought planning was all about. For him, the planner collected data, determined the optimal scenario, and acted upon that information. While it would appear that Bartholomew chose poorly, his choice was shaped by a discernible rationale. Since the hodgepodge of building styles and sizes made the area seem to him an unlikely candidate for rehabilitation, Bartholomew chose to retain the industrial uses along the northern flank, believing that the proximity of a major thoroughfare (Chouteau) and the rail yards made it better suited to industrial, as opposed to residential uses—a decision that has been a bane for neighborhood "gentrifiers" for thirty years.

Housing: Three Areas, Three Programs

The next section of the plan, Bartholomew's housing plan, was—and has been—the most controversial part of the plan. In it, Bartholomew presented ideas that he had been working on for more than a decade to refashion the city. It was a bold statement. No other master plan in postwar America proposed as massive an undertaking as Bartholomew was proposing. His plan called for a total rebuild of 7 percent of the city and a substantial rehabilitation of another 27 percent. In total, Bartholomew's plan mandated the renovation of over twenty square miles of St. Louis.

But in Bartholomew's mind, there was no other choice. As he opened his discussion, Bartholomew declared,

"We cannot truthfully say that St. Louis is a good place in which to live *when*—

- We spend $4,000,000 general tax funds annually to maintain our obsolete areas. (This sum represents the difference in cost of governmental service and tax collections annually in these areas.)

- We have 33,000 dwellings still dependent on outside privy vaults.

- We have an additional 25,000 dwellings where toilets are shared by several families.

- We have 82,000 dwellings in structures built before 1900" (Bartholomew 1947, 27)."

Figure 3. Obsolete and Blighted Districts.
***Comprehensive City Plan*, Plate 13.**

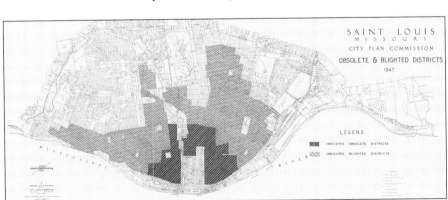

For Bartholomew, these were intolerable conditions. Unless they were addressed, the city faced ruin. The longer St. Louis waited to address these problems, the worse they would become.

In an almost scolding tone, Bartholomew explained to St. Louisans that the housing problems which they faced were their own fault. "We have obsolete and blighted districts because our interest has always been centered in the newest and latest houses and subdivisions in areas of new development," he declared. Instead of maintaining what they had, St. Louisans were constantly moving to newer areas of the city, allowing the existing housing stock to deteriorate. "We have had *no Housing Policy* and *no Housing Program*," Bartholomew lambasted his fellow citizens, "other than that of abandonment of old areas and of moving to new fringe areas." As he concluded, "this is no way to build a sound city" (Bartholomew 1947, 27).

For Bartholomew, this lack of a housing program was not only bad policy, it had the potential of destroying St. Louis as a community. "This is a frightfully wasteful policy," Bartholomew informed St. Louisans, hoping to shame them into action, "of which we have not yet reckoned the full cost. It is a tragic policy because of the poor housing conditions which must be endured by those unable to move to new outlying areas" (Bartholomew 1947, 27–28).

Like many of his contemporary planning colleagues, Bartholomew saw this physical decay leading to social and economic pathologies that would spread from one neighborhood to the next. Like a metastasized cancer, Bartholomew warned his readers, "our obsolete and blighted districts . . . will continue to expand until the whole city is engulfed unless we remove the causes of this condition" (Bartholomew 1947, 28).

However, Bartholomew told his readers, there was hope. "There is no reason," he said, "why the older neighborhoods cannot be kept wholesome and attractive" (Bartholomew 1947, 28). Moreover, he explained, such a course of action would benefit the whole city, not just the poor who were trapped in the city's slums. "We can redirect our attention," he pronounced, "to creating good living conditions in older central areas with much advantage and profit" (Bartholomew 1947, 28). In other words, urban renewal was not just the right thing to do, it was smart business. Concluding his opening remarks on why St. Louis needed to embark on this massive undertaking, Bartholomew came full circle, exclaiming, "it is not difficult to visualize complete transformation of the city by a new housing policy and a bold program" (Bartholomew 1947, 28). Bartholomew was ready to show how St. Louisans could not only save their city, but make it great once again. What came next was the division of the city into eighty-two residential neighborhoods and seventeen industrial districts which were further separated into three different categories. "As a result of these studies," Bartholomew told his readers, "a definite constructive housing plan and policy is suggested herewith" (Bartholomew 1947, 28).

Obsolete Areas

Bartholomew began his housing plan by examining the most distressed areas. The term that he used in describing these areas was "obsolete." It was a very interesting—but very deliberate—choice of words. While most of his contemporaries used the word "blighted" to describe severely dilapidated housing conditions, Bartholomew saw blight as a process and, consequently, saved the term to characterize neighborhoods just beginning to show distress. What Bartholomew meant to imply with the term "obsolete" was that a block of housing or a neighborhood was no longer capable of being rehabilitated. It was either too dilapidated or too outmoded to be refitted to modern standards. In terms of housing stock, what this usually entailed was a lack of inside toilets and/or kitchens. Such housing and the neighborhoods in which it was located were, for Bartholomew, beyond saving. In his mind—to use a biological metaphor—neighborhoods that contained obsolete housing were dead. The only recourse that a planner had was to tear everything down and start anew.

From the opening lines of his housing strategy for obsolete areas, Bartholomew made it explicit that his underlying project was not just to remake the physical plan of the city, but to remake its social body as well. Like most city planners since the 1907 plan, Bartholomew believed that industrialism and the modern economy had torn the social fabric of the city apart. It no longer operated as a coherent whole. For Bartholomew and all the master planners before and after him, the entire point of a master plan was to coerce the various pieces of the city back together so that the city would reflect and serve the interests of all citizens. In short, the purpose of the plan was to make the citizenry—even those who lived in obsolete areas—a community.

But for a scientific or rational planner such as Bartholomew, extensive study of cities had revealed that there were natural laws that described how communities operated, just as there were natural laws which governed traffic flow. While particular circumstances—age, topography, climate, history, ethnic composition, etc.—made each city unique, Bartholomew believed that there were general principles that shaped urban life wherever it took place. The job of the planner was to use that knowledge to put the city back together so that the citizens could realize their natural potential to exist as a community.

According to Bartholomew, there was a natural—and obvious—connection between poor living conditions and social/economic pathologies. "Present obsolete areas must be cleared and reconstructed," Bartholomew explained, because it "is a social necessity as well as an economic essential" (Bartholomew 1947, 28). While critics of the type of urban renewal which Bartholomew espoused would laughingly declare in the 1950s and 1960s that "better toilets make better people,"[2] Bartholomew anticipated present-day social theorists, such as William Julius Wilson, who speaks of a "culture of poverty" by arguing that there was a direct connection between poor living conditions and such things as crime, poor health, and disinvestment (Wilson 1990). Although the word "slum" is no longer used, Bartholomew believed that the slums of St. Louis not only pulled down the people who lived in them, but the whole city. "The City of St. Louis cannot continue to thrive and prosper where there is nothing but progressive decadence in its housing supply," he stated matter-of-factly, "any more than is [sic] could with polluted water supply or smoke laden air" (Bartholomew 1947, 28).

Because Bartholomew viewed obsolete areas as not just diseased, but essentially dead, he argued that reconstruction had to take place at the neighborhood level because it was "necessary to create a new environment," which, he maintained, could "be accomplished only by large scale operations." The goal for Bartholomew was not just to replace deteriorated housing but to change the whole tenor of a neighborhood. "Obsolete neighborhoods must be rebuilt, not merely with houses of good design and construction," Bartholomew told St. Louisans, "but with more open space, more park and playground facilities, a good school and community center" (Bartholomew 1947, 28).

The question was how this was to be accomplished. For housing reformers since the Gilded Age, there had always been two huge hurdles. One was land acquisition and clearance. Dilapidated housing was often situated on the densest land. This made it extremely expensive to acquire since it was so valuable for its owners. Once the land was acquired, existing structures had to be demolished and hauled. This was also very expensive. The second problem involved new construction. If the new housing was for low-income people the question was, how could they afford it? But if the housing was meant for middle- or upper-income people, the difficulty

---

[2]For an insightful overview of the urban renewal movement, see Jon Teaford, *Rough Road to Renaissance: Urban Revitalization in America, 1940–1985* (Baltimore: Johns Hopkins University Press, 1990).

involved financing and attracting developers, as well as investors who were willing to take a risk in a new market.

Bartholomew had led the way in addressing these issues. In 1946, three years prior to the path-breaking 1949 Housing Act, Bartholomew had lobbied the state legislature to pass a measure—Chapter 353—that permitted cities to authorize the use of eminent domain to acquire "blighted properties" for the purposes of redevelopment. Unlike Title I of the 1949 Housing Act, which used federal funds to write down two-thirds of acquisition and clearance costs (with municipalities picking up the remaining third), Chapter 353 provided incentives to investors to undertake development in "obsolete" areas by offering them partial tax abatements on the new projects not to exceed twenty-five years. As Bartholomew remarked, this Act, in conjunction with a new Urban Redevelopment Corporation Act "should make possible considerable large scale reconstruction" (Bartholomew 1947, 29).

However, in Bartholomew's mind, financing low-income housing was still a problem. Even though St. Louis had taken advantage of the United States Housing Act of 1937 and used federal funds to build the first two public housing projects in St. Louis—Carr Square on the north side (dedicated for African Americans) and Clinton Peabody on the south side (dedicated for whites)—in 1942, the Missouri legislature had still not passed the legislation allowing the St. Louis Housing Authority to take advantage of federal funds. "Such legislation," Bartholomew said, "[was] imperative if St. Louis is to participate as do other American cities in any future Federal public housing programs" (Bartholomew 1947, 29).

Next Bartholomew turned his attention to selling his program. Because the economy was still feeling the inflationary pressures of the postwar period, construction costs were high. But Bartholomew pointed out, "as construction costs become lower the city must be in a position to encourage wholesale reconstruction of these obsolete areas" (Bartholomew 1947, 29). The costs of the program would be high, Bartholomew admitted, but he argued that it would be a good investment. Maintaining that the "the total cost of clearance would scarcely exceed public expenditure during the past twenty-five years for other types of public work such as streets, sewers, and airports," Bartholomew claimed that "unlike these, however, ownership of the land would be a sound investment" (Bartholomew 1947, 29). Streets and sewers could not be bought and sold, but blighted land could. Consequently, "much if not all of the expense involved could be recovered." According to Bartholomew, the city and the citizens could recoup their costs through "(1) elimination of the present $4,000,000 annual deficit, (2) a long term increment in taxable revenues on private housing projects, and (3) participation in Federal subsidy programs" (Bartholomew 1947, 29–30).

To demonstrate how he envisioned the reconstruction of these obsolete neighborhoods, Bartholomew presented two model plans. One was for the DeSoto and Carr neighborhoods on the city's north side. The other plan was for the northern portion of the south side Soulard neighborhood. In terms of urban design, what is noteworthy about the two proposals is that each called for replatting the neighborhoods with irregularly shaped superresidential blocks. Inspired by Henry Wright and Clarence Stein's *Radburn*,[3] a model new town in New Jersey built in 1929, Bartholomew saw the superblocks as a means of enhancing social interaction and discouraging through traffic. Both suggested treatments provided for widening major thoroughfares, which would outline the neighborhoods and the grouping of commercial uses in designated shopping centers. In addition, both model plans called for extensive landscaping, recreational facilities, and community centers. As Bartholomew noted in speaking of the model plan for DeSoto and Carr, "the effectuation of this plan would result in a good standard of housing with ample open space, freedom from multiplicity of small streets, attractive environment, small concentrated shopping areas, and a large neighborhood park and community center would replace one of the worst slums in the city" (Bartholomew 1947, 30).

Since 1947 there have been numerous criticisms of Bartholomew's proposals and the urban renewal approach in general. Bartholomew's 1947 strategy for obsolete housing has been accused of everything from destroying viable neighborhoods, to wasting valuable historical resources, to paving the way for the fiasco of Pruitt-Igoe.

However, what would appear to be the most damning criticism of Bartholomew's urban renewal construct was that it was implicitly classist and racist. Although Bartholomew never discussed race, virtually all of the residents in the areas labeled obsolete were poor African Americans. So while Bartholomew had left St. Louis before any of his strategy could be implemented, the massive urban renewal projects which the city undertook in the 1950s that displaced thousands of African American families can be partially attributed to him and the 1947 plan.

The Mill Creek Valley Project, for example, totally cleared a 2.5-square-mile area in the midtown area except for four buildings. The devastation was so complete that the project was known locally as "Hiroshima Flats"

---

[3]See Clarence Stein, *Toward New Towns for America* (Cambridge: Massachusetts Institute of Technology Press, 1966).

(Teaford 1993). Hiroshima Flats, or Mill Creek Valley, was the largest African American neighborhood in St. Louis with hundreds of African American businesses, institutions, and churches. From the vantage point of many of its critics—both past and present—the demolition of Mill Creek was nothing less than cultural genocide.

Figure 4. Soulard Neighborhood District. Site Plan—Preliminary Study.
***Comprehensive City Plan*, Plate 16.**

Seemingly, however, it could be argued on the other hand that to have left Mill Creek standing would have been even more classist and racist. The majority of the housing had been built before 1900 and two-thirds of the units did not have indoor toilets. As part of its justification of the project, the city claimed that the rat population of the neighborhood exceeded that for humans. If this were indeed true, the city had a moral imperative to act. Speaking of the Carr Square/DeSoto Park neighborhood which was adjacent to Mill Creek, Bartholomew argued that "the effectuation of this plan would result in a good standard of housing with ample open space, freedom from multiplicity of small streets, attractive environment, small concentrated shopping areas, and a large neighborhood park and community center would replace one of the worst slums in the city" (Bartholomew 1947, 30). As Bartholomew's urban renewal strategy was implemented, mistakes were made—as Pruitt-Igoe attests (but Bartholomew was always against high-rise public housing). Yet it would also be wrong to totally discount the motives of the "urban renewers" as being nothing more than propaganda to advance the agenda of various real estate interests. Bartholomew was not interested in "black removal" as many of his critics claim. As he clearly stated with respect to the DeSoto plan, "this is an area occupied by low income families, many of whom should be rehoused here" (Bartholomew 1947, 30). The scientific planners, like Bartholomew, should have made more of an effort to elicit the input of residents of neighborhoods such as Mill Creek. But the main reason they wanted to rebuild obsolete neighborhoods was that they thought it was in the best interest of both the residents affected and the city as a whole.

Blighted Districts

Even though most of the controversy about the 1947 plan revolved around Bartholomew's ideas concerning obsolete or the most distressed areas, for him the rehabilitation of neighborhoods just beginning to show signs of distress or blight was "more important than reconstruction of obsolete areas" (Bartholomew 1947, 33). In his mind, the time to act was when a neighborhood could be saved, not when it was already dead. As he told St. Louisans, "this is both a social need and an economic essential because of high rates of juvenile delinquency, crime, and disease found in areas of poor housing" (Bartholomew 1947, 31). Moreover, as Bartholomew pointed out, "without a definate [sic] plan for the rehabilitation of the present blighted areas new obsolete areas will develop faster than present areas can be reconstructed" (Bartholomew 1947, 33).

Bartholomew's ideas concerning blighted neighborhoods emphasized conservation. Outlining his basic agenda for these aging St. Louis communities, Bartholomew said that "obsolete buildings should be removed, some streets should be closed, new park, playground and recreation areas created, small concentrated shop areas established, and individual buildings should be repaired and brought up to a good minimum standard" (Bartholomew 1947, 32). Looking at his mock plan to rehabilitate a blighted neighborhood, nothing is especially striking in terms of design except for his ideas of how to create small interior parks inside of existing blocks and his approach to street closures.

But the heart of Bartholomew's approach to blighted neighborhoods was not a particular design notion or a call for new construction. It was a plea for a minimum standards housing ordinance. As Bartholomew told St. Louisans, such an ordinance would provide for occupancy standards to reduce overcrowding; construction requirements pertaining to windows, lighting, flues, and the like; the prohibition of basement rooms as dwelling units; a mandate for the elimination of privies in six years; and the strict enforcement of sanitation codes. Though he seldom italicized anything else in the plan, Bartholomew concluded his remarks on the proposed ordinance by italicizing the entirety of his last sentence. As if he was shouting at St. Louisans, Bartholomew wrote that "*unless and until such an ordinance has been adopted and enforced, most housing areas in St. Louis will continue to deteriorate and blighted districts and obsolete areas will reach much greater proportions than at present*" (Bartholomew 1947, 33).

New Residence Areas

The last section of Bartholomew's housing plan was only two paragraphs long. In this brief discussion, Bartholomew spoke of new housing construction in St. Louis. As he noted, there was relatively little vacant land in St. Louis. However, he did point out that "there are still many good, comparatively new residential areas in the northern, western, and southern sections of St. Louis" (Bartholomew 1947, 34). Though he did not expressly say it, it was implicit in his comments that these new neighborhoods were composed of detached single-family housing built for the middle class. What he did say, and say rather forcibly, was that "there is great need for better protection, improved standards, and greater confidence among property owners in the future stability and character of these districts" (Bartholomew 1947, 34).

Figure 5. Rehabilitation of a Blighted Area.
Comprehensive City Plan, Plate 17.

St. Louis Plans

In Bartholomew's mind, St. Louis needed to do two things to protect these middle-class communities. One was to enact his revised zoning ordinance that would provide for a separate category for single-family residences. The second need, Bartholomew felt, was "the encouragement for the formation of strong neighborhood associations interested in protecting their character and environment." St. Louis already had several neighborhood associations, but Bartholomew felt that they could work better and be better organized. "The City Plan Commission," Bartholomew told his readers, "is giving assistance in this field" (Bartholomew 1947, 34).

The housing plan is not only the most controversial section of the 1947 plan, but also the most telling in terms of Bartholomew's ideology and the ideology of the rational planning movement. From the standpoint of the twenty-first century, it is not so much what Bartholomew is proposing, but how he is proposing it, that is startling to the contemporary mind. Confronted by the unraveling of the central city brought about by the automobile and suburbanization, Bartholomew and his fellow master planners desperately tried to keep the city together as a unified whole. Knowing already what the rest of the country would discover twenty years later, Bartholomew realized that the distressed areas of the city had the potential for ripping the city apart. St. Louis, as a community, not only had a moral and a civic responsibility to address these ills, it was in its best interest to do so. But for Bartholomew, St. Louis—like any city—did not emerge as a community through the joint endeavor of solving its problems. It was a community only because of the plan. In his mind, the city had become too large, too complex to be left alone. The only way that it could operate as a system was if the planner engineered—coerced—the pieces together. The problem, therefore, was not that Bartholomew's plan called for poor people to live in one place and the middle class to live somewhere else. It was that they were not asked where they wanted to live. Even in the newer, more affluent neighborhoods, Bartholomew felt the need to show the residents how to have neighborhood associations.

Streets and Trafficways: Four Basic Types Proposed

The next section of the plan was devoted to Bartholomew's long-term plan for improving St. Louis's street system. After the housing plan, this was the most controversial part of the plan. While it contained only five pages of text and two plates, it laid out a scheme that would totally revamp the city's transportation system in ways that are being felt today.

Bartholomew began his street plan by observing that "840,000 people in St. Louis owned 165,000 automobiles and trucks in 1946" and that "by 1970 it is estimated that there will be about 230,000 automobiles and trucks" (Bartholomew 1947, 35). As he noted, this did not include streetcars, buses, and the cars of suburban residents who used St. Louis streets. Using calculations from the Missouri State Highway Department, Bartholomew pointed out that "the annual traffic in St. Louis will be increased from 1,531,000,000 to 2,403,000,000 vehicle miles by 1960. This is a lot of traffic" (Bartholomew 1947, 35). For him, there was only one conclusion. All of this traffic "cannot be accommodated on our present street system. It will require new and enlarged adequate flow channels as well as a high degree of regulation and control" (Bartholomew 1947, 35).

According to Bartholomew, St. Louis had already done a great deal to enlarge its flow channels. "Since 1916 [his arrival in St. Louis]," he told St. Louisans, "St. Louis has expended over $40,000,000 in opening, widening, connecting, and extending the system of major streets" (Bartholomew 1947, 35). Major projects had included making Gravois, Natural Bridge, Olive, and Washington streets as radial thoroughfares into the central business district.

From the beginning, Bartholomew's goal had been to create a street system with different categories of streets serving different functions. Bartholomew envisioned a system resting on four types of major streets. The first, which he labeled secondary streets, were generally four lanes wide and primarily served residential areas. The second category was major streets that were six lanes wide. These streets were generally cross-town routes and carried substantial traffic, including buses and streetcars (Bartholomew 1947, 36).

While Bartholomew argued that a few of the major streets needed to be widened, he felt that the first two levels of the street system were adequately in place. Now what he wanted was to take advantage of new federal highway funds to create two additional street categories, both of which would carry substantially more traffic. The first of these new "flow channels" were extensions of the three major federal highways serving St. Louis: US 40, US 66, and US 50. These extensions were to be routed into the central business district and were to be separated grade expressways with limited access and were to be eight to ten lanes in width. In addition to these interstate extensions, Bartholomew's plan called for six additional six-to-eight-lane surface grade expressways. Two of the six were improvements to two of Bartholomew's original radial thoroughfares: Gravois and Natural Bridge. One was a strictly local expressway that would take traffic from the business district to the western edge of the city. This would eventually become Forest Park Parkway. The other three expressways would run north to south and would connect the three interstate extensions. The first of the three proposed north-south expressways would be situated at the far edge of the city primarily using the existing McCausland-Skinker-Hodiamont roadbed. The second would travel through the center of St. Louis following Morganford from the south, running underneath Tower Grove Park, and connecting with the northern leg of the interstate system via Tower Grove, Whittier, and Adelaide avenues. The last of the north-south distributors would use 18th Street to create a loop around the business district. It was an incredibly bold plan that would shape St. Louis for the next generation (Bartholomew 1947, 40).

Figure 6. Proposed Interstate and Urban Distributing Routes, January 1947.
***Comprehensive City Plan*, Plate 20.**

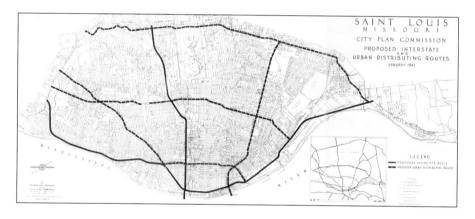

Like Bartholomew's urban renewal plan, his interstate and expressway plans have elicited a firestorm of criticism over the years. One criticism often leveled at Bartholomew and his plan was that he wantonly proposed cutting through St. Louis neighborhoods on the north and south sides. Again, as with the largest urban renewal projects, the interstate highways were built long after Bartholomew had left St. Louis and deviated tremendously from his original proposals. When they were finally built, there were four interstates instead of three. Interstate 55, which replaced US 66 from Chicago, was split in half when it reached St. Louis. I-55 continued south to Memphis and New Orleans with I-44 roughly following the US 66 route to the southwest. What is now I-64 approximately replaced US 50 and initially ended in St. Louis. In the 1980s, the section of US 40 from St. Louis to Wentzville that had been constructed between the early 1930s and mid-1960s was made part of I-64. Interstate 70 replaced US 40 nationally and was routed in a direct northwest angle to St. Charles.

As can be seen from the map on page 137, these routes were much different from what Bartholomew suggested and were much less sensitive to existing land use patterns. Bartholomew saw the new interstates as a means of separating industrial and residential areas. Both his northern and southern interstates ran along the Mississippi, keeping commercial and residential districts on one side with industry and warehousing on the other. Instead of cutting through a number of residential neighborhoods to create a direct path to Lambert Airport, Bartholomew routed his northern interstate due north toward Alton. In like manner, his design for US 40, which roughly parallels the present-day I-44 route, hugged the industrial corridor along the east-west rail corridor instead of cutting through residential neighborhoods to the south. Consequently, the damage done to a number of St. Louis neighborhoods—particularly Compton Heights and the Hill—can be laid at Bartholomew's feet.

However, this is not the case with his expressway plans. Bartholomew's proposed central distributor that would have run underneath Tower Grove Park, if constructed, would have decimated the heart of the city. While it was never built, preparations for the interior north-south distributor (dubbed the North/South Destroyer), have left a five-square-block pockmark west of the business district. But even here, it would seem that Bartholomew's intentions have been misunderstood. What he was proposing was not limited-access freeways, like those of the interstates, but on-grade thoroughfares, like Forest Park Parkway.

Ultimately, the real critique of Bartholomew's street plan is not what was built where, but whether or not the freeways and the interstates should have been built at all. One of Bartholomew's most noteworthy activities as a planner was his central role in formulating the policy that would lead to the 1956 National Defense Highway Act. The act had been in the making since the 1930s, and Bartholomew was at the heart of the fray. Bartholomew had been active promoting the interests of those who wanted the freeways to extend into the heart of the city. Unlike the farm lobby, which wanted the interstates to serve primarily rural needs, Bartholomew represented the view that the proposed interstates offered the means to enhance entrance and egress to the central cities from the suburbs. Fearing that cities like St. Louis would choke to death from increased congestion caused by suburbanites driving their cars into the city, Bartholomew wanted enlarged "flow channels" to carry suburbanites in and out of the city.

What Bartholomew did not envision was that these improved "flow channels" would make it possible for jobs and shopping to flow out of the cities altogether. While he would have been appalled by the suburban sprawl of today, Bartholomew is very much responsible for what came to be. Like many planners, Bartholomew anticipated that the central cities, like St. Louis, would grow in population only marginally, if at all, as more and more people lived in the suburbs. But in his mind, however, what the interstates would do is allow the central cities to hold on to their dominant economic role. Bartholomew never imagined that two-thirds of suburbanites would both live and work in the suburbs.

Public Recreation Facilities: Many New Neighborhood Parks, Playgrounds, and Playfields Needed

With what he considered the major sections of the plan in place, Bartholomew turned his attention to the less important components. The first of these minor plans was the one for open space and public recreation.

Although not a major focus of the plan, the parks and recreation plan reflected Bartholomew's overriding premise that the city should exist as a system. Like streets, the city needed different kinds of parks to serve different needs. In his mind, it was clear that St. Louis already had outstanding large parks like Forest Park. "Large parks," Bartholomew argued, "are very useful but they supply only one part of the city's recreation requirements." What it lacked were smaller, neighborhood parks. "There is a surprising deficiency," Bartholomew told his readers, "in neighborhood parks, playfields, and playgrounds" (Bartholomew 1947, 41). According to him, these smaller parks and playgrounds were perhaps more important than a city's large parks. They were not only important in providing recreational opportunities for the city's residents, they were key in stabilizing neighborhoods. "If stability and improved environment in the various residential areas of St. Louis is to be assured," Bartholomew emphatically declared, "it is imperative that adequate local recreational areas be acquired" (Bartholomew 1947, 41).

According to Bartholomew, "each of the eighty-two residential neighborhoods in the city should have a neighborhood park, and playground" (Bartholomew 1947, 41). Bartholomew felt that "modern neighborhood design principals and standards" called for an approximately twenty-acre park to be located near the center of the neighborhood, preferably adjacent to the elementary school serving the neighborhood (Bartholomew 1947, 41). What this meant, of course, was that if a neighborhood was already built out and did not have a park, the land to build one had to be acquired and cleared. Bartholomew justified this huge acquisition and clearance program on the grounds that St. Louis was woefully deficient in comparison to other midwestern cities in terms of park acreage per person. As Bartholomew noted, "St. Louis has but one acre of park for each 263 persons (1940), as compared with one acre of park for each 90 persons in Cincinnati, 92 persons in Minneapolis, and 109 persons in Kansas City" (Bartholomew 1947, 42). In his mind, Bartholomew felt that "the park acreage of St. Louis should be more than doubled within the next twenty-five years" (Bartholomew 1947, 42).

Mass Transportation: Extensions, Reroutings, and Use of Expressways Proposed

The least ambitious section of the 1947 *Comprehensive City Plan* dealt with mass transportation. While Bartholomew was instrumental in the design and construction of the Washington, D.C., subway system, he did not feel that St. Louis had a sufficiently dense population to justify a subway. Moreover, he maintained that "despite receivership, re-organization and several changes of ownership the mass transportation facilities have been kept fairly well abreast of the city's needs" (Bartholomew 1947, 44). As a result, Bartholomew's proposals for mass transit were extremely modest.

Although he did not say so explicitly, it was clear that Bartholomew thought—like most of his contemporaries—that the streetcar would eventually be phased out. Bus lines were much more flexible and could take advantage of the proposed new freeways and street openings. As Bartholomew declared, "with the opening and widening of Third Street and its connections to Florissant Avenue on the north and Gravois Avenue on the south there will be need for no further provision of main arterial approaches for accommodation of mass transportation to the central business district" (Bartholomew 1947, 45). Unlike streetcars, buses could jump directly to "the northern and southern parts of the city in which live 70 percent of the city's total population" (Bartholomew 1947, 46). According to Bartholomew, mass transit issues in St. Louis had largely been solved. The only real remaining impediment to improving travel time and congestion was reducing the amount of downtown parking.

From the vantage point of the present, Bartholomew's viewpoint seems extremely shortsighted and unimaginative. By placing so much attention on the freeways, Bartholomew ensured that St. Louis would never have the density to create the type of system that would have slowed down the movement to the suburbs.

Air Transportation: Five Types of Airfields Proposed

While Bartholomew may have been too cautious in his mass transit planning, he has been ridiculed for what now seem like totally unrealistic expectations concerning the evolution of air travel.

As with the rest of the 1947 plan, Bartholomew took a systemic approach to the air transportation needs of St. Louis. Just like with streets and parks, St. Louis needed different airports for different needs. Bartholomew's transportation plan was a metropolitan plan that proposed thirty-five airfields grouped in five categories: 1) three major airports that would handle the bulk of commercial passenger travel, 2) a feeder airport that would presumably handle spill-over traffic, 3) fifteen minor fields that would provide freight service, 4) thirteen local personal fields for private plane, and 5) three congested area airports that would offer facilities for "autogyros" and heliocopters (Bartholomew 1947, 52–53).

The plan retained Lambert as a major field, but added two additional airports—one in Missouri and one in Illinois. The new major airport in Missouri would have been situated inside the southern side of the confluence of the Missouri and Mississippi rivers. The new major airport proposed for Illinois would have been located east of Horseshoe Lake, close to the Cahokia Mounds. The feeder airport would have been located close to where Parks College used to be in the city of Cahokia.

What is interesting about the minor and personal fields is not how many Bartholomew proposed but presumably how small most of these fields would have been. Three of these fields would have been in built-up areas inside city limits. One of these small fields would have been east of Morgan Ford at the southern city limits. Another would have been located on the western edge of the city at Hampton Boulevard north of Columbia Avenue. The third minor airport proposed for inside the city was actually operational for a period. It was located between Broadway and the Mississippi on the city's north side.

Even though he was trained as a civil engineer and was probably fascinated by advances in aviation, Bartholomew was conservative enough to hedge his bets concerning helicopters and other kinds of experimental aircraft. While they seemingly had huge potential to reshape intra-urban transportation, these new aircraft were still extremely expensive. As a result, Bartholomew said that site selection for what he called "congested area airports" would involve great cost and "should await further technological developments in design and operation" of these experimental aircraft (Bartholomew 1947, 52).

Figure 7. Airport Plan for the St. Louis Region.
Comprehensive City Plan, **Plate 27**.

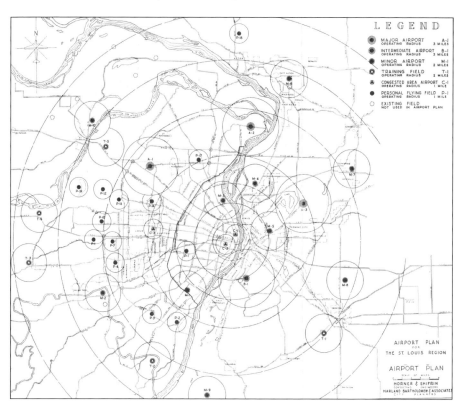

Although it is easy to make fun of Bartholomew for his heliports and park-size, personal airports, it would seem in hindsight that the region should have followed his lead in planning for one, if not two additional, major airports. Already in 1947, Bartholomew could anticipate that Lambert Airport, built in the 1920s, would not be able to accommodate future air travel demands. While Lambert has been recently expanded, it has come too late and at too high a cost. Although Bartholomew's suggested confluence site would have been submerged under two stories of water during the 1993 flood if it had been built, he showed great vision in also proposing a site on the eastern side of the Mississippi. In the early 1970s, federal funding had been designated for a new airport near Columbia, Illinois. Because of resistance on the western side of the river, particularly in St. Louis County, the airport was never built and the funds that were earmarked for St. Louis went to Houston for the building of what is now George Bush Intercontinental Airport; it has been a boon to the Houston region. If the airport had been built in St. Louis at that time, it might have been possible to make the region equally balanced and to retain the city as a hub (Primm 1990). By the time Scott Air Force Base in Troy, Illinois, had been expanded in the 1990s, the project was twenty years too late, with the center of regional population five miles west of I-270, the western bypass of the St. Louis interstate system. As a result, the project has been a fiasco.

The Central Business District: Improved Access Required for Greater Traffic Volume and/or More Parking Facilities

The last design component of the plan was Bartholomew's proposals for the central business district or the downtown. Although he declared in the central business district plan that the district was "the heart of the city and of the metropolitan district," Bartholomew's thinking about the district would ultimately lead to its demise (Bartholomew 1947, 54).

According to Bartholomew, the central problem facing the central business district (CBD) was congestion. As he explained to St. Louisans, "the close concentration of offices, retail stores, wholesale houses, banks, government buildings, and other facilities is highly advantageous and a great public convenience" (Bartholomew 1947, 54). But, as he went on, "if congestion is permitted to become so great and so protracted as to necessitate broader scattering of these buildings and facilities . . . the public convenience would be seriously impaired" (Bartholomew 1947,54). Consequently, the whole thrust of Bartholomew's CBD plan was to reduce congestion.

In Bartholomew's mind, mounting CBD congestion was the result of four things: 1) city and regional population growth which increased the number of persons entering the CBD, 2) new construction downtown, 3) drastic increase in automobile and truck traffic, and 4) the inability to widen CBD streets. (Bartholomew 1947, 54) But he did not think that expanding the CBD was necessary or desirable. The CBD had already been expanded northward by widening Delmar and Franklin. For Bartholomew, "no further expansion [was] necessary" (Bartholomew 1947, 55) In his mind, the area bound by Franklin, Tucker, Market, and Third (a little more than a square mile) was "sufficiently large to satisfy the demands of a metropolitan population of 2,000,000 people" (Bartholomew 1947, 55). The key, Bartholomew thought, was to 1) provide adequate parking, 2) build new expressways, and 3) improve traffic control measures (Bartholomew 1947, 55).

The most important of the three was to provide more parking. As he noted, 375,000 people entered the St. Louis CBD every day. However, the problem was being able to project how many more people would be in the CBD with anticipated regional population growth. To better gauge what impact population growth might have on St. Louis, Bartholomew compared St. Louis with ten other cities. What Bartholomew discovered was that "the number of persons entering by automobile in St. Louis exceeds that in all but four of the cities shown" (Bartholomew 1947, 55). He also concluded, in comparing St. Louis with these other cities, that the city should anticipate a daily influx of 450,000 into the CBD by 1970. While he acknowledged that twenty-five years earlier such a number of people would have necessitated subways, he argued that "the introduction of automobile traffic however has produced an entirely new situation" (Bartholomew 1947, 58). Instead of taking streetcars, most people now entered the CBD in either a private automobile or motor bus.

For Bartholomew, this had not only created more congestion because private automobiles took up six to eight times more space per passenger than public transportation, it created a new problem—where do you put the cars when the passengers are at work? But instead of planning to encourage people to take public transit, Bartholomew argued that the new task of the planner was to find a place to put all of these new automobiles. "A vast amount of parking space for the accommodation of individual automobile traffic is imperative," Bartholomew said (Bartholomew 1947, 59). But as he pointed out, people could not be permitted to park on the public streets. This would only further increase CBD congestion. The only solution, for Bartholomew, was creating off-street parking. "Provision of this parking space," he remarked rather matter-of-factly, "if not undertaken by private enterprise, may be forced upon the city as a public function. It is the modern substitute for subway construction" (Bartholomew 1947, 59–60).

But where could the city put this new parking? Assuming that one square foot of parking space was needed for each square foot of commercial space, Bartholomew calculated that the city needed at least 37,000 parking spaces to satisfy anticipated need. This was nearly 20,000 more than it already possessed. To create this much new parking inside the CBD would involve hundreds of existing department stores and office buildings. The only solution realized was to provide large parking garages on the fringes of the CBD and provide public transportation into the district (Bartholomew 1947, 61).

However, while Bartholomew saw parking as a major challenge for the CBD, he anticipated that actual traffic on CBD streets would actually decrease. He felt that the proposed interstates and local express highways would route traffic away from the downtown. He also thought that downtown traffic flow would be greatly enhanced by reducing curb parking—especially during rush hours, one-way streets, and by rerouting streetcars and buses (Bartholomew 1947, 62-63).

But he should not have worried. By kowtowing to the automobile, Bartholomew had made the downtown "obsolete." Parking space for parking space, the CBD would never be able to match suburban shopping centers. Moreover, with so much parking inside the CBD, it no longer provided the convenience which had been its sole reason for being. By 1970, the CBD had only a fraction of its 1947 daily population instead of the additional 75,000 that Bartholomew had projected. As contemporary planners struggle to revitalize downtowns across the country, the first thing they try to do is to increase congestion by reducing parking.

Carrying Out the Comprehensive Plan: Plan Is of No Value Unless It Is Followed

Although the plan also contained a section that listed City Plan Accomplishments (i.e. Bartholomew's accomplishments) from 1916 to 1947 and an appendix (Bartholomew 1947, 70–74, 75–77), the last component of the plan was a non-design discussion of plan implementation. As is the case in most of his master plans, Bartholomew argued in the St. Louis plan that the most crucial thing was giving the plan official status. But for Bartholomew, it was not enough for the plan to be recognized as law. It had to have both the power of being enforced as well as the flexibility to adapt to changing conditions. According to Bartholomew, this was only possible through the creation of an independent planning commission as outlined in the Standard City Planning Enabling Act, a model created by the profession in the 1920s (Bartholomew 1947, 65–67).

From Bartholomew's perspective, St. Louis had been a pioneer in the city planning movement. Not only had St. Louis prepared the first comprehensive plan in 1907, it was one of the first cities in the country to have a planning commission when an official City Plan Commission was appointed in 1912. However, according to Bartholomew, St. Louis's planning commission was flawed in that it was a creature of the city's executive branch. As a result, it was only effective as long as the administration was interested in or capable of following the provisions of the plan.

For Bartholomew the way around this problem was to make the commission independent of both the mayor and the city council as proposed by the Standard Act. As Bartholomew patiently explained to St. Louisans, "the purpose of this Act [is] to require public officials to give careful consideration to officially adopted city plans and to establish a systematic procedure whereby an official city plan would have to be considered before any official action could be taken on any matter affecting the plan" (Bartholomew 1947, 67). Moreover, as Bartholomew pointed out, by making the Commission the caretakers of the plan, they could change or modify it at will. "By having the City Plan Commission adopt the plan as a general guide rather than to be officially adapted as a fixed and arbitrary legal instrument," Bartholomew observed, "it would be possible to keep the plan flexible and dynamic and to meet changing conditions without the necessity of passing various amendatory ordinances for minute changes of detail" (Bartholomew 1947, 68).

Although the Standard Act from Bartholomew's view addressed the chief defect in most planning commissions, it manifested the fatal flaw in the comprehensive planning movement. As he had to realize, the Standard Act did not really give the power over the plan to the planning commission, but to its staff and the professional planners like Bartholomew. While the plan was suppose to reflect the will of the people, it actually came to reflect the will of the planners who created it. For Bartholomew, this was exactly what gave the plan its power and made it a tool for democracy. As a professional who possessed the scientific knowledge of how cities worked, the planner was freed from the constraints of partisan politics. Instead, the planner acted objectively to mold the city in a way that benefited all citizens. Believing that the city only existed as a coherent whole, planners like Bartholomew were blinded by their assumption that there was only one correct way to address a problem and that this best solution benefited all the citizens equally. While Bartholomew and the other master planners of his generation may have seen themselves planning with the best of intentions, the kind of power that they sought made them nothing less than the dictator of the city. Eventually, they would discover that they would be even less encumbered without a plan at all.

In any case, Bartholomew must have been persuasive, for the appendix is a copy of a new ordinance adopted two months after the release of the plan which created a new planning commission modeled directly on the Standard City Planning Enabling Act.

The Plan's Legacy

How are we to assess the 1947 *Comprehensive City Plan*'s legacy for St. Louis? Clearly, the 1947 plan has had—and continues to have—a tremendous impact on St. Louis and the St. Louis region. But has this impact been harmful or positive?

Looking at Bartholomew's ideas concerning the region, one would have to argue that he had a great deal of value to say. It would be difficult, if not impossible, to suggest that the lack of a metropolitan planning agency and a metropolitan plan has been a good thing for St. Louis. Though the East-West Gateway Coordinating Council has done a yeoman's job in trying to facilitate joint efforts in the region, it has never been given all of the power that Bartholomew felt was necessary for such an agency.

While Bartholomew's population projections might appear crazy now, it is necessary to recognize the two preconditions that Bartholomew assumed: 1) that the region would grow at the same pace as the nation, and 2) that the city would take steps to retain a larger percentage of its middle class. Neither condition occurred. The region has not grown as fast as the nation over the last generation due to the region's dependence on industrialization in an age of deindustrialization. Perhaps if the region had placed more emphasis on planning, it would have been positioned to counter such a trend. Moreover, one has to wonder if the city would have moved earlier to develop suburban-like, single-family attached housing as with the new Botanical Heights and St. Vincent Place developments if it would have held on to a greater percentage of its population base.

Likewise, while Bartholomew has been criticized over the years for having almost a fetish concerning single-family housing and starkly segregated land uses, maybe he simply better understood what contemporary Americans want and what central cities needed to adjust to those market forces to compete with the suburbs. In any case, the constant march of developers to obtain zoning variances would seem to support overwhelmingly Bartholomew's contention that zoning needs to be grounded firmly in a land use plan if it is to be effective.

Obviously, the greatest amount of criticism of Bartholomew and the 1947 master plan has been leveled against his housing and highway strategies. It cannot be denied that urban renewal and highway construction in the 1950s and 1960s greatly traumatized St. Louis. Indeed, if some of the tactics in the 1947 plan that were not implemented had been—such as the three north-south distributors or the rebuilding of Soulard—St. Louis could have been even more scarred. However, many of things which the plan and Bartholomew have been accused of were simply not their fault. Bartholomew never advocated high-rise public housing complexes and his placement of the proposed interstates would have been much more sensitive to existing neighborhoods. While Bartholomew has been wrongly blamed for many of the failings of the urban renewal era, it would appear that he has not been credited with many initiatives that are now considered planning best practices. He has not been given nearly enough recognition for his ideas concerning neighborhoods. Although the 1947 plan is usually seen as the quintessential urban renewal plan, the plan outlined strategies for neighborhood preservation, discussed the role of neighborhood parks, and emphasized the importance of neighborhood associations a quarter century before most planners even thought about neighborhoods.

In hindsight, Bartholomew's ideas concerning transportation almost seem absurd. But even here, Bartholomew might have been ahead of his time and his advice could have helped St. Louis if it was only followed. Most St. Louisans today shake their heads when they view Bartholomew's map with the thirty-five regional airports. The proposed second major airport seems especially ludicrous in light of the fact that the first airport is currently underutilized and that the proposed airport, if it had been built, would have been underwater during the 1993 flood. But Bartholomew correctly anticipated the importance of air facilities to the success of a region, as the new airports for Denver and Houston clearly illustrate. If Bartholomew can be blamed for anything concerning transportation in the 1947 plan, it is that he totally omitted rail, trucking, and river facilities in the plan. That he did so is surprising since he suggested their importance in the regional guide he prepared for the Metropolitan Plan Association in 1948. The document's mass transit plan is also uninspiring. However, Bartholomew was right in suggesting that St. Louis simply did not have the density to support rapid transit options available in 1947.

In retrospect, perhaps the most damaging legacy of the plan was Bartholomew's ideas—or the lack thereof—concerning the downtown and the overall economy of the city. Bartholomew simply did not anticipate the devastating impact that the proposed expressways would have on the Central Business District specifically, and St. Louis business in general. Once built, the interstates became huge straws that sucked retail, industrial, and office activity out to the suburbs. Bartholomew's proposed parking garages were no match for the centrifugal forces that the expressways created. While his suggested placement of these "mega-traffic flows" would have been more sensitive than what was actually built, Bartholomew was at the head of the pack nationally in getting the concept of the interstates accepted in the first place.

It would seem that on balance the legacy of the plan for St. Louis has been positive. Because of changing international economic conditions, St. Louis would probably have slid into the second tier of American metropolises no matter what, interstates or no. However, maybe some of the insights of this giant of the planning profession might lead St. Louis and the region to regain some of its past glory.

References

Abbott, Mark. "The Master Plan: The Life and Death of an Idea." Ph.D. diss., Purdue University, 1985.

Bartholomew, Harland, and Associates. *Guide Plan: Missouri-Illinois Metropolitan Area—An Overall Analysis of the Major Development Problems with Some Tentative Proposals for their Solution*. St. Louis: Author, 1948.

Jacobs, Jane. *The Death and Life of Great American Cities*. New York: Random House, 1961.

Johnson, Norman J. "Harland Bartholomew: Precedent for the Profession." In *The American Planner: Biographies and Recollections*, 2nd ed., edited by Donald A. Kruecheberg. New Brunswick, NJ: The Center for Urban Policy Research, 1994.

Lovelace, Eldridge. *Harland Bartholomew: His Contributions to American Urban Planning*. Urbana: University of Illinois, 1992.

Primm, James Neal. *The Lion of the Valley: St. Louis, Missouri*. 2nd ed. Boulder, CO: Pruett, 1990.

St. Louis City Plan Commission, and Harland Bartholomew. *Comprehensive City Plan: St. Louis, Missouri*. St. Louis: St. Louis City Plan Commission, 1947.

Stein, Clarence. *Toward New Towns for America*. Cambridge: Massachusetts Institute of Technology Press, 1966.

Teaford, Jon. *Rough Road to Renaissance: Urban Revitalization in America, 1940–1985*. Baltimore: The Johns Hopkins University Press, 1990.

———. *The Twentieth-Century American City: Problem, Promise, and Reality*. 2nd ed. Baltimore: The Johns Hopkins University Press, 1993.

Wilson, William Julius. *The Truly Disadvantaged: The Inner City, the Underclass, and Public Policy*. Chicago: University of Chicago Press, 1990.

Chapter 5
Planning Since the 1970s in the City of St. Louis

Charles Kindleberger

The Housing and Community Development Act of 1974 (U.S. Congress 1974) introduced a new playing field for American cities.[1] Out were the categorical grants associated with specific urban renewal plans, open-space plans, and, soon, in the form of the 701 planning program, even direct support for city planning.[2] In its place a new lump sum award program was instituted. In the case of cities with a population of more than 50,000, the annual allocation was to be given on an "entitlement" basis (U.S. Department of Housing and Urban Development 2006a).

This chapter is about city planning as practiced in the city of St. Louis since the 1970s. With new federal programs, a new department locally, and a growing set of demographic, social, and economic challenges, the profession took on a new focus and gave up on some of its traditional roles. The chapter traces some of the accomplishments and shortcomings experienced by planners and their colleagues during the last three-plus decades.

In 1974, a new department was created to take advantage of the change in funding opportunities. With backing from the "young turks"[3] on the Board of Aldermen, the St. Louis Community Development Agency (CDA) was created by merging four previously separate entities: the city Plan Commission, the Office of Business Development, the Beautifica-

---

[1]The Housing and Community Development Act of 1974 combined seven previously separate programs into a flexible community development fund distributed by a formula that considered population and various measures of community distress.

[2]The Comprehensive Planning Assistance Program, authorized under Section 701 of the 1954 Housing Act provided matching grants (2/3—HUD, 1/3—local). The program shifted direction during the 1970s from long- or medium-range land use planning to short-term projects, and was finally terminated in 1980 with the arrival of President Reagan. The City of St. Louis received relatively modest amounts.

[3]These individuals included Richard Gephardt, James Komareck, John Roach, and Milton Svetanics.

tion Commission, and the Model Cities Corporation (St. Louis Board of Aldermen 1974).[4] In most respects the planning function carried out by the new CDA Commission was similar to that of the previous city Plan Commission. Review and approval of proposed zoning changes, redevelopment or neighborhood plans, and street closings were still the order of the day but there were some important differences.

Planning was no longer an independent activity. Instead, it became part of a "Planning and Programming" division that was also charged with obtaining state and federal funds and then allocating them to other departments and nonprofits in order to carry out community development initiatives. Other divisions within the agency were responsible for promoting housing development, economic development and monitoring.

The advent of the federal Community Development Block Grant (CDBG)[5] program administered by a new CDA had a number of impacts both positive and negative for actual day-to-day planning. Twenty percent of the block grant could be used for administration and planning, so there was some money with which to hire both planning staff and consultants (U.S. Department of Housing and Urban Development 2006a). However, the presence of money created a whole new set of tasks, especially when a revised formula more favorable to troubled cities like St. Louis resulted in a jump from approximately $15 million to $30 million annually. Planning staff was caught up, along with a Community Development Advisory Group, in working with neighborhood groups and aldermen defining projects, reviewing large numbers of proposals to spend CDBG funds, and preparing the necessary work programs and contracts to carry out the activities.

Inevitably, CDA and the new process for receiving and spending development funds from Washington, D.C., was not without pain for other organizations that no longer had a direct link to the U.S. Department of Housing and Urban Development (HUD). The Model Cities program

---

[4]The City Plan Commission was created in 1911; the Mayor's Business Development Commission (MBDC) was created in 1960 (Ordinance 49776); the Beautification Commission was created in 1965 (Ordinance 53609) and first directed by Mel Beauchamp; the Model City Comprehensive City Demonstration Program was approved in 1968 (Ordinance 5660) and directed by Don Bourgeois, followed by Margaret Bush Wilson.

[5]CDBG applications for funds are submitted annually to the U.S. Department of Housing and Urban Development (HUD), after a process that involves public hearings and review and approval by the Board of Aldermen and mayor. HUD must approve the application as long as the proposed activities meet one of the three broad national objectives—for the benefit of low- and moderate-income people (at least 70 percent of funds), removal of slums and blight, or, dealing with an emergency, funds are not to be spent on ordinary municipal functions.

shut down, even as new CDBG funds were needed to close out many of its initiatives. The Land Clearance for Redevelopment Authority (LCRA)[6] now had to come to CDA for its urban renewal funds, and inevitably encountered frustration. Perhaps most dramatic was the decision by CDA and the mayor's office that the LaSalle Park urban renewal plan should be modified. The first phase of the plan, immediately south of Chouteau and east of Tucker, had involved clearance and the construction of new commercial, institutional, and residential uses. Unhappily, the replacement housing looked like the low-income housing that it was. LCRA was informed that the second and third phases of the plan would emphasize historic rehabilitation with a middle-class orientation, an approach that was sold to Ralston Purina as well. This would not be the last evidence of tension between established agencies like LCRA and the new CDA.

In 1977, the Conway administration[7] brought with it a new director to CDA, Donald Spaid, a professional planner with considerable experience in Indianapolis and then St. Paul. He soon initiated two large-scale planning exercises to be undertaken by national planning consultants—an Economic Development Strategy led by Hammer, Siler, George Associates, and a Housing Strategy led by Barton-Aschman Associates. The resulting documents set forth a series of initiatives that, while not particularly of interest to the Board of Aldermen, provided a direction for the agency.

The Housing Strategy (Barton-Aschman 1978) called for helping private developers willing to build low- and moderate-income housing and able to demonstrate a need for public financial support. The Economic Strategy (Hammer, Siler, George Associates 1978) highlighted industrial and housing development and other concerns that would continue for the next several decades:

- Development Administration—Managing the planning/development process

- Information—Providing planners and developers with necessary data

- Area Planning—Focusing on key geographic areas of the city

---

[6]LCRA was created in 1951 (Ordinance 45977) in order to conduct urban renewal projects. Charles Farris was director from 1953 to 1966, and 1969 to 1989. The Authority continues to exist, but its staff moved into the Economic Development Corporation (1988) and then the St. Louis Development Corporation (1990).

[7]Mayor Conway served one term, from 1977 to 1981.

- Downtown Development—Energizing the historic heart of the region
- Neighborhood Commercial Development—Updating outdated commercial strips

The rest of this chapter will consider planning issues from the perspective of these general topics, supplemented with two additional categories:

- Functional plans that focused on a particular topic such as Forest Park or the riverfront
- Strategic plans especially those concerned with city government operations.

Development Administration

Coordinating planning and development in any city, let alone one with a weak mayor form of government, involves interaction with many organizations. There is the need to coordinate the operating departments of city government (those that pave the streets, cut the weeds, and maintain the parks, for example) with those that attempt to encourage and direct private investment. There is the need to guide government entities only indirectly controlled by the mayor (the urban renewal authority, housing authority, land reutilization authority, etc.) and to interact with even more separate groups like the public schools or the public transportation agency.

Beyond public agencies, a host of nonprofit groups both help and complicate the development process. Some have a specific geographic focus (the Downtown Partnership and countless neighborhood groups) and others embrace a special interest (the Landmarks Association, concerned with historic preservation; Trailnet, concerned with the development of biking and pedestrian trails; etc.).

The mayor is, of course, only one of many elected officials who help shape planning and development. In the city of St. Louis, with its 28 aldermen, each representing around 12,500 citizens living in a ward of little more than two square miles, individual members of the legislative body can exert strong control on planning and development. In recognition of this power, city departments rarely act on specific transactions without securing aldermanic approval. Those wanting, for example, to purchase land from the Land Reutilization Authority (LRA)[8], receive tax abatement or some other subsidy, or those wanting to obtain a zoning variance had better obtain a letter from the relevant alderman.

The tradition of "aldermanic courtesy" reinforces the power held by individual members of the Board. Even in situations where most representatives think that a proposal makes eminent sense, they rarely vote against the position held by the alderman whose ward would be affected. To do so would invite future retribution.

Government

The board overseeing CDA was the Community Development Commission (CDC).[9] It was designed to extend the mayor's control in this decentralized environment. Unlike the typical planning commission, the fifteen-person body did not consist of volunteers chaired by one of their own. Instead, the Commission consisted of three categories of individuals: three aldermen—the chair of the Housing and Urban Development Committee, the Zoning Committee, and the president of the Board of Aldermen; five citizens appointed by the mayor; and seven city officials who served by virtue of their office, including the Directors of Streets, the Board of Public Service, Public Safety, Land Clearance for Redevelopment Authority, Housing Authority, Community Development Agency, and the Mayor's Director for Development. The Commission was chaired by the Director of CDA (St. Louis Board of Aldermen 1974).

Like its predecessor (the city Plan Commission) and its successor (the Planning and Urban Design Commission), the CDC was an organization where the mayor could command the votes when necessary. It was also an organization designed to allow knowledgeable, if not necessarily independent, people to discuss specific planning and development proposals, most of which would then go before the Board of Aldermen for approval by ordinance. The monthly meetings were open to the public, which occasionally showed up in large numbers, and while individuals were sometimes allowed to speak, formal public hearings were rarely held. Instead, they were typically the province of Board of Aldermen committee

---

[8]The Authority holds around ten thousand parcels of land and buildings that have been foreclosed and offered unsuccessfully at auction to anyone willing to pay the back taxes. The Authority also accepts donated property and purchases properties for future development.

[9]The Commission met once a month. Initially there were also subcommittee meetings to deal with specific issues like rezonings or street vacations, but these were discontinued in the early 1980s. The Commission reviewed CDBG applications, proposed redevelopment plans, proposed housing assistance projects, and more.

meetings, which considered rezoning petitions, redevelopment plans, and other matters prior to consideration by the full board.

Most mayors saw the need for an additional forum in which to examine development issues more broadly. Sometimes chaired by the mayor and other times by his director of development, these were opportunities not so much to talk about specific projects as about interdepartmental communication, redevelopment policy, and specific development challenges. Often called the Development Council, these meetings were most effective when they occurred on a routine basis, were attended by the mayor, and had an advance agenda. At their worst, they were forums for small talk and for department heads to show off. At their best, they were opportunities for policy alternatives to be debated, with clear follow-up directions provided by the mayor.

Business Relations

Effective public planning and development involves routine interaction with the private sector. On a day-to-day level, this requires responding to businesses that have problems with permits, parking, crime, or similar concerns. It also includes identifying and encouraging those who might be willing to invest either in a new business or expansion of an existing one. During the last thirty years, mayors also wrestled with how best to involve the business community at the policy level.

Mayor Conway decided to create a Mayor's Economic Development Advisory Commission (MEDAC).[10] Don Lasiter, then president of Mercantile Bank, was convinced to head the initiative, which included a cross section of business leaders. A professor on sabbatical (John Eilers) was hired to provide staff support. The meetings were informative but soon there were organizational issues (e.g., was it acceptable for a member to send an associate when he or she could not attend) and mission issues (e.g., what exactly should the group address and how). The organization did engage in some useful studies as to how the city might best promote itself, but its life did not extend beyond Mayor Conway's one term.

The more typical interaction with the business community involved requesting support from Civic Progress, the Regional Commerce and

---

[10]Unlike most of the organizations discussed in this chapter, MEDAC was not approved by ordinance; instead it was simply an advisory group.

Growth Association (RCGA), Downtown St. Louis Inc., later known as the Partnership[11] and other business groups. Specific projects like the Lucas Heights development, and later the domed stadium and Forest Park, were assisted by Civic Progress or individual companies within the thirty-member group. For the most part, however, Civic Progress showed little interest or capacity for an ongoing commitment to the city.

By contrast the Chamber of Commerce of Metropolitan St. Louis, St. Louis Regional Industrial Development Corps, and the St. Louis Research Council, which merged to become the RCGA, had both interest and staff able to promote development. What it asked for was funding support. A recurring issue within the city government was the extent to which the city was getting its money's worth in return for the annual support (usually around $150,000) of RCGA's marketing efforts. Inevitably, each of the jurisdictions contributing to this effort felt that other counties were receiving a disproportionate share of the leads.

Neighborhoods

A neighborhood planner is pulled in many directions. He or she may be responsible for preparing or updating a traditional plan, complete with statements of goals and objectives, examination of alternative futures, and specific recommendations. Carrying out such a project is hard enough at any time, but when the CDBG program provided money that could be spent in neighborhoods, a whole new set of tasks were required. The planner was asked to help a neighborhood group put together a proposal for funds, to help decide on potential sites for a mini-park, or to identify those blocks to receive concentrated code enforcement. Traditionally, aldermen have not had individual staffs in the city of St. Louis, but soon the more assertive members of the Board were asking neighborhood planners for all kinds of assistance. Multitasking became the order of the day.

In the early 1980s, Mayor Vincent Schoemehl changed all that.[12] Soon after his inauguration, he came to believe that CDA had become bloated,

---

[11]There are far more business groups today than earlier. The most influential have been Civic Progress (traditionally the thirty largest corporations in St. Louis, plus the heads of Washington University, St. Louis University, the mayor, and the county executive), RCGA (open to all businesses and supported with a large staff), and Downtown St. Louis Partnership (a nonprofit that promotes the Central Business District and manages the Downtown Community Improvement District.

[12] Mayor Schoemehl served three terms, from 1981 to 1993.

non-responsive, and inefficient. In the summer of 1981 and again 1982, large cuts were made resulting in the reduction of an organization that, counting vacancies, had had around 180 positions to one with under 50. Traditional neighborhood planning ceased, but the role of the planner as "firefighter" and aldermanic helper continued with the creation of a Neighborhood Liaison Office (NLO)[13] reporting to the Mayor's Office.

Schoemehl recognized that it is often easier to create a new organization with new people than to redirect an existing department. With help from his sister, he created Operation Brightside[14] to take over and expand on the landscaping duties run by CDA and, before it, the Beautification Commission. Operation Impact[15] was created to provide staff support for newly created neighborhood housing corporations. The corporations were charged with identifying and redeveloping so-called problem properties and the Impact staff was expected to help with the technical work associated with real estate transactions, housing investments, tax abatement, and more.

In the mid-1980s, convinced that there were certain neighborhoods that needed special intervention in order to prevent further disinvestment, the mayor created Operation Conserv.[16] This was, in effect, a group of individuals with NLO skills but assigned to a limited number of "Phase 1" neighborhoods. Operation Conserv staff were expected to prepare "plans" for their respective neighborhoods, but with a focus on immediate, not long-range, challenges. These individuals were asked to "drive the alleys" so that they truly understood conditions and to recommend practical approaches for dealing with crime, abandoned cars, derelict property, and other symptoms of blight. In many respects, this was the "broken window" approach that Mayor Rudy Giuliani made famous in New York City. If one could focus on the often small problems that suggested indifference or deliberate disregard for the neighborhood, then more positive behavior would result on the part of all neighborhood residents.

Directing resources at neighborhoods that appeared to be at risk of "blight" meant less money for neighborhoods in even worse shape, and not

---

[13]The NLO was staffed initially with individuals who had been laid off from CDA. It was first headed by Al Nerviani, a former Building Division official.

[14]Operation Brightside was created largely under the leadership of the mayor's sister Lucille Green. Best known for the explosion of daffodils that happened each spring along city streets and highways, the organization was replicated in many other cities.

[15]Operation Impact was headed first by Gee Stuart, a former housing activist from the Skinker-Debaliviere neighborhood of the city.

[16]Operation Conserv was first headed by Don Roe. As part of this initiative, all city neighborhoods were divided into two phases. Operation Conserv declared its intent to focus on Phase 1 neighborhoods with the understanding that Phase 2 neighborhoods would receive special attention at a later time.

everyone liked that. For example, one of the largest developers, McCormack Baron, was assembling a large amount of land in the St. Louis Place neighborhood, north of Cass and east of Jefferson. But their approach to redevelopment in a largely abandoned neighborhood was understandably clearance and new construction, all of which required heavy subsidy. In a series of tense meetings, they learned that there was not enough in the way of public support for projects of this scope and the more customized approach in the Operation Conserv neighborhoods. They subsequently sold much of their inventory.

With the election of Mayor Bosley in the early 1990s, the approach to neighborhood planning turned once again. Operation Conserv (targeted neighborhoods) and the NLO (aldermanic support) merged into a new thirty-person Neighborhood Stabilization Office (NSO).[17] The new office addressed previous concerns that some neighborhoods in need received considerably less attention than others. The NSO has continued through the present, albeit with some changes in focus and leadership. One of those made in the last few years has been to organize staff services along the twenty-eight wards rather than the seventy-eight neighborhoods. In general, the city's planners have viewed this geographic shift with skepticism, worrying that the staff would be pressured to become more political and less professional in their day-to-day work.

Information

City planning has long struggled with the extent to which it was more an art or a science. There are good arguments for both sides, but most planners, whether they emphasize intuitive decision making or decisions based more on empirical evidence, demand information.

As Mark Abbott discusses in Chapter 4, the 1947 City Plan illustrated the importance that Harland Bartholomew gave to information about community conditions and assets. A strong interest in a quantitative approach to planning grew in the 1960s, reflecting perhaps a national interest (articulated by Robert McNamara and others) in systems analysis, as well as the development of computer-based transportation models in the planning field. The federal Community Renewal Program, and to a lesser extent the 701 Planning Program, provided considerable funding for data assembly and research. The St. Louis Development Program

---

[17]The NSO was led initially by Ron Igoe, and then Anna Ginsburg. It includes the Citizen Service Bureau and continues to this present day.

(city Plan Commission 1973)[18] stands out as one of the best and most polished profiles of the city in terms of both data and graphics.

Evidence of interest in community conditions and trends in the mid-1970s could be found in a newly constructed "war room" in City Hall across from the Mayor's Office. Around the walls were backlit transparencies portraying conditions in planning and program areas throughout the city. A rearview slide projector represented the latest in audio-visual technology.

Over time the war room was used less and less until the space was commanded for some other purposes. This was in part because CDA had moved from the Civil Courts Building to a downtown office building considerably further from city Hall. But it was mostly because keeping the data current was beyond the resources and eventually the will of the department.

In the 1970s, planners increasingly recognized that to stay current with regard to information like land use, building activity, and public safety incidents, they had to be consumers of data from other departments in government. Yet many of these departments had antiquated computing systems if they had any at all. Accordingly, in the late 1970s an initiative was put in place to design an integrated information system that could meet the operational needs of many of the Mayor's key departments (the Assessor's Office, the Building Division in the Department of Public Safety, etc.) as well as independent "county level" departments (e.g., the Recorder of Deeds, the License Collector, the Collector of Revenue).

The basic concept, if not all the details, survived the transition from the Conway to the Schoemehl administrations. HUD was convinced that block grant funds were eligible for this purpose, and the Grant Thornton consulting firm was hired to carry out the work. The result was a Land Records Management System (LRMS)[19] running on the city's mainframe that met most of the needs of the operating departments and that could provide, given sufficient time, "printouts" of relevant planning information. However, the portion of this project that would have allowed a

---

[18]Under the direction of James Schoonover, the St. Louis Development Program was a follow-up to the Challenge of the Seventies organized by Mayor Cervantes and led by his brother. The St. Louis Development Program was funded mostly with a HUD Community Renewal Program grant. Consultants included Alan Voorhees and Associates, Robert Gladstone and Associates, and others.

[19]LRMS was developed in "total" from an IBM database system. It enabled a major improvement to the parcel records (used by the Assessor's Office), the permit records (used by the Building Division in the Public Safety Department and others), and license records (used by the License Collector's Office).

Geographic Information System (GIS) with which to analyze and map information was cut out of the budget.

In 1982, IBM issued its first personal computer. Planners in St. Louis and elsewhere immediately recognized the opportunity to reduce their reliance on the central Information Technology (IT) office and the potential to do their own information analysis on their own schedule. The bureaucratic battles were fierce, especially given the organization of city government. The Comptroller's Office housed the Information Technology (then data processing) office. They controlled the city mainframe and could see no reason why other departments needed a computer, even if it was a small one that they could afford. A separate microcomputer operation was set up by the Mayor's Office, some LRMS functions were recreated on the microcomputers, and tempers flared.

By 1985, the planners at CDA had a few of their own microcomputers and some very rudimentary mapping software that allowed a set of relatively crude thematic maps to be contained in a new demographic profile titled *St. Louis 1985: A Profile at Mid-Decade* (Community Development Agency 1985). Yet in many respects the city was still in the nineteenth century in terms of public service. A citizen, for example, could not go to the zoning office and obtain an up-to date zoning map. The ability of the city of St. Louis to create and print computer-generated maps did not yet exist.

Then in the late 1980s several fortunate events occurred. First, the Apple Computer company tried to gain a foothold in the computer mapping world. The city of St. Louis was selected to participate in a program that provided a Macintosh computer, a mapping package (MapGraphics), and a Hewlett Packard map plotter, all at substantial discounts. Soon the CDA graphics department was creating electronic parcel maps for different neighborhoods.

Second, the Comptroller's Office recognized the desirability of doing a feasibility study to define a Geographic Information System that could meet the needs of the city. AT&T was hired and while the resulting report was not particularly groundbreaking, it did help raise awareness. At roughly the same time, Union Electric and then the Metropolitan Sewer District realized that it was in their interest to collaborate in the development of base maps.

The 1993 flood was an opportunity to demonstrate the importance of up-to-date, accurate maps in dealing with both the event and the post-disaster cleanup. With help from the mayor's chief of operations and the city budget director, and considerable pushing from planners and other city employees who recognized the potential of GIS, the Board of Aldermen approved two successive allocations of $100,000 in the Capital

Improvement Program. Finally, it was possible to purchase new GIS software licenses, computers able to run the software, training courses, and a small amount of application development work by consultants.

The 1990s were also an opportunity to assemble data and a mapping capability on the World Wide Web. A number of federal, corporate and state grants (e.g., Enterprise Community, Corporation for Public Broadcasting, HUD Ounce of Prevention) enabled GIS capability to be built into both the St. Louis Community Information Network (CIN) and the Geo St. Louis internet sites.

Currently, those who work in planning and development for the city of St. Louis and many of those in other departments have ready access to specific land and building information, and some ability to analyze the information. Routinely placing data on the internet (currently weekly) has substantially simplified some tasks. Yet there is much more to be done including supplementing the parcel database with an accurate inventory of buildings, dwelling units, and addresses.

Area Plans

The traditional planning goal for U.S. communities is to have a "comprehensive," "master," or "general" plan for the whole jurisdiction, and then to have more detailed plans for individual neighborhoods. It is a hard goal to achieve. In the early 1970s, the City Plan Commission decided to prepare a new comprehensive plan for the city, one that would be more realistic than the more than twenty-year-old Bartholomew plan of 1947. With federal 701 planning funds, a local young consulting firm, Team Four,[20] was hired and began to prepare a series of background papers.

As so many plans had before, there was recognition that conditions varied widely across the city. Some neighborhoods were in relatively strong shape, needing continued investment and maintenance but not too much more, while others were in considerably more desperate straits, and candidates for major renewal. Previous plans since the early 1900s had made

---

[20]Team Four originally consisted of Richard Ward, Jerome Pratter, Bill Albinson, and another. Jack Pyburn, Austin Tao, Larry Marx, and Bob Lewis soon joined. The company exists today under Bill Albinson; many others joined Development Strategies. One of the firm's technical memorandums prepared for the Plan Commission characterized the City in terms of "Conservation, Redevelopment and Depletion" areas. The suggestion was made that effective economic investment was not currently possible in the depletion areas. This concept became known as "the Team Four Plan."

similar observations, especially the 1947 plan, which called for large-scale clearance. However, this time the climate was different.

By the early 1970s, the city had experienced fifteen years of active urban renewal, some of which was incomplete and most of which had been controversial. Many of those who had been displaced now lived in neighborhoods which were identified as candidates for additional "renewal." Moreover, a growing segment of the poor and minority community in St. Louis had been galvanized during the civil rights struggles of this era.

Perhaps most galling was the concept of "triage," the idea that, as on the battlefield in Vietnam, those who are wounded need to be divided into three groups: those in relatively good shape, those likely to die, and those in the middle where priority intervention could make a difference. When this analogy was applied to neighborhoods, the inevitable conclusion was that resources should go to a limited number of areas under "threat" of distress and abandonment. Other even poorer neighborhoods that had already lost many of their affluent residents would have to wait. Some residents in these neighborhoods thought that they were being asked to experience "benign neglect," a term used by Patrick Moynihan in a 1970 memorandum to President Nixon.

There is reasonable debate about the details of the early drafts, but soon the planning effort was being referred to with derision as the "Team Four" plan (Team Four 1973). The Plan Commission members let the consultants take the heat. A draft *Interim Comprehensive Plan* (City Plan Commission 1975) was published containing mostly sensible land use recommendations for portions of the city. The new CDA then sought to continue the comprehensive planning effort but without much enthusiasm or support. With the arrival of Mayor Schoemehl and the large number of layoffs, the initiative was discontinued. It would take twenty years for the concept to be revived, and then in a different form. With the arrival of Mayor Slay in 2001, a significant effort was begun to develop a new city-wide land use plan (Planning and Urban Design Agency 2005).

The new land use plan avoided references to targeting or priority setting between different neighborhoods, as well as traditionally controversial subjects like residential density. Most importantly it was drawn up in close consultation with each of the twenty-eight aldermen, with very little in the way of public participation. In 2005, the Planning and Urban Design Commission approved the new plan, replacing the 1975 Interim plan and the last formally adopted plan—the 1947 *Comprehensive City Plan*. The combination of "staying below the radar," astute political interaction with individual aldermen, avoiding certain controversial topics, and a different, quieter era made possible a new citywide plan. For the first time in a long time, the city had taken a major step toward compliance with state planning law.

While citywide planning was controversial, there were some calls for plans for large areas of the city. A group of north side aldermen convinced the Conway administration to initiate a large-scale planning process under the shared direction of Irma Lawrence's North Side Preservation Project and CDA. Joyce Whitely of Whitely and Whitely, a minority planning firm in Cleveland, was hired. Large area plans were also endorsed by some aldermen, especially on the near north side and the near south side of downtown. Typically these involved a request for proposals, the hiring of a planning team, and an attempt to identify investment opportunities. Most succeeded in describing problems and articulating citizen needs and desires. Few, however, occurred in an environment where there was much in the way of market demand. Inevitably, many plans gathered the proverbial "dust on the shelf."

Much of the planning activity consisted of the preparation and review of plans necessary to help assemble land and convey tax abatement—and later, tax incremental financing—assistance to private developers. Planners at LCRA (now staffed by the St. Louis Development Corporation) prepared Chapter 99 and Chapter 100 plans,[21] while planners at CDA—and subsequently PDA—reviewed these and Chapter 353 plans[22] as prepared typically by planning consultants for potential developers. These were reviewed by the Community Development Commission (subsequently Plan Commission) and recommended to the Board of Aldermen and mayor for approval. More recently, historic tax credits,[23] brownfield tax credits[24,] and especially tax increment financing also became of major importance to many redevelopment projects.

---

[21]Ch. 99 of the Missouri Revised Statutes is the Land Clearance for Redevelopment Law. It allows a Land Clearance for Redevelopment Authority to make findings that areas are "blighted" and to prepare plans for their renewal. Ch. 100 enables a community's Planned Industrial Expansion Authority to conduct similar studies and prepare similar plans, but they relate only to industrial land.

[22]Ch. 353 of the Missouri Revised Statutes allows a community to review and approve a plan that conveys tax abatement and eminent domain powers to a developer. The developer must show that its proposal for the "blighted" area is in the public interest, that it has the ability to carry out the proposal, and that, "but for" the tax abatement and eminent domain, the proposal would not be possible.

[23]Since 1998, the State of Missouri has offered an investment tax credit equal to 25 percent of approved costs that are part of a qualified rehabilitation. Income-producing buildings may qualify for both state and federal tax credits. The Missouri Department of Natural Resources states that more than $2.3 billion has been invested in historic rehabilitation projects since the program's initiation, making the state one of the leaders in the nation.

[24]The Missouri Department of Economic Development may issue tax credits for up to 100 percent of the cost of remediation of a project, or 100 percent of demolition of a site. Businesses that then relo-

The mixed record of city-initiated area plans, as opposed to redevelopment plans, can be illustrated in the experience of the near north side, the neighborhoods roughly north of Delmar and Convention Center Plaza to around St. Louis Avenue, between Interstate 70 on the east and Jefferson on the west. The giant Pruit-Igoe public housing complex came down in the early 1970s, the large Falstaff Brewery at the base of St. Louis Place Park was empty, and Section 235 housing (HUD subsidized with low-interest financing and almost no down payment) built in the 1960s was becoming abandoned. There was a high degree of neighborhood frustration especially in the late 1970s when it became evident that the Missouri Department of Transportation still envisioned a circumferential freeway through the area that would bypass the riverfront west of downtown. Some called it the "North-South Destroyer."[25]

This portion of St. Louis was the site of Model Cities, a 1960s War-on-Poverty-era program that focused funds on a small area within an eligible municipality, when and if there was a high degree of grassroots participation. The Fourteenth Street Mall, Courtney Street Health Center, Carr Square Community Center, and other facilities were made possible with Model Cities funding. However, many observers concluded that the real impact of the Model Cities program was to provide some citizens in the neighborhoods with jobs and income that allowed them to move to another location.

The strategy drawn up by CDA during the Conway administration (Hammer, Siler, George Associates 1978) designated the area "Centrum," presumably because of its proximity to downtown. Funding for a plan was called for, a request for proposals issued, and a selection committee assembled. The head of CDA and the Mayor's Office exerted insufficient control/direction and a consulting team was selected by the committee that was not the director's choice.

A contract was prepared, approved, and signed, but the initial bad blood with the designated consulting firm proceeded to get worse. Little useful guidance was provided to the consultants. After several contentious meetings over a few months, the director used his powers to cancel the contract. The half-completed document was not released.

In the early 1980s, a new firm, Fleming Associates, was hired to begin a new plan for the area. There was strong support from Fifth Ward Alder-

---

cate to a clean site may qualify for credits based on new jobs created, capital investment made, and a 50 percent income exemption.

[25]The official name was the North South Distributor. Opponents included neighborhood leaders in the Jeff-Vander-Lou and the Downtown West neighborhoods. Alderman Bruce Summers and associates from the Americans for Democratic Action were also very much involved.

woman Mary Ross, but again there was little in the way of implementation. Neighborhood-based plans were occasionally developed, primarily through the input of volunteers. Inevitably, these would conflict with ideas proposed or favored by the alderman. In the early 2000s, still another new plan was undertaken (Schwetye Architects 2002) for the area, this time with the support of a new alderman, April Ford Griffin of the Fifth Ward.

For the most part, these plans made little difference. To some degree the process gave sustenance to residents who cared about their neighborhoods and were able to dream collectively about improvements. But the real changes happened because of private development. In some cases, this was highly subsidized by the federal government. HUD funds for the Vaughn Demonstration Project,[26] with its three stages of mixed-income housing, and the Falstaff Brewery Urban Development Action Grant (UDAG) redevelopment project before it, enabled McCormack Baron to make a major transformation. At the same time, private development by Judy Woolerton of Choate Construction created new, market-rate, single-family housing north of Cass Avenue with little subsidy.

Similarly, major public development projects occurred with little reference to plans. The Gateway School complex was placed on the southern half of the Pruitt-Igoe site, and the fire department headquarters and a new police station were built on Jefferson Avenue. These developments contributed to the growing confidence in the investment climate.

Even bolder plans would be prepared for the area, including a proposed golf course in the mid-1990s. Designed for both sides of Cass Avenue, the idea was to stimulate adjacent residential new construction, as with suburban developments. Finding private investors and the political again proved difficult.

Downtown Development

Downtown St. Louis in the early 1970s was still the downtown for much of the region. There were two department stores and stand-alone clothing stores like Boyds and Brooks Brothers. There were several movie theaters (the Ambassador and Lowe's) and great cafeteria restaurants (Maryland

---

[26]Vaughn Demonstration Project, a high-rise public housing complex located along 21st Street, just east of the Pruitt-Igoe site, was demolished with special federal funds provided by HUD with the backing of Senator Bond. The success of this demonstration is credited with leading to HUD's Hope VI program, which has enabled the conversion of troubled public housing projects across the country.

Kitchen and Miss Hulling's). Buildings that were soon to become vacant were still occupied (the Security Trust, the Merchandise Mart, the Paul Brown, the Ambassador, and many more). The Arch and the new Busch Memorial Stadium had recently been completed. The major banks were committing to new headquarter buildings.

But there had been a net loss in the city of around 170,000 people during the previous two decades, and businesses were starting to follow. Office development occurred along Route 40 and I-270. New construction came to Clayton. Industrial warehouse developments sprang up along I-70, most notably in Earth City, a massive development in the flood plain of the Missouri River. Downtown had growing competition.

There were five general CBD-wide planning efforts during the last thirty years. All involved a combination of consultants, staff, and committees of individuals known today as "stakeholders." They include:

- 1973: This Peckham Guyton Albers & Viets (PGAV) consulting effort recommended a Locust Street Transit Mall, skywalks between buildings and more (Peckham Guyton Albers & Viets 1974).

- 1982: The staff and consultants of Harland Bartholomew and Associates' (HBA) effort was shelved after failing to retain priority during an administration shift (Harland Bartholomew and Associates 1982).

- 1986: Tom Martinson, an architect from Minneapolis, recommended a north-south green space south of the Gateway Mall, downtown housing, and more (Martinson 1986).

- 1993: A large group led by Tom Purcell, director of the Lalede's Landing Redevelopment Corporation, and Don Royse, director of design for SLDC, had difficulty resolving key issues.

- 2000: A new umbrella organization, Downtown Now[27,] raised more than a million dollars and hired a consulting team led by EDAW, Inc. (EDAW 2000). While the effort ended in a squabble with the consultant (resulting in very few copies of the final document), the plan has formed the basis for the remarkable set of downtown investments during the last decade.

---

[27]Downtown Now, a newly created group was established to help engage the business community and to overcome tensions between the City's SLDC and the Downtown Partnership. It was headed by Tom Reeves.

The development decisions in downtown were inevitably shaped by the interaction of property owners, investors, civic and political leaders, and the bureaucracy. Battles were fought over issues both large and small.

Historic Preservation

Led by the Landmarks Association, there has been a fight to save buildings from demolition over the last thirty years. The record is mixed. The most controversial debate was in the early 1980s over the International, Title Guarantee, and Buder buildings in the Gateway Mall, but there were plenty of others before and since—the demolitions of the Demenil Building, the Ambassador Theater, the Century Building, and others and the proposed multidistrict nomination to the National Historic Register. Given the highly charged politics, planners entered these debates at their own risk, but in some cases helped clarify the debate as they processed the plan reviews.

Fortunately, much of the historic downtown environment has survived. In some situations this was due to the courageous acts of individuals (e.g., Mayor Schoemehl's decision to stand up to Anheuser-Busch's desire to demolish Cupples Station for a new arena) or the persistence of individuals (e.g. Austin P. Leland's fight to save the Old Post Office, which has recently been renovated for the second time). Perhaps of greater import were the relative lack of demand for new construction (and hence land) and the advent of state historic tax credits and local tax increment financing that together have enabled the dramatic conversion of largely vacant Class C office buildings to condominiums and apartments.

Parking and Circulation

Many planners argued that the parking facilities, especially surface lots, were a major blight on downtown, and that instead they should be encouraged on the fringes of downtown rather than in the heart of the area. Developers, property owners and retailers in general thought quite the opposite, and, as they showed willingness to invest, they generally carried the day. The urban renewal authority (LCRA), the Treasurer's Office, and the state of Missouri all developed parking structures as well.

Like everyone else, planners can be caught up in the fad of the day. Most today are pleased that the skywalks suggested in the 1974 plan were not built, and that the "People Mover" competition in the late 1970s was won by Detroit and Miami and not St. Louis. Less clear is the question of the Locust Street Bus Mall, especially when one thinks about the transit mall in Denver. The big circulation successes on the last thirty years have been the MetroLink and streetscape on Washington Avenue. Both were made possible with hard-to-come-by federal transportation dollars. Among the remaining challenges are constructing a lid over Memorial Drive to the Gateway Arch grounds and general landscaping and street enhancements.

Aesthetics

Many property owners tend to think that the exterior of their building or lot—its cleanliness, paint, repair, signage, and landscaping—is their business and no one else's. In general, planners and others concerned with the whole community see the world differently. They argue that property owners have a responsibility to build, maintain, and repair their property in a tasteful, respectful manner. Inevitably, this costs more money than doing nothing or other inexpensive solutions.

Often planners had little leverage in these debates, especially when design review authority was eliminated for proposed projects within three hundred feet of a park and transferred to the Building Division for Minex reviews.[28] But for developments receiving tax abatement or TIF subsidy in urban renewal areas (i.e., Chapter 99 or 100 plans), planners had authority to see that design standards spelled out in the plan were observed. Planner/architects like Al Karetski and Dale Ruthsatz fought for these standards, sometimes not only against a developer but also city Hall, either in the form of an alderman or the mayor and his associates in Room 200. Often the issues appeared subjective—the size of signage, signs above the roof line, or the width (caliper) of new trees. Those planners who achieved the most success over time worked to educate others about the importance of design principles; they also carefully chose their battles.

As this is written, downtown appears in better shape than it has been in a long time. All the major sports venues have been resolved, the failed St. Louis Centre has new promise, and Washington Avenue and the Old Post Office District are experiencing massive development. All but a relatively few of the Class C office, industrial, and warehouse buildings have been purchased for conversion to condominiums or apartments. Even some of the big, unintended consequences of previous projects have begun to right themselves. For example, the northwest quadrant of downtown is coming back after being partially emptied when federal employees were moved to the Congressman Young Federal Building, on Tucker south of the Police

---

[28]The Minimum Exterior Standards (MINEX) program requires a basic architectural review of all commercial, industrial, and residential structures containing more than four units that are proposed for an area that is not in a city historical district or redevelopment area.

Station, after it received a massive renovation in the 1980s. With help from the Missouri Historic Tax Credits, Tax Increment Financing, and a new generation of entrepreneurs, that section of downtown is rapidly mending.

Neighborhood Commercial Development

The automobile changed everything. Where once people shopped for groceries and other goods by foot, carriage, and then streetcar, the car allowed them to go much farther—initially to other parts of town, but then to the suburban malls and the "big box" national brand stores.

In the mid-1970s, one could shop at a Sears store on North Kingshighway or on South Grand. The Southtown Famous-Barr store anchored the intersection of Chippewa and Kingshighway. Some family restaurants and retail shops still seemed to prosper.

Older cities like St. Louis seemed to have endless miles of arterial streets lined by underused, "undesirable," or abandoned commercial establishments. Wig shops, Karate studios, and used goods stores increasingly replaced more traditional shops. Planners were assigned the task of doing something to remedy the situation. It wasn't easy.

Outreach

Planners were asked to meet and in many cases help form a merchants association that was affiliated with a given "strip." Routine meetings were encouraged with the police, license collector, and other city offices that could provide help.

Market Analysis

Planners also conducted studies designed to show that the density of the city offset its lower median income as compared to suburban locations. As the use of computers and GIS improved, it became easier to help retailers and potential investors appreciate the size of the market that needed consumer goods and services.

Marketing

Mayor Schoemehl pushed the planners to come up with themes for different areas. If the Hill conjured up images of Italy, and South Grand concentrated on Asian restaurants and shops, he wondered if comparable themes could serve as a basis elsewhere for retail revival.

Design Services

In the late 1970s, formal design plans were prepared for South Grand, Cherokee, and several other locations. Under the guidance of Jim Praprotnik, Bill Fronick, and Earl Zellsman, these contained elaborate elevations illustrating existing building facades and how they might be renovated. However, they took a long time to prepare, and within a few years, massive staff cutbacks left no staff to continue them.

Façade Program

The Delmar Loop in University City became an outstanding example of how a strip commercial area could combine improvements to the exteriors of its buildings with new street trees, curbs, and sidewalks. Mayor Schoemehl pushed to establish a program whereby building owners willing to put up their own money could receive a like sum from the city, subject to certain conditions. Funds had to be spent on removing ugly signs, installing new awnings, repairing windows, or otherwise fixing the exterior of the building. All improvements were subject to architectural review.

Landscaping / Infrastructure

Complementing these investments, the city was prepared to redo the public right of way, often with new trees, sidewalks, and tree lawns. Gravois, Jefferson, Cherokee, North Kingshighway, and West Florissant were just some of the arterial streets that received help. Each spring new flowering Bradford pear trees seemed to be everywhere.

Zoning

Residential neighbors didn't just want better looking physical environs. Many clearly preferred certain uses to others. They didn't like convenience stores, pawn shops, and similar shops that some claimed encouraged "loitering." Some aldermen tried to achieve land use changes by tinkering with the zoning ordinance, often requiring a conditional use permit that would give neighbors an opportunity to complain before the Board of Zoning Adjustment. Some went so far as to list non-permitted uses in redevelopment plans, even though they were not regulated in the zoning ordinance.

Demolition

A more direct way to deal with "undesirable" land uses was to purchase the property, sometimes with federal funds, and to have it renovated into another use or demolished. Convenience stores on Thirty-ninth Street south of I-44 and movie theaters on South Grand got this treatment. A less dramatic way of dealing with loitering and even drug dealing was to have the public phone removed from in front of a store.

The commercial development picture in St. Louis remains mixed. The Façade Program has made a visible difference in many neighborhoods where aldermen have been cooperative and property owners have been willing to invest. National brand stores have continued to be hard to attract, and securing large grocery stores remains a challenge. Fortunately there are exceptions in downtown and many neighborhoods where coffee- houses, restaurants, and some small businesses seem to be succeeding.

Functional Planning

Most traditional city planning involves dealing with a particular proposal or concentrating on all aspects of a neighborhood or corridor. Other plans look at a particular subject. Three topics have recurred in recent years: parks, riverfront, and transportation.

Parks Planning

The Parks Department faces a mix of challenges. With around one hundred parks, from the 1,300-acre Forest Park to a series of minute parcels, around a dozen recreation centers, and responsibility for recreation programming, street trees, weed cutting, and debris removal, the department has constantly been stretched. In an environment characterized by extensive demands for day-to-day maintenance and thin budgets, its management had little time for planning. There were some important exceptions.

Forest Park is perhaps the best example of planning success. With the zoo, Muny Opera, history museum, science museum, tennis, golf, and many additional playing fields, there have always been diverse clients. Some want passive areas for walking or picnics; others are interested only in venues for active sports. Some want nearby parking; some want fewer roads and parking facilities.

In the late 1970s, a serious planning effort began with participation from a steering group, CDA planning staff, and a team of consultants. There was considerable initial enthusiasm, but some of the basic conflicts were not worked out. In any case, the new Schoemehl administration did not perceive this as a priority. The planning process ended with a whimper.

Major debates continued about the park—a proposal for a "farm" near the zoo; additional parking behind the art museum; a shared Forest Park budget and governance with St. Louis County. Other planning and fund-raising efforts were initiated, but the one that succeeded began in the mid-nineties led by John Hoal and a group of planner/architects in the St. Louis Development Corporation. With enthusiastic help from Mayor Bosley, stakeholders were involved, a friends group (Forest Park Forever) was created, and real money was raised. An outpouring of corporate and individual contributions, combined with a new capital improvements tax directing some funds to the largest parks in the city, allowed implementation to become reality. As a result, the park has been transformed into one of the nation's most attractive and modern centerpiece urban parks.

Other park planning initiatives were made possible because of federal programs. The Urban Park and Recreation Recovery program required that communities have a "Recovery Action Plan" for their parks. In other cases, the triggering factor was the hope for a private-public partnership, especially in running the recreation centers, or even, in the case of Carondelet Park, a congressional earmark. As always there have been trade-offs—should fewer parks be upgraded at a higher level of quality or a greater number of parks helped at a more basic level? Should restrooms and water fountains be repaired given the almost-certain vandalism?

Riverfront Planning

A constant refrain during the past thirty years has been the need to "return to the river." The argument is that first with the railroads, then with interstate highways, St. Louis cut off its physical access, and in some respects its symbolic connection, with its Mississippi river heritage. Progress has been made: It is no longer easy to get stuck on the levy side while a long freight train negotiates the central riverfront; substantial improvements have been made to Leonor K. Sullivan Drive; Eads Bridge provides a dramatic vista for pedestrians and bicyclists as well as automobiles.

Yet a series of plans for the central riverfront (between Laclede's Landing on the north and Chouteau's Landing on the south) have failed to take hold. Lots of private and public investment occurred (e.g., the Santa Maria, Mine Sweeper, Admiral, McDonalds, Robert E. Lee) without lasting success, and many other ideas were explored (e.g., a marina, a Jacques Cousteau Center, currently floating islands) that went nowhere.

To the north and south, the planning has tended to focus more on industrial land and the ways that new infrastructure and investment might be attracted. Exceptions would be plans for Bellerive Park, resulting in a partially realized lower level; North Riverfront Park; and, perhaps most successfully, the plan and partial implementation of a riverfront bike path.

In some respects the bike path represents planning at its best. A small group of planners at CDA, led by Jim Pona, combined forces with a small group of bicyclist volunteers, and with Grace Hill, always on the lookout for something to do in their Old North St. Louis neighborhood. The group found federal money, enabling a conceptual plan and then an engineering study, and obtained the support of Mayor Schoemehl. Inevitably, riverfront industries said that it was impossible—that people would get hurt and that there would be insurance issues. Within the city government, the Streets Department was dubious about providing the gravel and asphalt, the Parks Department didn't want or need another project requiring maintenance, and the Water Division was concerned about people getting too close to their operations.

However, the combination of a good idea backed by a small number of passionate supporters with a long view and a creative political leader enabled real progress over the past twenty years. Today the combination of Great River Greenways (a public district) and Trailnet (a nonprofit) ensure that the path and trail system will continue to grow.

Transportation Planning

In St. Louis, transportation planning has had many dimensions. It has been an ongoing battle between those who want to widen streets and highways for traffic that may or may not materialize and others who do not want to give into the power of the automobile. The debate has been complicated because much of the power to conduct transportation planning resides at the regional (East-West Gateway Council of Governments) and state (Missouri Department of Transportation or MODOT) level,[29] and because within the city, the Streets Department and to a lesser extent the Board of Public Service (public works) Department perceive this as their responsibility.

---

[29]The East-West Gateway Council of Governments or EWGCG is the regional planning agency in St. Louis. Its twenty-one person board of directors consists of elected representatives of cities and counties in eight counties. The Missouri Department of Transportation is directed by a commission consisting of six individuals appointed for six-year terms by the governor. No more than three members may be of the same political party.

The most intense transportation fight during the last thirty years occurred in the late seventies when MODOT tried to revive the concept of a North-South Distributor highway that would connect I-55 and I-44 on the south with I-70 on the north by a freeway to the east of Jefferson. Mayor Conway and his head planner (Donald Spaid, head of CDA) encountered an angry group composed of JVL and Downtown West residents, their respective aldermen, Missouri Coalition for the Environment members, and assorted anti-establishment advocates from the 1960s. Scaled back alternatives were proposed. After about twenty years of laborious land assembly and construction, the Truman Parkway connected I-55 and I-44 with Eighteenth Street and downtown. In the process, it further divided Lafayette Square from the Clinton Peabody public housing to the east, but arguably improved the viability of redeveloping the long vacant City Hospital and adjacent areas.

North of Highway 40, the solution called for the state to make improvements up to Market Street, and the city to continue with the construction of a Twenty-second Street Parkway to a business district in and around the old Pruitt-Igoe site.[30] Again there was extensive planning and land assembly, but with the prospect of rising costs and no strong advocates, the Slay administration discontinued the project.

Inevitably, various Streets directors argued for widening certain arterial streets. Usually these projects were not implemented because of the extensive maintenance costs associated with the existing street network (in recent years, finally shared in part by the state) and the redevelopment challenges especially of bridges and viaducts across the River Des Peres and Mill Creek Valley.[31] Street reconstruction and beautification was often an important component of big development sites (e.g., Kingshighway next to the BJC complex; Chouteau next to the Arena site).

As with most American cities, St. Louis discontinued its trolleys in the 1960s and yet failed to give up on the dream of fixed rail public transit. During the early 1970s, an expensive proposed system was drawn up by Parsons Brinckerhoff that would have connected downtown with Clayton. There was little enthusiasm or any obvious source of funding.

By the late 1970s, a more creative and affordable planning effort began. A small group led by John Roach, the first director of CDA, recognized

---

[30]The Pruitt-Igoe public housing complex was designed in 1951 on approximately 60 acres at the southeast corner of Jefferson and Cass avenues. After extensive management problems, its 33 eleven-story buildings were demolished in 1970.

[31]River Des Peres is a large open ditch that flows generally from south of Forest Park along the southwestern border of the City of St. Louis to the Mississippi River. Mill Creek Valley is the low-lying area, containing principally railroad tracks and industrial uses, that extends southwestward from just south of downtown to the city limits.

that the Norfolk and Western Railroad no longer used the tracks that meandered from downtown to Forest Park and then turned north, passing through Wellston near the University of Missouri–St. Louis and near the airport. Using the "stone soup" approach (where the soldiers start with nothing and gradually convince others to add separate food items, finally gathering enough to create a great soup), control of the track right-of-way and Eads Bridge was used to obtain matching funds from the federal government. In the face of considerable skepticism, the regional planning authority (EWGCG) and the regional transit authority (the Bi-State Development Authority, now Metro), the first link was designed and built. It attracted more riders than most observers thought possible.

Planning for a larger light-rail system has proved controversial. Voters in St. Charles County turned down the idea of extending the line across the Missouri River, and the federal transit funds became much harder to obtain. Extensions were built, first east to Scott Air Force Base, and second, with local monies, to Clayton and Shrewsbury. Additional transit corridors were planned, but the lack of not only federal funds but interest on the part of the state blunted promise of additional expansion in the near future.

Strategic Planning

Traditionally, strategic planning examines a complicated, large-scale situation and considers the problems, goals, and costs and benefits of alternative avenues for achieving success. One thinks of a strategic plan as having a bigger focus than a tactical plan, and a concern with process not evident in a static or site plan. In practice, the word has been overused, so that it has little precise meaning.

Over the past years, there were a number of collaborative planning efforts that focused primarily on the performance of city functions, and less on what a particular neighborhood or transportation corridor ought to look like. Five "strategic" planning exercises are summarized below.

Irv Smogii. A retired chemist from Monsanto, Dr. Smogii was hired in the 1970s to encourage city departments to track their performance. He believed that any organization should select a set of indicators and then plot the changes on a month-to-month, year-to-year basis. He brought enthusiasm, wit, and persistence to his work.

Mid-1980s Planning. Inspired by *In Search of Excellence* by Tom Peters and Robert Waterson, Mayor Schoemehl initiated a process of routine, cross-departmental meetings to examine broad subjects like public safety, quality of life, and economic and housing development. Emphasis was placed on measuring conditions in the community, defining new initiatives, detailed quarterly reports, and general "thinking outside of the box."

Inside City Hall. Early in Mayor Harmon's administration, Focus St. Louis (the civic group that had been created by merging Confluence and Leadership St. Louis) was invited to study the performance of departments. Volunteer professionals conducted extensive interviews with both managers and ordinary employees. The result was a detailed report full of ideas for reform and modernization. Task forces composed of city employees were subsequently created in order to follow up, and annual progress reports were generated.

Vital Few. Mayor Harmon also sought to motivate his departments by asking them to identify a "critical few" goals that they would address each year. With help from a consultant used by United Van Lines, departments were encouraged to separate their routine, day-to-day responsibilities from a limited number of priority goals/objectives for the year. Department heads, commissioners, and other senior managers met periodically as a group to review progress.

City View. Early in Mayor Slay's first term, a new process for motivating departmental improvements was initiated based on similar efforts in New York City and Baltimore. City View required departments to prepare spreadsheets measuring their "outputs" and "outcomes" and to make quarterly presentations to a panel composed of the mayor, his chief of staff, chief of operations, development director, and representatives from the personnel, law, and IT departments. Some meetings involved cross-departmental issues such as dealing with lead paint; others focused simply on one department. A two-person staff helped the departments prepare their databases, reports, and an overall report card. The City View process is ongoing.

Those experienced in business will see nothing particularly new in these various initiatives. Yet in the world of local government they were often greeted with skepticism, fear, and even anger. Inevitably, there were complaints that these efforts were a waste of time, too much additional work, or misleading because of the implication that significant changes were possible in an environment of scarce resources and constant politics.

City planners interested in modernizing the government tended to have a more positive view about the various experiments. Some believed that forced introspection and communication between departments could only be helpful. In a government without a city manager and with regular turnover of elected and appointed officials, each initiative ran out of energy as the mayor lost interest or left office.

Conclusions

The nature of city planning varies depending upon the jurisdiction in which it operates. In many locations, including much of suburban St. Louis, the planner is asked primarily to review proposed development activity. In these settings, much of the planner's work involves negotiating with home builders and commercial developers to resolve questions of density, common ground, landscaping, sidewalks, and all the other issues that can determine the difference between a high-quality or lower-quality subdivision or office park.

Planning in an older community that is experiencing weak demand tends to be a different game. In this environment, the planner is much more likely to be opportunistic, anxious to take advantage of state and federal programs, and challenged to stimulate, rather than regulate, development.

Power

In every community, the professional planner needs to be sensitive to political winds and the extent to which would-be investors are close to the political leadership. First and foremost, he or she needs to recognize the power of the mayor and his immediate staff, but there is also the legislative body, the business community, major cultural and educational institutions, advocacy groups, and neighborhood organizations.

In general, there is less legislative involvement in those communities with newer charters, and hence usually fewer members of the council, some of which may be elected on an "at-large" basis. By contrast, St. Louis has twenty-eight aldermen, many of whom depend on the job as their major source of income. With a strong tradition of aldermanic courtesy and a relatively small geographic and demographic area (around 2 square miles and 12,000 residents per alderman), these elected officials tend to get very involved in the decisions that planners and economic and housing specialists would more likely make on their own elsewhere. In the City of St. Louis, planners and development specialists have been challenged to advise and educate elected officials about professional design and planning standards.

During the past thirty years, planners came to recognize the importance, and power, of large businesses and institutions. Understandably, these organizations tended to focus on their surrounding neighborhoods. And few would argue about the extent of their impact. The Washington University Medical Center, Saint Louis University (both the main campus and the medical center), and the Missouri Botanical Garden stand out among those that have made long-term, dramatic investments, but there are more—AmerenUE, Nestlé (formerly Ralston), Sensient (formerly Warner Jenkinson), and Ranken Technical College, among others. Those organizations that had the most impact often formed and staffed their own redevelopment corporations. Occasionally these businesses/institutions engendered friction with the typically much less affluent residents and small businesses that surrounded them. Fortunately, most developed alliances with neighborhood leaders, enabling them to sponsor positive, if sometimes controversial, investments.

Culture and Aesthetics

A great city is defined by the quality of its cultural institutions and the design of its built environment. Recent mayors recognized the first point more than the latter. Unsuccessful efforts were made to create a St. Louis Museum in the Switzer Building on Laclede's Landing and later the Ambassador Building next to St. Louis Centre. During the 1980s, there was a push to convince the Smithsonian to establish a branch in St. Louis, and still later by some to convince the Art Museum to have a branch in the Old Post Office.

Tax support helped. An increase in 1994 allowed the library system to renovate or replace almost all of its fourteen branches and to plan a major upgrade to its central headquarters. Help from the Zoo Museum District contributed to dramatic expansions at the Saint Louis Zoo, Saint Louis Art Museum, Missouri Historical Society, Saint Louis Science Center, and the Missouri Botanical Garden. A sales tax earmarked for capital improvements provided significant public support for the transformation of Forest Park.

Above all, the generosity of families and foundations enabled a new set of institutions—the City Museum, the Pulitzer and Contemporary Arts museums, the Regional Arts Commission building, and the Centene Center for the Arts.

Planners have traditionally had a major role in the quality of design, as well as land use, decisions. In the 1970s, a volunteer Landmarks Review Board received planning staff support, examining proposed improvements or demolitions in historic districts within three hundred feet of a park and, under the Minimum Exterior Standards ordinance (Minex) all residential structures containing more than four units, as well as commercial and other non-residential structures. Planners within the urban renewal authority (LCRA) reviewed compliance with the design standards contained in Chapter 99 redevelopment plans, and building inspectors reviewed compliance with signage and other aspects of the zoning code. At the beginning of the 1980s, the process shifted somewhat with the creation of the Heritage and Urban Design Division within the Department of Public Safety. In the late 1990s, the historic review function came back in the form of a Cultural Resources Office to the newly created Planning and Urban Design Agency.

Regardless of the bureaucratic structure, there were continuing mixed messages from the city's political leadership regarding design review. Most mayors came into office with a bias in favor of less, or at least more flexible, design review. This reflected the fact that city businesses constituted a large source of campaign contributions and a source of complaints about alleged insensitive or impractical bureaucrats. Often the balance changed as the mayor or alderman gained experience in office, hearing more from those neighborhood residents (and voters) who worried about poor design and shoddy construction. Mayor Schoemehl made perhaps the most dramatic transition. Toward the beginning of his three terms he argued that a chat (gravel) parking lot was fine. After greater exposure to design forums, especially the Mayors' Institute on City Design,[32] the architectural community, and individuals like Joe Riley Jr., the mayor of Charleston, South Carolina, he converted. Soon parking lots at least in downtown and other visible locations were to be surrounded by brick and iron railings.

Inevitably, property owners and developers with more political clout and a willingness to spend it could achieve some consideration, especially with the threat that they might invest elsewhere. CEO of HBE Corporation Fred Kummer[33] agreed to put a few small ground floor windows on the east side of his new Adams Mark Hotel, but grudgingly. He shifted to an exterior of brick, rather than dryvit (stucco) only when a $5 million Urban Development Action Grant became possible. Southwestern Bell (now AT&T) agreed to ground-level storefront commercial space in its new tower and data processing facility only if the activity could be placed in outside corner kiosks (built but not successful) that kept customers outside of their buildings.

---

[32]The Mayors' Institute on City Design was created in 1986 and has continued with the backing of the National Endowment for the Arts, the American Architects Foundation, and the United States Conference of Mayors.

[33]The HBE Corporation is one of the largest privately held, design/build companies in the country. It has concentrated on the construction of hospitals and other medical facilities. Some wags have suggested that its hotels bear a resemblance to hospitals.

Motivation

Over the last thirty years, there were many reasons behind planning initiatives. Good government and state law accounted for some, but there were other factors. Planning projects were used to energize residents, to build community consensus, and sometimes to create the impression of development activity. More progressive mayors and aldermen used the planning process to excite existing residents and to market the area to new home buyers and businesses. More traditional political leaders (one thinks of Louis Buckowitz[34] of the Tenth Ward) had little use for planning, with its potential for upsetting the status quo.

Some planning exercises were undertaken as a state or federal obligation. The Community Development Block Grant program required a multiyear "consolidated plan" that analyzed problems and made recommendations on a variety of topics. So did major grant initiatives such as the 1994 and 1998 Empowerment Zone proposals.[35] These planning documents tended to be more important in soliciting funds and/or keeping state or federal employees content than in guiding local development decisions.

The motivation for planning initiatives could also be intertwined with basic local politics. Consultant engagements initiated before an election might spur interest in political contributions. Contracts initiated after an election might reward political donors or individuals who had been led incorrectly to believe that they might receive a postelection employment opportunity.

Summary

In some respects, the planning profession had less impact during the last thirty years than earlier in the century. It was a time when there were no planning professionals with the stature of a Harland Bartholomew or Charles Ferris at the Land Clearance for Redevelopment Authority. With

---

[34]Louis Buckowitz represented the Tenth Ward on the south side of the city for a long time. In the manner of old time ward-heelers, he looked after his constituents and had little interest in redevelopment activity that might attract more affluent and independent voters.

[35]The Clinton administration held competitions in 1994 and 1998 for cities that could demonstrate an understanding of the economic and social problems in their poorest census tracts, and could recommend creative solutions. St. Louis won a second prize designation in 1995 as an "Enterprise Community," and in 1999, along with portions of East St. Louis and St. Louis County, the Empowerment Zone award. Unfortunately, the promised full funding ($100 million) did not prove to be forthcoming.

few exceptions, the public planners followed the lead of the mayor and his development director, some of whom lacked planning experience, let alone professional training.

However, rank and file planners could and did make a difference. Examples are plentiful—plans were central to the private-public partnerships that have led to the revival of Forest Park, downtown, and a number of neighborhoods. The Riverfront Bike Path, the city's Community Information Network website, Geographic Information Systems, and numerous successful grant proposals exemplify the kinds of "below the radar" projects that captured the passionate interest and time of city planners and resulted in important contributions to the city. The vast majority of private investment activity was approved with the help of planners in processing and negotiating the redevelopment plans, tax increment financing plans, housing assistance, neighborhood commercial façade program assistance, and many other government programs. In summary, much was accomplished. Much more remains to be done.

References

Those interested in learning more about planning and development in the City of St. Louis are encouraged to review the Five-Year Consolidated Plan Strategies (1994, 1999, 2005) and the Consolidated Annual Performance and Evaluation Reports (CAPERS), all on the internet in the Government Documents section of the St. Louis Community Information Network (CIN). The CIN also contains a synopsis of historic plans relating to St. Louis and a book on Harland Bartholomew. Finally, a large number of planning documents are housed in the library of the St. Louis Planning and Urban Design Agency.

Barton-Aschman Associates. *St. Louis Housing Strategy*. Chicago: 1978.

City Plan Commission. *History of Renewal, Technical Report—St. Louis Development Program*. St. Louis: Author, 1970.

———. *St. Louis Development Program*. St. Louis: Author, 1973.

———. *1975 Interim Comprehensive Plan*. St. Louis: Author, 1975.

EDAW, Inc. *Downtown Now Revitalization Master Plan*. St. Louis: Author, 2000.

Focus St. Louis. *Inside City Hall*. St. Louis: Author, 1997.

Hammer, Siler, George Associates. *1978 Economic Development Strategy Recommendations for the City of St. Louis*. Washington, DC: Author, 1978.

Harland Bartholomew and Associates. *Preliminary Draft Plan for Downtown St. Louis*. St. Louis: Author, 1982.

Martinson, Tom. *A Plan for Downtown St. Louis: Visions of the Future*. St. Louis: City Plan Commission, 1986.

Peckham Guyton Albers & Viets, Inc. *A Plan for Downtown St. Louis*. St. Louis: Author, 1974.

Planning and Urban Design Agency. *Strategic Land Use Plan: Connecting the City*. St. Louis: Author, 2005.

Roach, John. "Special Report on Community Development Issues." St. Louis, September 1976. Western Historical Manuscript Collection, University of Missouri–St. Louis, Box 10. www.umsl.edu/~whmc/guides/whm0557.htm.

Schwetye Architects. *Fifth Ward Neighborhood Plan*. St. Louis: Author, 2002.

Sedway Group. *St. Louis Economic Development Plan—Interim Report*. San Francisco: Author, 1998.

St. Louis City Board of Aldermen. St. Louis City Ordinance 56708, sections 3.48.010 to 3.48.210, 1974.

———. St. Louis City Ordinance 64687, Board Bill No. [99] 52.

St. Louis Community Development Agency. *St. Louis Neighborhood Betterment Program*. St. Louis: Author, 1977.

———. *St. Louis 1985: A Profile at Mid-Decade*. St. Louis: Author, 1985.

St. Louis Development Corporation. *Forest Park Master Plan*. St. Louis: Author, 1995.

Team Four. *Preface, Bibliography, and Technical Memorandum 6B on City Wide Implementation Strategies: The Draft Comprehensive Plan*. St. Louis: Author, 1976.

———. *Technical Memorandum on City Wide Implementation Strategies: The Draft Comprehensive Plan*. St. Louis: Author, 1973.

U.S. Congress. *1974 Housing and Community Development Act*. Public Law 93-383. Washington, DC: GPO, 1974.

U.S. Department of Housing and Urban Development. "Community Development Block Grant Entitlement Communities." 2006a. www.hud.gov/offices/cpd/ (accessed June 6, 2007).

———. "Community Development Laws and Regulations." 2006b. www.hud.gov/offices/cpd/communitydevelopment/rulesandregs/ (accessed June 6, 2007).

Chapter 6
Ahead of the Curve?:
Planning in St. Louis County, 1930–2000

E. Terrence Jones

By 1930, it was quite evident that change would be a constant in St. Louis County for the decades ahead. Although the City of St. Louis still had four times the population, the county itself had quadrupled during the century's first three decades, rising from 50,040 in 1900 to 211,593 in 1930. Within the next forty years, it would quintuple, increasing almost twenty thousand annually. Between 1950 and 1970 alone, it added 545,000 residents, about the combined size of today's Jefferson and St. Charles counties.

Qualitative change accompanied quantitative growth. Rural settings with a few scattered communities like Florissant and Kirkwood were joined by inner ring suburbs in the pre–World War II period. That war spurred significant industrialization, the postwar brought hundreds of suburban subdivisions, and the interstate highways lowered density. As the service sector began to outpace manufacturing, office centers like Clayton and office parks like those along U.S. 40/64 developed. Between 1950 and 1990, the number of jobs more than tripled, going from 156,526 to 507,771. By century's end, the county had become the region's dominant jurisdiction, housing over one-third its population and containing almost half its jobs.

To what extent did St. Louis County government planning anticipate these changes? Did county planners see over the horizon, detect the trends, alert leadership about consequences, shape future policies? This chapter traces that story from the late 1920s to the turn of the century.

The Origins of Planning

Systematic planning in St. Louis County began as a voluntary partnership between county government and the then approximately fifteen
municipalities. Initiated in 1928 by Albert P. Greensfelder, the chair of the
University City Plan Commission, the St. Louis County Plan Association's
bylaws called for the St. Louis County presiding judge to serve as honorary
chair.[1]

The Association's charge called for it to focus on "continuity . . . of
streets and highways, establishment of park and boulevard systems, coordination of sewer and drainage systems, . . . and the harmonizing of zoning
restrictions in adjacent territories" (St. Louis County Plan Association
1940). Working under the leadership of the St. Louis County Chamber of
Commerce, it also supported state legislation that would enable the county
to have a legally binding planning mechanism.

After four years without legislative success despite persistent lobbying
by the Chamber and the Plan Association, the Missouri General Assembly finally passed a law in 1939 authorizing St. Louis County to form a
planning commission. Noting that it was no longer needed, the Plan Association then disbanded. That turned out to be premature. The 1939 law
was challenged, largely for apparently covering only St. Louis County.[2]
Two years later, the General Assembly passed a second proposal, now
dubbed the "County Planning and Zoning Enabling Act," with sounder
constitutional footing. Nevertheless, it was also challenged but ultimately
upheld by the Missouri Supreme Court on March 25, 1943.

Although the County Court had appointed a Planning Commission
in October 1941, the legal uncertainties and the preoccupation with the
war effort slowed its work. With assistance from Harland Bartholomew
and Associates Incorporated, it published its first report in September 1943

---

[1]Prior to its adoption of a home rule charter government in 1950, the County was governed by
a three-person commission as dictated by state law. The commission, termed the County Court
despite having both administrative and judicial roles, was headed by a presiding judge elected
County-wide. In addition to playing a prominent local role in planning matters, Greensfelder was
also one of the original members of the State of Missouri Conservation Commission, established
in 1937, and was later appointed by President Harry S Truman to the National Capital Park and
Planning Commission. Greensfelder Park in western St. Louis County is named for him.

[2]Then and now, the Missouri Constitution prohibits the General Assembly passing "any local
or special law . . . creating offices, prescribing the powers and duties of officers in, or regulating
the affairs of counties, cities, townships, election or school districts." See *Missouri Constitution,*
Article III, Section 40.

St. Louis Plans

entitled *It's Your County, It's Your County Plan.* The report took pride in several accomplishments, most notably a major highway plan (December 1942), regulations for new subdivisions in the unincorporated areas (January 1943), a major airport plan (March 1943), and a postwar plan for public works (June 1943).[3]

Much of the report stressed the need for professional planning. It argued for a "master plan" that will specify a "designed and coordinated arrangement of highways, airports, sewers, schools, parks, and transportation to serve the county" (St. Louis County Planning Commission 1943). Predicting that the county's population would be a half million by 1970, it warned about the dire consequences if planning did not occur, predicting that then "blighted areas and even slums will appear and spread rapidly . . . , haphazard and illogical county development . . . will require excessive taxes to maintain, . . . (and that) we will have a far poorer place in which to live at a much greater cost" (St. Louis County Planning Commission 1943).

The next summary report did not appear until 1951 after planning had become one of the departments established by the home rule charter approved by the voters a year earlier. Perhaps reflecting a more definitive place with the governmental bureaucracy, including a larger budget, the thrity-five-page document, *Look for Tomorrow Today*, was printed on slick paper. It noted that the Planning Commission's zoning ordinances enacted during the 1940s had successfully required developers to pay for added streets and utilities, no small matter in a county that had added 130,000 more people during that decade. It also officially noted that the county had moved well beyond being largely a bedroom community, announcing that "a certain amount of industrial development (was necessary) to produce a sound economy" (St. Louis County Department of Planning 1951).

Although the first county master plan would not appear for still another decade, the planning unit produced occasional analyses about trends and consequences, all intended to provide a context for the yet-to-be-produced general plan. In 1952, *Let's Get Together: A Report on the Advantages of an Integrated Community*, came as governmental fragmentation was at a historic high. More than fifty municipalities had incorporated between 1945 and 1952, raising the total to ninety-four. The report argued that "this multiplicity of incorporated areas is creating problems of integration of effort in meeting common problems" (St. Louis County Planning

---

[3]The challenge was led by Stanley Wallach, the County's separately elected prosecuting attorney. See *State ex rel. Wallach v. Loesch,* 350 Mo. 989.

Commission 1952) and warned that "the recent trend toward a multiplicity of incorporated areas may lead to waste and administrative and political chaos" (St. Louis County Planning Commission 1952). It suggested setting a minimum assessed valuation for incorporation, proposing a standard that fifty-five of the existing ninety-four cities did not meet.

Three of its recommendations had an impact. First, it encouraged the county to oppose additional incorporations where there was an inadequate tax base. Working partially through state legislation, the county started successfully to do just that (Jones 2000).[4] Second, it employed the then thirty-nine separate sewer districts as the poster child for service integration, helping pave the way for the 1954 formation of the Metropolitan Sewer District. Third, it urged smaller municipalities to contract with the county for services, helping legitimize this approach in St. Louis County and anticipating the Lakewood Plan in California by two years.[5]

In a more dramatic fashion, the County Planning Commission sounded the alert in 1954 that the county was changing rapidly and fundamentally. The 100-plus-page *Metropolitan Metamorphosis: The Story of the Change of St. Louis County, Missouri from a Rural to an Urban Area* proclaimed that a "completely new St. Louis County with changing environment is breaking forth . . . on a scale beyond realization (St. Louis County Planning Commission 1954). Far from waiting until 1970 for the population to hit 500,000, the county was soaring past the half million mark in 1955, creating "a complete change of attitude on the part of citizens (who) . . . are demanding more regulation of property, a reversal of their original views" (St. Louis County Planning Commission 1954).

This transformation, the report argued, called for more planning conducted by professionals, complete with aerial maps and a block-and-lot numbering system. Repeating some of the language of *Let's Get Together*, it warned that "local patriotism can become . . . a force which divides the county into small units as to make the continuation of community func-

---

[4]See E. Terrence Jones, *Fragmented by Design: Why St. Louis Has So Many Governments* (St. Louis: Palmerston and Reed, 2000), 31–35. In the St. Louis County segment of a booklet on metropolitan development, Alfred H. Kerth, the Planning Commission chair, and M. Eugene Baughman, the Commission director, boasted that "since the publication of the report *Let's Get Together* . . . , the County Council has succeeded in delaying the establishment of twelve new municipalities." See *Guide Book 1954: Metropolitan St. Louis Area Development* (St. Louis: Metropolitan Plan Association, 1953), 32.

[5]Lakewood, California, in Los Angeles County was the pilot experiment for a newly incorporated suburban municipality that contracted with county government for most of its services. See Vincent Ostrom, Charles M. Tiebout, and Robert Warren, "The Organization of Governments in Metropolitan Areas: A Theoretical Inquiry," *American Political Science Review*, 55, no. 4 (December 1961), 831–842.

tions impossible" (St. Louis County Planning Commission 1954). Toward the end it floats the idea of a "Metropolitan Federation," consolidating the county into seven areas, each containing both incorporated and unincorporated territory. Each district would be governed by a professional administrator jointly chosen by the municipalities and the appropriate county councilperson.

Guide for Growth

Although the 1941 state legislation authorized the county "to make, adopt, and . . . publish an official master plan . . . for the purpose of bringing about coordinated physical development in accordance with present and future needs" (*Missouri Revised Statutes*, Section 64.040), it was not until two decades later that anything beyond a zoning ordinance was put forth. Prepared over an extended period in the late 1950s and early 1960s, it appeared in four overlapping documents: *A General Land Use Plan: St. Louis County* (St. Louis County 1960), *Guide for Growth: The Land Use Plan* (St. Louis County Planning Commission 1961), *Guide for Growth: Research and Analysis of the Land Use Components* (St. Louis County 1962), and *Guide for Growth: Land Use Diagram by Study Area* (St. Louis County 1962). Harland Bartholomew and Associates were significantly involved in the plan's preparation.

The county's population had just passed 700,000 living in approximately 180,000 residential units. The plan projected that, by 1980, the population would rise to 1,175,000 in about 340,000 dwellings. It was 200,000 too high on the head count but remarkably close to the mark (358,000) on residences. Other stated assumptions undergirding the plan included extending recent patterns forward: socioeconomic levels rising and interstate highways expanding with the City of St. Louis maintaining its role "as the core for urban cultural activities" (St. Louis County Planning Commission 1961). Less realistically, especially considering the 1959 electoral rejection of the City/Country District Plan, *Guide for Growth* anticipated the development of a comprehensive plan "coordinating the social, economic, and physical development of all urban and non-urban places within the metropolitan area" (St. Louis County Planning Commission 1961).

Among the principal problems identified by *Guide for Growth* were inadequate transportation, proliferation of strip commercial development, insufficient open space, a shortage of public facilities, and job growth not keeping pace with population increases within the county. In addressing these problems, the plan suggested, the county needed to treasure certain core values, especially "stimulating individual creativity" and, in a bow to public choice, providing "a reasonable diversity of living, working, and recreational areas, maximizing the choice of location" (St. Louis County Planning Commission 1961).

The plan presented a set of principles for residential, commercial, industrial, and open-space usage, many pitched at a general and non-controversial level. Examples include "residential blight should be eliminated" (St. Louis County Planning Commission 1961), and "incompatible uses (e.g., residential) should not be located within industrial areas" (St. Louis County Planning Commission 1961). Others had more of an edge such as a plea for reserving more open space before it was all developed and sharp limitations on more commercial strips.

The limited number of policy proposals represented a more structured approach to development. The major one recommended clustering the county into seven "regional business centers" containing, in total, twenty-six "community business centers" which, in turn, would collectively have 116 "neighborhood business centers" (St. Louis County Planning Commission 1962). The plan's summary also proposed that, if possible, most urbanization within the county be within eight miles of its border with the City of St. Louis, noting that there was enough vacant land in this segment to accommodate a million people.

These latter proposals for land use created confusion about whether *Guide for Growth* was a precursor to a new zoning ordinance or the beginnings of a comprehensive master plan. Among others, the Home Builders Association of Greater St. Louis raised this point. The group expressed concern that, if taken literally and translated into specific zoning classifications, *Guide for Growth* could "infringe upon the rights of individuals, particularly the rights of owners of private property" and, raising what is now called the "takings" issue, cautioned that "nothing should be undertaken which will tend to interfere with an individual's rights to his property without due process and fair compensation to such individual" (Home Builders Association of Greater St. Louis 1962).

With all the ensuing controversy, the county Council ultimately never endorsed *Guide for Growth*. Instead, it instructed the Planning Commission staff to use it as a basis for a new zoning map, one that was ultimately adopted by the Council in April 1965. The eight-mile boundary did not prevail, and urbanization spilled ever outward. Throughout the late 1960s, rezoning petitions for residential developments were approved, especially in the county's western and far northern areas.

General Plan (1973)

Although twelve years elapsed between *Guide for Growth* and another comprehensive plan, a maturing planning unit whose staffing more than doubled during the 1960s conducted numerous studies in addition to executing its ongoing zoning responsibilities. Not surprisingly in a county adding a quarter million population during that decade, most addressed housing issues, both rental (e.g., *Multi-Family Housing in St. Louis County*, released in 1965, and *Apartments in St. Louis County*, published in 1971) and single family (e.g., *Strategy for Community Development: Emphasis Residential*, produced in 1968). Even as the housing boom was at its peak, with new construction accelerating toward the county's outer edges, concern about deterioration emerged (e.g., *Areas of Deterioration and Blight in St. Louis County*, published in 1964, and *Housing Conditions, Needs, and Programs in St. Louis County*, issued in 1970).

This attentiveness to the darker side of urbanization continued during the 1970s and beyond. As concern mounted about blight, the Department of Planning embarked on a series of *Community Evaluation Reports*. The first, issued in October 1972, focused on municipalities and concluded that "in looking at the total county, a picture emerges of growth and health in newer, more affluent areas on the outer rings or fringes of urbanization, and of creeping deterioration as a result of age, obsolescence, marginal or low income persons, increasing crime rates, etc., in the inner rings of municipalities surrounding the City of St. Louis" (St. Louis County Department of Planning 1972). The second, published in April 1973, reached similar conclusions about portions of unincorporated county (St. Louis County Department of Planning 1973). Together, these two reports helped the county allocate the federal Community Block Grant Development funds that started to flow in the mid-1970s.

Housing did not consume the agenda, however. In 1969 and 1970, respectively, business was the topic for, first, *Strategy for Community Development: Emphasis Industrial* and, second, *Strategy for Community Development: Emphasis Commercial*. Also in the study spotlight were parks (*The Challenge of Growth: A Study of Major County and Regional Park Needs*, released in 1965), and transportation (*Highway Sufficiency and Preliminary System Classification*, issued in 1967).

Lawrence K. Roos, the county supervisor who did more than any other chief elected executive to modernize county government, saw the need for a new and expanded comprehensive plan.[6] In his January 1971 State of the County address, he called for preparing a fresh version.

As befits the profession's deliberative style, four months later the Department of Planning published a plan for planning (St. Louis County Department of Planning 1971). *Guide for Growth* is applauded for its good intentions but criticized for its narrow scope ("the concerns of poverty, pollution, racial prejudice and injustice, crime, subsidized housing, employment, welfare and life style are only hinted at if addressed at all") (St. Louis County Department of Planning 1971) and further chastised for its mistaken assumption that most development would be contained within eight miles of the county's border with the City of St. Louis. Procedurally, the Department pledged to make full use of a Citizen's Participation Committee and, "beyond it, (involve) residents' associations, special interest groups and even local political association. . . ." (St. Louis County Department of Planning 1971).

The *General Plan* was published in August 1973 in three separate documents: *History Element*, *Land Element*, and *People Element*. The inside cover of each referred to a fourth installment (*Summary Document*) but it never appeared. *History Element* set the scene by reviewing the history of planning in St. Louis County, providing a history of key events in the county and the region from 1764 forward, and giving a taxonomy of thirty-two studies conducted between 1930 and 1972.

Land Element devoted over forty pages to a detailed technical description of the county's geology and hydrology. The prose is dense and nearly impenetrable, filled with passages like "these older alluvial deposits are thinner than those of the flood plain and are underlain by Ordovician limestone and dolomite bedrock" (St. Louis County Department of Planning 1973b). The document concluded with one or two paragraphs of general land use advice for each of nine planning areas such as "the rolling upland area around Fenton has considerable prime vacant land suitable for medium and high intensity development" (St. Louis County Department of Planning 1973b). It offered no countywide recommendations about physical development.

People Element marked the first time county planning had moved beyond land and physical matters that tended to treat residents as an undifferentiated mass, with few considerations other than how many individuals and how many households. This breakthrough made humans the center of

---

[6]St. Louis County's chief elected executive title was "county supervisor" until changed to "county executive" in a 1979 Charter revision.

analysis, giving more attention to their needs and aspirations rather than concentrating on land and its development.

Nevertheless this portion of the *General Plan* was all diagnosis and no proposed cures. It raised issues and suggested questions to be addressed but provided no preferred answers. It specified seven issues: managing growth, maintaining an appropriate mix of housing options, providing employment, lessening poverty, improving government service delivery, enhancing citizen-government communications, and protecting the environment.

It pointed to key trends. Population had increased over 50 percent per decade since 1900. It projected that the rate of growth would decline but predicted that, by 1980, the county would have 1,127,000 residents, 176,000 more than there were in 1970. It noted that poverty was on the rise, both in absolute numbers and population share. It remarked that the county was becoming more diverse with African American residents, as of 1970, approaching 50,000. It pinpointed the county's heightened role in the region's economy, going from 6 percent of the metropolitan area's employment in 1950 to 31 percent in 1970.

It expressed concern that the county's housing stock was becoming less affordable to middle- and lower-income households. It described both in prose and with charts how urbanization had contributed to more crime and traffic congestion, both in turn causing citizens to demand more local government services that placed more stress on tax revenues, especially the property tax. It mused that greater service demand had not led to higher support for consolidation and observed, with some apparent disappointment, that "the majority are relatively satisfied with existing arrangements" (St. Louis County Department of Planning 1973c).

Written at a time when Watergate and Vietnam had the nation in a collective funk, the substantive segment ends with both a comment on the times ("a tendency to distrust the status quo and feel alienated from established organizations has been voiced by both young and old people who express a desire to participate in the formulation of new direction and priorities in the county") and a plea that local government can be part of "all levels of government re-emphasizing personal communications, whether in the form of police courtesy, returning a phone call, or meeting and listening to citizen groups" (St. Louis County Department of Planning 1973c).

The *Prospectus for a Revised General Plan* had proposed a "document (that) will attempt to suggest both general policies and specific programs that could improve condition" although it worried aloud that "more concrete the proposals in a general urban plan, the more heated has been the debate and the less likely any real possibilities of consensus" (St. Louis County Department of Planning 1973c). In the end, it avoided proposing even a sketchily detailed map for the county's future, confining itself instead to issues and exhortations.

General Plan (1980)

Revisions to the St. Louis County Charter passed in November 1979 mandated that the existing general plan be reviewed "not less than twelve months after the adoption of this charter and thereafter not less frequently than once every five years."[7] Despite the tight deadline, the Department of Planning continued the trend toward broader public consultation and produced a ninety-six-page document, *General Plan*, by early November 1980.

The 1980 plan projected accurately that after eight decades of steady increases, the county's population would stabilize at about 1 million for the indefinite future. It would be a county with a higher share of older adults, an aging housing stock, smaller household sizes, and a considerably greater role in the region's economy—all estimates that ultimately came to pass. Unlike the 1973 plan, however, the 1980 version made no comments about poverty households or the increase in the African American population share.

The plan addressed eleven separate topics: transportation, government, housing, land use, business and industry, environmental quality, recreation/culture/open space, energy, health, human services, and criminal justice. Within each, it departed from earlier practice and made multiple policy recommendations. Most were mundane and obvious (e.g., "encourage compatibility between land use and site characteristics") (St. Louis County Department of Planning 1980), but several were more controversial and others led to new policies or approaches.

Under government, the plan stressed the advantage of a county-wide approach for providing selected services (e.g., tax collection) and encouraged adding to the list although it did not make any specific suggestions. Perhaps anticipating the future incorporations of Chesterfield (1988) and Maryland Heights (1985), the plan proclaimed that "county government recognizes that certain future incorporations may ultimately serve the best interests of the directly affected citizens and the county as a whole" (St. Louis County Department of Planning 1980).

---

[7]See *St. Louis County Charter,* Article 2, Section 2.180.33.

Within housing, the plan promoted higher densities for more afford-able units albeit with the politically cautious caveat that this would require "careful planning to protect existing neighborhoods and areas" (St. Louis County Department of Planning 1980). Two of its business/industry rec-ommendations ("strengthen and coordinate the county's business and industrial information services and research capability" and "through mar-keting programs promote the St. Louis region's advantages for businesses and industries") laid the groundwork for the establishment of the St. Louis County Economic Council in 1982.

Stern language about flood plain development (e.g., "retain flood plains . . . for use as linear parklands and storm water control easements" and, more gently, "encourage the use of unprotected flood plains for open space and agricultural use") (St. Louis County Department of Planning 1980) were subsequently and repeatedly ignored. Conversely, the goal for "an effective solid waste management system emphasizing regional cooperation and an effective resource recovery system" (St. Louis County Department of Planning 1980) was an early step toward the 1991 found-ing of the St. Louis–Jefferson Solid Waste Management District, initially a cooperative effort with the City of St. Louis and Jefferson County, which now also includes St. Charles County.

The plan concludes with a four-page to-do list. Labeled "imple-mentation," it assigned a series of tasks to various county government departments. A recurring theme within these guidelines is the need to coordinate the county's effort more closely with regional bodies (e.g., East-West Gateway), private entities (e.g., Home Builders Association), and municipalities.

General Plan Update (1985)

Although containing "update" in its title, this ninety-six-page plan empha-sized its independence ("the Update is independent from the 1980 Plan with respect to goals, policies, and implementation strategies") while simultaneously acknowledging continuity ("however many of the goal and policy statements from 1980 continue to be relevant.") (St. Louis County Department of Planning 1985). It maintained the same eleven topics but added a theme, "the challenges of transition," prominently displayed on the document's cover. Reflecting the move away from comprehensive planning toward strategic planning, it also added a "strategies" segment to each set of goals and policies.

It pointed to the same trends as enumerated in 1980 although often in a somewhat bleaker tone. It was even more pessimistic about population growth, doubting that the county would reach 1 million before the end of the century. It expressed even more concern about aging housing stock and infrastructure along with the limited financial resources available to counter their negative effects. Like the 1980 version, it continued to project a lower job growth rate than actually occurred, predicting 501,600 when the ultimate total became 611,000. Also identical to 1980, there is neither information about nor discussion of poverty or minority population trends.

Laying the groundwork for the late 1980s plan proposed by county executive Gene McNary to reduce sharply the number of municipalities and to clarify service roles and responsibilities between county and municipal governments, the plan was sharper in its criticism of the status quo. It argued that "fragmentation of authority makes resolution of area-wide problems difficult, numerous small and overlapping jurisdictions result in an inequitable distribution of resources available to address public needs, [and that] citizens are confused and frustrated by multiple overlapping jurisdictions and regulations, contributing to public apathy" (St. Louis County Department of Planning 1985). Among the strategies proposed was establishing a "Boundary Review Commission," a remedy that was instituted late in 1989 after the Board of Freeholders formed in 1987 to consolidate governments within the county was ruled unconstitutional (Jones 2000).

The plan repeated the aspiration to "encourage the use of unprotected flood plains as farmland, parklands and storm water control easements" but, on the same page, also recommended that the county "promote economic development in the flood plain of the Missouri River that takes into consideration" developments that "would be unique to the St. Louis County area," "would not be able to occur elsewhere in St. Louis County," "would preserve some natural areas," and "would minimize the negative impact to the environment" (St. Louis County Department of Planning 1985).

With the existence of the St. Louis County Economic Council and the county's growing place in the region's economy, the plan listed several concrete steps to strengthen its competitive standing. These included seeking state legislation giving the county more tax subsidy options, forming an enterprise zone in the Wellston area, and establishing one or more small business incubators.

Noting the decline in patients at the St. Louis County Hospital, the plan blessed the movement toward a city/county approach, including "implementing the contractual agreement for inpatient hospital services with the St. Louis Regional Medical Center" (St. Louis County Department of Planning 1985). Reacting to the possible erosion of the county Police Department through annexations and incorporations, it urged that unit to improve its services in the unincorporated areas and to increase its providing contract patrol services to municipalities.

Adopting some of the elements of strategic planning, the document concluded with a table outlining fifty separate tasks enumerated by time (Years 1–2, Years 2–4, Years 4–5) and responsible units within county government, starting with "study and develop closer linkages between county and municipal governments" (St. Louis County Department of Planning 1985), a diplomatic approach that would soon come asunder with the county-led movement to shrink the number of municipalities.

General Plan Update (1993)

Work on what was to have been the 1990 update started promptly but, in the end, the next countywide plan was years in the making. When ultimately published in 1993, it bore a confusion of titles. The cover has "Shaping the Future Together: St. Louis County/Strategic Plan" while the title page read "The Future Belongs to Those Who Prepare for It: General Plan Update 1993." Begun in 1990 when Republican H. C. Milford was county executive, the process spilled over into the early years of Democrat Buzz Westfall's administration, after he had defeated Milford in the November 1990 election.

This plan marked the end of a traditional comprehensive approach and the full flowering of a strategic planning paradigm. For each topic (environment, land, transportation, economic development, housing and neighborhoods, health and human services, public safety, government), there is a vision statement and a series of action items that, cumulatively, total 130.

The process was much more elaborate using multiple methods to gather opinions. Every county household received a two-page questionnaire, almost seventy-thousand of which were returned. The Department of Planning sponsored thirty-two community forums, there was a one and a half day deliberative citizens conference with about one hundred participants, and a probability survey of five hundred county residents.

Along with materials prepared by county departments, all this input was digested by eight action committees, one for each topic. Their charge was to produce a twenty-year vision and to devise five-year action plans for moving toward that vision. As a direct consequence of this decentralized approach, the 1993 version is much more a set of eight separate strategic plans than it is an overarching master plan.

Not surprisingly, the vision statements are platitudinous but word choice often reveals a tilt toward equity and regionalism. The housing and neighborhoods vision, for example, is "increasing housing choices for all" and its public safety counterpart is "serve and protect all citizens equitably and dependably" (St. Louis County Department of Planning 1993). Signaling the county's sense that it had become first among equals within the St. Louis metropolitan area, assuming more of a leadership role in regional matters, the economic development vision is "diversity, strengthen, expand the region's economy" while the transportation vision is "meet the region's transportation needs safely, clearly, efficiently, (and) reliably" (St. Louis County Department of Planning 1993).

The Government Structure and Finance Action Committee generated the most controversy with a proposal to shift the primary local government revenue source from a sales tax to an earnings tax. The county had adopted a 1 cent sales tax in 1978. At that time, municipalities were given two choices: They could keep all the sales tax collected within their boundaries (point-of-sales cities) or participate, on a per capita basis, in a countywide pool (pool cities).

Cities like Crestwood and St. Ann with high retail activity understandably opted for point-of-sales status while those with less sales, including unincorporated county, entered the pool. By 1990, the point-of-sales cities were capturing about half the revenues despite having only one-quarter of the residents. This perceived inequity along with the county's needs for additional revenue sources, especially if the county became fully incorporated, sparked the move to reform the system.

The Government Structure and Finance Action Committee championed eliminating the 1 percent sales tax and adopting a 1 percent earnings tax, which would be distributed to the municipalities and unincorporated county on a per capita basis. That, the Committee argued, would be "the simplest and best way to provide a basic and consistent level of funding . . . [that would] lessen regressivity and increase responsiveness of the tax base to economic growth and inflation" (St. Louis County Department of Planning 1991). Although the earnings tax as a cure did not materialize, the maldistribution of the county sales tax—an inequity that had a majority receiving less than what they regarded as their fair share—was acknowledged and county and municipal officials negotiated revisions where the point-of-sales cities would share some of their revenues with the pool participants. The Missouri General Assembly blessed this arrangement in 1993 and it went into effect in 1994.[8]

Other action plans that bore fruit were enacting a recycling ordinance for the unincorporated areas, establishing a hazardous materials collection program, and forming the World Trade Center. Improving the supply of affordable housing received considerable emphasis although subsequent progress has been a challenge. Taken as a whole, the 116 action plans did not constitute a coherent agenda united by a common vision. Instead, they were a mix of platitudes (e.g., "support . . . effort to develop regional transportation plan"), favored projects (e.g., "acquire property and develop trail along north bank of Meramec"), or special interest pleading (e.g., "lobby legislature to provide more funds and programs at UMSL") (St. Louis County Department of Planning 1993).

St. Louis County Strategic Plan (2000–2004)

The delay in publishing *Shaping the Future Together*, a plan ostensibly for 1990 to 1995 but not formally released until 1993, led to the county foregoing a plan for the decade's second half. Instead it started preparations for a 2000–2004 version in 1998. This effort was more self-consciously focused, using what by then had become the standard routine for strategic planning including an environmental scan for trends and a SWOT (strengths, weaknesses, opportunities, threats) assessment, all leading to identifying a limited number of strategic issues that should dominate the county's action agenda for the next five years.

Both active and passive citizen involvement expanded. Community forums were more publicized and better organized. Neutral third parties—FOCUS St. Louis, the region's citizens league, and Development Strategies, a highly respected consulting firm—conducted the sessions. Focus groups were held both early (issue identification) and late (testing the draft proposals) in the process. Simultaneous with each round of focus groups, a probability survey was administered to county residents.

---

[8]See *Missouri Revised Statutes*, Sections 66.620 and 66.630. This arrangement was noted in the final publication of the strategic plan. See Shaping the Future Together (St. Louis: St. Louis County Department of Planning, 1993), 85. Also see James Brasfield, "Local Revenue Sharing Reform: The St. Louis Case," paper delivered at the Midwest Political Science Association Annual Meeting, Chicago, April 3–6, 2003. Brasfield cochaired the Government Structure and Finance Action Committee.

The plan saw "a mature, nearly fully developed urban county" (St. Louis County Department of Planning 2000). It stressed that not only will the number of residents remain static—a point recognized in earlier plans—but that the number of jobs had also stabilized. For the first time, a plan not only acknowledged African Americans statistically, noting the number had increased 27 percent since 1980, but emphasized diversity as a value ("racial and ethic diversity creates character and adds cultural opportunities to the fabric of our communities") and an issue ("St. Louis County must become increasingly sensitive and responsive to the increase in minority populations") (St. Louis County Department of Planning 2000).

What had been governmental fragmentation in many earlier plans was now characterized as more of a blessing ("St. Louis County is a community of 'hometowns'—a big place with a small town feel" and "a large number of local governments may help ensure that governance is closer and more accountable to its citizens") than a curse although its downside ("may also fragment decision-making processes and inhibit cooperative regional initiatives") was also mentioned (St. Louis County Department of Planning 2000).

The 2000-2004 plan took pride in narrowing the agenda to just four strategic issues: reinvestment in older communities, St. Louis County's role in the region, transportation, and unincorporated services. Task forces were formed and, with some staff and consultant assistance, were asked to develop action plans for the forthcoming five years that would effectively address each issue.[9]

Collectively, forty-eight of the task force action plans were included in the final document. The community reinvestment proposals included finding new revenue streams for this initiative. The Missouri General Assembly passed the Community Comeback Act in 2000, authorizing the county to pass a use tax for this purpose.[10] But the county electorate soundly rejected it in an April 2001 election with 81,009 "no" votes versus 58,534 "yes" tallies. Following the plan's recommendation, the County Council did adopt a residential reoccupancy permit program for the unincorporated areas.

Most of the recommendations for enhancing the county's role in the region were exhortations to interact more, both within the county (e.g., "strengthen the relationship between St. Louis County, municipal leaders, and the St. Louis County Municipal League") and externally (e.g., "estab-

---

[9]The author served on the task force examining the County's role in the region.
[10]*Missouri Revised Statutes,* Section 144.757. A use tax is a sales tax on out-of-state purchases.

lish an educational liaison within St. Louis County Government to work on regional public education and workforce development issues") (St. Louis County Department of Planning 2000). None of the more concrete proposals has ever been put forward, much less adopted and implemented.

Most of the transportation recommendations addressed lessening congestion. The emphasis was on utilizing advanced technology (e.g., Geographic Information Systems, intelligent transportation systems) to accomplish this objective. It also urged more mass transit and the expansion of bicycle and pedestrian projects. The unincorporated services segment was essentially a reminder to the county bureaucracy that, in addition to providing certain services (e.g., public health) for the entire county, it was also the de facto municipal government for over 300,000 residents.

Concluding Comments

Over the past seventy-five years, planning in St. Louis County has gone from a voluntary collaborative venture to a professionally staffed operation. Throughout this era, whatever the format, the planners have done three things quite well. First, more often than not, they have been accurate about demographic trends. They saw the population boom coming well in advance and they forecast its end even while the trend line pointed upward.

Second, they were astute about the county's urbanization and its consequences, especially for the housing stock. Even as tens of subdivisions were being developed during the 1970s, for example, the planners were calling attention to actual and potential deterioration. They were also continuously alert to housing affordability and diversity.

Third, they understood early that the county was destined to become the region's economic engine, that as the residential boom went on, commercialization and industrialization were bound to follow. They helped generate the studies that made this transition easier and they contributed to establishing the governmental infrastructure, especially the Economic Council, to guide its evolution.

Planning also had some paradise lost moments. The most notable was the *Guide for Growth*'s 1961 recommendation that urged, as the county grew to a million population, an estimate that was right on the mark, that zoning be used to keep almost all of it within eight miles of the county's boundary with the City of St. Louis, an area that now roughly corresponds to everything inside Interstate 270. This quickly became a futile attempt to contain the growth machine.

Chronicling planning over the better part of a century also reminds us about how its procedures have changed. What began with land as its focus now has people at the center. What was once labeled comprehensive, even though it never was, is now termed strategic. What was done solely by professionals—government employees and consultants—now involves extensive citizen participation.

It still seems that planning in St. Louis County has not fully become a permanent element of policymaking. At times, general plans were a key ingredient either in getting a policy proposal on the agenda or moving it up to the action phase. At other times, planning has been treated as a sideshow, something that good governments are supposed to do but not something that needs to be taken seriously. That, in part, accounts for the irregular timing in a process that, according to the County Charter, should be on a strict five-year timetable. Planning's challenge in the years ahead is to expand its place at the policy table.

References

Brasfield, James. "Local Revenue Sharing Reform: The St. Louis Case." Paper presesnted at the Midwest Political Science Association Annual Meeting, Chicago, IL, April 3–6, 2003.

Home Builders Association of Greater St. Louis. *Comments Regarding the Proposed Land Use Plan (Guide for Growth)*. St. Louis: Author, 1962.

Jones, E. Terrence. *Fragmented by Design: Why St. Louis Has So Many Governments*. St. Louis: Palmerston and Reed, 2000.

Metropolitan Plan Association. *Guide Book 1954: Metropolitan St. Louis Area Development*. St. Louis: Author, 1953, 32.

Missouri Revised Statutes, Section 64.040.

Missouri Revised Statutes, Section 144.757.

Missouri Revised Statutes, Sections 66.620 and 66.630.

Ostrom, Vincent, Charles M. Tiebout, and Robert Warren. "The Organization of Governments in Metropolitan Areas: A Theoretical Inquiry." *American Political Science Review* 55, no. 4 (December 1961): 831–842.

St. Louis County Charter, Article 2, Section 2.180, p. 33.

St. Louis County Department of Planning. *Community Evaluation Report 1*. St. Louis: Author, 1972.

———. *Community Evaluation Report 2*. St. Louis: Author, 1973a.

———. *General Plan: Land Element*. St. Louis: Author, 1973b.

———. *General Plan Update*. St. Louis: Author, 1985.

———. *Look for Tomorrow Today*. St. Louis: Author, 1951.

———. *Prospectus for a Revised General Plan*. St. Louis, Author, 1971.

———. *Prospectus for a Revised General Plan*. St. Louis: Author, 1973c.

———. *Recommendations of the Government Structure and Finance Action Committee*. St. Louis: Author, 1991.

———. *Shaping the Future Together*. St. Louis: Author, 1993.

———. *St. Louis County Strategic Plan: 2000–2004*. St. Louis: Author, 2000.

St. Louis County Plan Association. *Twelve Years of Unofficial St. Louis County Planning: 1928–1940*. St. Louis: St. Louis County Plan Association, 1940, 4.

St. Louis County Planning Commission. *Guide for Growth: The Land Use Plan*. St. Louis: Author, 1961.

———. *It's Your County, It's Your County Plan*. St. Louis: Author, 1943.

———. *Let's Get Together: A Report on the Advantages of an Integrated Community*. St. Louis: Author, 1952.

———. *Metropolitan Metamorphosis: The Story of the Change of St. Louis County, Missouri from a Rural to an Urban Area*. St. Louis: Author, 1954.

Chapter 7
Civic Planning in St. Louis: The Case of St. Louis 2004

William E. Winter

In most discussions of urban policy, "planning" refers to the duties of professionals undertaken in the public sector or allied private sector organizations; in reality, planning activities have always involved a broader cast of characters. In the City of St. Louis, as in many other American cities, the input of other stakeholders in planning is both a function of the fragmented and substantially privatized nature of local decision-making and the need of local elites to cooperate across sectoral boundaries to initiate projects. In this sense, local planning reflects patterns of local governance, particularly the need for leaders in local cities to organize the capacity to get things done in the face of complexity, conflict, and social change (Kearns and Paddison 2000).

Civic organizations and civic entrepreneurs have been important participants in contemporary local planning (McCoy 2002; Walters 1998; West and Taylor 1995). Civic organizations are groups representing the "third arm" of local public policymaking, outside the public sector and business/corporate interests (Rifkin 1998; Salamon 1994). These include both formal organizations—nonprofit interest groups, neighborhood organizations, civic improvement associations and advocacy groups around specific issues—as well as looser and less permanent networks of individuals and organizations. The term "civic planning" refers both to the participation and the leadership of planning activities by members of this sector of the local environment. Civic sector elites bring to the planning table not only a unique set of skills but also a set of connections to the local political culture different from the norms guiding activities in either the public or private sector (Henton et al. 1997).

In St. Louis, civic planning emerged with force in the 1990s, as local debates around the city's continuing economic and demographic change intensified. While the St. Louis 2004 effort is the best recognized of these, under it came a wide range of additional activities and organizations, undertaken by a grouping of individuals and organizations outside the political and corporate organizations conventionally seen as dominating local policymaking. Besides advocating new development-oriented planning, St. Louis 2004 initiated plans on a wide range of local policy issues—from a regional park system to youth violence—and began or assisted in the beginning of a number of projects and organizations. This chapter discusses the planning process undertaken by St. Louis 2004, with particular emphasis on planning activities around two of the initiatives chosen: the Sustainable Neighborhoods Initiative and the Regional Parks Initiative. The two initiatives chosen for specific review reflect the attempt, on the one hand, to foster collaborative activity at the neighborhood level and link it to a regional set of resources and, on the other, to foster a regional plan linked to regional resources and local projects. By focusing on these two projects, this chapter places the St. Louis 2004 initiative in the context of two different structures of local decision-making. Within these projects it evaluates whether civic planning succeeded in encouraging new participation in local decision-making and substantially reorienting the capacity of local leaders to advance new solutions to persistent urban issues.

Defining the Scope and Impact of the Civic Sector in Planning

Capacity-building is a critical task for local leaders, given the factors that constrain local governance. Key among them is a pervading ethos of privatism in American political behavior (Barnekov, Boyle, and Rich 1989; Squires 1991) and a structural framework of local governments that confines their ability to restrict private economic matters, privileging private interests in local policymaking (Robertson and Judd 1989). At the same time, local capacity is also a function of the structural makeup of local authority, and, in St. Louis particularly, its pervasive fragmentation. For St. Louis leaders, fragmentation stems from the formal structure of local politics in its charter and regional organization (Stein 2002); thus, in St. Louis, local policymaking fragmentation is particularly intense, with structural fragmentation in the region's political institutions resulting in fragmentation in the city's governing institutions (Laslo and Judd 2006).

The participation of the civic sector in planning represents one mechanism for expanding decision-making capacity. The civic sector represents a list of institutions broader than just traditional nonprofit groups; it includes organizations and networks generally outside of elected political leadership or corporate/business elite—local universities, foundations, citizen leagues, neighborhood groups, and human service organizations. One feature of these types of institutions is that they are explicitly organized and responsive to a broader range of interests and incentives than the political calculations of elected officials or the economic returns of corporations and development interests (Bradley 1998). As a practical matter, civic sector participants in planning may bring new skills and access to resources unavailable in the public or the private sector—for example, volunteer energy and funds to jump-start local initiatives. The emphasis on "civic" also takes seriously the claims of these efforts in promoting new forms of collaboration as a method of creating new solutions to problems rooted in past urban policy failures (McCoy 2002). This is a major theme in the writings of advocates who promote civic planning and other community visioning efforts as a method of creating civic space for dialogue and collaboration that overcomes past political dysfunctions (Putnam 1996; National Civic League 2000; Helling 1998; Shipley et al. 2004). This was a significant goal for St. Louis 2004's proponents (Tucci 1996).

It is necessary to evaluate the extent to which St. Louis 2004 activated a broader range of local interests, as compared to the more typical land use planning exercises. As significant, however, is whether this participation extended the range of policy priorities addressed in local decision-making or fundamentally incorporated these changes into new institutions—either by recasting existing organizations or creating new ones. The political impact of the civic sector has been underappreciated, even as enthusiasm for civic planning has increased. Some political scientists have examined the impact of civic interests within a discussion of community development organizations and other advocacy, activist-oriented groups (Ferman 1996). Related to this are a set of studies within the planning literature concerning the ability of planners to assist in the mobilization of grassroots interests in order to challenge traditional business-oriented development interests (Grengs 2002; Fainstein 2000). Scholars have also investigated the role of nonprofit organizations generally in local political activities, including the ability of "governing nonprofits," to participate in local public policymaking and to restructure local political agendas (Hula and Jackson-Elmoore 2001; Orr 2001; Smith 2001; Hula, Jackson, and Orr 1997). This literature defines governing nonprofits as a class of organizations not focused on service provision, policy advocacy, or narrow procedural issues of governmental efficiency or transparency, but organized directly to provide "a context for collective decision-making, policy formulation and policy implementation" (Ferris 1998).

This broader context links civic planning under St. Louis 2004 to questions of local decision-making in the St. Louis metropolitan region. The initiative's leaders directly posed local capacity-building as a chief element of the planning process, eschewing the need to start a new organization and instead focusing on acting as a catalyst to bring existing resources together (Mihalopoulos 1996; Mihalopoulos 1997b; Smith 2004). With the organization scheduled to shut its doors on December 31, 2004, the long-term impact of the initiative would play out in a number of other organizations and initiatives. This work would be spread out over a broad range of issues, including downtown development, after-school programming for children, youth violence, and neighborhood social services. St. Louis 2004 provides a test case of the ability of the civic sector to create and maintain the sort of social capital that informs collaborative activity and is necessary for planning and implementing solutions in the face of political and institutional fragmentation. However, capacity can be achieved on a number of different levels—regional, metropolitan, municipal, interorganizational, and neighborhood (Kearns and Forrest 2001)—across a number of different issue areas. St. Louis 2004 operated on each of these levels, often within the same initiative, and its successes and failures say something about the ability of civic planning to transform local decision-making across them.

Planning Under St. Louis 2004

The call in 1996 to create St. Louis 2004 came out the frustration of some corporate and civic leaders in the region over a constellation of issues and the desire to create a mechanism to provide solutions to the city's and the region's seemingly intractable problems. These problems included continuing demographic decline in the city and stagnant population growth across the metropolitan area, persistent political fragmentation, racial polarization, and a lack of innovation in political, social and economic terms. At the time of St. Louis 2004's initiation, regional leaders under the Regional Commerce and Growth Association (RCGA) supported a public and extensive examination of the region in the Peirce Report, coauthored by national urban experts Neal Peirce and Curtis Johnson, published in the *St. Louis Post-Dispatch* in March 1997. Chief among the report's recommendations were a strengthening of the activity of the area's civic and nonprofit organizations and a ringing endorsement of the then-fledgling 2004 effort as a natural place for "civic experimentation" (Peirce and Johnson 1997a).

While the Peirce Report in turn launched a series of meetings and debates about St. Louis (*St. Louis Post-Dispatch* 1997; Desloge 1997), by far the most significant outcome from it was the boost given to St. Louis 2004 to continue discussions and to define implementation strategies (LaSala and Danforth 1997). A 1996 speech by Andrew Craig, outgoing president of Civic Progress and chair of Boatmen's Bank, called on local leaders to plan a series of civic improvements and events to celebrate the one-hundred-year anniversary of the city's 1904 World's Fair in 2004 (Craig 1996). The speech was written by Alfred Kerth, a public relations official at Fleishman-Hillard and the main staff person for Civic Progress. Kerth subsequently led St. Louis 2004 in its earliest phase. Kerth's departure from St. Louis 2004 brought former Republican Senator John Danforth in as chairman of the organization and JoAnne LaSala, a senior vice president at Fleishman-Hillard, in as the organization's first director. A month later, Peter Sortino, a lobbyist with the St. Louis mayor's office, joined as vice president of governmental affairs. Over the course of the fall, the staff grew to fifteen members with a budget of $2.3 million. The new team retooled the effort's public outreach, creating a series of action teams around key regional issues (Tucci 1996) and hosting a series of "visioning" sessions in December 1996 to gather public input (Mihalopoulos 1996).

The participation of Danforth typified the fact that at the top of St. Louis 2004 were some of the better-known names in local leadership. Joining Danforth on the board of St. Louis 2004 were John Baricevic, board chairman of St. Clair County in Illinois, Charmaine Chapman, president of the United Way of Greater St. Louis, Andrew Craig, of Boatmen's Bank, and John Jacob, an executive vice president at Anheuser-Busch. Danforth brought not only many years of political experience as a national Republican leader, but also considerable connections through both his family and the Danforth Foundation, capitalized with a total of $400 million in assets (Tucci 1998). The role of the foundation in St. Louis initiatives heightened after Danforth assumed chairmanship of the foundation in the spring 1997 and the foundation announced that it was changing its mission from a nationally oriented educational foundation to a foundation focused exclusively on the St. Louis region (*St. Louis Post-Dispatch* 1997; Danforth Foundation 1997). In announcing the change, foundation leaders noted "a renewed sense of optimism in the region" and specifically mentioned St. Louis 2004 as a sign of willingness among

St. Louis area citizens to define and solve a number of the region's major problems (Danforth Foundation 1997).

The change in the mission brought significant resources to local projects, including those initiatives supported by St. Louis 2004, as well as the interest of the foundation's board and staff. While some outreach work preceded Danforth's chairmanship at St. Louis 2004—including limited focus groups and a "Think 2004" public relations campaign—the new staff intensified the group's work and outreach activities.[1] St. Louis 2004 was restructured into six action teams, each led by a staff member and a volunteer chair—Citizenship, Culture, Learning, Work, Environment and Health—with multiple taskforces under each team (twenty-seven in total) reflecting specific issues to be resolved (Tucci 1996).[2] The group also retooled the public outreach strategy by holding a series of visioning sessions around the region in December 1996 (Mihalopoulos 1996), utilizing the public comments at task force meetings to identify best practices on specific issues from St. Louis and elsewhere. The initiative's leaders set a deadline of April 1998 for release of the 2004 action plan to the general public in order to create the impetus for task forces to move quickly into project implementation.

Danforth presented a report back to the visioning participants in April 1997, summarizing some of the key findings from the sessions. This presentation began the process of preparing a draft report with proposed initiatives, with staff working from recommendations from the task forces and other ad-hoc committees. Titled *Ideas for Change*, the plan was released to volunteers and political leaders privately in July 1997, and following revisions, released to the public in August 1997. The draft listed twenty-eight key points under the rubric of four main goals—Safe and Healthy Citizens, Children Prepared for Life, Economic Security and Opportunity, and Rich and Vital Lives—with some specific recommendations listed under each. St. Louis 2004 provided some greater detail on the proposals in a September 1997 report *A Report from the St. Louis 2004 Volunteers*, listing a total of 116 proposals taken from all of the existing task forces and committees. Both documents were a central focus of a second round of public engagement held by St. Louis 2004 and FOCUS St. Louis, the regional citizenship group, throughout 1997. These included twenty-eight

---

[1] Deborah Duggan's 2005 publication *Looking Back—Moving Forward: A Report to the Community on the St. Louis 2004 Effort* discusses in greater detail the planning processes and the various stages of the process built upon each other to produce the 1998 action plan.

[2] Appendix I lists all of the task forces established by St. Louis 2004 in fall 1996. As discussed below, additional committees, subcommittees, and task forces were added as needed.

forums held in locations across the twelve-county region and round tables on key regional issues, such as race and difference, neighborhood-economic development, and downtown.

This second round of public input was matched by continued work around key project goals by action teams and task forces throughout the fall 1997. Both of these processes were intended to pare down the list of projects to a doable list of initiatives to be completed before 2004. St. Louis 2004 staff and committee/task force leaders met in January 1998 to vote on a list of eighteen key projects (Schlinkmann 1998). Organizers then held a third round of public input in January and February 1998, with staff reviewing the additional input before finalizing the list of initiatives. Finally on March 10, 1998, Danforth announced St. Louis 2004's Action Plan, listing key areas in which St. Louis 2004 would focus its energies (Mihalopoulos and Schlinkmann 1998). The eleven areas[3] included:

- race and economic opportunity
- hate crimes and bigotry
- youth violence and gang activity
- safe places for children after school
- health insurance for low income residents
- downtown and riverfront redevelopment
- improving regional air quality
- sustainable neighborhood redevelopment
- a regional park system
- new technology business startups
- women and minority business development.

While these priorities would shift slightly, they represented the main issues that St. Louis 2004 pursued until the organization voluntarily closed its doors at the end of 2004. The issue of regional air quality was resolved when the state repealed a ban on the sale of the cleaner reformulated gaso-

---

[3]Two additional initiatives are often included in this list. Celebration 2004 was a yearlong series of events during 2004 commemorating the anniversary of the 1904 World's Fair. Team St. Louis provided small grant funding to St. Louis area nonprofits and initiatives to accomplish short-term community goals and projects.

line in the summer of 1998. Other initiatives gradually were added to the list as community support and leadership emerged. In 1999, Faith Beyond Walls, a project designed to encourage the work of local congregations in community issues, was launched. In 2000, a Families and Learning Initiative was formed to encourage the growth of quality childcare centers. St. Louis 2004 also worked to initiate the Greater St. Louis Land Development Trust, which provided financial resources to accumulate and clear vacant industrial properties for redevelopment.[4]

The Infrastructure of St. Louis 2004 Planning and Implementation

While some criticized St. Louis 2004's public engagement strategy as window dressing, there is some evidence of the opposite. For example, public opinion largely killed a more enhanced version of the land trust, which some African American residents regarded as a scheme to assemble land for large-scale residential development by suburban developers. Public input also validated strong support for the regional parks initiative (Mihalopoulos, 1997c), spurring St. Louis 2004 to tout it as one of their premier efforts. However, since the Action Plan only detailed the general guidelines for implementation, planning effectively continued past spring of 1998. Because the task forces and key staff members were mostly responsible for this work, it accelerated St. Louis 2004's shift toward the constituent groups and individuals who were actively involved in the various focus issues.

Thus, it is within the discussions and deliberations of the task forces that one must look to determine who participated in the St. Louis 2004 initiative and how that participation shaped specific initiatives. Early on, some commentators regarded the effort as more or less an extension of Civic Progress, pointing to the role of Craig and Kerth in founding the effort and the role of Civic Progress corporations in funding the effort and many of its initiatives (Mihalopoulos 1997a, 1A). However, while corporate actors and political officials can be found throughout the planning process, the participation of other types of actors is equally important, particularly on the task forces that largely shaped the initiatives in 1998 and 1999. This

---

[4]Appendix II summarizes the fourteen initiatives, who is implementing them, and their major outcomes.

can be seen in the examples of two of the St. Louis 2004's initiatives that will be examined here: the Sustainable Neighborhoods Initiative and the Regional Parks Initiative.

Sustainable Neighborhoods Initiative

The Sustainable Neighborhoods Initiative first emerged out of discussions within the Sustainable Neighborhoods task force, formed in the fall of 1996 as a part of the Environment action team. St. Louis 2004 staff selected the initial membership of the committee and asked four individuals to co-chair the effort, including Richard Baron, CEO of McCormack Baron, a private development company known nationally for innovative community-building efforts. However, as is the case of other task forces, the meetings were generally open to anyone who wanted to be there. Thus, the task force's membership reflected a broad grouping of neighborhood activists, community development corporation leaders, local officials and representatives of human service agencies. Meetings of the task force included presentations on model ideas in neighborhood redevelopment and long brainstorming sessions on a wide variety of ideas—from neighborhood community courts, to public-private development partnerships, to neighborhood school initiatives, to individual development accounts and other wealth-building strategies.

The cochairs and St. Louis 2004 staff were primarily responsible for winnowing down proposals and creating the structure for the continued work in this area after the publication of the draft action plan in August 1997. At this point, however, the work of the larger group ended and was placed in the hands of a smaller Sustainable Neighborhoods Steering Committee that did more detailed planning work. The Steering Committee combined the work of both the original task force and a number of other task forces—the Access task force of the Health Action Team and the Sustainable Neighborhoods/Wealth Creation task force of the Work Action Team—that were concerned with place-based strategies to increase the ability of neighborhood residents to access services and improve their lives. The Steering Committee continued to hold meetings through the remainder of 1997 and 1998 to iron out details of the initiative, in the process forming a number of additional working groups to tackle specific issues.

The Sustainable Neighborhoods Steering Committee reflected the self-interested nature of participants in the planning process. It included leaders and staff at some of the city's larger and more active social service groups like the Urban League, Grace Hill, Paraquad, and OASIS.

It also consisted of organizations and individuals interested in promoting physical redevelopment in neighborhoods, including McCormack Baron, as well as local banks and city officials. Particularly important in the planning effort were staff members at two organizations that would ultimately become implementers of the initiative—the Regional Housing and Community Development Alliance (RHCDA) and St. Louis Community Partnership (later Area Resources for Community and Human Services, or ARCHS). RHCDA was an amalgam of a number of local nonprofits founded in the 1980s and 1990s to facilitate housing development in the city. The organization and its predecessors had received support from Civic Progress corporations (Linsalata and Novak 1991; Todd 1994). By the time of St. Louis 2004, the organization's increasing staff included both former city development officials and nonprofit development experts and had a track record of housing development in city neighborhoods. St. Louis Community Partnership—the other major organizational sponsor of the initiative—was formed in 1997 as a partnership for implementation and funding of five state agencies. Its work was partly based on the Caring Communities model, an initiative that located outreach and social services at elementary schools.

Initial plans for the Sustainable Neighborhoods Initiative developed during the spring of 1998 and a plan released to the public later in December 1998 reflected the input and priorities of these different organizations. St. Louis 2004 assisted in preparing a white paper in April 1998 that laid out main features of the initiative, including a compact between St. Louis 2004 and the St. Louis Community Partnership that highlighted the principle of resident involvement in planning (St. Louis 2004 1998a). The plan proposed a series of physical and human service planning processes to be piloted in key neighborhoods in the region, the establishment of Neighborhood Leadership Teams to implement the priorities detailed in neighborhood plans, and linkages between neighborhood leaders and a Resource Committee under the initiative to leverage existing and identify new resources to implement the plans (St. Louis 2004 1998b). The initiative eschewed direct grants to existing neighborhood-based entities in favor of a facilitated approach led by the two implementing organizations, with other neighborhood-based nonprofits providing resources as detailed in neighborhood plans. Steering Committee members also were responsible for the arduous process of choosing the participant neighborhoods—ultimately nine clusters of contiguous areas located in St. Louis City, St. Louis County, and across the Mississippi River in East St. Louis.

The announcement of the initiative in December 1998—replete with promised commitments of hundreds of millions of dollars for designated clusters—set off planning processes within the nine clusters, with the implementing organizations, and ARCHS (formerly St. Louis Community Partnership) particularly, overseeing planning efforts (Parish 1998b). Under the original plan, RHCDA and ARCHS were to work together to facilitate planning and development in the clusters; a third organization, the Sustainable Neighborhoods Development Organization (SNDO) was formed in 1999 by St. Louis 2004 staff to specifically find and direct resources to neighborhoods to complete projects. However, despite this coordination, the initiative's implementation was based more on the existing conditions within the nine clusters than on a function of the coordinated approach by the implementing organizations. Even as Sustainable Neighborhoods secured commitments for investment in the clusters, access to these resources depended upon the ability of neighborhood-based organizations to plan and implement projects, including the development of projects prior to the Sustainable Neighborhoods designation. Thus, some of the variations in outcomes of the initiative reflect the existing capacity of organizations in each of the clusters, the presence of existing projects attractive to partnering organizations, and the ability of residents to quickly organize in order to access Sustainable Neighborhoods resources.

A number of the clusters quickly began planning—some funded through a grant from the Daughters of Charity Foundation—with the city's Forest Park Southeast neighborhood completing a draft plan by the summer of 1999 (Hines 1999b). By 2000, five of the clusters had completed planning or had planning under way (St. Louis 2004 2000). In other areas, by contrast, planning lagged, with one cluster not holding social service planning meetings until 2002, relatively late in the process. The plans varied in their goals and proposed projects, and implementation of the projects likewise varied. In retrospect, the $751 million price tag of the initiative became an albatross around the necks of its organizers as they overpromised results without clearly annunciating under what conditions that investment would occur.

Implementation of physical redevelopment projects by RHCDA and other developers depended upon the lining up of a number of complex political and economic factors. By 2004, RHCDA had worked in at least four of the nine clusters (Mihalopolous 1998; Parish 2000; Thomas 2006; RHCDA 2004), with physical redevelopment activities occurring in a fifth sponsored by McCormack Baron (Smith 2004). RHCDA generally benefited from St. Louis 2004 sponsorship, both in terms of staff funds to plan projects and grant and other equity funds to implement development deals (Parish 1998a; RHCDA 2004; Sustainable Neighborhoods Development Office

2004). RHCDA also worked in additional ways to fill development-related needs in the participating clusters, including a small business loan program and a loan program for completing improvements on residential buildings.

Similarly, the social service planning undertaken by ARCHS had mixed results. In some of the clusters achieving consensus took a long time and required a longer commitment from ARCHS both in terms of planning funds and staff time. While a number of clusters continued to meet as Neighborhood Leadership Teams well past St. Louis 2004's end date, the larger goal of the establishment of a neighborhood cabinet, with representatives from each of the clusters continuing resident-based planning work, never achieved viability and largely ended when Sustainable Neighborhoods ended in 2005 and 2006. ARCHS's involvement was also hampered by its reliance on state funding, with budget cuts and the resulting staff turnover complicating the process. State cuts first hit the group in 2001, negatively impacting the group's ability to continue planning work; other cuts in 2002 and 2003 additionally complicated the relationship between ARCHS and its affiliated Caring Communities group, largely leading to the latter's curtailment. More generally, state cuts and program changes in key aspects of the region's social service net further hampered the ability of neighborhood residents to meaningfully participate in long-term planning activities. While most of the clusters could point to social service initiatives that reflected the desires of residents as articulated in their neighborhood plans, the broader vision of participatory planning and a holistic approach to community-building as first articulated in the spring of 1998 eluded both the initiative's leadership and participating residents.

The Regional Parks Initiative

As in the case of the Sustainable Neighborhoods Initiative, St. Louis 2004's Regional Parks Initiative was strongly backed by a grouping of organizations and stakeholders that had been working on local bike trails and parks for a number of years. These included some of the region's prominent environmental groups—the Coalition for the Environment, the Sierra Club, and others—as well as local groups that had been specifically involved in past trail development. Among these were Trailnet, an organization founded in 1988 to support the development of trails regionally, including a riverfront trail along the Mississippi; Grace Hill, whose Americorp trail ranger project created a portion of the trail in the 1990s; and the Greenway Network, a land conservancy group based in St. Charles County. Trailnet in particular had a long history in working to complete local trails; the

1997 Peirce Report mentioned its work as one of the few unifying visions of the metropolitan region (Peirce and Johnson 1997b). Members of the three groups had been collaborating on a regional plan for trails prior to their participation in St. Louis 2004, and their "Confluence Greenway" plan—detailing trails from the Missouri River and St. Charles County on the north to the downtown area along the Mississippi River—was released in 1997 during the planning process.

Representatives of the organizations were among the thirty members of the Parks and Open Space task force under the Environment Action Team that participated in the first phase of St. Louis 2004's planning process to come up with initial ideas for the organization. The Confluence Greenway proposal was a significant part of the Task Force's recommendations provided to St. Louis 2004 in the spring and summer of 1997. When the 1997 draft plan announced a regional parks and trails system as one of the preliminary goals of the initiative, members continued to meet throughout fall 1997 and provided the central energy to the Regional Parks Initiative. Over time, this core group was joined by other interests from elsewhere in the region, which were generally outside the scope of the Confluence plan, including trail advocates in St. Louis County, where Trailnet's previous efforts had fostered both support and opposition, and in St. Charles County, where booming real estate investment was spurring population growth. St. Louis County officials particularly became active supporters of the project; Bob Hall, the former director of county parks, became the executive director of Gateway Trails and Parks, an interim organization founded in 1999 to implement the initiative. Over time, St. Louis 2004's championship of the issue would create new organizations to carry out the plan—building upon the initial interest of environmentalists and trail proponents and securing support for regional trails from suburban politicians, developers, and residents.

St. Louis 2004's proposal for the regional trail system, released preliminarily in spring 1998, planned trails across the region at a total cost of $80 million and called for new tax increases or fees to fund their development (Schlinkmann 1998). Over the short term, the inclusion of the regional parks initiative energized support for trails, bringing new resources and support for projects. Danforth specifically lobbied in Washington, D.C., for federal support for the plan in 1998 and 1999, securing millions in funding (Uhlenbrock 1998). St. Louis 2004 also helped trail proponents secure the support of the area's Republican representatives, who had previously opposed designation of the Mississippi River as an American Heritage River. Most important, St. Louis 2004 staff lead an effort to secure public financing for the plan's implementation—first lobbying in the Illinois and Missouri state houses for authorization to set up local taxing districts, then securing county legislative support for the districts, and then heading an electoral effort to secure public approval for the districts in November 2000.

As a part of this, in 1999, St. Louis 2004 established and largely funded a new organization, Gateway Parks and Trails, to publicize a regional trail and park plan and conduct the campaign for a regional sales tax to finance it. Besides Hall, the group included a board of the publisher of the *St. Louis Post-Dispatch*, the director of the Missouri Botanical Garden, and a number of prominent civic and corporate leaders. The contributions of this group were specific to the process of securing public support for the tax as well as more generally instrumental in shifting the discussion of the plan away from the initial Confluence Greenway proposal. St. Louis 2004's Sortino assisted Hall in leading the group's lobbying efforts. St. Louis 2004 also targeted additional funding from St. Louis Heroes, a civic fund-raising group with ties to St. Louis 2004, to pay for a regional poll of public funding in 1999 (St. Louis 2004 2000) and helped secure other private support to pay for a campaign in support of the November 2000 vote.

Public financing for the regional parks planning combined the unusual bi-state tax with a brokered political agreement on the Missouri side of the river that garnered municipal and county support for the plans. Under the plan, the public tax would be split between a newly created Metropolitan Parks and Recreation District, county governments, and municipal governments, effectively giving local governments a new source of funding for general park improvements and maintenance (Sutin 2000a). Trail supporters played up state authorization of the financing scheme in spring 1999, leading to a joint appearance by the governors of Missouri and Illinois meeting on the Chain of Rocks Bridge—a linchpin of the trail system—to sign the legislation and kick off the local campaign (Hines 1999a). Support by various county governments followed in 2000, including Madison County and St. Clair County on the east side and the City of St. Louis, St. Louis County, and St. Charles County on the west side.

The lopsided campaign for the park tax, where proponents raised over $900,000 in support of the plan (Sutin 2000b), led to victory in all five counties, creating a conduit for an estimated $20 million annually for the three participating Missouri counties to plan and implement trail projects (Riley 2000). The tax victory also led to a second shift in organizational structure over the initiative—in this case, the initiation of a Metropolitan Parks and Recreation District created in January 2001 to oversee spending of the public funds. In creating the group, the Park District further regionalized management and coordination of the trail and greenway planning, formally incorporating representatives from St. Louis County, St. Charles County, and City of St. Louis government to serve on the organization's board (Dimmitt 2001). While the new organization strongly endorsed the Confluence Greenway plan, pledging $36 million of the organization's future resources to the project (Sutin 2001), the district's plans quickly grew to encompass a broader range of projects across the metropolitan region; significantly, the role of the organization expanded beyond the financing of improvements to become the lead agency for overseeing trail and park development. The district's planning culminated in a name change—to Great Rivers Greenway (GRG)—and a comprehensive regional plan called the River Ring, incorporating a local trails plan into an interconnected trail system along the Mississippi, Missouri, and Meramec rivers and the Cuivre River/Western Greenway at the western edge of St. Charles County (*St. Louis Post-Dispatch* 2004).

GRC's access to resources and leadership over trails and parks issues has also led to an expansion of the organization's work in other local recreation matters. GRC staff have played a leadership role in the funding and planning for a new riverfront park, coordinated planning for new on-street designated bicycle lanes in the city of St. Louis, and purchased the initial pieces of property for a planned Chouteau's Pond adjacent to downtown (Van Der Werf 2005; O'Neil 2006). GRG's ascension has also prompted a shift in the work of existing trails groups from planning and development of new trails to advocacy and promotion of the regional trail system. While GRG has not been immune to local challenges—political leaders in some St. Charles County municipalities were initially opposed to the plan (Harris 2000) and some St. Charles developers objected to initial proposals as antidevelopment (Schlinkmann 2004)—the group's leaders were able to overcome those objections and find compromises that maintained the plan's original intent.

St. Louis 2004 and Local Decision-Making

These examples illustrate how the detailed planning and implementation strategies of St. Louis 2004 emerged from conversations among participants in the various interests groups around the specific issue areas. In terms of the Sustainable Neighborhoods Initiative, steering committee participants, and particularly representatives from the St. Louis Community Partnership (ARCHS), developed the idea of joining physical planning and human service planning, a concept that was largely accepted by other stakeholders in the process despite reservations around its breadth and comprehensiveness. While full implementation of the initiative faced challenges—including both external funding problems and internal organizational difficulties—the initiative heightened the role of RHCDA and ARCHS in local community building. The example of the Regional Parks Initiative indicates how St. Louis 2004 linked to the existing work of a number of environmental and recreational organizations to craft a regional plan for parks. St. Louis 2004's sponsorship of the plan created a regional political consensus around the goal, creating a new regional body to implement the plan, and convinced voters on both sides of the river to pass a sales tax to fund park and trail improvements.

The role of issue-specific participants in formulating and implementing plans is similarly evident in other St. Louis 2004 initiatives. The youth violence initiative, referred to as Ceasefire, existed prior to St. Louis 2004 as a joint effort of the U.S. Attorney's Office, local law enforcement authorities, and local social service agencies, particularly those focusing on urban youth and antigang activities. By including the initiative in the planning, St. Louis 2004 staff brought additional resources to the existing committee, including visits to model practices elsewhere. Inclusion of the plan also heightened interest in the activities, but did not substantially change the operation of the initiative. Similarly, activism by faith leaders led to the inclusion of the Faith Beyond Walls program after the announcement of the action plan in spring 1998; members of the primary organizations supporting the initiative, the St. Louis Clergy Coalition and the Interfaith Partnership, had participated in the planning process and had been initially distressed that their proposals had not been incorporated in the eleven initiatives named. Support for the initiative followed the activism by local clergy around a series of hate crimes in the region and the participation of clergy in the Roman Catholic papal visit in 1999. The initiative also matched the interests of Senator John Danforth, an ordained Episcopal minister and the supporter of the "I Dare You" Award through the Danforth Foundation, given annually to a local congregation that demonstrated outreach efforts aimed at improving the community.

Retrospectively, the ability of St. Louis 2004 to effectively mobilize and negotiate among such diverse coalitions of interests is no small feat; as a planning process, St. Louis 2004 set a new local standard. St. Louis 2004 also demonstrates the key role that civic leaders can play in local decision-making and how their involvement can bring new energy and initiatives to local policy areas, including those focused upon poor neighborhoods and their residents. Consequently, implementation of these initiatives built upon existing civic organizations and established new frameworks—in some cases, new organizations—to coordinate activities, and, on an inter-organizational level, helped improve local capacity. These intermediary agencies benefited from the prominence of St. Louis 2004 in both funding and civic and corporate support; their participation in St. Louis 2004 made them central actors within each of the issue areas. In this way, a specific part of the St. Louis 2004 strategy was to create institutions that could continue to organize local decision-making, provide capacity-building where needed, and mobilize the often disparate resources and agencies—including service providers in the field—to advance their broadly defined goals.

The practical effect of this strategy was that the success and failure of specific initiatives would rest upon the capabilities of the implementing partners and their ability to navigate around internal and external threats and barriers. Over time, the success of these distinct elements of the plan would evolve increasingly separately from each other and the clarity of the call that motivated civic planners in the first place. The danger of this separation—a reflection of both St. Louis 2004's organizational structure and the fragmentation of policymaking generally—is not that the St. Louis 2004 plan would fail but that initiatives would succeed or fail in a manner that reflected existing divisions within St. Louis's politics.

In this sense, the two initiatives analyzed here show how the ability of St. Louis 2004 to foster local capacity varied across different levels of local decision-making. On the one hand, the leaders of the Regional Parks Initiative were able to develop a regional vision for parks and trails, convince a majority of citizens regionally to fund it, and create an organization with regional representation to implement it. While regional differences in the plan emerged, the Great Rivers Greenway largely has navigated through them, finding unlikely allies for the plan. On the other hand, efforts under the Sustainable Neighborhoods Initiative show how difficult it is to foster collaboration at the neighborhood level and link that collaboration with regional resources. While the model of Sustainable Neighborhoods worked for organizations and residents who were able to quickly advance their concerns to the initiative's partners, the harder vision of promoting citizen participation remained unfulfilled. In this sense, the vision that St. Louis 2004 set for itself was probably far more radical than one would think looking at the cast of characters that started the process in 1996, and probably not realistic. Ultimately, the inability to foster meaningful neighborhood-level participation and capacity in project planning and implementation remains an intractable problem that is not solved through civic planning alone and generally is not addressed through other avenues of local decision-making.

Appendix I: Action Teams and Task Forces Established by St. Louis 2004, Fall 1996

CITIZENSHIP

Vice President: Peter Sortino

Chair: Kathryn Nelson, Former Director, Danforth Foundation

Task Forces:

Values Education

Business Ethics

Living Together in the Community

Rearing and Nurturing Youth

CULTURE

Vice President: Marvin Anderson

Chair: Robert Archibald, President, Missouri Historical Society

Task Forces:

Religion

Arts

Civic Identity

Sports

LEARNING

Vice President: Valerie Bell

Chair: Blanche Touhill, Chancellor, University of Missouri–St. Louis

Task Forces:

Families

Teacher Preparation and Development

Formal Learning

Informal Learning

WORK

Vice President: Sandra Moore

Chair: Richard C. D. Fleming, President, St. Louis Regional Commerce & Growth Association

Task Forces:

Business Expansion

Innovation and New Business

Workforce Training

Sustainable Neighborhood Economic Development

ENVIRONMENT

Vice President: Marc Solomon

Chair: Peter Raven, Director, Missouri Botanical Garden

Task Forces:

Neighborhoods

Planning and Urban Design

Infrastructure

Regional Environment

Parks and Open Space

Measurements

HEALTH

Vice President: Mark Hayes

Chair: Fred Brown, President and CEO, BJC Health System

Task Forces:

Access

Prevention and Wellness

Resources

Appendix II: Summary of St. Louis 2004 Initiatives

Issue	Description	Implementing Organization(s)	Implementation
Racism and economic opportunity	Hold annual conference to promote workforce diversity	RCGA, Civic Progress, Regional Business Council, St. Louis Minority Business Council	St. Louis Business Diversity Initiative formed in 2000 to coordinate existing efforts by promoting best practices, minority businesses and networking/training of minority employees
Hate crimes and bigotry	Sponsor "race response" to hate crimes and train law enforcement	U.S. Attorney's Office, St. Louis 2004 Hate Crimes Task Force	Facilitated training among law enforcement, lobbied for tougher penalties against hate crimes. St. Louis 2004 supported the initiation of the diversity
Youth violence and gang activity	Initiate "Cease Fire" program of law enforcement and social services for youth	U.S. Attorney's Office, Eastern Division, and others	Some aspects of program exist (night watch at juvenile justice center and anti-gang task force in local police)
Safe places for children after school	Build on existing programs, develop networks of service providers and provide training	St. Louis for Kids	St. Louis for Kids continues to exist and work on primary mission
Health insurance for low income residents	Assist uninsured to purchase health insurance and eliminate other barriers to treatment	St. Louis Regional Health Commission	Full coverage for uninsured not realized; RHA continues to exist to coordinate health delivery and access strategies
Downtown and riverfront redevelopment	Encourage market-rate housing, Washington Ave., entertainment, and riverfront development	Downtown Now!	Downtown plan completed in 1999, implementation ongoing. Downtown Now! folded into Downtown Partnership in 2006
Improving regional air quality	Repeal ban on reformulated gasoline	RCGA, East-West Gateway Council of Governments	MO legislature repealed ban on reformulated gas (1998)
Sustainable neighborhood redevelopment	Coordinate neighborhood planning for physical redevelopment and human services	RHCDA, Area resources for Community and Human Services	Planning largely completed in all clusters, with physical development primary outcome and some resident leadership teams active
Regional greenways and park system	Create 200 mile regional trail system	Green Rivers Greenway, Confluence Greenway, Trailnet	GRG continues implementation of plan; public funding secured for system in 2001
New industries and emerging technology	Create regional technology alliance and support seed money fund for new ventures	RCGA, East-West Gateway Council of Governments	Formed the Coalition for Plant and Life Sciences to build capacity in the bio-tech sector
Minority and women-owned business growth	Strengthen business opportunities and raise capital to support development of businesses	St. Louis Minority Business Council, National Association of Women Business Owners	Capital fund never started due to economic and philanthropic downturn, and initiative ended
Faith and community	Involve congregations in community work	Faith Beyond Walls	Organization continues to exist and follow mission; merged with Interfaith Partnership in 2005
Greater St. Louis land development fund	Land-bank parcels for redevelopment	RHCDA	Secured state fund for tax credit to fund assembly of land, funding industrial projects
Families and learning	Encourage access to high quality, safe child care centers	United Way of St. Louis	Initiative part of Success by 6 project, providing assistance in starting, accrediting, and improving child care programs

References

Barnekov, Timothy, Robin Boyle, and Daniel Rich. *Privatism and Urban Policy in Britain and the United States.* New York: Oxford University Press, 1989.

Bradley, Bill. "The Importance of the Civic Sector." *National Civic Review* 87, no. 2 (1998): 157–162.

Craig, Andrew. "Craig: 'Transcend . . . Traditional Boundaries.'" *St. Louis Post-Dispatch*, January 9, 1996, p. 5B.

Danforth Foundation. *The Danforth Foundation 1997 Annual Report.* St. Louis: Author, 1997.

Desloge, Rick. "Leaders Commit to Study Peirce Report's Findings." *St. Louis Business Journal*, March 7, 1997, p. 1.

Dimmit, Ralph. "Ortwerth Appoints Ash, Zerr to Parks District Board of Governors." *St. Louis Post-Dispatch* (St. Charles County Post), January 5, 2001, p. 2.

Fainstein, Susan. "New Directions in Planning Theory." *Urban Affairs Review* 35, no. 4 (2000): 451–478.

Ferman, Barbara. *Challenging the Growth Machine: Neighborhood Politics in Chicago and Pittsburgh.* Lawrence: University of Kansas Press, 1996.

Ferris, James. "The Role of the Nonprofit Sector in a Self-Governing Society: A View from the United States." *Voluntas* 9, no. 2 (1998): 137–151.

Grengs, Joe. "Community-Based Planning as a Source of Political Change." *American Planning Association Journal* 68, no. 2 (2002): 165–177.

Harris, Mihal. "St. Peters Aldermen Oppose County Tax Initiative for Parks." *St. Louis Post-Dispatch* (St. Charles County Post), August 15, 2000, p. 1.

Helling, Amy. "Collaborative Visioning: Proceed with Caution." *Journal of the American Planning Association* 64, no. 3 (1998): 335–349.

Henton, Douglas, John Melville, and Kimberly Walesh. "The Age of the Civic Entrepreneur: Restoring Civil Society and Building Economic Community." *National Civic Review* 86, no. 2 (Summer 1997): 149–157.

Hines, Michael. "Missouri and Illinois Governors Sign Park Legislation Together." *St. Louis Post-Dispatch*, July 14, 1999a, p. B3.

———. "Area Near Forest Park Will Get 5 New Homes." *St. Louis Post-Dispatch*, July 20, 1999b, p. B2.

Hula, Richard, and Cynthia Jackson-Elmoore. "Governing Nonprofits and Local Political Processes." *Urban Affairs Review* 36, no. 3 (2001): 324–358.

Hula, Richard, Cynthia Jackson, and Marion Orr. "Urban Politics, Governing Nonprofits and Community Revitalization." *Urban Affairs Review* 32, no. 4 (1997): 459–489.

Kearns, Ade, and Ray Forrest. "Social Cohesion and Multilevel Urban Governance." *Urban Studies* 37, no. 5–6 (2001): 995–1017.

Kearns, Ade, and Ronan Paddison. "New Challenges for Urban Governance." *Urban Studies* 37, nos. 5–6 (2000): 845–850.

LaSala, JoAnne, and John Danforth. "Giving Life to a Community's Hopes." *St. Louis Post-Dispatch*, March 16, 1997, p. 3B.

Laslo, David, and Dennis Judd. "Building Civic Capacity Through an Elastic Local State: The Case of St. Louis." *Review of Policy Research* 23, nos. 6 (November 2006): 1235–1255.

Linsalata, Phil, and Tim Novak. "Housing Proposal Backed." *St. Louis Post-Dispatch*, December 22, 1991, p. 1A.

McCoy, John. "Leading and Learning: Multisector Collaboration Yields Civic Change and Lessons on the Nature of Progress." *National Civic Review* 91, no. 3 (2002): 269–281.

Mihalopoulos, Dan. "A Speech, a Vision, and 2004 Lifts Off; One Critic Calls It Just Expensive PR." *St. Louis Post-Dispatch*, December 15, 1996, p. 1D.

———. "St. Louis 2004 Pursues Area's Renewal." *St. Louis Post-Dispatch*, April 20, 1997a, p. 1A.

———. "St. Louis 2004 to Go to the Next Level." *St. Louis Post-Dispatch*, August 17, 1997b, p. 1A.

———. "Ideas Float, Pop, Sparkle at 2004 Forums." *St. Louis Post-Dispatch*, September 28, 1997c, p. 1D.

———. "Plans for East St. Louis Apartments Advance." *St. Louis Post-Dispatch*, May 18, 1998, p. B4.

Mihalopoulos, Dan, and Mark Schlinkmann. "2004 Outlines Its Plan; Finding the Money Poses Next Challenge." *St. Louis Post-Dispatch*, March 11, 1998, p. A1.

National Civic League. *The Community Visioning and Strategic Planning Handbook*. Denver, CO: National Civic League Press, 2000.

O'Neil, Tim. "Linked Bicycle Trails Are Taking Shape Across St. Louis Region." *St. Louis Post-Dispatch*, December 4, 2006, p. B3.

Orr, Marion. "BUILD: Governing Nonprofits and Relational Power." *Policy Studies Review* 18, no. 4 (2001): 71–90.

Parish, Norm. "Houses Being Built in Wellston Can Provide a Foundation for the City's Future." *St. Louis Post-Dispatch*, January 28, 2000, p. B1.

———. "Local Firms Support $3 Million Housing Plan." *St. Louis Post-Dispatch*, February 19, 1998a, p. A5.

———. "Plan Hopes to Revitalize Neighborhoods." *St. Louis Post-Dispatch*, December 17, 1998b, p. B1.

Peirce, Neal, and Curtis Johnson. "A New Century, a New Challenge." *St. Louis Post-Dispatch*, March 16, 1997a, p. 1B.

———. "A Unified Region?" *St. Louis Post-Dispatch*, March 16, 1997b, p. 7B.

Putnam, Robert. "The Strange Disappearance of Civic America." *American Prospect* (Winter 1996): 34–48.

Regional Housing and Community Development Alliance (RHCDA). *Annual Report [2003]*. St. Louis: Author, 2004.

Rifkin, Jeremy. "A Civil Education for the Twenty First Century." *National Civic Review* 87, no. 2 (1998): 177–181.

Riley, Marianna. "Region Probably Sees First Benefits from New Tax for Parks in Early 2002." *St. Louis Post-Dispatch*, November 15, 2000, p. B1.

Robertson, David Brian, and Dennis Judd. *The Development of American Public Policy: The Structure of Policy Restraint*. Glenview, IL: Scott, Foresman, 1989.

Salamon, Lester. "The Rise of the Non-Profit Sector." *Foreign Affairs* 73, no. 4 (1994): 109–123.

Schlinkmann, Mark. "Greenway Agency Backs Off Land Use Regulation After Objections." *St. Louis Post-Dispatch*, January 26, 2004.

———. "2004 Group Releases Its List of Top Priorities." *St. Louis Post-Dispatch*, January 23, 1998, p. C1.

Shipley, Robert, Robert Feick, Brent Hall, and Robert Earley. "Evaluating Municipal Visioning." *Planning, Practice and Research* 19, no. 2 (2004): 195–210.

Smith, Bill. "St. Louis 2004 Can Take Credit for Solid Achievements." *St. Louis Post-Dispatch*, January 4, 2004, p. A1.

Smith, Steven Rathgeb. "Nonprofit Organizations in Urban Politics and Policy." *Policy Studies Review* 18, no. 4 (2001): 7–26.

Squires, Gregory. "Partnership and the Pursuit of the Private City." *Urban Affairs Review* 39, no. 2 (1991): 196–221.

St. Louis Post-Dispatch. "Group Follows Report," March 16, 1997, p. 9B.

____. "Rivers of Green [editorial]," June 28, 2004, p. B5.

St. Louis 2004. *Sustainable Neighborhoods: A White Paper*. April 10, 1998 Final Draft. St. Louis: Author, 1998a.

____. *Purpose of the Sustainable Neighborhoods Initiative*. July 24, 1998 Draft. St. Louis: Author, 1998b.

____. *Annual Report*. 1999–2000. St. Louis: Author, 2000.

Stein, Lana. *St. Louis Politics: The Triumph of Tradition*. St. Louis: Missouri Historical Society Press, 2002.

Sustainable Neighborhoods Development Office. "IRS 990." 2004. www.guidestar.org (accessed January 15, 2007).

Sutin, Phil. "Schools, Recreation, Waste Management: Special District Says Tax Increase Would Keep Services." *St. Louis Post-Dispatch*, October 15, 2000a, p. B1.

———. "Regional Tax Backers Raise More than $900,000." *St. Louis Post-Dispatch* (South Post), November 2, 2000b, p. 1.

———. "Funding Sought for Meramec Greenway." *St. Louis Post-Dispatch* (South Post), June 7, 2001, p. 1.

Thomas, Susan. "Rebuilding Old North St. Louis." *St. Louis Post-Dispatch*, October 20, 2006, p. B1.

Todd, Cynthia. "City, County Launch Housing Program." *St. Louis Post-Dispatch*, April 20, 1994, p. 1B.

Tucci, Linda. "$2.3 Million Budget, Staff of 15 for St. Louis 2004." *St. Louis Post-Dispatch*, November 1, 1996, p. 1.

———. "Two Foundations, Two Missions; Danforths and McDonnells Go in Different Directions." *St. Louis Business Journal*, April 20, 1998, p. 1.

Uhlenbrock, Tom. "Millions are Earmarked for Regional Trail Plan." *St. Louis Post-Dispatch*, July 2, 1998, p. B1.

Van Der Werf, Martin. "First Greenway Lake Might Be Dry for About Six Years." *St. Louis Post-Dispatch*, June 21, 2005, p. C1.

Walters, Jonathon. "Cities and the Vision Thing." *Governing* (May 1998): 32.

West, Harry, and Zach Taylor. "Stimulating Civic Change in Metropolitan Regions." *National Civic Review* 84, no. 3 (1995): 225–238.

Chapter 8
Economic Development Planning in Metropolitan St. Louis

Robert M. Lewis

There is economic development, and then there is the planning for economic development. While planning should precede action, this is not always the case. Indeed, planning is a relatively new concept in economic development. Actions like business attraction and industrial park construction have long been staples of the discipline—but often without the benefit of community-based planning. The trend, however, is forcibly toward more planning to support more comprehensive action.

St. Louis is both a leader and a follower in planning for economic development. Many planning initiatives of the last two decades in the metro area have demonstrated cutting-edge efforts in American economic development. The *St. Louis Economic Adjustment and Diversification Program* of 1991 (also known as the Defense Adjustment Plan) is a perfect example. Faced with massive job layoffs at McDonnell Douglas Corporation (now Boeing) because of large U.S. defense budget cuts, regional economic development officials in both Illinois and Missouri mounted a visionary review of economic development opportunities for the region. This bi-state, multicounty cooperation was virtually unprecedented, especially at that scale, not only for Greater St. Louis but for the nation. In many ways, this success story led to another visionary effort—formation of the Greater St. Louis Economic Development Council.

On the other hand, much of what passes for economic development planning in St. Louis is often more reactive than proactive—and often is neither, instead describing economic conditions without prescribing. But St. Louis has also found that planning and being proactive better prepares the region for those times when reaction is necessary.

Some economic development planning focuses on small-scale projects that, from a public sector point of view, simply play to the existing tax structure (e.g., retail projects to generate sales taxes, high job creation to generate earnings taxes, or high property values to generate real estate taxes) without attempts at diversifying the economy against business cycles. Other planning often focuses on immediate crises that might have been avoided with longer-term planning or that should have been used as a rationale to mount longer-term planning. All too often, economic development planning, or its implementation, is myopic for the presumed benefit of a single city or county but without consideration of regional, national, or global forces that affect and are affected by local economic circumstances.

Defining Economic Development

Before embarking on a review of trends in economic development planning in Greater St. Louis, it is important to define economic development and to describe broader forces in the still-emerging and relatively young discipline of economic development planning. While this summary is simplified, it describes the national, if not international, context of economic development within which Greater St. Louis, the nation's eighteenth-largest regional economy, has been operating.

Economic development is variously defined as wealth creation, job creation, land development, tax base enhancement, and other purposes that attempt to justify why economic development should be formally pursued at all. A specific definition is not necessary here because the primary purpose is to discuss historic trends during which formal definitions have also evolved. Today's generally accepted definition, which revolves around "wealth creation and sustainability," was not necessarily appropriate for earlier times. But, of course, a common theme is that people, corporations, and cities all pursue economic development generally to become richer.

The modern era of economic development starts with the post–World War II period. But its foundation goes back much further to the formation of cities. There is a great deal of literature and research that clearly equates the creation of human settlements, eventually to become cities and regions, with the need to promote economic development—though perhaps it is not stated quite so overtly. In effect, the whole became greater than the sum of the parts when specialized labor, pooled human and financial resources, and common defense, among other factors, enabled civilizations to advance the material and social well-being of humankind. Indeed, the entrepreneurial spirit thrives best where there are diverse resources and stable societies and where humans have the time and relative leisure to envision and pursue, profitably, a higher order of well-being. The organization of cities provided this context by removing people from subsistence living.

One can argue that the U.S. Declaration of Independence is a statement in support of economic development. "Life, liberty, and the pursuit of happiness" became the fundamentals of national governance and philosophy, defining government as a creator and protector of, in part, a probusiness climate. Certainly, common defense is a major factor in this regard, from the protection of shipping from piracy to opening western lands free of foreign incursions and hostile native peoples.[1] The central government and the states went even further, of course, by sponsoring and helping to finance major transportation systems such as canals, shipping ports, national roads, and railroads—many times imposing the constitutional eminent domain provision to justify transportation corridors "for public use." Such practices continue to the present with most transportation corridors in the United States (and globally, for that matter) built, financed, operated, regulated, and/ or subsidized by government. Few can argue that transportation networks do not promote economic development. All roads leading to Rome was purposeful for the empire's economic expansion and full employment of the citizenry, thus promoting material wealth while minimizing the chances for revolution. The United States is a great and diverse economy in no small part because of its intricate and expansive transportation networks.

It is those networks, in fact, that lay the cornerstone for economic development as a profession and, eventually, a public responsibility. Canal building, for example, required a great many financial resources that could be repaid, in part, by charging fees for use of the canal. Thus, it was necessary to find users—or to promote local economic development. This resulted in manufacturing plants, mills, shipbuilders, and haulers locating in what we might call, today, industrial parks adjacent to the canals. Communities actively sought such users in order to create jobs, exploit the transportation system, and generate tax revenues that, in turn, were directed toward improving the collective economic climate of the community. An owner or operator of a canal, therefore, sought economic development from a profit motivation or at least to pay back certain debts or to raise public revenues.

---

[1] The author does not necessarily condone some of the specific practices in the pursuit of the economic development component of Manifest Destiny, but the realities reflect an American priority for economic growth, whether moral or ethical in today's terms or not.

Railroads and electric utility companies followed suit. It is one thing to be chartered by the government to build a railroad or a power grid; it is another to have customers who will pay the freight over time. Railroad and utility companies, therefore, became aggressive economic developers in their own right. At the time, this was probably called "marketing" but, in fact, this marketing directly led to real estate development and, thus, economic development. Real estate assets added wealth to the owners and created places of employment for willing workers who, in turn, were paid for their services, often earning more than they could have as subsistence farmers or cottage businesses.

Many of the forces outlined above became even more focused in the United States and St. Louis after World War II. But they weren't evenly distributed. For the most part, the United States enjoyed world economic supremacy virtually into the 1970s. The nation couldn't help but grow economically since the world depended on U.S. managerial and labor capabilities. When things are going well, however, societies frequently fail to plan ahead and, therefore, fail to anticipate changes in the business cycle and, consequently fail to timely adapt to new circumstances.

Such was true for the nation as a whole, but not for all parts of the nation. Notably, many southern states had suffered economically since the Civil War and were not as prepared to contribute to the World War II effort as many other places. Much of the south, therefore, emerged in the late 1940s as still economically disadvantaged compared to places like Greater St. Louis, which prospered with strong manufacturing sectors (e.g., automobiles, chemicals, and aerospace), a capital of midwestern finance, a center of higher education, and with all the multiplier effects therefrom. Southern states, therefore, initiated the modern era of economic development by literally planning how to exploit the strengths they had. Strengths tended to be their relatively mild weather (though summer heat was a problem until air-conditioning became widespread in the 1960s), low-cost labor, plenty of land, and low taxes. The mantra of economic development became "business attraction," luring firms from other locales where costs, especially labor costs, were higher. A great migration of manufacturing facilities ensued, especially as firms tired of labor strife (and costs) and aging plants. The south offered lower cost, non-union labor with newer facilities.[2] Planning for economic development "from within" was rarely considered.

---

[2]This trend continues to this day, especially with the automobile assembly industry. But it less involves domestic automakers and more involves the attraction of foreign auto companies that are attracted because of low costs and because of U.S. import restrictions that, therefore, encourage production inside the United States.

Pressure mounted in other parts of the country to counter the migration. The race was on to "steal" firms from elsewhere in order to backfill locations where companies used to be located. If a manufacturer from St. Louis was lured to Mississippi, St. Louis authorities might try to attract existing firms from, say, New England—forwarding such advantages as lower cost labor in St. Louis (relative to New England, anyway), an existing business infrastructure, an experienced workforce, and so on. Too many localities and states, however, treated economic development as a zero-sum game, failing to either nurture internal growth or to equitably support their existing businesses.

This certainly was the basis of economic development as practiced by private railroads and utility companies. When firms they had served moved elsewhere, capacity in the local transportation and power networks deprived these railroads and utilities of major revenues, so it was in their interest to mount formal attraction programs.

Even today, Ameren, the St. Louis area (both Missouri and Illinois) electric utility company, maintains a sizable staff of trained economic developers. Their interests are clearly to support Ameren's current business electricity users, but these people are also active participants in regional economic development initiatives, both to contribute their expertise to the good of the whole and to obtain intelligence on economic development opportunities that might be exploited by Ameren itself.

Scores of Studies

Where was St. Louis as these trends and forces altered the U.S. economy? Right in the middle, for the most part. Little formal planning took place until the 1970s as St. Louis rode the wave of postwar American prosperity. Planning became ever more important, however, as St. Louis suffered from business out-migration—a consequence, in no small way, of a failure to modernize economic facilities, processes, and leadership.

As the graph in Figure 1 illustrates, population in metropolitan St. Louis[3] grew at the same pace as the national population between 1940 and almost 1970, as it had in many decades prior to World War II. As the nation's economy expanded, Greater St. Louis regularly got its fair share. Why plan for additional or different kinds of economic development? It seemed automatic.

---

[3]Metro St. Louis today is formally defined as comprising 16 counties, 8 in Illinois and 8 in Missouri. The data shown on the graph reflect all 16 counties for all of the years shown, even though the formally defined metro area in 1940 effectively consisted of just 4 or 5 of those counties.

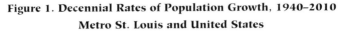

Figure 1. Decennial Rates of Population Growth, 1940–2010
Metro St. Louis and United States

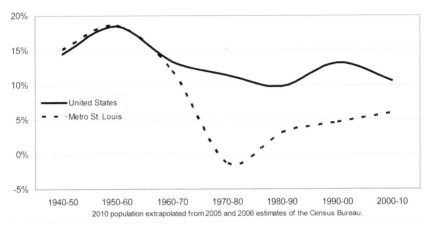

2010 population extrapolated from 2005 and 2006 estimates of the Census Bureau.

Until the late 1960s, the rest of the world started to become more competitive, especially in manufacturing, as new plants and equipment came online from postwar reinvestment. The south attracted St. Louis companies (and those from other "Rust Belt" cities) to newer and cheaper circumstances. Air-conditioning and the expanded interstate highway network leavened the trend. After growing as rapidly as the country for decades, metro St. Louis suddenly lost population in the 1970s. The region has been growing ever since, but at rates much below those of the nation.

An early attempt to address some of these changes was not a plan but a study of the metro St. Louis economy by Ben-Chieh Liu of the St. Louis Regional Industrial Development Corporation. His 1969 paper on St. Louis, *Employment Multipliers and Projections*, was a detailed approach to better understanding the underpinnings of the economy and how it could change during the coming decade. As it turned out, Liu quite accurately projected total employment for the year 1980 in the then five-county metro area at just over 1.2 million jobs. But he overstated the manufacturing sector by almost 100,000 jobs, projecting that manufacturing would remain the major job sector that it had been. Instead, the shift to non-manufacturing jobs was already under way, yet "hidden" in a sense even in the large amount of data that Liu had at hand.[4]

---

[4]Source of historic data on actual employment trends in metropolitan St. Louis is the U.S. Department of Commerce, Bureau of Economic Analysis, Regional Economic Information System (REIS), 1969 through 2004.

Hit hardest by these shifts was the City of St. Louis and, although less attention was paid to them at the time, the inner ring of St. Louis County and the river cities of Metro East. These were all locations of heavy manufacturing establishments and related sectors. As the American economy experienced enormous competitive adjustments in manufacturing, St. Louis was certainly among the most dramatically affected regional economies.

Thus, it is not surprising that the earliest efforts to plan for economic development start in the City. Again, when times are good, planning is often ignored. When times get tough, leaders try to determine what went wrong, unfortunately too often in hindsight, and how to swing the trend into a positive direction. An indicator of this change in approach was the lengthy process to prepare the *St. Louis Development Program* of 1973, a comprehensive planning process and set of documents that focused on the need for stemming urban decay and reattracting orderly growth in the City (St. Louis City Plan Commission 1973). The *Development Program* did not solely address economic development,[5] but it is clear that a driving force behind the need for the plan was not only the age of the existing comprehensive plan (1947) but also the need to address the many new ills affecting the City, including its declining labor force, out-migration of jobs, and rapidly deteriorating tax base.

For a variety of political reasons, this plan was never adopted by the Board of Aldermen as city policy, however, so planners and policymakers could` not officially follow the plan's recommendations. In hindsight, many of the economic-related findings and recommendations were acted upon nevertheless (notes from interviews of Bannister and Coleman), but the formal policy void also demanded that economic development planning be addressed without the baggage of other issues facing the city.

One answer was the report *Recycling of Urban Land and Economic Development Policy: St. Louis, A Case Study*, by the Economic Development Division of the St. Louis Community Development Agency (CDA) in 1975 (Langsdorf 1975). The *Recycling* report summarized a range of already-enabled economic development incentives available to St. Louis and how these might be more aggressively applied in the face of so much real estate abandonment. These incentives had been established by Missouri enabling legislation and, with some minor amendments since then, still exist and are used widely in St. Louis:

---

[5]It has a nine-page subchapter entitled "Economic Development Strategy," which was a meek, albeit early, attempt at approaching the true economic problems faced by the City at the time.

- The Land Reutilization Authority Law, Chapter 92.700-.920, RSMO (1969)

- The Land Clearance Law, Chapter 99.300-.660, RSMO (1969)

- The Missouri Redevelopment Law, Chapter 353, RSMO (1969), as amended

- The Planned Industrial Expansion Law, Chapter 100.300-.620, RSMO (1969), as amended.

Known more colloquially as simply LRA, LCRA (Land Clearance for Redevelopment Authority), 353, and PIEA (Planned Industrial Expansion Authority), respectfully, these state-enabled statutes were to be put to the test in subsequent years in order to promote growth and change in the City. Indeed, most were already used heavily as Missouri's contribution to the "urban renewal era" of postwar America. All of these are still relied on frequently today, not only in St. Louis but also in St. Louis County as its economy has likewise aged. A widely used addition to these laws is tax incremental financing (TIF), amended to Chapter 99, which has, for the most part, supplanted Chapter 353 as a primary incentive for private redevelopment projects.

Again, however, the *Recycling* report was more descriptive of conditions and tools not proscriptive in the form of a plan. The 1978 publication of *Economic Development Strategy Recommendations for the City of St. Louis* for CDA (Hammer, Siler, George Associates 1978) created such an agenda. As the consultants immediately pointed out, "the subject is a complex one" (Hammer, Siler, George Associates 1978). At almost 250 total pages, the complexities are dealt with rather comprehensively and result in a set of specific "major strategies." There was, for instance, a recommendation for development of a "Centrum Complex" as an "innovative, nine hundred-acre, multi-use activity complex" on the near north side "to create new jobs, new housing, and an expanded tax base" (Hammer, Siler, George Associates 1978). The plan also recommended acquisition of land for industrial development, employing "the city's structurally unemployed work force" to rehab as many as three thousand housing units per year, undertaking a demonstration program for adaptive reuse of downtown buildings, and pursuing a comprehensive neighborhood commercial district strategy—a recommendation that continues to be implemented (interview of Bannister). While impressive, these strategies partially overwhelmed a city that was already struggling with reduced public and private resources. Indeed, St. Louis wrestles with many similar issues today, especially in light of the lack of an appropriate federal urban policy that could help equalize resources for America's older cities (interviews of Bannister and Koepke).

The 1978 Hammer, Siler, George report, very importantly, also dealt more deeply with fundamentals of economic development, what the consultants termed the city's "economic development muscle." Actions and strategies are only part of the game; having the institutional structure to take action is, perhaps, more crucial. The consultants recommended, for instance, increasing the political and institutional capacities of the city, including greater integration of economic development planning with land use and transportation planning—a relatively new concept at the time to actually make economic development a formal component of city planning.

The same report also urged that the City increase its participation in regional planning to assure that maximum attention would be paid to the City's economic development needs through greater attention to regional utility and transportation systems and through cooperative efforts to attract federal economic development funds. If the integration of economic development with land planning was a new idea, conceiving of planning in the City within a regional context, let alone cooperatively with other jurisdictions, was almost radically different from past behavior. Moreover, the plan's recommendations go on to recommend more public-private collaboration in order to leverage more resources toward economic development.

In essence, these and other strategy recommendations directly addressed the profession's changing philosophy of economic development, from simply attracting someone else's firms to looking internally and building on the city's particular strengths and to working as a partner with other public entities and, increasingly, with private developers, employers, and the labor force. Economic development had never really been conducted that way in most places, however, especially in St. Louis.

The First Crisis Response Plan

These 1978 strategy recommendations were abruptly put to the challenge by the implosion of the American automobile industry during the recession of the early 1980s, which grew in part from the energy price hikes and gasoline shortages of the mid- to-late 1970s and America's slow response to the need for more fuel-efficient cars. Symbolic of the big but increasingly uncompetitive manufacturing sector of the United States, the auto industry's problems hit St. Louis hard. At the time, metro St. Louis was second only to metro Detroit in terms of the number of automobiles built (Team Four 1983a). There were six auto assembly lines in St. Louis. General Motors (GM) operated three aging plants at Union and Natural Bridge roads on the city's northwest side, including one that produced the famous Corvette sports car. These plants were becoming too small and too old to be competitive in the international market, so GM built a new plant "way out west" in Wentzville, Missouri, in an undeveloped part of St. Charles County,[6] and it relocated the Corvette manufacturing to Kentucky (one of those southern, or near-southern, states that was aggressively touting its low costs). Meanwhile, Ford Motor Company operated a plant in suburban Hazelwood that survived the 1980s crisis but was shuttered in 2006. And Chrysler had, and continues to operate (now under the DaimlerChrysler banner), two plants in suburban Fenton. Still, the recession effectively cost Greater St. Louis half of its auto-related jobs as out-migration and robotic technology reduced the labor force (Team Four 1983a). And the City of St. Louis lost virtually all of its auto-related manufacturing, including a number of major parts providers.

A response to this economic crisis was the *St. Louis Auto Community Adjustment Program* (ACAP), led by the consulting firm of Team Four (1983b). Overseen by the St. Louis CDA, this regionally based plan, funded mostly with federal dollars, delineated the problems facing the auto sector in the region, including the potential loss of thousands of skilled and experienced workers. It then identified a number of alternative "growth sectors" for which collective regional resources should be used in order to reemploy that labor force, thus retaining proven workers, while promoting growth in more promising sectors.

ACAP, however, was crisis-driven. But, through a regional planning process, involving all communities with auto-related businesses in the bi-state area, it was the region's first comprehensive economic development plan to cope with issues that readily transcended political boundaries. While the Hammer, Siler, George plan urged interconnectivity between economic development and other planning responsibilities along with more regional leadership by the City of St. Louis, ACAP tested the willingness of the City to be this regional leader and challenged the entire region to recognize that economic development planning was not an issue just for the aging city center but a high priority for everyone.

---

[6]Importantly, especially for long-term changes in the St. Louis area's approach to economic development planning, the metro area was able to retain this major auto plant when it could very well have been built somewhere else. The City lost the jobs while St. Charles County gained some, but this attests to GM's desire to continue using at least some of its experienced metro St. Louis area labor force.

Indeed, in the years following ACAP, both St. Louis County and St. Charles County markedly increased their economic development planning and implementation capacities with expanded agencies (St. Louis County Economic Council and St. Charles County Economic Development Corporation). The Leadership Council of Southwestern Illinois also formed in 1983 to unify economic development efforts in Madison and St. Clair counties (Koepke interview). Notably, these economic development organizations are at least partially independent of elected officials. Terms like *council* and *corporation* try to distinguish them from, say, departments or agencies under direct government management. The City's economic development, for instance, is managed by the St. Louis Development Corporation (SLDC) with oversight from the Mayor's Office but with a board of directors separate from the Board of Aldermen and with most employees not subject to the city's civil service rules. The St. Louis County Economic Council and the St. Charles County Economic Development Corporation have similar formations. The Leadership Council of Southwestern Illinois is, like the Regional Chamber and Growth Association (RCGA), a fully private organization, though both accept public agency memberships.

In other words, economic development in most of St. Louis (and many other parts of the country) has not yet become such an integrated part of planning that it has a "cabinet" position directly answerable to, say, the mayor or county executive. Still, economic development often is treated as "cabinet level" but is provided sufficient independence to insulate it from direct politics.

The population and job losses of the 1970s and the auto industry's shrinkage in the early 1980s put the scare into economic leaders of Greater St. Louis. Not only were economic development councils and corporations born in some cases, or nursed into adolescence in others, but a flurry of economic development planning and activity ensued. For instance, the St. Louis County Department of Planning began producing a series of annual reports on the County's economic development trends (St. Louis County Department of Planning 1984–1996). Not plans, exactly, but these status reports or profiles provided a great deal of information for planners, policy-makers, and the private sector in identifying forces and opportunities.

St. Louis County, of course, was looking out for itself, but other counties had help. The St. Louis Regional Commerce and Growth Association, now the St. Louis Regional Chamber and Growth Association, produced an *Economic History and Profile* for every county in the region as early as 1976 under contract with the East-West Gateway Coordinating Council (now the East-West Gateway Council of Governments). Again, these weren't plans but they offered consistent measures of economic status and history across all counties—useful for comparisons and, if so inclined, as a basis for strategic thinking. But strategic thinking was not yet a high priority as the region continued in a form of shock over the weakening of a once powerful and leading economic region.

A Push Toward Regional Planning

In addition to the auto industry recession, Greater St. Louis got a needed kick in the pants from what is informally known as the Fantus report and formally named *Regional Economic Development Study*, prepared for the RCGA by the management consulting firm Fantus, based in Chicago (Fantus Company 1981). This publication has three main parts:

- "Compendium of Selected Past Reports, 1975–1980," which reviews related plans, studies, reports, and profiles about all or parts of metro St. Louis in order to pull together common themes.

- "Regional Assessment of Assets and Liabilities," which builds on the compendium by clarifying the strengths and weaknesses of greater St. Louis so that strategic planning would have a foundation.

- "Economic Development Growth Strategy," which is, perhaps, the first comprehensive regional economic development plan for the metropolitan area.

Fantus shook St. Louis by proposing that a growth strategy should revolve primarily around "organizing for implementation of key economic development programs that have regional impact." Fantus cites the slightly earlier study by the Wright and Manning public relations firm that had reviewed thirty previous economic development–oriented studies of the City of St. Louis alone toward creation of a marketing campaign to attract jobs. Wright and Manning's conclusion was "that successful economic development must be a product of a comprehensive, coordinated effort." While Wright and Manning had focused on the City of St. Louis, Fantus effectively applied the same principles for the entire region. Fantus found that regional St. Louis was not organized, emphasized that it needed to move in that direction, and suggested means for doing so.

Fantus proposed that an "Economic Development Coordinating Council" be formed under RCGA leadership, including representation of all regional agencies.[7] The Council was to link academic, business, and labor interests to the RCGA, while the RCGA in turn would capture information from the Bi-State Development Agency (now called Metro), East-West Gateway, Southwestern Illinois Area Planning Commission (SWIMPAC), all the counties of the metropolitan area, both states, and, separately, the City of East St. Louis and Southern Illinois University at Edwardsville (SIUE).[8]

Fantus also suggested other strategies for regional economic development. One was to create attractive incentive features for industry on a regionwide scale. In other words, define incentives to lure business to Greater St. Louis, and the economy will diversify itself. Perhaps this idea has most manifested itself in the widespread use of state and federal tax credits for use in raising equity for certain types of developments (interviews of Koepke, Fleming, Johnson, and Leonard). Fantus further recommended the establishment of regionwide "growth increment tax sharing" that would encourage all jurisdictions to help all others because everyone would benefit from an equitable distribution of the "new" tax base. Alas, only St. Louis County has implemented such an idea, limited to local retail sales taxes, but this program does not go as far as Fantus would have liked.

Fantus also proposed "pollutant emission offsets to attract new manufacturers," a nod to the environmental pollution problems suffered by St. Louis while conceding that St. Louis's future still lay heavily in the manufacturing sector. The early 1980s recession that started just as the Fantus report was released, however, may have put an end to such projections.

Additional strategic recommendations of Fantus were to make far-reaching image improvements, to accelerate efforts to establish better labor-management relations, to stimulate foreign trade activity, and to enhance regional data retrieval mechanisms.

Image improvements became an immediate priority for the RCGA and what became the St. Louis Partnership, a poorly funded, early joint

---

[7]In effect, this council was finally created in 1994 as the Greater St. Louis Economic Development Council, as described later.

[8]Why the University of Missouri–St. Louis and other universities were not included is not explained in this 1981 document, but it is historically interesting to see that, while all counties and both states would be involved, Fantus chose also to call out three Illinois-only organizations: SIUE, East St. Louis, and SWIMPAC. Perhaps this reflects the relative lack of unified economic development leadership in Metro East at the time compared to Metro West prior to the 1983 formation of the Leadership Council Southwestern Illinois.

initiative of the RCGA, St. Louis County, and the City of St. Louis to demonstrate regionalism in economic development (interview with Joyner). Emerging from the Partnership's efforts were such programs as "Sold On St. Louis," which was largely aimed at regional St. Louisans in order to encourage positive thinking about the region and thereby to create a couple of million "ambassadors" for St. Louis (Kittner et al. 1993; Greenburg et al. 1993). The Partnership also made early efforts to create a common "lead tracking" system wherein information learned by one jurisdiction about a possible corporate location or expansion in greater St. Louis could be shared with others so that joint marketing could reinforce the unification of the region. Lead tracking also attempted to create a common data system that every jurisdiction could utilize (interviews with Joyner, Ward, Fleming).

Image building remains a regional priority, as demonstrated by the increased presence of St. Louis on "best places" lists (Fleming interview). The "St! Lou¡s: Perfectly Centered, Remarkably Connected" campaign continues this clever promotion of the region (Johnson interview). Lead tracking also remains a priority, though the proprietary nature of most such information keeps it from the public spotlight.

A key lesson from these efforts was that a tremendous amount of trust had to be developed between all the economic development organizations of the region, if the programs were going to succeed. Sharing information with another county, for instance, might be ceding competitive advantage in case that other county wanted to make independent overtures to the prospect corporation. Pooling resources to sell a common, positive image also had to overcome perceptions that regional resources would just be used to advance the interests of Downtown St. Louis or the entire City of St. Louis since these locations represent the middle of the region, where most outsiders obtain their strongest and earliest images of the region. Quite quickly, then, trust or lack thereof became an obstacle to regional organization, something that the Fantus Company said was paramount for successful economic development.

Also in 1981, the City of St. Louis formed a Task Force on Economic Development that advised the new mayor, Vincent C. Schoemehl Jr. on actions that city government needed to take to stem the tide of net economic disinvestments (St. Louis Task Force on Economic Development 1981). Building in large part on the *Economic Development Strategy Recommendations* from 1978 (Hammer, Siler, George Associates 1978), the task force outlined specific steps that City Hall should undertake, including a comprehensive communications program to assure that all relevant departments and agencies had sufficient information to act quickly, decisively, and collectively to exploit an opportunity or avoid a major problem. The task force also suggested creation of special taxing districts where extra funds could be used for added services. One outcome of this recommendation was that the Missouri Community Improvement District (CID) enabled legislation (Ward interview). The task force further recommended certain public relations efforts, creation of enterprise zones that would allow businesses to take advantage of a range of state and federal incentives, and more aggressive use of general obligation bonds to improve the City's economic infrastructure.

Partly in response to this pressure for better regional cooperation and how to get there, the three entities composing the St. Louis Partnership— St. Louis City, St. Louis County, and RCGA—commissioned a comprehensive economic development study on "regional best practices" (Joyner interview; Team Four Research 1986). The goal was to identify regional economic development best practices in other metropolitan areas and to borrow the best ideas for implementation in Greater St. Louis.

Three regions emerged as having components of what could be an ideal economic development organization for St. Louis. The Kansas City area had implemented a model information sharing, or lead tracking, system. Greater Cleveland had the best, if early, network of economic development organizations, and the Philadelphia area had, at the time, the best corporate-led economic development model for promoting the region. All three, moreover, were years ahead of St. Louis, as were about ten others that were studied less broadly, in regional cooperation, marketing, and strategic planning (Team Four Research 1986).

The plan that emerged from this study for the St. Louis Partnership was hard hitting and radical for the metropolitan area, but no organization had, or was willing to put up, the resources necessary to implement the recommendations—yet. Sometimes plans simply may be ahead of their times (Chicago is still implementing the "Burnham Plan" of the early 1900s while Washington, D.C., continues to implement the principles of the "L'Enfant Plan" commissioned by President George Washington). As it turned out, the regional plan for St. Louis found traction a few years later, but that story awaits other notable advances in economic development planning.

Other organizations got into the act. The relatively new Confluence St. Louis produced a detailed task force report, *Entrepreneurship in Metropolitan St. Louis* (Confluence St. Louis 1985). Starting with a premise that had been painstakingly researched for the ACAP a couple of years earlier, Confluence urged regional action to promote small business growth since small businesses were proven to be the most significant job creators in the American economy. One result of such efforts has been the emergence of business incubators in the region—two in the City of St. Louis, three in St. Louis County, and one in St. Charles County (Coleman, Koepke interviews). Another was longer in coming but built on the same entrepreneurship findings to support business growth in the inner city. The *St. Louis Inner City Competitive Assessment and Strategy Project* of 2000 took the findings of a national study on overlooked inner city competitiveness by the Initiative for a Competitive Inner City (ICIC) and applied them to St. Louis through a new organization hosted by the RCGA.

The United Way of Greater St. Louis prepared a series of socio-economic profiles of the region's counties in an effort to better inform social service agencies about conditions and trends affecting their clientele, especially those losing jobs because they no longer had skills in demand. Confluence St. Louis's successor, FOCUS St. Louis, produced a task force report in 2001 titled *Preparing the St. Louis Region for the 21st Century Economy*. FOCUS determined that the most important factor to address was the region's ability to attract and retain "younger adults," those in their twenties and thirties, in order to create economic demand for "fresh ideas" and to build a cadre of young leaders devoted to St. Louis who would become the top leaders of business and civic life in years to come. Metro St. Louis ranks near the bottom of major metro areas in the number and retention of younger adults in the economy, as many who grow up and/or attend college in St. Louis are attracted to other regions perceived as more conducive to their lifestyles.

In 2004, RegionWise, an organization formed by the Danforth Foundation to promote regional thinking and cooperation, produced a report on economic development strategy in St. Louis by assessing key industry sectors that should be the strengths of the region on which to build a stronger and more self-sustainable economy. In fact, RegionWise evaluated in some crucial detail the sectors that were already the primary marketing and planning focus of the RCGA (Leonard interview).

St. Louis 2004, an organization also initiated by the Danforth Foundation, got into the act itself in October 1997 with a summary of studies on technology-based economic development in St. Louis between 1991 and 1997. During that period, the report's author, Eva Klein and Associates, identified almost thirty tech-based reports, plans, and studies that had been conducted or were under way. This was a clear sign that economic development planning in Greater St. Louis was growing in sophistication with an awareness of the need to be thinking about future forces in the world, not about past glories.

Thus, the interest in planning for Greater St. Louis's economic future is not limited to the formal economic development organizations. Still, that's where the biggest resources for planning and implementation lie. In the mid-1980s, as the region was still trying to figure out how to emerge from the malaise of economic stagnation when compared to many other regions, the RCGA sponsored several of its own "strategic task forces" that studied opportunities for growth in four discrete, though certainly interconnected, sectors affecting regional competitiveness:

- Transportation, which studied the networks of systems for moving people and goods into, out of, and around St. Louis with the added advantage of being located at the population center of the United States (RCGA Transportation Task Force 1986).

- Government affairs, which addressed the "fragmentation" of local government in Greater St. Louis, how this both hindered and helped economic development, and how the two states and various localities could better work together to promote economic development (RCGA Government Affairs Task Force 1986).

- Labor, which concluded that successful, homegrown programs to improve labor management relations in several sectors needed to be promoted outside of St. Louis to enhance the region's economic development image (RCGA Labor Task Force 1986).

- Technology, which identified metro St. Louis as a "major Midwest research cluster" and recommended a series of technology initiatives for improving the Missouri Research Park in St. Charles County, finding a permanent home for what was then called the St. Louis Technology Center (now the Center for Emerging Technologies in midtown St. Louis), and assisting SIUE with its research park, among other ideas (RCGA Strategic Task Force on Technology 1986).

These task forces were, essentially, a prelude to what is now an on-going program of the RCGA, through the Greater St. Louis Economic Development Council, to periodically review key growth sectors in the world economy and what St. Louis contributes to those sectors so that they can be expanded and reinforced through overt economic development initiatives. The life and plant science sector today is perhaps the most notable of these targeted industries pursued by RCGA for the benefit of the region, but there are four others that currently have plans being implemented at various stages (Fleming, Johnson, and Leonard interviews): St. Louis as a regional financial center, St. Louis as an international logistics hub (transportation and distribution), St. Louis as a center of advanced manufacturing (high-tech processes and highly paid labor force), and St. Louis as an information technology center.

Simultaneously, Metro East began a study of its own strengths. Under the umbrella of the Southwestern Illinois Corridor Council, the consulting firm of Laventhol And Horwath produced *Linked Industry Identification Study* (1987) that identified how Metro East economic sectors were intertwined not only internally but with the greater region and the State of Illinois. The intent was to better understand where and how Metro East might exploit its own economic strengths to support other parts of the regional economy while empowering some of its own companies with knowledge for business opportunities.

The Second Crisis Response Plan

These exciting initiatives were interrupted by negative economic consequences of the end to the Cold War. With the demise of the Iron Curtain and related improvements in international governance, the U.S. Department of Defense, which had expanded spending in part to put an end to the Cold War, began cutting unnecessary expenses in the late 1980s. The impact on St. Louis was a pending massive layoff of thousands of highly educated and experienced aerospace and fighter aircraft workers at McDonnell Douglas Corporation (now part of the Boeing Company) in St. Louis and St. Charles counties, with all the attendant negative ripple effects on households, suppliers, retailers, and so on. The region certainly did not want to lose thousands of good workers, so the St. Louis County Economic Council was able to obtain planning funds from the federal government to study the possible impacts and to identify actions to ameliorate them. The Economic Council, in turn, convened economic development officials from the entire bi-state region to address the issue collectively since the ripple effects would spread across many jurisdictions. The Economic Council hired a consulting team led by Development Strategies, Inc., to assist in the research, analysis, and recommendations (Development Strategies, Inc., et al. 1991).

This was the most extensive and comprehensive economic development planning effort ever undertaken in metro St. Louis (Coleman interview).

Surveys were conducted of displaced workers and of defense contractors in the region. Forecasts of economic and occupational trends were produced. Other defense-dependent regions were studied. Opportunities in international business growth were identified. The region's business development and labor force assistance programs, including existing incubators, were evaluated. An extensive assessment of the region's information technology was conducted, and it discovered, remarkably, that St. Louis, most specifically Washington University, was a national leader in the development of technology that was the early throes of the internet.

As a result, the plan published in November 1991 unveiled an aggressive program of economic development changes in the region (Coleman, Fleming, Anderson, Johnson, and Leonard interviews). The World Trade Center of St. Louis was established in Clayton to expand and support St. Louis businesses in international opportunities. The business incubator program was expanded, in part to address the survey finding that 5 percent of laid-off McDonnell Douglas workers had started their own businesses. Regional job training and placement clearinghouse activities were coordinated, especially within the community college network. Venture capital and related business financing voids were identified and means adopted to expand the network of investors. A technology transfer program was initiated to more efficiently link academic research with commercial applications in St. Louis. A biomedical/technology incubator was proposed and soon became the Nidus Center on the Monsanto campus in Creve Coeur; it was soon followed by the Donald Danforth Plant Sciences Center, also on Monsanto-owned land. Relatedly, more intensive efforts were put into the transformation of the "triangle" between the Washington University Medical Center, the Saint Louis University Medical Center, and the Missouri Botanical Garden into a biomedical "technopolis," a project that is now in full swing and renamed Cortex (Ward interview).

More mundane but crucial economic development activities were reinforced and expanded, too. The network of the region's economic development professionals that sponsored the "Defense Adjustment Plan" continued to meet right away as the St. Louis Regional Economic Adjustment and Diversification Committee but eventually it became the foundation for the Greater St. Louis Economic Development Network under the yet-to-come Greater St. Louis Economic Development Council. As a result, regional economic progress is more routinely and thoroughly monitored than in the past while state and federal legislative priorities to support regional economic development are now more unified.

Engaging the Private Sector

None of this may have resulted if a more structured—and private sector driven—solution had not emerged. A clear outcome of the Defense Adjustment Plan was that the Greater St. Louis economic development professionals were both willing and able to act collectively for the good of the whole. But that effort had been led by St. Louis County, not necessarily a neutral participant in regional matters. The permanent solution had to be taken on by a regional body. In this case, the Regional Chamber and Growth Association took up the charge, though not without a great deal of disruption in the old ways of doing things.

Notably missing from much of the defense adjustment planning process was, in fact, the RCGA. Not only its leadership, but even significant participation of staff was almost conspicuous by its absence. The RCGA had initiated the various technology task forces in the mid-1980s but did not carry this momentum to higher levels. It seemed to relegate one of the biggest regional economic crises ever experienced in St. Louis—the McDonnell Douglas downsizing—to public sector economic development authorities. That is, the primary private sector business organization in the region was a weak and reluctant player.

After the Defense Adjustment plan's completion, new leadership took over the RCGA's board of directors, chaired by Earl Harbison, recently of Monsanto and, by the early 1990s, in business for himself. A man with worldwide business experience, Harbison quickly realized that regional economic development in St. Louis was in its infancy at best and that the RCGA itself was barely in the game. He insisted on improvements, and two previous planning efforts helped him to realize the goal.

One was the defense adjustment planning process itself. That process had demonstrated that capable regional leaders were able to address the region's common problems logically, objectively, and equitably. But the private sector had not been a strong presence even though the private sector makes up more than 80 percent of the economy.

The other planning effort was the outcome of the comparative best practices plan sponsored by the St. Louis Partnership in the late 1980s (Team Four Research 1986). Harbison had it dusted off and effectively re-validated by graduate business students at Washington University. Most of those best practice findings were reinforced and provided new energy under the wing of a now-reorganizing RCGA.

Harbison also realized that plans and professionals weren't enough. The top leadership of the region needed to be spearheading economic development; economic development simply had to be a top priority for the top people. Thus, he led formation of a new organization, to be housed and managed by the RCGA, called the Greater St. Louis Economic Development Council (GSLEDC). The Council was to include two private sector members of Civic Progress, the region's organization of top corporate, academic, and political chief executives. It would also include the chief political leaders of the larger counties in the region along with representation from organized labor, small business organizations, and the like. The initial GSLEDC included eleven of the region's most notable business and government leaders from both states.

Harbison went further. He recognized that these leaders may be brilliant at their jobs, but that they knew relatively little about regional economic development. He, therefore, put them through a five-course training program, led by Development Strategies, to "teach" them about the Greater St. Louis economy, the importance of metropolitan areas as economic entities, and how regional economic development should be addressed. The Council, as a result, became the most powerful advocate of economic development in Greater St. Louis.

As the GSLEDC was incorporated, it was necessary to hire professional leadership, a process that attracted Richard C. D. Fleming to St. Louis from similar posts held in Denver and Atlanta. Fleming, who was hired in 1994 and was still the CEO of RCGA in mid-2007, assumed the role as the region's principal economic development official while also taking on the leadership of the region's largest chamber of commerce. The formal *Strategic Plan for Economic Development* of the GSLEDC was published in 1995 with six primary objectives focused on world trade, tourism and conventions, technology development, transportation and distribution, business attraction of targeted economic sectors (headquarters operations, high-performance manufacturing, and financial services), and a high-quality labor force.

But planning did not entirely shift to RCGA. A remarkable effort was initiated in the early 1990s to focus this region more intently on its growth in high technology. Under the administration of President George H. W. Bush in the late 1980s and early 1990s, two biannual national panels were convened of top scientists in the nation to identify the "critical technologies" of the future where the United States could and should play the leading roles. A major intent of these panels was to assure that the United States maintained its leadership in technology growth and that national resources were funneled where they would have the most leverage.

Unfortunately, these studies were ended with the Clinton administration, but the second panel was chaired by a St. Louis scientist, Dr. William

Phillips, of Washington University. His acquaintance with then CEO of Monsanto, Richard Mahoney, led to an in-depth study of the critical technologies available in Greater St. Louis.[9] In essence, Mahoney asked experts in metro St. Louis to study the national critical technologies and to identify which of those were strengths in St. Louis. Six major categories emerged, which became six task forces of academic and corporate scientists and researchers that met to discuss the capabilities of Greater St. Louis. From these were to emerge recommendations for national growth on a number of fronts that, of course, could lead to regional growth as well (Development Strategies, Inc., and Phillips 1993).

With the termination of the national critical technologies panels, however, the depth of review of technology capacity in St. Louis faltered as well. But this does not mean that technology is not studied and pursued. Quite the contrary. RCGA, in particular, continues to evaluate international trends and forces with a particular emphasis on the strengths that St. Louis can offer for growth in that technology while also leading to job creation and economic development in St. Louis (Fleming, Johnson interviews). As noted earlier, such evaluations presently support priority initiatives of the region in biotechnology, advanced (high-tech process and equipment) manufacturing, and information technology.

Planning Through Networking

Perhaps the most important element in the evolution of economic development planning in St. Louis has been the growth in cooperative meetings, actions, communications, and decision-making on opportunities or threats affecting the entire region (Coleman, Koepke, Fleming interviews). The dramatic drop in the national economic leadership of Greater St. Louis during the 1960s caught everyone off guard and it did not affect just the central city. All parts of the region suffered because the labor force lives all over the region, and small businesses that supply the big businesses are all over the region, and the retailers where household income is spent are all over the region. The recession of the early 1980s opened regional eyes about this collective problem. The defense cutbacks, combined with a national recession of the early 1990s, pulled regional

---

[9]Greater St. Louis, in this case, extended to the University of Illinois at Urbana-Champaign and the University of Missouri–Columbia because of their scale, research capacities, and vital role in supporting the St. Louis economy.

economic developers together. With obvious success emanating from a well-conceived and jointly sponsored plan, St. Louis was well on its way as a national example of regional cooperation.

This cooperation is the mantra of the Greater St. Louis Economic Development Council. But it is probably no better embodied than in the Greater St. Louis Economic Development Network, which is the group of professionals whose job it is to promote economic development on a day-to-day basis from every corner of the metropolitan area. By meeting and communicating regularly, the Network has been a powerful tool for achieving economic diversification and growth.

The threatened closure of the Ford Motor Company's assembly plant in Hazelwood in 2002 is an example of how this networking can play out. The plant's closure was delayed for a few years by the immediate response of the City of Hazelwood, St. Louis County, RCGA, and Missouri officials who, by now, were accustomed to communicating with one another. This history enabled all officials to move swiftly and cooperatively, having established that ever-important trust from years of meeting together on common issues. One notable result was passage of needed incentives by the Missouri General Assembly much more quickly than is the legislature's habit.

Note, however, that these efforts did not prevent the plant's closure, which finally occurred in 2006. In part, the network of economic developers foresaw that closure was inevitable in light of Ford's own corporate financial difficulties. But the team of officials working on the project used the opportunity to plan for other improvements in north St. Louis County, where the plant is located, and to obtain at least starter funding for such improvements. Chief among these may be a revised roadway network that can better serve the needs of manufacturers and their suppliers, thus making the Hazelwood area more competitive, especially in light of the RCGA's current emphasis on transportation logistics as a strength for Greater St. Louis.

Networking goes further. The regional network's success demonstrated to St. Louis County officials that the region was better prepared for a collective crisis than the municipalities in the County itself. Thus, in 2006, the St. Louis County Economic Council initiated the St. Louis County Economic Development Collaborative (Leezer interview). The Collaborative is a network of economic development officials from every city and chamber of commerce throughout the County. Its goal, like the regional network, is to improve communications and response so that opportunities and challenges within the County can be more efficiently addressed. Much of the agenda for the Collaborative lies in the *St. Louis*

County Comprehensive Economic Development Strategy, or CEDS (Development Strategies, Inc., 2005). CEDS is a national program promoted through the U.S. Department of Housing and Urban Development to encourage communities to adopt economic development plans. CEDS enables easier access to federal funds for those locales that have adopted them—including five-year updates. St. Louis County, in fact, relied on the 1991 Defense Adjustment plan as its CEDS that year and for two subsequent updates, but commissioned a full review of the county's economy for the latest edition (Coleman interview).

That most recent CEDS purposefully involved substantial input from the public and, notably, from the various chambers of commerce and incorporated cities in the county. Acting on a clearly identified need, therefore, the Economic Council created the Collaborative to continue this all-important dialogue and trust-building among the county's business and political leaders.

Greater St. Louis has come a long way in economic development planning. From virtually none at all while the region grew despite itself, to floundering for many years to find a better way, to a clear recognition that comprehensive planning is vital to long-term regional prosperity, St. Louis has benefited from broad-based leadership that, though often mal-informed and even occasionally lost in the mire, remained determined to regain an economic leadership position for the region. Cooperative planning, even under competitive conditions, has matured well in St. Louis. Still, planning is only a beginning and, while having to be renewed now and then, it is the implementation of good plans that reveals economic development advances. Forty years of trial and error have helped to identify the best means for progress.

Acknowledgments

The author interviewed the following people for background on the history and changes in economic development planning in metro St. Louis. Many thanks go to each and every one of them for insights they provided, perhaps often without knowing they did so. The economic development professionals in St. Louis represent the best in skills, knowledge, experience, and dedication. Their assistance and professional collegiality are greatly appreciated.

Steven J. Anderson, Vice President, Business Development, St. Louis County Economic Council

Patrick M. Bannister, Director of Economic Development, St. Louis Development Corporation

Dennis G. Coleman, CEcD, President and CEO, St. Louis County Economic Council

Richard C. D. Fleming, President and CEO, St. Louis Regional Chamber and Growth Association

Karin M. Hagaman, CEcD, Associate, Development Strategies

Steven S. Johnson, CEcD, Senior Vice President for Economic Development, St. Louis Regional Chamber & Growth Association

Dee Joyner, Senior Vice President, Director of Organizational Development and Community Relations, Commerce Bank of St. Louis

Michael S. Kearney, CEcD, Manager of Economic Development, Ameren Services

Robert L. Koepke, PhD, CEcD, Retired, Southern Illinois University at Edwardsville

David A. Leezer, CEcD, Vice President, Economic Development Collaborative, St. Louis County Economic Council

Linda Leonard, CEcD, Vice President for Economic Development, St. Louis Regional Chamber & Growth Association

Libbey R. Malberg, CEcD, Assistant City Administrator for Economic and Community Development, City of Chesterfield, Missouri

Michael J. Pierceall, CEcD, AICP, Executive Director, Alliance for Edwardsville & Glen Carbon, Illinois

Richard C. Ward, CEcD, AICP, Senior Principal, Development Strategies

References
Confluence St. Louis (now FOCUS St. Louis). *Entrepreneurship in Metropolitan St. Louis: A Report of the Entrepreneurship Task Force,* October 16, 1985.
Development Strategies, Inc. *Report on the Feasiblity of a St. Louis Biomedical Technopolis.* Prepared for the St. Louis Development Corporation. February 1992.
———. *St. Louis County Comprehensive Economic Development Strategy.* Prepared for the St. Louis County Economic Council. 2005.
——— and Dr. William D. Phillips. *Report of the St. Louis Critical Technologies Task Force and Appendices.* Sponsored by Civic Progress, Inc., and the St. Louis Regional Economic Adjustment & Diversification Committee, September 1993.
——— et al. *St. Louis Economic Adjustment and Diversification Program.* Prepared for the St. Louis Economic Adjustment and Diversification Task Force. November 1991.
Eva Klein & Associates. *Technology-Based Economic Development in St. Louis: Summary of Studies 1991 to 1997.* Prepared for St. Louis 2004. October 1997.
Fantus Company. *Regional Economic Development Study.* Prepared for the St. Louis Regional Commerce and Growth Association. May 27, 1981.
FOCUS St. Louis. *Preparing St. Louis for Leadership in the 21st Century Economy.* St. Louis: Author, July 2002.
Franklin County, Missouri. *Overall Economic Development Program (OEDP).* November 1995.
Greater St. Louis Economic Development Council (GSLEDC). *A Strategic Plan for Economic Development.* St. Louis: Author, 1995.

Greenberg, James A., et al. *Sold On St. Louis—Best Image: An Analytical Approach to City Image.* St. Louis: Washington University John M. Olin School of Business, 1993.

Hammer, Siler, George Associates. *Economic Development Strategy Recommendations for the City of St. Louis.* Prepared for the Community Development Agency, City of St. Louis, Missouri. June 1978.

Initiative for a Competitive Inner City (ICIC). *St. Louis Inner City Competitive Assessment and Strategy Project: Creating Jobs, Income, and Wealth in the Inner City.* St. Louis: Author, September 2000.

Kittner, Dorothy, Jometric McIntyre, Ingrid Ruiz, and David Weiss. *Sold On St. Louis Marketing Strategies Best Practices.* St. Louis: Washington University John M. Olin School of Business, December 21, 1993.

Langsdorf, Kenneth R. *Recycling of Urban Land and Economic Development Policy: St. Louis, A Case Study.* Economic Development Division, St. Louis Community Development Agency. Working paper developed for a National Council for Urban Economic Development seminar in St. Louis, April 17–18, 1975.

Laslo, David H. *Economic Development Strategy in St. Louis: An Assessment of Key Industry Clusters.* Prepared for RegionWise by the Metropolitan Information and Data Analysis Services, Public Policy Research Center, University of Missouri–St. Louis. February 2004.

Laventhol & Horwath. *Linked Industry Identification Study.* Prepared for the Southwestern Illinois Corridor Council. July 1987.

Liu, Ben-Chieh. *Employment Multipliers and Employment Projections: An Economic Base Study for the St. Louis Region.* Prepared for the East-West Gateway Coordinating Council. Paper presented at the Annual Meeting of the Missouri Academy of Sciences, May 5, 1969.

McCarthy & Associates, Inc. *A Mandate for Strategic Action: 2004–2008.* Prepared for the St. Louis County Economic Council. June 2003.

RCGA Governmental Affairs Task Force. *Report of the RCGA Governmental Affairs Task Force.* St. Louis: Author, November 19, 1986.

RCGA Labor Task Force and Michael F. Shanahan. *Report of the RCGA Labor Task Force: St. Louis Regional Commerce and Growth Association.* St. Louis: Author, October 23, 1986.

RCGA Strategic Task Force on Technology. *Report of the RCGA Strategic Task Force on Technology.* St. Louis: Author, November 19, 1986.

RCGA Transportation Task Force. *Report of the RCGA Transportation Task Force.* St. Louis: Author, November 19, 1986.

Sedway Group. *St. Louis Economic Development Strategic Plan.* Prepared for the St. Louis Development Corporation. February 1999.

St. Louis City Plan Commission. *St. Louis Development Program.* June 1973.

St. Louis County Economic Council. *Comprehensive Economic Development Strategy.* June 2003.

———. *Comprehensive Economic Development Strategy: St. Louis Economic Adjustment and Diversification Program 1991–1999.* St. Louis: Author, updated August 1999.

St. Louis County Economic Development Study Committee. *St. Louis County Economic Development Report.* St. Louis: Author, January 1982.

St. Louis County Planning Commission. *St. Louis County Economic Development Report.* St. Louis: Author, December 7, 1981.

St. Louis Regional Commerce & Growth Association. *Campaign for a Greater St. Louis Business Development Plan: 1995–1996.* St. Louis: Author, October 17, 1995.

———. *Economic History and Profile of Jefferson County, Missouri.* Prepared for East-West Gateway Coordinating Council, June 30, 1976.

———. *Economic History and Profile of St. Charles County, Missouri.* Prepared for East-West Gateway Coordinating Council. June 30, 1976.

St. Louis Task Force on Economic Development. *Report to the Mayor: Vincent C. Schoemehl, Jr.* October 1981.

Team Four, Inc. *St. Louis Technology Center: Summary Location Analysis and Facility Evaluation and a Proposal for an Urban Science and Innovation Center.* Prepared for the Regional Commerce & Growth Association High Tech Task Force. 1983a.

Team Four Planning & Economic Research Consultants. *St. Louis Auto Community Adjustment Program.* 3 vols. Prepared for the City of St. Louis, Missouri, Community Development Agency. January 1983b.

Team Four Research. *Update Report: St. Louis Auto Community Adjustment Program.* Prepared for the St. Louis Office of Business Development. September 1986.

Wright & Manning, Inc., Price Waterhouse & Co., and Team Four, Inc. *Job Retention and Creation: A Marketing and Promotional Program for the City of St. Louis.* First Interim Report and Appendices prepared for the St. Louis Community Development Agency and Local Development Company. November 1979.

Chapter 9
Aspects of Educational Planning for Public Schools in St. Louis County

Carole Murphy
Helene Sherman
Chris Wright
Diana Bourisaw

Introduction

The most important resource we have in St. Louis County is our children. The ways in which we plan for our schools and for the preparation of future school leaders and teachers is extremely important to educate all students to achieve their fullest potential. It is impossible to discuss the educational planning that is taking place in St. Louis County without some understanding of what is happening statewide and nationally. Mandates from the federal government such as No Child Left Behind and State of Missouri certification and standard requirements impact every decision in the planning process. Although in this chapter we will focus on St. Louis County and St. Louis Public Schools, most of what we present is also applicable to schools across the state.

To begin this discussion, we must ask some important questions: Can public schools meet the growing educational needs of students in the face of societal and global trends, and can public schools continue to have relevance, maintain adequate funding levels, and meet the ever-increasing demands of federal, state, and local mandates? The way we answer these questions will determine the future success of our local public school systems (MacDonald 2006, 669).

Today's school leaders and teachers face many challenges. They must address local, state, and federal reform initiatives. They must deal with competition from charter and "for-profit" schools, as well as from home-schooling, vouchers, and school choice. School leaders must handle negative media attention and an increase in diverse populations with varied student needs while dealing with lower public financial support. And most important, they must be accountable for the success of the children under their care. These challenges require insightful planning and knowledgeable leadership from both administrators and teachers (MacDonald 2006).

In this chapter we present the aspects of educational planning that contribute to successful schools, and the preparation of effective school administrators and teachers. Successful schools cannot go it alone. Springer (2006) discusses the ramifications of who controls education in his book *American Education*. He states that the important thing to understand is that the political structure of education determines the content of education that in turn directly affects what a student learns (Springer 2006, 182). This understanding has implication for community educational leaders as they work to meet local, state, and federal requirements while involving all of the community's stakeholders in the planning process.

This chapter is divided into four parts and will focus on changes that are impacting St. Louis County and City schools. Part 1 discusses the preparation of school leaders and is written by Dr. Carole Murphy, associate professor and former chair of the Division of Educational Leadership and Policy Studies, College of Education, University of Missouri–St. Louis. Part 2 discusses teacher preparation and its impact on St. Louis County and City and is written by Dr. Helene Sherman, associate dean for Undergraduate Education and professor in the College of Education, University of Missouri–St. Louis. Part 3 is written by Dr. Chris Wright, superintendent, Hazelwood School District, and discusses the planning that is taking place by superintendents in St. Louis County suburban schools. Dr. Diana Bourisaw, superintendent of the St. Louis Public Schools, writes Part 4. Dr. Bourisaw discusses her vision for the St. Louis Public Schools and the plans that are being implemented to raise academic achievement.

Part 1: Preparing Administrators for Tomorrow's Schools

In an attempt to improve the preparation of principals and superintendents in the state, the Missouri Department of Elementary and Secondary Education (DESE) has, along with other stakeholders, created a statewide planning committee. Five St. Louis County universities currently participate in this planning effort. They are the University of Missouri–St. Louis (UMSL), St. Louis University (SLU), Webster University, Maryville University, and Missouri Baptist University. St. Charles County is represented in this cooperative planning effort by Lindenwood University.

St. Louis County consists of twenty-three school districts (see Table 1), plus the Special School District and St. Louis Public Schools (SLPS). Because of its size, data regarding the SLPS system are normally documented separately from other St. Louis County school districts. However, for the purpose of this chapter, it will be included as part of St. Louis County. These twenty-five school districts have a total of 60 high schools, 10 junior highs, 51 middle schools, and 240 elementary schools. One hundred and eighty-seven thousand, six hundred and thirty-three (187,633) children are served by public schools in St. Louis City and County. Combined, they spend $45,303,453,834 on education (see Table 2). This count does not include charter schools, private schools, or children who are home-schooled (DESE 2006).

Table 1. Number of Schools in St. Louis County

St. Louis County School Districts	No. Elem. Schools	No. Middle Schools	No. Jr. High Schools	No. High Schools	Total No. Students
Affton	2	1	0	1	2,507
Bayless	2	0	1	1	1,592
Brentwood	2	1	0	1	816
Clayton	4	1	0	1	2,529
Ferguson-Florissant	18	3	0	3	12,869
Hancock Place	1	1	0	1	1,855
Hazelwood	20	0	3	4	19,556
Jennings	5	0	1	1	3,264
Kirkwood	6	2	0	1	5,303
Ladue	4	1	0	1	3,357
Lindbergh	5	1	0	1	5,479
Maplewood-Richmond Heights	2	1	0	1	971
Mehlville	10	4	0	2	11,308
Normandy	8	1	0	2	5,526
Parkway	18	5	0	5	18,787
Pattonville	8	2	0	1	5,994
Ritenour	6	2	0	1	5,887
Riverview Gardens	11	1	0	1	8,096
Rockwood	20	6	0	4	22,326
Special School District	7	0	0	3	2,105
University City	7	0	1	1	3,674
Valley Park	1	1	0	1	1,042
Webster Groves	8	1	0	1	1,355
Wellston	2	1	0	1	622
St. Louis	63	15	4	20	40,813
Total	**240**	**51**	**10**	**60**	**187,633**

Source: 2006–2007 Missouri School Directory.

Table 2. St. Louis County Schools' Tax Assessment Valuation

St. Louis County School Districts	Tax Levy	Assessed Valuation
Affton	5.0811	377,812,480
Bayless	3.5800	160,617,960
Brentwood	3.3716	173,073,420
Clayton	3.7726	907,163,910
Ferguson-Florissant	4.9561	992,345,230
Hancock Place	4.4454	62,716,130
Hazelwood	5.6327	1,896,863,180
Jennings	4.8542	110,281,110
Kirkwood	3.8850	1,059,901,680
Ladue	2.8600	1,289,135,600
Lindbergh	3.1597	1,189,806,160
Maplewood-Richmond Heights	5.2554	229,286,320
Mehlville	3.6443	1,594,286,320
Normandy	5.5852	242,972,590
Parkway	3.5151	3,931,783,390
Pattonville	4.0560	1,326,945,140
Ritenour	4.5091	545,254,520
Riverview Gardens	5.7077	255,771,330
Rockwood	4.4177	2,913,395,160
Special School District	0.8235	20,917,764,888
University City	4.6108	550,433,150
Valley Park	4.6592	139,126,370
Webster Groves	5.3174	633,524,120
Wellston	5.3666	20,153,380
St. Louis	4.0193	3,783,108,406
Total		45,303,453,834
Source: 2006–2007 Missouri School Directory.		

Education literature strongly supports the concept that effective leadership can substantially boost student learning (Waters, Marzano, and McNulty 2004). There is a substantial amount of qualitative data that provide evidence that school leaders influence learning "by galvanizing effort around ambitious goals and by establishing conditions that support teachers and that help students succeed " (Leithwood and Riehl 2003, 3). At local, state, and national levels, school administrators are being held accountable for how well teachers teach and how much students learn. In a report by the National Commission for the Advancement of Educational Leadership Preparation (NCAELP), two recommendations were made that affect the preparation of administrators. They are: "preparation programs should continually develop their programs round the rigorous standards and learning processes that develop leaders who can support the learning of all children," and "multiple stakeholders should be involved in program development and licensure policy" (Hull 2003, 3).

With the evidence that improved leadership in schools produces increased student learning, and with the accountability demands of No Child Left Behind and the Missouri School Improvement Program, the Missouri Professors of Educational Administration (MPEA), the Missouri Department of Elementary and Secondary Education, and the Wallace Foundation joined together to form the Higher Education Evaluation Committee (HEEC) collaborative partnership. The goal of this collaborative is to positively impact student performance by inspiring and developing highly effective school leaders. Seventeen Missouri universities and colleges, along with staff from DESE and the Wallace Foundation, participate in this partnership. As mentioned earlier, five universities from St. Louis County and one from St. Charles County serve on the planning committee of HEEC. The role of HEEC, as defined by its members, is to:

- participate in the development process for adoption of new Interstate School Leaders Licensure Consortium (ISLLC) standards

- raise the School Leaders Licensure Assessment (SLLA) cut scores for administrators

- work with national consortiums on current research that develops future school leaders, including organizations such as the Council of Chief State School Officers (CCSSO), the University Council for Educational Admistration (UCEA), and the National Council for the Accreditation of Teacher Education (NCATE)

- work with the Missouri Administrator Mentoring Program

- participate in a backward mapping project of effective school leaders

- implement a statewide system of professional development geared to the needs of educational administration faculty

- implement an online scoring of the SLLA and State's Superintendents Assessment (SSA) exams to better inform and compare Missouri university educational administration programs

- raise Missouri educational administration programs' entrance requirements

- increase rigor for candidates in Missouri educational administration programs

- increase minority participation in educational administration programs
- develop a common follow-up survey for all institutions that prepare school leaders (HEEC, 2006).

St. Louis County school leaders face daunting higher-stakes testing and greater pressures from state school accountability mandates. Although university preparation programs of school principals and superintendents have never been better, much remains to be done to increase the quality and relevance of leadership programs (Hoyle 2005).

The ISLLC Standards

Since most of the policy for educational administration in the last ten years is based on the ISLLC Standards, it is important to understand these standards and how they were developed. The National Policy Board of Educational Administration (1994) was the major organization behind the creation of the original ISLLC Standards, and in 1996 the Interstate School Leaders Licensure Consortium Standards for School Leaders was published. This was the most innovative plan for "recalibration of educational administration programs" in decades (CCSSO 2006). Its designers created an instructional leadership framework whose vision of effective school leaders was as follows:

> The ISLLC Standards acknowledge that effective leaders often espouse different patterns of beliefs and act differently from the norm in the profession. Effective school leaders are strong educators, anchoring their work on central issues of learning and teaching and school improvement. They are moral agents and social advocates for the children and the communities they serve. Finally, they make strong connections with other people, valuing and caring for others as individuals and as members of the educational community (ISLLC 1996, 5).

Missouri was one of the approximately forty-one states that adopted or implemented the ISLLC Standards as a model for their licensure and certification policies. In order to be an administrator in Missouri, entry-level school administrators must pass the School Leaders Licensure Assessment examination. These standards form the framework for a common language for the field of educational leadership and are currently used in Missouri (CCSSO 2006). Critics have identified several problems with the original ISLLC Standards. The two main objections are that they are "vague ideas rather than prescriptions for practice" (Hess 2003, 23), and that they leave out critical information or underemphasize such important issues as technology (Murphy 2003). These two issues are currently being addressed by the HEEC.

In compliance with the ISLLC Standards, St. Louis County administrators are held accountable for six responsibilities of school leadership. They are that a school administrator is an educational leader who promotes the success of all students by:

- facilitating the development, articulation, implementation, and stewardship of a vision of learning that is shared and supported by the school community

- advocating, nurturing, and sustaining a school culture and instructional program conducive to student learning and staff professional growth

- ensuring management of the organization, operations, and resources for a safe, efficient, and effective learning environment

- collaborating with families and community members, responding to diverse community interests and needs, and mobilizing community resources

- acting with integrity and fairness, and in an ethical manner

- understanding, responding to, and influencing the larger political, social, economic, legal, and cultural context.

The ISLLC Standards are presently being updated. CCSSO has begun a formal process of working with state education agencies and therefore the formation of the HEEC Collaborative.

Using Research to Improve Leadership Preparation Programs

Through the HEEC Collaborative, several local research projects were set into motion during the last five years that impact the preparation of St. Louis County administrators. The goal of the research is to gather data that will lead to improvement of leadership preparation programs within Missouri and thereby within St. Louis County. In the following narrative, four of these research projects are discussed.

In 2005, at the request of the University Council for Educational Administration, the HEEC Collaborative, and the Missouri DESE, three national researchers conducted a study of five, university-based leadership preparation programs. This research had three goals:

- To compare program elements.

- To gather information on the aspects of leadership learned.

- To investigate the career intentions and advancement of graduates.

A comprehensive description of this research can be found in the proceedings of the 2006 Annual Conference of the American Educational Research Association. In brief, the results showed that the five programs studied, while adhering to many of the innovative program features recommended by experts, did vary in challenge and coherence. They also varied in the use of active student-centered instructional practices and internship length and quality, which positively associated to the extent to which graduates learned to lead learning and foster organizational learning. The findings of this research are currently being woven into the leadership preparation programs of the five St. Louis County universities that are members of the HEEC.

A second study begun in 2006 with the specific goal of improving Missouri administration preparation programs was the Backward Mapping Project. This study, conducted by the Missouri Professors of Education Administration, seeks to learn from highly effective school principals, many from the St. Louis County area, how Missouri institutions of higher learning can improve their school leader preparation programs. School principals were selected from schools that had demonstrated significant improvement in student achievement over the last five years. Principals are observed on the job and interviews are conducted with various members of the school community, looking for the characteristics that make these principals effective instructional leaders.

In the summer of 2005 a third research project was begun when four researchers from major Missouri higher education institutions canvassed more than 250 Missouri principals on their opinions of administration preparation programs within the state. A grounded theory design was used to systematically gather qualitative data that could be used to generate a theory that explained, at a broad conceptual level, the quality of administration preparation programs in Missouri. UMSL was one of the four universities that led the project. These data gave Missouri universities feedback on the effectiveness of their programs, and also connected theory and practice.

Approximately forty principals and assistant principals from St. Louis County were members of the group. Participants were all members of the DESE Satellite Leadership Academy. Members of the Academy were first divided into two groups: aspiring principals and practicing principals. Practicing principals included assistant principals as well as currently serving principals. They were asked to work in focus groups, posting their responses on chart paper. Their responses were gathered and categorized, and a general discussion followed with all groups reporting out to the whole group. The three questions posed were:

- What are some of the things you liked about the classes you have taken in your principal preparation program?

- What are some of the things you disliked about the classes you have taken in your principal preparation program?

- If you could change one thing about your principal preparation program, what would it be?

After reviewing comments from participants in the 2005 Academy, it was decided to ask certain groups of participants in the class of 2006 about their perceptions of their own university preparation programs. Participants were asked to write a narrative about their perceptions and to comment on their likes, dislikes, and how they would change their programs to best meet their own needs.

Through analysis of the focus group responses and the narratives, the researchers were able to hear the voices of more than four hundred practicing and aspiring Missouri principals. In summary, participants requested that university preparation programs in Missouri provide faculty who are up to date with their knowledge and course content and who provide a balance between practice and theory. In addition, participants requested the following:

- That curriculum not be redundant.

- That internship experiences be hands on, meaningful, and well coordinated between universities and local schools.

- That sufficient opportunities for networking be provided.

- That there be more flexible scheduling of classes.

- That requirements for admission to leadership preparation programs be increased.

The information provided by the participants was shared with all seventeen Missouri universities that were members of the HEEC. The five universities in St. Louis County immediately began restructuring their programs to incorporate relevant suggestions made by the participants of the study.

In 2003, four different task forces from within the MPEA membership researched and developed white papers with the hope of influencing program planning and state policy related to the recruiting, retention, support, and preparation of Missouri school leaders. The topics of the white papers included (1) the improvement of administrative preparation internship programs; (2) mentoring programs for principals and superintendents; (3) alternative preparation and certification programs; and (4) social conditions impacting administrative practice. The results have been most encouraging.

On December 14, 2004, the Missouri State Board of Education adopted rule changes for the certification of school leaders based on feedback from stakeholders. Changes include the requirement that new principals and superintendents participate in a mentoring program (two years for principals and one year for superintendents). St. Louis County university internship programs are being reevaluated for relevance and hands-on experiences, and money is being provided by the State for career transition programs. UMSL and SLU are both working with the St. Louis Public Schools in these areas. UMSL has also initiated a social justice program to create an understanding within its faculty of the social conditions that impact practice and urban institutions.

Of note is the professional development opportunities provided to St. Louis County administrators by the Satellite Leadership Academy. Each year, approximately forty St. Louis County administrators participate in both the St. Louis Principal's Academy and the Satellite Leadership Academy. The Missouri Leadership Academy is the parent organization for statewide leadership preparation. Nine Principal Academies are housed at Regional Professional Development Centers around the State. In addition, other Academies, such as a St. Louis Teacher's Academy, have been created to meet regional and local needs. Faculty from Missouri universities are encouraged to participate in the Academies. For more than twenty years, the Leadership Academy has been bringing together master practitioners, DESE representatives, and faculty from higher education institutions to exchange and share ideas. In 2004, the Missouri Leadership Academy was recognized by Stanford University as one of the most effective organizations providing professional development for leaders in the United States. This professional development has a major impact on St. Louis County schools, and numerous doctoral students are currently trying to tease out the impact that this professional development, as well as administrative preparation, has on the academic achievement of students in St. Louis County.

An ongoing dialogue among St. Louis County stakeholders to improve school leadership is still raging. Naturally, this has a great effect on educational planning. Currently all stakeholders are represented in this dialogue, which tends to keep lines of communication open concerning policy and quality issues related to the preparation of school leaders. St. Louis County is in a time of change and accountability. Each year, schools are evaluated on their academic progress by DESE. It will be interesting to see how schools rise to the call of providing quality leadership that contributes to and fosters quality education for all children.

Part 2: Creating New Visions for Teacher Preparation

Teaching children to read a story, write their name for the first time or add a column of numbers offers a lifetime of opportunity and personal reward for instructors and their students. The nation's future depends, in large part, on "how well its citizens are educated by a qualified and effective teaching force"—National Commission of Teaching and America's Future (1996, 5)

Teacher preparation or training programs are responsible for designing course work in teaching principles, theory, methods, and classroom applications. As well as preparing individuals to successfully meet state certification standards as teachers of prekindergarten through twelfth-grade students, programs strive to ensure that their teacher candidates build a solid theoretical and content foundation upon which to base classroom practice. "The importance of preparing teachers to exercise trustworthy judgment based on a strong base of knowledge is increasingly important in today's society" (Darling-Hammond and Bransford 2005, 2.). In more than 1,300 large and small, public and private colleges and universities, including teacher preparation programs offered by Fontbonne University, Harris-Stowe State University, Maryville University, Missouri Baptist University, St. Louis University, University of Missouri–St. Louis, Washington University, and Webster University in St. Louis County and City, teachers must be educated to meet increasing professional demands and expectations. Complex information must be gathered from a wide variety of sources using current educational tools and skills to motivate and enrich all children (Wilson et al., 2001).

The purpose of this section is to describe important issues impacting teacher education preparation and to identify future directions for the profession, specifically, for St. Louis City and County students and teachers.

National and State Standards-Based Reform Movements

During the late twentieth century, the effort to objectively evaluate teacher preparation programs led to the development of standards-based assessments by organizations such as the American Association of Colleges for Teacher Education (AACTE 2006). This consortium of approximately eight hundred private and public higher education institutions encourages teacher preparation programs to address established levels of institutions' and students' data-based performance.

The National Council for the Accreditation of Teacher Education (NCATE) is the profession's mechanism for voluntary national-level professional accreditation of schools, colleges, and departments of education. Founded in 1954, NCATE currently accredits 623 colleges of education and represents a coalition of thirty-three member organizations of teachers, teacher educators, content specialists, and local and state policymakers. The United States Department of Education and the Council for Higher Education Accreditation recognize NCATE as a professional accrediting body for teacher preparation. NCATE accredited teacher preparation programs in St. Louis County and City include those at Fontbonne University, Harris-Stowe State University, Missouri Baptist University, Maryville University, University of Missouri–St. Louis, and St. Louis University.

Preparation and accreditation procedures to meet national standards are planned by each St. Louis higher education institution individually. National accreditation visits are scheduled for each college or school of education in a seven-year cycle. Standards for assessing education colleges or schools (units) focus on unit resources, faculty qualifications, nature of practical field experiences, recruitment of a diverse student body and faculty, and candidates' knowledge, skills, and commitment to teaching all children assessment systems.

In Missouri, DESE is responsible for state certification. DESE requires detailed descriptions of each certification program in teacher education. Missouri assesses its teacher education programs using requirements of the Missouri Standards for Teacher Preparation (MoSTEP) program. Certification program assessments include data such as content taught, graduation rates, graduates' job performance, and demographics of students, as well as the unit's procedures for assessing its certification candidates. Individual teachers are certified, upon recommendation from an accrediting institution or from DESE directly, also based upon MoSTEP Teacher Certification standards. Twenty-three St. Louis County school districts reported to the Department of Elementary and Secondary Education that, as of the 2005–2006 school year, 97 percent of all teachers hired were fully certified. St. Louis Public School District provided data that 80.9 percent of district teachers were classified as fully certified.

Planning for the development of Missouri's statewide standards began in 1990 with the purpose of producing a performance-based assessment system for teacher and program certification. A task force of the state's thirty-six teacher preparation institutions, as well as pre-kindergarten to grade 12 educators, administrators, and representatives from two-year colleges and the Coordinating Board for Higher Education (CBHE) completed the standards document in 1995, based on the NCATE model. The Missouri State Board of Education approved the MoSTEP standards in 1999.

Piloting of the requirement of a capstone experience, the certification portfolio, began in St. Louis County in 1999 at the University of Missouri–St. Louis College of Education. This effort to design performance-based assessments is an example of collaborative planning undertaken by DESE and the College of Education. Teacher candidates generated a portfolio of MoSTEP standards-based artifacts and reflections and their efforts were evaluated by the university. These perspectives were shared with DESE. Following the pilot program year, portfolio requirements for both candidates and program evaluation were continued. Faculty at each institution are invited annually to comment to DESE regarding the usefulness and implementation of the standards-based assessment system and are also invited to yearly DESE training sessions to update information and further refine the system. As a result of educator input, DESE now requires a capstone experience that is not necessarily a portfolio but one proposed by an institution and approved by the state accreditation office.

The Transfer and Articulation Planning Group, which involves the collaboration of St. Louis Community Colleges and the University of Missouri–St. Louis, provides a specific example of higher education planning in St. Louis County to meet state accreditation standards. Teacher education representatives have been meeting regularly since 2000 to articulate courses that transfer and satisfy the DESE two-year and four-year institutional teacher preparation program requirements. Educators work to provide a smooth transition for students' pursuit of state certification at the four-year institutions from two-year college programs. As well, institutions share and plan for portfolio assessment, evaluation of common course content, necessary teaching skills and student dispositions, and best practices for providing experiences with technology and issues of diversity. These planning sessions have made it possible to come to institutionalize agreements for coursework and current teaching practices supported by the partnership.

Preparing Teachers to Teach in Diverse Settings

Many of America's large city school districts enroll students from a wide range of racial/ethnic groups and from high poverty socio-economic levels. In terms of diversity, Feistritzer and Chester (2000) note that 26 percent of students represent minority populations, yet nine percent of teachers are minority individuals. Another fourth of the nation's students are enrolled in rural areas where very small school districts struggle to hire teachers for fields such as physics, when a full day of classes cannot be offered. The fastest growing group of non-white teachers is persons of Hispanic origin (Council of Chief State School Officers 2006). The chart below illustrates recent data on Missouri teachers' demographics. Data specific to St. Louis County and City are not available but are represented in state totals in Table 3.

Table 3. Gender and Race/Ethnicity Trends, 1993–2004

	1993	1994	1995	1996	1997	1998	1999	2000	2001	2002	2003	2004
Total Teachers	54,221	55,912	57,686	58,254	60,381	61,728	63,092	64,791	65,429	66,705	67,826	66,646
GENDER												
Female	76.7%	77.0%	77.3%	77.5%	77.7%	77.9%	78.1%	78.2%	78.3%	78.4%	78.3%	78.5%
Male	23.3%	22.9%	22.7%	22.5%	22.3%	22.1%	21.9%	21.8%	21.7%	21.6%	21.7%	21.5%
RACE/ETHNICITY												
WHITE	91.2%	91.4%	91.6%	91.8%	92.0%	92.1%	92.1%	91.9%	92.3%	92.2%	92.0%	92.1%
Female	69.6%	70.1%	70.6%	71.0%	71.3%	71.6%	71.9%	71.9%	72.3%	72.3%	72.1%	72.3%
Male	21.6%	21.2%	21.0%	20.9%	20.6%	20.5%	20.3%	20.1%	20.0%	19.9%	19.9%	19.8%
BLACK	8.1%	8.0%	7.7%	7.5%	7.4%	7.2%	7.2%	7.4%	7.0%	7.0%	7.2%	7.0%
Female	6.6%	6.5%	6.2%	6.1%	5.9%	5.8%	5.7%	5.8%	5.5%	5.5%	5.6%	5.5%
Male	1.6%	1.5%	1.5%	1.4%	1.4%	1.4%	1.4%	1.6%	1.5%	1.55%	1.6%	1.5%
OTHER	0.6%	0.6%	0.6%	0.7%	0.7%	0.7%	0.7%	0.7%	0.7%	0.7%	0.8%	0.9%

The objective of teacher preparation programs is to prepare future teachers to understand and effectively teach all their students, as identified by both state and national certification organizations, DESE and

NCATE. Certification programs in Missouri are designed to meet that goal by addressing the MoSTEP standard to plan for and implement strategies for recruiting and retaining a diverse student body as well as faculty. Many university programs in St. Louis County prepare education students by involving them in field experiences and internship/student teaching semesters scheduled in urban, near urban, suburban, and rural school districts. By observing instruction, tutoring groups of students, working in internships, and student teaching in a variety of districts throughout the teacher preparation curriculum, future teachers become familiar with classroom settings and daily instructional responsibilities in diverse settings. Education students often seek employment in the districts in which they completed the internship and/or student teaching semesters.

The Career Transition program, offered at UMSL since 2000, is an example of a teacher preparation program specifically designed for the urban experience. The program employs students who have already earned a college degree. The students teach full-time for three years while certification is earned. Upon completion, the newly certified teacher remains in the classroom for two more years to fulfill financial obligation and become tenured in the St. Louis Public School District. Course work and field experience provide future teachers with the knowledge base and teaching skills they will need to relate to and successfully instruct their students.

Establishing University/School Collaborative Partnerships

Partnerships are a critically important vehicle for connecting education students to a variety of instructional settings during their training. Collaborative projects also serve to meet state and national program standards by providing opportunities for teaching and working in diverse communities. For example, teacher education programs and classrooms in St. Louis County have participated in the Professional Development School (PDS) project since the mid-1980s (Holmes Group 1990): "The intentions for such schools are consistent with learning theory that emphasizes inquiry about practice" (Darling-Hammond and Bransford 2005, 414). By partnering with prekindergarten to grade twelve classroom teachers and projects during their university experience, interns and student teachers are able to relate their college-based course work to daily teaching practice. Education students gain direct, everyday experience in making learning relevant to their students. Programs of this type make it possible to bring "into play a national coalition of school university partnerships for the simultaneous improvement of schools and the education of educators" (Sirotnik and Associates 2001, 6).

Planning for PDS work takes place across universities and school districts under the auspices of each teacher preparation program. One successful partnership between UMSL and the Parkway School District has been ongoing since 1992. The formal PDS partnership between the university and Parkway Central Middle School (PCMS) was formed in 1994, with direction and leadership from the National and the South-Central Holmes Group. The partnership engaged in various projects and areas of research study, including tutoring, in-class observations, action research projects, and courses taught by PCMS teachers. "A core of both the UM–St. Louis faculty and staff (from the Dean of Education to non-tenured instructors) and PCMS faculty and staff (from the principal to rookie teachers) took an active approach to the developing PDS" (Ambrose 2004, 13). Teachers and university faculty meet during the academic year to plan for professional development projects and the integration of teacher candidates in prekindergarten to grade-twelve classrooms. An additional PDS partnership exists between UMSL and Compton Drew Middle School.

Planning for PDS programs also takes place in conjunction with the Regional Professional Development Center Development Collaborative. The purpose of the center is related to supporting the work of schools and districts to focus on enhanced teacher skills and increased student learning. The St. Louis Regional Professional Development Center (RPDC) operates under contract with the Cooperating School District, (CSD) and combines CSD staff development resources with Missouri DESE resources. The St. Louis RPDC is one of nine regional centers created by DESE as part of the educational reform act of 1993. Its programs include professional development for St. Louis County teachers through conferences, video and online resources, and forums for university and districtwide collaborations.

Fostering opportunities for university/prekindergarten through grade-twelve collaboration and student achievement are also the goals of St. Louis In-Gear for Success (SLINGS). The College of Education at the University of Missouri–St. Louis and St. Louis Community College launched a $60 million initiative in 2005 to increase high school graduation and college enrollment rates in seven St. Louis County school districts and the St. Louis Public School District. Nearly half of the funding for the program is provided by a six-year, $28 million grant secured by UMSL from the U.S. Department of Education and is devoted to professional development for classroom instructors and university faculty. Implementation is ongoing through joint programs, classroom coaching, and university credit course offerings. More than six thousand low-income and underrepresented students will be mentored and coached by public school teachers, university faculty, and teacher education students, on-site, in the students' classrooms.

Retention of Teachers in the Profession

The 2005 missouri recruitment and retention report states that approximately one-third of teachers leave the field within the first three years of work. Specifically, in 2003, teachers leaving the classroom after only one to three years increased from 26.0 percent to 29.2 percent, an increase of 3.2 percent over the previous year: "Teachers leaving the classroom after only one to five years increased 0.8 percent" (Hirsch et al. 2001). Filling teaching positions in high-need subjects such as mathematics, science, technology and special education, as well as art and music, continues to be of concern to the field. Retaining teachers is a high priority for both the classroom and university programs. An experienced, consistent, and focused job force is of utmost importance to the quality of education. Table 4 provides statewide data that include St. Louis County and are illustrative of the patterns described above. Table 5 lists those subjects for which qualified teachers in the area are needed.

One of the reasons offered for the high attrition rate for new teachers is that they receive too little or infrequent professional development support (Darling-Hammond and Bransford 2005). In response to that need, Missouri's DESE mandated that universities offer a university-based Beginning Teacher Assistance Program (BTAP). Since 2002, the University of Missouri–St. Louis College of Education has been offering a unique yearlong experience to first- and second-year prekindergarten to twelfth-grade teachers. Induction and mentoring programs are also available at other St. Louis universities in partnership with area school districts. DESE assesses teacher education institutions on data reporting the number of their graduates remaining in their profession for at least five years.

Table 4. Teachers Leaving Missouri's Public School Work Force, 1993–2004

	1993	1994	1995	1996	1997	1998	1999	2000	2001	2002	2003	2004
Total Teachers	54,221	55,912	57,686	58,254	60,381	61,728	63,092	64,791	65,429	66,705	67,826	66,646
First-Year Teachers	2,401	3,223	3,429	3,424	3,804	4,030	4,313	4,646	5,064	4,802	4,439	3,428
Percent of First-Year Teachers Who Left the Classroom												
After 1–3 Years	19.5%	19.3%	18.6%	21.7%	24.3%	25.3%	24.8%	26.0%	29.2%			
After 1–5 Years	26.9%	27.2%	27.7%	33.8%	36.5%	35.1%	35.9%					

Table 5. Critical Teacher Shortage Areas, 1991–2001

1990–91 thru 1993–94	1994–95	1995–96 & 1996–97	1997–98	1998–99	1999–00	2000–01 & 2001–02
Foreign Language K-12 • French • German • Hebrew • Italian • Latin • Russian • Spanish Science • Chemistry 4-12 • Physics 7-12 Special Education K-12 • Behavioral Disordered • Blind/Partially Sighted • Deaf/Hearing Impaired • Early Childhood Special Ed. • Educable Mentally Retarded • Learning Disabilities • Orthopedically/Health Impaired • Remedial Reading • Severely Developmentally Disabled Speech Language Specialist K-12	Chemistry 4-12 Foreign Language K-12 • French • German • Hebrew • Italian • Latin • Russian • Spanish Physics 7-12 Special Education K-12 • Behavioral Disordered • Blind/Partially Sighted • Deaf/Hearing Impaired • Early Childhood Special Ed. • Educable Mentally Retarded • Learning Disabilities • Orthopedically/Health Impaired • Remedial Reading • Severely Developmentally Disabled Speech Language Specialist K-12	Foreign Languages Gifted Industrial Arts Mathematics Reading (special) Science • Biology • Chemistry • Physics Special Education • Behavioral Disordered • Deaf/Hearing Impaired • Early Childhood • Learning Disabilities • Mentally Handicapped • Other Speech/Language Pathologist	Agriculture Computer Science English Speakers of other Languages Industrial Arts Journalism Music, instrumental Reading (special) Science • Biology • General • Chemistry • Earth/Physical • Physics Special Education • Behavioral Disordered • Blind/Partially Sighted • Deaf/Hearing Impaired • Early Childhood • Learning Disabilities • Mentally Handicapped • Orthopedically Impaired Speech/Language Pathologist Speech/Theatre	Agriculture English Speakers of other Languages Foreign Language • Latin • Japanese • German • French • Spanish Gifted Industrial Tech. Journalism Mathematics, middle school Music, instrumental Reading Science • Physics • Chemistry • Biology • Earth Science • Middle School • Family/Consumer Science Special Education • Behavioral Disordered • Cross Cat. • Early Child. • Learning Disabilities • Mentally Handicapped • Severe Developmental Disorder • Blind/Partially Sighted Speech/Theatre	Agriculture English Speakers of other Languages Foreign Language • Latin • Japanese • German • French • Spanish Gifted Industrial Tech. Journalism Mathematics, sec. Mathematics, middle school Music, instrumental Reading (special) Special Education • Behavioral Disordered • Cross Category • Deaf/Hearing Impaired • Early Child. • Learning Disabilities • Mentally Handicapped • Physical/Other Health Impaired • Severe Developmental Disorder • Blind/Partially Sighted Speech/Language Specialist Speech/Theatre Technology Ed.	Agriculture Art Business Education Driver's Education English for Speak. Of Other Languages Foreign Languages • Spanish • French • German Gifted Health Industrial Tech. Journalism Mathematics, sec. Mathematics, middle school Music, instrumental Music, vocal Reading (special) Science • Physics • Chemistry • Middle School • Biology • Earth Science • Family/Consumer Science Special Education • Deaf Blind • Severe Develop. Disorder • Deaf • Blind • Behavioral Disordered • Speech/Lang. Specialist • Cross Cat. • Learning Dis. • Mentally Handicapped Speech/Theatre Technology Ed.

Alternative Certification Initiatives

The term "alternative teacher certification" has referred to a variety of avenues to becoming licensed to teach, other than through traditional four-year university-based programs. In 2005, forty-seven states, plus the District of Columbia, reported 122 alternative routes to teacher certification being implemented by 619 providers of individual programs around the country (NCEI 2004). The National Center for Education

Information (NCEI) estimates that more than 250,000 persons have been licensed through alternative routes since the mid-1980s; the majority of these have been in the last decade and are individuals who are transitioning into teaching from occupations outside the field of education. These programs are designed for non-traditional students seeking teacher certification and alternative certification and are designed to address today's demand for teachers in both the high-need subject areas and in districts in inner cities and outlying rural areas. Approximately 35,000 individuals are entering teaching through alternative teacher certification routes each year (NCEI 2004).

Identifying programs in St. Louis County that are classified as alternative options to traditional four-year teacher education programs is somewhat problematic. The DESE recognizes both "alternative and innovative" programs though no specific criteria are established; each institution offering routes toward certification defines its own program components. There are no current statewide or St. Louis County data on the specific number of alternatively certified teachers. However, Missouri Baptist University, University of Missouri–St Louis, and the Department of Education at Washington University in St. Louis County are approved to offer alternative certification programs in various formats.

The previously described Career Transition programs, as well as the Temporary Authorization Program offered by DESE. are examples of alternative programs that are already in place in St. Louis County. Requirements for alternative certification vary by program and institution across Missouri. Some programs accelerate certification by combining courses to offer them more quickly, some offer programs at the schools at which certification students are the full-time instructor, and others provide online and video course work to provide more educational access to students.

An ongoing debate within the profession exists regarding the effectiveness of alternative routes toward certification as compared to more traditional programs offered in four-year institutions. The measure of effectiveness is often stated in terms of which type of program, traditional or alternative, most affects prekindergarten to grade twelve student achievement. Some proponents suggest that alternative certification programs offer the chance to circumvent inadequate schools of education and to increase the number of minorities entering the teaching profession. Opponents counter that less preparation is hardly an answer to concerns about teacher quality (Darling-Hammond and Bransford 2005). Each institution designs its own programs so that future teachers have options for accelerated programs. Programs vary with regard to the amount of time spent on campus versus classes offered in a combination of real and online time. There is no formal venue for areawide planning for such programs but they do offer students a variety of paths leading to teacher certification.

Teacher Education Programs' Impact on Student Learning and Assessment

The purpose of formal teacher education programs, clinical training, and certification processes is currently under state and national scrutiny with regard to impact on student learning. In recent years, research on teaching effectiveness has reported a direct relationship between teaching quality and student learning (Darling-Hammond and Young 2002). However, a clear definition of teaching effectiveness is needed in educational literature in order to make research relevant to practice. For example, there is debate in terms of measuring teachers' impact on their students' performance, considering the wide variety of factors that affect achievement (Ding and Sherman 2006). In a report published by the Education Commission of the States in 2003, ninety-two studies were used to describe eight challenges to the teacher education profession (Allen 2003). These included the role of subject knowledge, teaching knowledge, and quality of field experiences. The author acknowledged the "relative thinness of the research" (Allen 2003 viii). In light of such uncertainty, more precise definitions of issues and types of data to be gathered are necessary to use assessment data accurately. Higher education faculty in research groups at the University of Missouri–St. Louis College of Education are studying the impact of teacher education programs in St. Louis County and City on pre kindergarten to twelfth grade students' academic achievement. St. Louis County classroom teachers are being surveyed and data collected to determine the values of formal teacher preparation. As the planning and analysis is completed in 2007, educators will be more fully informed to prepare future teachers and better able to design effective curriculum and practice experience.

Conclusion

Many pivotal issues face teacher educators in terms of program structure and assessment. St. Louis County offers a rich array of university- and school-based collaborations. More St. Louis County–based research, along with data driven conclusions, can provide directions to improving specific aspects of teacher preparation program quality. Whereas individual institutions strive to improve teacher education effectively in practice and theory, partnerships of all stakeholders, including community leaders, parents, teachers, and academic administrators should form the basis for policy commitments for research-based educational change. A significant increase in work toward areawide planning, collaboration, and resultant initiatives are essential ingredients for teacher education program improvement in St. Louis County and City.

St. Louis County policymakers and educators should assess how to and whether they can implement mutually beneficial goals, plans, and connections between teacher preparation programs. The most effective aspects of teacher preparation should be defined, evaluated, and practiced in and through both traditional and alternative routes toward teacher education and certification. "The need is more urgent for research that looks at the conditions under which an array of policy levers helps improve teacher preparation" (Wilson et al. 2001, 25). Making certain that all children learn, and educating professionals to accomplish that goal, is of utmost importance to our nation's health and future and, of course, to students' academic success at all levels of education in St. Louis County and City.

Part 3: Possibilities and Challenges: Planning for St. Louis County Suburban Schools

The task of describing the future for the large and diverse population of school districts in St. Louis County is daunting at best. St. Louis County contains twenty-four school districts that educate close to 150,000 students. Close to 17 percent of the children in the state of Missouri are educated in these districts. They are as different as their students, ranging from the very small Brentwood School District, serving just over 800 students, to the suburban Rockwood School District with 22,336 (2005–2006 Annual Report of the Public School, State Board of Education 2006). And, as they differ in size, so too do they differ in demographic composition, financial structure, educational programming, and student needs. A description of the future needs of all twenty-four districts in one short chapter would be inadequate at best. What might be productive is a description of the current realities and the challenges these realities pose for all St. Louis County districts.

Current Realities

Public education has arguably never been under greater scrutiny or greater pressure. The multiple initiatives and efforts outlined earlier in this chapter to prepare educators for the changing needs of today's schools reflect the complex needs of the profession and the challenges educators face. These initiatives are complicated, and their results jeopardized, by changing and short-term leadership. This turnover in the profession is quickly becoming a factor that frames the entire context of schooling. From the classroom to the superintendency, changing personnel have become the norm rather than the exception throughout the county, the state, and the nation.

Changing Leadership

As baby boomers reach retirement, the average tenure of classroom teachers in the area continues to decline. The average tenure of classroom teachers has declined in the past five years from eighteen to twenty years in most districts to an average length of service closer to ten years. The ranks of teachers in their first five years of service have increased significantly for almost every district. For school administrators—particularly superintendents—the political nature of these leadership positions has caused a significant level of turnover in recent years. Although districts outside the City of St. Louis have for the most part avoided the revolving door and controversy of the city, succession planning in suburban districts is a topic to explore. In the county, only three districts—Clayton, Kirkwood, and Lindbergh—have had the same superintendent for ten years or more. While the others show considerably more stability than the St. Louis Public Schools (now on their sixth superintendent in the last ten years), all but the three mentioned earlier have had two or three superintendents during the last decade. This trend is suspected to continue. The public school retirement system recently reported that as many as 50 percent of the administrators (principals and superintendents) in the state could retire in the next three years.

This change in district leadership has both positive and negative implications. First, as districts are held to increasingly high standards of performance, the need for change becomes more and more imperative. Change in leadership, or systemic change as it is sometimes called, quite often requires new people. Those who have held positions of authority and influence in districts are not always able to see the need for change in systems that have traditionally functioned very well by most accounts. A colleague new to the superintendency in one of these suburban districts shared this story: "Not long ago I was meeting with one of my assistant superintendents. In my four years in the district, she has been a loyal partner—supporting change, communicating issues, and helping me navigate the culture of a district that hangs on desperately to the 'way it's always been.' This bright, committed, forward-thinking professional and I were discussing how much was going on and how overwhelmed she was feeling. I made several suggestions for streamlining activities including delegating more decision-making responsibility to teachers rather than having everything come through her office. She looked at me blankly and said, 'But we have a form.'"

And there's the problem. While school officials talk about change, work hard to make it happen, and, sometimes, even have the "right people on the bus" (Collins 2001), it gets overwhelmed or sabotaged by the system. The greatest challenge facing school leaders is that of transforming school districts to insure the success of every child. This is complex work. Change in one part of the organization inevitably affects another. What seems like a simple change can create widespread organizational ripples that go way beyond the initial impact.

For the districts in St. Louis County, a number of factors can and will ensure an adequate pool of candidates for these critical leadership positions. Affordable housing, quality of life, and competitive salaries are among the factors that continue to attract good candidates to the public schools of the metro area. In most districts, positive relationships between superintendents and the elected Boards of Education serve as a drawing card for those seeking to make a positive change. Ultimately, the future of districts in St. Louis County, and elsewhere, will depend on successful transitions in leadership.

Other factors impact the current reality facing St. Louis County school districts. The American Association of School Administrators (AASA), in a recent forum on the issue of leadership and change, provided an opportunity for school leaders to come together to discuss these issues and the implications for schools. The best summation was provided by the 2005 National Superintendent of the Year, Monte Moses, who identified a dozen new realities confronting public education. These realities are:

- Revenue and expenditure limitations
- Increasingly diverse and complex students and families

- High public expectations and accountability for student achievement

- Rapid advances in knowledge and technology

- Business and political concerns about public education

- International competition in education

- More legal and law enforcement issues

- Violence, racism, and substance abuse

- Choice and vouchers

- Growing state control of education

- Increases in student enrollment

- Erosion of public confidence and common agreement about public education (AASA 2005).

While all of these realities certainly have implications for districts in St. Louis County, and all have significant implications for the recruitment and selection of teachers and school leaders, some are particularly relevant for districts in the county. These include revenue and expenditure limitations, high public expectations and accountability for student achievement, choice and vouchers, and growing state control of education. We will explore each a bit further.

Revenue and Expenditure Limitations

The State of Missouri has been in the throes of a battle to define adequate and equitable support for public schools for many years. In 1990, school districts, students, and taxpayers filed lawsuits, later consolidated, claiming that Missouri's school finance system violated the state constitution's equal protection and education clauses on both "equity" and "adequacy" grounds. The districts in St. Louis County found themselves on opposite sides of the issue, with those with greater local property wealth joining the State in defending the system, and those with lower local wealth asserting constitutional violations. Ultimately, the trial court declared the funding system unconstitutional and held that the State must provide the same educational opportunity to children living in rich and poor districts (Cole County Circuit Court 1993). The General Assembly responded by passing the Outstanding Schools Act of 1993, which increased school funding by raising taxes, improving funding equity, and instituting a number of educational reforms. All was well for about ten years.

In January 2004, a group of school districts reinstituted a new Committee for Educational Equality that once again filed an equity and adequacy lawsuit against the State, claiming that the Missouri finance system has once again become unconstitutional. This time, the districts in St. Louis County have almost all weighed in with the same argument that students are being harmed by underfunding of essential resources, including teachers, programs, facilities, and equipment (Hunter 2004). The argument is that even for districts with significant local wealth, the demands of accountability and ever-growing state and federal requirements have outpaced state financial support.

Complicating this issue of state revenue for some county districts is the future of the voluntary desegregation program. Through 2003–2004, participating districts were paid at their respective tuition rates for each transfer student. Starting in 2004–2005, tuition was funded through the same state funding mechanisms as all other public schools in Missouri, and was capped at about $7,000 per student (VICC 2006). Since this payment is significantly lower than the per pupil cost at many of the participating districts, the change has caused these districts to reexamine the viability of their participation, and, in some cases, has caused districts to reduce the number of transfer students they accept.

Add to these concerns a growing dissatisfaction among voters with local property taxes, personal property taxes, and other sources of revenue for schools, and the financial pressures for all school districts continue to escalate. With a few notable exceptions, county school districts have not generally been successful in addressing their financial concerns through local action. At the state level, though the General Assembly once again made an effort to address funding by passing a new formula in 2006, the fact is that very few of the districts in the metropolitan area will see significant financial relief upon its implementation. In fact, the formula eliminates several sources of categorical funding, thereby hurting some local districts even more. The formula's eight-year roll-out sends a strong message that state relief is a remote possibility.

High Expectations and Accountability for Student Achievement

With the passage of No Child Left Behind (NCLB), St. Louis County districts—like others throughout the country—were called to ever-greater demands for accountability and performance. For most county districts, these were not new challenges. The DESE and the State Board of Education had been enforcing standards of performance since the passage of the Outstanding Schools Act of 1993 (Public School Laws of Missouri 2005). Most county districts had been meeting these high state standards for some time. Some were struggling. NCLB ensured that districts started to look beyond overall student performance, to pay attention to, and focus efforts on, individual schools and groups of students as well. In the county, this had special implications for those districts with large populations of traditionally underperforming students—African Americans, English language learners, special education students, and others. It also caused some careful review of the performance of students participating in the area desegregation program—the largest choice program in the history of the state.

Recent efforts by suburban districts to close achievement gaps, increase student performance for all children, and further improve programs and services are notable. In fact, of the twenty-four districts in St. Louis County, only three have not fully met the high standards established by the State of Missouri. Districts throughout the area have largely embraced the notion of accountability and have redoubled efforts to meet increasingly high standards for student achievement. Discussions at professional gatherings of superintendents, board members, and other school leaders typically focus on how to improve their districts, not whether or not they should.

In spite of the positive attitude of local school officials, they nevertheless worry about the implications of NCLB and the public demands for accountability they face. As parents and community members come to rely on a "scoreboard" approach to assessing the progress of their schools, teachers and administrators find themselves caught up in a competition that has more to do with accumulating points than it does educating children.

Choice and Vouchers

St. Louis County is home to the country's longest lasting, and some would argue, most successful desegregation settlement and choice program. Since its inception, close to 60,000 students have chosen to transfer to a different school district in the county for at least a portion of their K-12 experience. Currently, about 10,000 African American students from the city have chosen to attend school in county districts; just over 500 county white students now attend St. Louis magnet schools. Students who have participated in the program are distinguished by a four-year college attendance rate of 77 percent—significantly above the statewide percentage of 47 percent—and a persistence to graduation rate of 49 percent—twice as high as their non-transferring counterparts.

In spite of this generally positive track record, the program has not been popular with everyone in the county. Many districts both in St. Louis County and in other parts of the state have expressed concerns about the resources directed into the desegregation program, stating that districts everywhere have paid a price for the remedy agreed to by a few county districts. Too, the inner ring districts of St. Louis County have experienced significant growth in African American student populations during the course of the desegregation program—without benefit of additional state funds.

Though not necessarily united around the voluntary choice program, all the districts in the area agree on the issue of charter schools and vouchers. St. Louis County districts oppose legislation allowing the creation of charter schools in school districts in Missouri other than those currently authorized in the cities of St. Louis and Kansas City. They also oppose authorizing the use of state funds to support charter school sponsors. Collectively, these districts have opposed legislation that authorizes tuition tax credits, tuition tax deductions, and/or educational scholarships (vouchers). While most educators support innovation, and all support legitimate efforts to improve educational opportunities for children, the issue of diverting already scarce public funds to private use—without accountability—is a volatile one.

There are several potential benefits of charter schools: freedom and equitable choice for parents; innovative opportunities for educators; explicit accountability for student achievement; and creation of a laboratory setting for local school districts. If charter schools reflect meaningful choice, autonomy, and accountability, they could become models for all public schools in Missouri. Current Missouri law allows for the establishment of charter schools only in the Kansas City and St. Louis school districts. For those charter schools currently operating in Missouri, data on student achievement are not yet available by which to judge their effectiveness. It is important to recognize that freedom from restraint and bureaucracy is no guarantee of quality or improvement. Just as there can be quality education and good student achievement within some bureaucratic systems, there can also be ineffectual, misguided efforts in an atmosphere of freedom. For this reason, area educators emphasize the importance of standards, evaluation, and accountability in the establishment of any charter school. Most leaders in the area would suggest that charter schools have clear, written objectives; equitable and non-discriminatory admission policies; free tuition; fiscal and educational accountability; staff and parent involvement in program design; accommodations for the disabled; adequate, safe, and healthy physical facilities; and staff who volunteer to work in the school. Such schools would find general support and might very well serve to fill the perceived need for alternatives to current school offerings.

Growing State Control of Education

A current reality facing area schools, and a trend that many find extremely alarming, is the relentless effort on the part of state and federal officials to erode the local control of schools. Local districts have worked hard in recent years to protect the ability to make decisions regarding the employment, assignment, compensation, or termination of school personnel; to maintain the ability to seek civil, equitable, judicial and/or other legal remedies; and to prevent other action that might impede local educational, instructional, financial and/or administrative decisions. Numerous bills in each of these areas have been filed in the past few legislative seasons, and some have come alarmingly close to passing. At the federal level, the mandates of NCLB have eroded both state and local authority in a variety of ways.

In some local districts, parents are starting to question this erosion of local control. Concerns about the emphasis on state testing, the growing reliance on property tax for funding, and the efforts to mandate everything from seat belts to salaries have caused many to express concerns. Many have started to look at the total contribution to the state general revenue coming from the metro area, in proportion to the resources and services received in return.

Cooperation Among Districts

While each of these issues poses challenges for the districts in St. Louis County, one of the greatest tools they have to address them effectively is their history of cooperation and collaboration. The Cooperating School Districts (CSD) of Greater St. Louis is a nonprofit educational service agency created some forty years ago to share resources, information, and ideas (CSD 2006). As financial resources become more scarce, demands for higher levels of student performance increase, and the need for new and more effective teaching strategies become apparent, County school districts have found it more important than ever to work together to find creative solutions to common problems. Cooperative learning has taken on new meaning as districts work together and learn from one another in efforts to ensure every child success.

CSD is, in fact, a unique organization. As a voluntary, membership-driven organization owned and governed by thirty public school districts in the St. Louis metropolitan area, and serving another thirty-one additional public school district members, CSD provides nationally recognized services in educational technology, cooperative purchasing, staff development, and more. Notably, CSD also serves as a proactive lobbying voice for education in St. Louis County and beyond. This level of cooperation is unusual among such diverse partners in education, or in fact, in any business. Legislative activity is framed by a statement of principle that states:

> We believe that every child should be given the opportunity to develop his or her talents to the fullest extent possible in order to attain access to the benefits of the American social, economic and political systems. We support the local autonomy of school districts and oppose the unfunded mandates of new programs. Furthermore, we urge that a moratorium be placed on mandating any new programs until all current programs are adequately funded. There are many factors, tangible and intangible, that affect the quality of education provided to children in Missouri. The Cooperating School Districts is committed to the principle that quality education is a shared responsibility of the home, school, community, state and nation (CSD Legislative Platform 2005, 2).

In addition, the districts of CSD—as diverse as they are in every way possible—have the distinction of actually coming together to agree on some priority legislative positions that they advocate strongly among local, state, and federal officials. These common legislative goals include a wide range of educational issues including funding, economic development, vouchers, transportation, testing, capital improvements, technology, and school safety. While the specific needs of the various districts drive strongly divergent views in many of these areas, the leaders of the CSD public schools have determined that their continued cooperation on common concerns has far greater impact than any individual district's efforts might. This penchant for collaboration is well grounded in the area and will continue to be more and more important in coming years.

Conclusion

The St. Louis County area is fortunate in its public schools. With few exceptions, the school districts of the area serve their children and their publics well. Challenges for greater accountability and higher performance have been met or exceeded in almost every district.

The educational future of the area appears bright. Teachers and administrators are better prepared and more focused on instructional improvement than ever before. As evidenced by the numerous studies and initiatives outlined in the first two sections of this chapter, the area is rich with cutting-edge research and professional development efforts sponsored by local universities and supported by various state and national agencies. Preparation programs, preservice experiences, and beginning teacher and administrator mentoring activities have enriched the profession in the County and throughout the State. Districts, universities, and other agencies are working together and learning new and more powerful ways to collaborate. The entire system of public education is undertaking change—in practice, in policy, and in people. Ultimately, the children of the area will be the beneficiaries of all this effort.

Part 4: Educating the Future: Building Toward 2011—What's Next in St. Louis Schools

With the abrupt resignation of Superintendent Creg Williams in July 2006, the St. Louis Public Schools (SLPS) entered another era of uncertainty. In the past four years, there have been six superintendents of the SLPS system. This lack of continuity has lead to frustration and inertia within the district. Many factors account for these changes in administration: low academic scores and high drop-out rates of students; the superintendent speaking out publicly against decisions made by the School Board; plans for improvement of schools being too expensive, and a lack of cooperation among School Board members. Regardless of these issues, the major problem that needs to be addressed is that children are matriculating through the SLPS system without receiving the education they need to be successful and competitive in college and in the rapidly changing job market.

For the past fifteen months, stakeholders in the SLPS have been working on a Five-Year Strategic Plan (the Plan). The Plan was in the process of being initiated when Dr. Williams left office.

On July 27, 2006, Commissioner of Education D. Kent King appointed a five-member special committee whose charge is to help find solutions to the continuing turmoil in the SLPS. However, remarked Commissioner King, "I would like to give the new administration and the school board some breathing room so they can stabilize the district and prepare for the opening of school on August 28" (SLPS 2006). Commissioner King said that he would ask the committee to gather information and make recommendations on topics such as the district's academic performance, identifying the steps to regain full accreditation, clarifying the financial condition of the school district, clarifying the primary concerns of parents and community residents, and recommending what the state's involvement should be with the school district. It is King's hope that the committee will help reduce tensions in the St. Louis community and focus stakeholders on the common goal of providing a safe and positive learning environment for children.

In order to describe some of the needs of the district, the following is a description of the Plan that centers on the goal to improve the academic performance of every child in the district. The Plan is the culmination of two years of planning and community involvement. Although the City of St. Louis faces an educational crisis of monumental proportion, the Plan was designed to offer a road map for future academic and personal success of children within the district and was begun before Dr. Williams took the superintendency. The Plan was developed through the analysis of historical data and educational trends, through an evaluation of the current state of the district and projected demographics and finances, and by consensus building among all its stakeholders. The SLPS team felt it could reach the attainable goal of achieving academic success for every student in the district by refocusing resources and talents on academic performance. Key to this success was the building of a consensus among stakeholders that included parents, guardians, business and civic leaders, teachers, staff, and others. It will take the sustained effort and input of the entire City of St. Louis to make any plan work and to ensure that it meets the changing needs of the district.

Students in SLPS have a wide range of academic needs. The foundation of the Plan centers on five core principles. These principles are:

1. Academic achievement

2. A safe and orderly environment

3. Community collaboration

4. Equity, and

5. Efficient and effective support operations.

According to the Plan, "The district's most important mission is to ensure that every child graduates from the St. Louis Public Schools with the academic, physical, mental, and emotional intelligence and skills to compete effectively in the global marketplace" (St. Louis Five-Year Strategic Plan 2006). The following is an explanation of how the Plan would make this goal a reality.

Principle 1: Academic Achievement

The goal of the first principle is to build the level of academic achievement in the district through multiple initiatives. These initiatives include a plan to increase the number of students participating in its sponsored preschool program by 10 percent per year for four years. To accomplish this, the district needed to expand the number of seats for preschool students by opening additional classrooms at three existing school sites and to expand the Parents as Teachers program by adding staff.

In addition, the Plan called for all students to demonstrate grade-level proficiency by the end of the third grade. In order to accomplish this goal, "Reading First" is scheduled to be implemented in fifteen of the district's lowest performing schools.

Next, the SLPS stakeholder team addressed the Adequate Yearly Progress (AYP) criteria set by No Child Left Behind's federal legislation. In order to cover this issue, the Plan set forth the following solutions:

- The district would open a middle school based on a nationally recognized model that includes extended school days
- Low-performing middle schools would be restructured to address AYP criteria
- An inclusive, data-driven model for school improvement would be implemented that provides effective strategies and resources to help schools meet AYP criteria
- Setting district targets for individual schools to create and put into place their own strategic actions.

The SLPS team also set the goal that 80 percent of students would achieve at or above proficiency levels on the Missouri Assessment Plan (MAP). In order to reach this goal, schools and programs are to be restructured to better meet the needs of students. For example, the district will create smaller, more nurturing, and community-based schools; expand its truancy and in-school suspension programs; and increase parent patrols in order to reduce violence and maintain a sense of discipline and order. The district will put into practice a model middle school program that addresses the social, emotional, and intellectual needs of the adolescent child. It will also implement new junior high academies that will offer students in the seventh through ninth grades in-depth exposure to a rigorous and challenging curriculum. A year-round instructional program for seventh- and eighth-grade students will be executed, and a ninth-grade unit summer recovery instructional program initiated. The Plan included new single gender schools that craft a learning environment specifically addressing the needs of learning styles of each gender. Programs that promote extended learning opportunities for students to excel beyond the identified core curriculum are included in the Plan. In addition, new alternative education schools are planned to provide instruction, programs, and services to address disruptive students' educational and behavioral needs.

Other activities included in the Plan to achieve 80 percent proficiency on the Missouri Assessment Program include the expansion of the eMINTS instructional model program in order to bring multimedia technology into inquiry-based, student-centered, interdisciplinary instruction throughout the district. Newcomer Academies and International Welcome Centers are included in the Plan that will offer services such as after-school classes to students with specific needs in the area of English as a Second Language (ESL) and remedial reading.

An electronic instructional data management system is to be created to provide the electronic tools necessary to share information among stakeholders. For example, parents will be able to access homework on-line, review report cards, or communicate with teachers and principals. In return, teachers and principals will be able to communicate more effectively with parents and community members.

The last goal under the principle of academic achievement is perhaps the most ambitious in its scope. That goal is to have 90 percent of all high school students graduate and be prepared for postsecondary educational opportunities. In order to reach this goal, it is planned for the district to implement a number of activities that specifically target problems that have been identified through analysis of data. First, smaller learning environments for ninth-grade students will be established in which a nurturing relationship will support students' academic achievement in the challenging transition from middle to high school. A new mandatory orientation for ninth-grade parents is part of the Plan to bring parents into active participation with the schools. Smaller high schools with a maximum of 500 students are being put into place that have a specialty focus and that partner with local corporations and universities. These high schools will align their curriculum across all schools in the district and will address the social, emotional, and intellectual needs of the young adult. Small "boutique" high schools were opened in 2005 on local college campuses (this partnership was already put into place with the University of Missouri–St. Louis and is currently in operation). Through this partnership, college credit and Advanced Placement (AP) classes are being made available to students who excel academically. Students are now being provided opportunities to investigate collegiate experiences in depth, and individual help is be given students to improve their scores on national exams. Opportunities for students to exchange ideas nationwide will be encouraged through the establishment of a new National Student Exchange program.

A new Senior Residency program is planned that will provide an opportunity for students to explore new methods of working independently and with others. In this same vein, districtwide summer jobs programs will give eligible students career readiness skills and professional experience. Career Prep programs are planned that will enhance students' awareness of professions in the areas of technology, law, transportation, health sciences, visual and performing arts, business, architectural design, and educational occupations.

A Student Success Center that would allow students to have input into academic, career, and postsecondary services has been eliminated from the plan.

Principle 2: A Safe and Orderly Environment

As stated in the Five-Year Strategic Plan, "This principle reflects the district's commitment to ensuring that every child and employee has the opportunity to learn, teach, and work in a safe and secure setting" (Williams 2006, 5). There are three goals in this area:

1. To decrease the number of serious incidents in the district by 20 percent per year for three years.

2. To install state-of-the-art working security systems, including video cameras and access cards for students and staff at the secondary school level.

3. To train district security personnel in the area of school safety and security.

The district plans to reach the goal of a safe and orderly environment by implementing a number of new programs that include parents and students in the solutions. Administrators are being required to attend the Character Education Leadership Academy and implement programs for students and staff that promote positive behavior. Conflict mediation and anger management programs are being implemented in all schools. A Parent Patrol program has been launched at the high schools that empowers parents to patrol the grounds and provide supplemental school monitoring services, and multiple student-run groups, such as Teen Court and Peer Mediation groups, have been instituted to address security and safety issues. The In-School Suspension (ISS) program has been expanded to reduce classroom interruptions and provide an alternative learning environment. The Truancy Department has been expanded and personnel increased to better serve the needs of students and parents. A uniform policy for schools is being discussed and a card access system is being reviewed. Security systems using digital security cameras and metal detectors are scheduled to be updated and upgraded, and assistance from local law enforcement agencies is being sought to identify best practices for identifying solutions to school crime issues. The stakeholders recognize that in order to build a high-achieving learning environment, children must feel safe (Williams 2006, 5). By being proactive and positive, and through programs such as character education and conflict mediation, the district hopes to reach its goal of providing a safe and orderly environment for our children.

Principle 3: Community Collaboration

This principle captures the importance of developing relationships with all of the SLPS stakeholders. In order to do this, the district has set three goals: First, all schools will implement Home/School/Community Councils with representation from school leadership, teachers, parents and community. The second goal sets in practice the building of community confidence in the SLPS by the convening of public forums and the dissemination of clear and concise information about the schools. In addition, it has been proposed that the district provide transparent financial information to stakeholders and foster community collaboration by implementing such things as quarterly breakfast meetings, electronic newsletters, quarterly district newspapers, periodic feedback from community groups, and surveys that enhance two-way communication between district and community. SLPS television programs are being expanded to target student needs and a segment from the Board president is being put into place.

The last goal is to have every school develop at least one partnership with a community or corporate body in support of its curricular and/or extracurricular offerings. To reach this goal, a districtwide partnership plan has been created that will track and align various district needs with potential community partners. Local business leaders are being asked to adopt a school and provide assistance, support, and encouragement for students and programs.

Principle 4: Equity

Ensuring that every child in the district receives the human and financial resources needed to be successful is the focus of this principle. Four goals have been set in order to reach equity:

- One hundred percent of our schools will have equity in facilities, programs, resources, and staffing
- One hundred percent of our principals, teachers, and paraprofessionals will be highly qualified and trained and will receive competitive salaries
- All students will have access to choices that include a wide array of high-quality educational programs and extracurricular activities

• A fair and flexible funding strategy will ensure equity across schools.

In order to reach the first equity goal, the district has implemented a districtwide capital improvement plan. Every building is being surveyed for needs and discrepancies. Capital improvement projects such as air-conditioning, window replacement, roofing repair, and classroom modifications, are being undertaken. A "balanced staffing" plan will be initiated based on student population and school needs.

To reach the second equity goal, the district is in the process of creating a Leadership Academy that includes a principal induction program and introduction to best practices. An effective recruitment and retention program is being established. In order to help with recruitment and retention, the following programs are being employed: tuition assistance for continuing education, and web-based resources for new teachers.

The districtwide extracurricular sports program is being enlarged to ensure that all SLPS students have access to choices. A Magnet School Fair that showcases various schools and highlights options for parents and students is being put into place, and the music and visual arts programs are being expanded.

The plan to ensure fair and flexible funding includes such strategies as (1) devising a system built on base-level and equalized funding per student, (2) developing a comprehensive fiscal recovery plan to eliminate the financial deficit, (3) implementing a scheme to generate sufficient funding to support and complete capital improvements, and (4) devising a development funding strategy targeting key foundations and other grant-making organizations for projects that support the strategic plan.

Principle 5: Efficient and Effective Support Operations

This principle focuses on ensuring that all human and capital resources are targeted toward driving academic achievement in an efficient and cost-effective manner. To do this, the district plans to develop and maintain a balanced budget that realizes the goals and activities of the Five-Year Strategic Plan. A zero-based budget process is being instituted, internal control procedures are being established, and a system for tracking and reporting time and attendance of both teachers and students is being established.

A plan to ensure that academic and operational support services to schools are timely, appropriate, and supportive of the instructional priorities of SLPS students is being put into place. A plan to improve vendors is being addressed, a database for accurately screening and placing volunteers is being established, and the fiber network is being upgraded in order to permit an IMS system, a web-based business system, a web-based student information system, and so on. The functions of the district office are being aligned to support schools.

To ensure effective operations, data will be gathered and analyzed to drive school goals and support school achievements. Student attendance, student achievement, and other pertinent data will be tracked on a six-week rolling basis and reported in a timely manner. An employee performance evaluation based on individual goal setting will be aligned to district goals, and the operations of each SLPS will be driven by the district's strategic plan and include an annual review of organizational impact and worker productivity.

Ultimately, the success of the SLPS will depend on the implementation of the Plan and its ability to foster student achievement. At the core of the Plan is the Education Covenant of the Board of Education. This Covenant sets forth the district's core beliefs, building principles, and a series of goals that it is committed to achieve by the year 2011. It is important to note that the Plan is a fluid document. Through ongoing dialogue with the community (parents, teachers, business leaders, concerned citizens, and students), the Plan will be modified to reflect fluctuations in needs and resources.

Striving for Excellence: Together We Can

As mentioned earlier in the chapter, public education is under greater scrutiny and greater pressure than ever before in its history. The multiple initiatives and efforts outlined in this chapter to prepare educators for the changing needs of today's schools reflect the complex needs of the profession and the challenges educators face. The authors have tried to give the reader a picture of how principals and teachers are being prepared to meet these complex needs in St. Louis County. In addition, we have tried to describe the challenges and possibilities that impact urban and suburban schools.

The education of a child is a complex undertaking. The rate of a child's progress depends on many variables, such as the expertise of the teacher, the competency of the school's administration, the amount of scholarly behavior his or her parents model at home, the involvement of the community and business in education, and whether the child wishes to reach for the stars (Plummer 1991). If we truly believe that our children are our most important resource, then all the stakeholders in St. Louis must join hands to ensure that our children get the best education possible. We have the resources; the question is, do we have the will? To quote Herbert Spencer, "The great aim of education is not knowledge, but action."

References

Allen, M. B. *Eight Questions on Teacher Preparation: What Does Research Say?* Denver, CO: Education Commission of the States, 2003.

Ambrose, A. *Parkway Central Middle School, University of Missouri–St. Louis Professional Development School PARTNERSHIP Annual Evaluation 2003–2004*. St. Louis: Parkway Central Middle School, 2004.

American Association of Colleges for Teacher Education (AACTE). "AACTE: Serving Learners." 2006. http://www.aacte.org/About_Us/default.aspx (accessed February 26, 2007).

American Association of School Administrators (AASA). *Leadership for Change*. Washington, DC: Author, 2005.

Cole County Circuit Court. *Committee for Educational Equality, et. al. v. State of Missouri*. Jefferson City, MO: Author, 1993.

Collins, J. *Good to Great: Why Some Companies Make the Leap . . . and Others Don't*. New York: Harper Collins, 2001.

"Cooperating School Districts of Greater St. Louis. 2006 (CSD)." http://csd.org/.

Council of Chief State School Officers (CCSSO). *Updating Educational Leadership Professional Standards in a Changing Public Education Environment*. Washington, DC: Author, 2006.

Darling-Hammond, L. D., and J. Bransford., eds. *Preparing Teachers for a Changing World: What Teachers Should Learn and Be Able to Do*. San Francisco: Jossey-Bass, 2005.

Darling-Hammond, L., and P. Young. "Defining 'Highly Qualified Teachers': What Does 'Scientifically Based Research' Actually Tell Us?" *Educational Researcher* 31, no. 9 (2002): 13–25.

Davis, S., L. Darling-Hammond, M. LaPointe, and D. Meyerson. "Review of Leadership: School Leadership Study—Developing Successful Principals." Stanford, CA: Stanford Educational Leadership Institute, 2005.

Ding, C., and H. Sherman. "Teaching Effectiveness and Student Achievement: Examining the Relationship." *Educational Research Quarterly* 29, no. 4 (2006): 39–49.

Evans, B. *Dictionary of Quotations*. New York: Delacorte Press, 1978.

Feistritzer, C. E., and D. Chester. *Alternative Teacher Certification: A State-By-State Analysis*. Washington, DC: National Center for Education, 2000.

Hess, F. M. *A License to Lead? A New Leadership Agenda for America's Schools*. Washington, DC: Progressive Policy Institute, 2003.

Hessel, K., and J. Holloway. *A Framework for School Leaders: Linking the ISLLC Standards to Practice*. Princeton, NJ: Educational Testing Service, 2002.

Higher Education Evaluation Committee (HEEC). Presentation to Board of Higher Education, 2006.

Hirsch, E., J. E. Koppich, and M. S. Knapp. "What States Are Doing to Improve the Quality of Teaching: A Brief Review of Current Patterns and Trends." Center for the Study of Teaching and Policy, 2001. depts.washington.edu/ctpmail/states_summary.html.

Holmes Group. *Tomorrow's Schools: Principles for the Design of Professional Development Schools: Executive summary*. East Lansing, MI: Author, 1990.

Hoyle, J. "The Good News About the Preparation of School Leaders: A Professor's View." *School Leadership Review*, 1, no. 2 (2005): 1–18.

Hull, A. *NCAELP Conference Report*. Columbia: University of Missouri/University Council for Educational Administration, 2003.

Hunter, Molly. "Missouri Committee for Educational Equality." 2004. www.governing.com/archive/2004/dec/schools/txt.

ISLLC Standards (see CCSSO, 2006).

Leithwood, K., and C. Riehl. *What We Know About Successful School Leadership*. Philadelphia: Laboratory for Student Success, Temple University, 2003

Leithwood, K. and R. Steinbach. "Toward a Second Generation of School Leadership Standards." In *Global Trends in School Leadership Preparation*, edited by P. Hallinger. The Netherlands: Swets and Zeitlinger, 2005.

MacDonald, J. H. "Community Education: Building Capacity in Public School Communities." In *Texas Public School Organization and Administration*, edited by J. A. Vornberg, 669–686. Dubuque, IA: Kendall/Hunt, 2006.

Missouri Department of Elementary and Secondary Education (DESE). News release July 27, 2006.

———. "2005 Missouri Recruitment and Retention Report." 2006. http://www.dese.mo.gov/.

Missouri School Board of Education. *Guidelines for performance based principal evaluation*. Jefferson City, MO: Author, 2006.

Missouri Standards for Education Programs. *Examiners' Handbook*. Missouri Department of Elementary and Secondary Education, Division of Urban and Teacher Education, Teacher Education and Assessment Section. Jefferson City, MO: Author, 2003.

Moses, M. "Superintendent of the Year Ceremony." Paper from meeting of the American Association of School Administrators, Leadership for Change, 2005.

Murphy, J. *Reculturing Educational Leadership: The ISLLC Standards Ten Years Out*. Washington, DC: National Policy Board for Educational Leadership, 2003.

National Center for Education Information (NCEI). "Profile of Alternate Route Teachers." 2006. http://www.ncei.com/part.html.

"National Commission for the Advancement of Educational Leadership Preparation." http://www.ccsso.org.

National Commission on Teaching and America's Future. *What Matters Most: Teaching for America's Future*. New York: Author, 1996.

Orr, Margaret T., Ruth Silverberg, and Brenda LeTendre. "Comparing Leadership Development from Pipeline to Preparation to Advancement: A Study of Multiple Institutions' Leadership Preparation Programs." Paper presented at the 2006 Annual Conference of the American Educational Research Association, San Francisco, California, April 10, 2006.

Plummer, Lynda. *Next Generation Schools: Providing Leaders for a Global Tomorrow*. Wichita Falls, TX: 1991.

Sirotnik, K., and Associates. *Reviewing Schools and Teacher Education: An Odyssey in Educational Changes*. Washington, DC: American Association of Colleges for Teacher Education, 2001.

Springer, J. *American Education*. 12th ed. New York: McGraw-Hill Higher Education, 2006.

Voluntary Interdistrict Choice Corporation (VICC). *The St. Louis Student Transfer Program: Historical Background*. St. Louis: Author, 2006.

Waters, J. T., R. K. Marzano, and B. McNulty. "Leadership That Sparks Learning." *Educational Leadership* (2004): 48–51.

Williams, Creg. *Building Towards 2011: St. Louis Public Schools Five-Year Plan*. St. Louis: St. Louis Board of Education, 2006.

Wilson, S. M., R. E. Floden, and J. Ferrini-Mundy. *Teacher Preparation Research: Current Knowledge, Gaps, and Recommendations*. A research report prepared for the U.S. Department of Education. Seattle, WA: Center for the Study of Teaching and Policy, 2001.

Wright, C. L. "School System Change: From the Inside Out." *New Superintendent E-Journal*, March 2006. www.aasa.org/.

Chapter 10
Social Planning in the St. Louis Region

Richard Patton

Overview

If the terminology is not politically incorrect, it might be fair to characterize social planning as the stepchild of the broader field of city and regional planning. Coming later to the table than physical planning—or many other forms of community and economic development planning—social planning lacks two of the primary characteristics that give other types of city and regional planning their appeal: glitz and apparent precision.

In the St. Louis region, this tension between earlier, traditional forms of city planning and social planning efforts—limited as they have been—that attempted to shoulder their way into the picture later in the game seems particularly acute. Amid the grandiose ambition of the nineteenth century, when St. Louis was the nation's fourth-largest city, plans were directed to propelling and securing St. Louis's place as the "future great city of the world" (Reavis 1875). In the twentieth century, as Heathcott and Abbott's earlier chapters detail, Harland Bartholomew's masterful plans were focused on establishing the position of St. Louis as a great American metropolis.

By the time social planning began to gain steam with the Great Depression, and certainly after midcentury, the focus and spirit of urban communities generally, and St. Louis particularly, were very different. These plans focused on what had gone wrong, who was left behind, and what difficult—and costly—things must be done to get us back to the point where, as always optimistic and sometimes naïve Americans, we felt we should be. By the mid-twentieth century, the problems of old age, fixed boundaries, overwhelming demographics, and arcane civic structures began to overtake the city of St. Louis and sneak up on other portions of the metropolitan region. Harland Bartholomew and Frederick Law Olmsted were not going to develop masterfully crafted plans or sketches of breathtaking urban landscapes that would get St. Louis or many urban communities out of the complicated circumstance in which they found themselves. Efforts to correct the situation fell to the murky and imprecise process of social planning. A limited number of individuals and groups were dedicated to that task, but for the most part communities did not embark on the business of social planning with great civic enthusiasm or confidence.

Social planning is not an arena in which the traditional civic notables operate. It is largely the bailiwick of do-gooders, academics, and government bureaucrats. Its focus is on people and problems not highlighted in promotional materials for the community. For the most part, it proceeds without benefit of political clout, public confidence it will produce results, or the surety of securing the resources required to implement the plans that are developed. Community efforts to put plans in place and reap their benefits are fueled not by the heady fumes given off by the nineteenth-century boast and belief that St. Louis, for example, was en route to becoming one of the great metropolises of the world. They are instead directed by the more low-octane hope articulated by current mayor Francis Slay, as well as the theme of his first mayoral campaign—that with sound planning, hard work, and a lot of luck, "St. Louis can be a great city again."

En route to examining social planning in St. Louis, this chapter also offers a brief review of the broad field of social planning. An effort is made to outline a general definition of social planning, as well as tracking how the concept has evolved over time.

The examination presented here of social planning[1] in St. Louis is offered from two perspectives. First, the chapter examines the long-term, historical view of social planning in St. Louis. This examination is rooted in a review of the literature and the author's work over nearly four decades on a wide range of community development and public policy issues, in the St. Louis region as well as nationally and internationally. That work was carried out from the base provided by a governmental research institute and two university public policy centers. It provides a perspective on how social planning "fits in" to the broader processes of planning and policy and program development in the St. Louis region—how it is perceived in the local civic landscape and the type of priority and resource support it is given.

The second perspective for this overview and analysis of social planning in St. Louis is from a vantage point that is narrower and more focused, but also more immediate and dynamic. On the latter count, a specific aspect

---

[1] It should be noted at the outset that in addressing the topic of social planning, the primary focus here is on what might be characterized as social and human services issues. Health planning is not addressed in any detail here. Although the roles of such organizations as the Health and Welfare Council of Metropolitan St. Louis are examined, despite its name and the fact it addressed some health issues, the organization's primary focus was on traditional social service concerns.

of social planning in St. Louis is examined over nearly two decades from the vantage provided by two closely related initiatives focused on promotion of the well-being of children: (1) Vision for Children at Risk and (2) the St. Louis Metropolitan Children's Agenda. These interrelated efforts involve a structured, research-based approach to strategically addressing the needs of the St. Louis region's most marginalized and imperiled young people. The model employed by the two initiatives is to link community assessment research with collaborative community action. Analysis of community needs, and the civic assets that are in place to address those problems, is coordinated with a broad-based collaborative process of planning, policy and program development, and strategy implementation to address the critical issues and service gaps that are identified. The lens provided by firsthand, day-to-day experience with these initiatives focused on at-risk children, youth, and families yields a variety of insights into how, in specific operational terms, social planning has been carried out in St. Louis in recent years, as well as how it is regarded in the broader civic landscape as it competes for pubic attention, credibility, and community resources.

What Is Social Planning?

Definitions of social planning have never been precise and, over the course of at least the past seventy years, have been in a state of regular, and sometimes rapid, evolution. Assistance in getting a handle on a definition—or at least sense—of social planning is provided by the 2004 report *A Review of Social Planning Activities in Toronto* (Zizys et al. 2004). The report provides both a conceptual and a historical look at social planning, and in so doing provides a framework in which social planning in St. Louis can be examined. In attempting to define and develop an understanding of social planning, this review draws heavily on the Toronto-based study.

Social equity might be established as the centerpiece of social planning. With that orientation, focus comes to rest on population groups who have been marginalized and are therefore at a disadvantage in efforts to get life needs met. There is a high degree of unanimity among the agencies engaged in social planning, both in the United States and internationally, that increasing social equity is one of the objectives. The populations on which agencies engaged in social planning are likely to focus include people living in poverty, children and youth, racial and ethnic minorities, refugees and immigrants, individuals with disabilities, women, older adults, and people who are gay, lesbian, and transgendered (NSW [New South Wales] Department of Local Government 1998).

There also is a fairly high level of consensus on the topical and functional issues involved in social planning. Those issues include health (including mental health); transportation and access; community inclusion, participation and empowerment; crime prevention; community safety; education and child development; employment and economic opportunity; housing; and intervention and treatment services related to problem behaviors.

Finally, with focus on the aforementioned population groups and issues, it has been suggested that the core strategies through which social planning is pursued include research, community engagement, and action (Zizys et al. 2004).

Still wanting for a comprehensive, coherent definition of social planning, we offer the following description, borrowing very heavily from the Australian NSW local government guidelines that define social and community planning:

> Social planning is the process of investigating and responding to the social needs and aspirations of all the people who live and work in a local community, with a particular focus on ensuring that resources and opportunities are provided equitably to those segments of the population whose needs often go unmet and aspirations unrealized. It is, ultimately, a process of collaborative planning on social and community issues in the local community and incorporates all types of activities that have an impact on community well-being (NSW Department of Local Government 1998).

Although the aforementioned is offered as a contemporary definition of social planning, it is important to understand that the concept of social planning is in constant, and on occasion rapid, evolution. To analyze social planning efforts in a given community and get a sense of where they stand, it also is useful to have a general sense of the primary stages through which social planning has progressed. Again, for assistance we look to the 2004 Toronto review of social planning.

The commencement of contemporary social planning is often marked by the transition from what is characterized in the Toronto study as individualized "charitable good works" to addressing social problems and needs through a more systematic approach. This systematic approach involves both government and a broad array of community stakeholders in structured processes that include data collection and analysis, community input, "best practice" research, and collaborative decision-making (Zizys et al. 2004). Simplifying and summarizing the historic stages of social planning offered in the *Review of Social Planning in the City of Toronto*, social planning since the Great Depression might be characterized as having four major stages:

Knowledge-based Social Planning—An approach that attempted to move beyond random, charitable good works as a response to social problems and develop empirical assessments as a foundation for "reasoned," structured interventions that were publicly supported.

Coordinated Social Planning—Focused on an integrated set of planning functions identified in the Toronto study as needs assessment, service planning, and program evaluation.

Community-based Social Planning—A process that moves beyond the orientation of simply providing services to address problems and needs that are identified empirically to engaging community members and organizations in identifying community needs and aspirations and developing strategies to address them.

Collaborative Social Planning—A planning approach adopted in response to what might be characterized as sea changes in recent decades in politics, government, the global economy, and popular perception of environmental issues. In this approach, proceeding under the aegis of such titles as "New Urban Planning" or "Alternative Social Planning," the focus is on an inclusive process that involves all stakeholders in collaborative efforts to identify common goals and implement jointly developed solutions. In the context of these collaborative efforts, it should be noted, however, that a clear focus is still maintained on ensuring that the needs of those who are disenfranchised are met, and that those constituencies are involved in the planning process.

In examining social planning in St. Louis, we will look back at these four stages in the evolution of the planning process and use them as benchmarks. With the above concepts and definitions in hand, we can proceed to an analysis of social planning in St. Louis.

Social Planning in St. Louis

Social plans and planning in the United States are likely to proceed in fragmented, even haphazard, fashion. Big cities may have comprehensive plans that touch on some social issues, or social development may appear as a component—though often peripheral—of traditional community and economic development plans. In large urban communities in the United States, the "social plan" is likely to be a conglomeration of the plans of a variety of governmental, civic, and community groups. St. Louis is squarely in this U.S. mold.

The 1947 *Comprehensive City Plan* under which the City of St. Louis operated for more than half a century had virtually no substantive provisions related to social planning. It made only a few passing references to slums and housing needs. It did note, "We have 33,000 dwellings still dependent on outside privy vaults." But it is not clear if that was seen as a social issue or simply a plumbing problem. There is a passing reference to "a comprehensive system of homogeneous neighborhoods" that may refer to standard zoning practice or something more insidious (St. Louis City Plan Commission 1947).

In roughly the same era, a 1954 planning report by the St. Louis County Plan Commission, *Metropolitan Metamorphosis*, examined the transformation of the county from a rural to an urban area. The report focused almost exclusively on physical and land use planning, as well as public works facilities and public utilities. There is a single page, plus a single paragraph, in the report that appears under the title "Sociological." In what would become a recurring theme for the next half century in developing plans to address the often-critical issues that faced the St. Louis region, the report strikes a note that now seems prescient. The report suggests that, "Unless we can recognize our common problems in developing a peaceful coexistence in the Metropolitan Area, we cannot expect to cope with any of the possible disasters which we have this far been fortunate in avoiding" (Baughman 1954). We will return to this theme later.

During the 1960s and 1970s, more attention was paid in local government plans to poverty, social disparities, and community dysfunction, but these things were rarely at the heart of the plans. The Department of Housing and Urban Development requires jurisdictions that receive certain types of federal funds to submit consolidated plans every five years. In recent years, the plans submitted by the City of St. Louis and St. Louis County focus heavily on such issues as public health, community development, population groups with special needs and, of course, housing. In 2000, as part of its plan, the city made a major effort to inventory and map community assets. Recent consolidated plans for the City of St. Louis have had a significant focus on children and youth. That approach is in line with strategies promoted in many national policy and academic circles that focus on the development of the community's young people to spur community and economic development, and improve the quality of community life. In contrast, the *St. Louis County Strategic Plan 2000–2004* (and its 2006 update) make essentially no reference to the needs and opportunities related to children and youth.

Beyond government, there has been a wide array of efforts in the St. Louis region to address social issues and human services needs. Many of those initiatives involve some type of planning component. The following review and analysis of social planning in St. Louis does not, therefore, have a precise target. It is instead based on a broad scan of the many social planning and development efforts carried out in the community. Usually, social planning initiatives have proceeded in an uncoordinated fashion. Efforts may be unconnected, duplicative, or even at cross-purposes.

The Broader Context for Social Planning in St. Louis

Activities in the philanthropic and religious sector, as well as the involvement of Civic Progress in community affairs, have all had a significant impact on efforts in St. Louis to address social and human services issues. While activities in these arenas do not usually constitute social planning per se, they often are only a short step removed and have an unquestionable impact. A brief analysis follows of some of the dynamics that set the context for social planning and development in the St. Louis area.

By virtue of their presence and the scale of their resources, philanthropic organizations and charitable giving have an inevitable and significant impact on efforts in any community to address social issues. Charitable and philanthropic giving in St. Louis is now in the area of $2 billion annually (Gateway to Giving Council 2004). Those funds come from a huge range of sources and are distributed through a wide range of mechanisms. Although expenditure of these funds has both an impact and ultimate direction, they are not collectively distributed according to any process that approximates a cohesive plan.

Monies distributed by foundations impact social planning and development efforts in two ways. On occasion, they are used to provide direct support to social planning initiatives, although historically in St. Louis only a small amount of support has been provided to such planning efforts. The greater impact on the community's social development efforts derive from the de facto effect that philanthropic giving has in the community. The donation of nearly $2 billion each year goes a long way to determining both what the community's priorities are related to social issues and the manner in which those problems and needs are addressed.

While the nature and impact of foundation giving can be tracked to some extent by the awards that are made, because foundation boards meet behind closed doors, the actual bases on which funding decisions are made are not usually known. From a social planning perspective, it is difficult to evaluate the intent and impact of funding decisions without knowing: (1) the priorities on which they are based; (2) who was consulted in the process of decision-making; (3) what data, if any, provide the basis for allocation decisions; and (4) if any effort was made to align funding awards with community priorities established in broader civic circles.

In recent years, there have been some efforts to connect local philanthropy more directly and strategically to broader, community-based efforts to address social problems and human services needs. The Deaconess Foundation, for example, in providing core support to Vision for Children at Risk and the St. Louis Metropolitan Children's Agenda, was intentional in trying to advance strategic, collaborative community action to address the needs of children, youth, and families. Focus was on support of joint community initiatives that were data driven, research based, and outcome oriented. In this framework, funding decisions were tied closely to the process of social planning. Usually, however, there is not such close alignment between the goals of foundations and the awards they make and broader community efforts to set priorities and develop policies and programs to address social issues.

A similar set of considerations come into play related to the charitable enterprises of religious organizations. Religious causes are, by far, the largest source to which St. Louis area households direct their charitable contributions, and those households are—once again, by far—the largest source of charitable giving in the region (Gateway to Giving Council 2004). It is clear that the impact of the faith community in addressing social issues in St. Louis is tremendous. To a great extent, however, it is individualized, random, and unplanned. Its collective intent and direction is hard to discern. Because of its large-scale and predominantly charitable orientation, it may be that the involvement of faith institutions and religious donations contribute to the dynamic discussed later: that the St. Louis region appears to be slow in evolving from a view of addressing social issues as charity to approaching this range of concerns as a community development exercise.

Civic Progress, in the same manner as the philanthropic sector and the faith community, has undoubtedly had an impact on the way social planning and development has been carried out in the St. Louis region. This impact derives from the large scale of its financial contributions, as well as from some of the issues it has addressed. In many ways, however, the involvement of Civic Progress in this range of issues has been involuntary and almost accidental. It was not an organization founded with the intent to engage in social planning or development.

Founded in the early 1950s, Civic Progress was formed as a civic organization dedicated to addressing such issues as the construction of new highways, housing, business and industrial development, and slum clearance (UMSL 2004). Beginning in the mid-1960s, the St. Louis public agenda and the ability to carry it forward became centered on Civic Progress (Judd 2006). As problems in the city of St. Louis, and broader metropolitan area, related to poverty, racial disparity, population loss, education, and housing began to worsen during the 1960s and beyond, the St. Louis region developed a strategy for attempting to deal with those issues. Faced with arcane, ineffective governmental structures that resulted in the concentration of social problems in certain jurisdictions and the resources needed to address those issues in others, the St. Louis region developed the almost reflexive habit of laying community problems at the feet of Civic Progress. Although well resourced and civic minded, social planning and development was not the business in which Civic Progress companies were engaged and, therefore, not the strongest skill set of its members. By its very structure, Civic Progress was not a broad-based and inclusive organization representative of the full range of interests and views in the St. Louis community, nor was its intent to solve the wide-ranging, deep-rooted social problems facing the region. Civic Progress was not equipped, nor did it intend, to take on the large, complex social problems that faced the St. Louis region. In the absence, however, of formal, effective civic structures for setting direction and allocating resources to address major regional problems, a community expectation emerged that Civic Progress would somehow provide for these needs.

Major Factors Affecting Social Planning in St. Louis

Four critical factors have affected—and continue to affect—social and human services planning in St. Louis. Those factors are (1) governmental fragmentation/civic segmentation and political exclusion; (2) extreme demographic disparities; (3) resistance to the strategic use of data and the lack of critical data; and (4) an orientation to social planning and development as a charitable exercise, rather than community and economic development functions.

While these factors are likely to arise to some extent in any major American metropolitan area engaged in community efforts to assess social problems and develop and implement solutions, the factors have been selected for examination here because, especially in combination, they seem to have significance in St. Louis. They present major challenges and obstacles that have, at least to date, proved largely insurmountable.

The four factors are grouped into two categories. The first two factors might be regarded as virtually inherent characteristics of the region. While not God-given, they are phenomena so deeply rooted and long standing that they can be regarded as structural issues—immutable "facts" of the civic culture. They are things that perhaps could (or should) be changed, but those changes would come about only with intense, committed action over time.

The last two factors are related more closely to the way the region has chosen to conduct its civic business. They, too, are related to the nature of the local civic culture but seem to be more procedural in nature, related to how the region has elected to conduct its civic business, rather than the indigenous nature of how things are.

Predictably, money—including the processes for securing and allocating financial resources, as well as the effect that possessing or lacking financial resources has on the interests and behaviors of individuals and organizations—also is a factor that has a significant impact on the social planning process. Rather than treating financial issues as a separate factor affecting planning, the impact of issues related to financial resources is addressed as a theme that runs throughout the social planning process. It is addressed in the context of the four other factors. While financial dynamics have an obvious impact on the way social planning is conducted in St. Louis, it is important to note that there has been relatively little direct financial support for social planning efforts. That fact is, of course, itself an issue of significance.

1. Governmental Fragmentation, Civic Segmentation, and Political Exclusion

In almost every way imaginable, St. Louis is—and long has been—a divided, segmented, and "exclusive" city and region. Myriad factors contribute to and reinforce the divisions and stratification: the city's old age and small geographic size; organization of the local community around strong ethnic neighborhoods; governmental fragmentation, beginning with the separation of the central city from its surrounding county; a civic culture with significant southern influences; and a business sector that was for many years dominated by large corporations. This is only a partial inventory of factors that have contributed to fragmentation in the St. Louis region. Moreover, as suggested by political analyst Terrence Jones in *Fragmented by Design*, St. Louisans have embraced a fragmented and stratified approach to community life and conducted their civic business and developed a host of structures and practices to give it expression (Jones 2000). The civic culture that results from this mix is at a minimum interesting—multilayered, rich, and complex—sometimes Byzantine. An argument can be made (and frequently has been) that this St. Louis model is well suited to certain aspects of local governance and the conduct of civic business. It makes government responsive to local needs, maximizes local control of financial resources so they are not "lost" to large-scale initiatives that serve what are perceived as someone else's interests, and builds and strengthens local communities and civic groupings.

What the St. Louis civic culture most assuredly does not do, however, is contribute to perception of common interests and development of shared community values. Similarly, it does not provide the foundation or infrastructure for community collaboration, joint community action, or aligning community resources and needs. At root, it establishes an "us versus them" civic paradigm.

The concept of "social capital" is very much at the center of current social planning and development models. Social capital revolves around social networks and the norms of reciprocity and trustworthiness that arise from them (Kawachi et al. 1999). From the perspective of social capital, addressing community problems and promoting community development requires face-to-face encounters (Beem 1999).

Social planning and development is, to a large extent, about bringing those who are marginalized into the social and economic mainstream and providing them with opportunities to share equitably in the assets and resources of the region. It is tied closely to building social capital. The fragmented and stratified civic culture in St. Louis does not facilitate—and usually impedes—that critical social planning process. At a broader level, it also undermines effective, strategic use of the community's resources. As was noted in the 1954 report *St. Louis: Social Life of a Modern Metropolis*, funded by the Carnegie Corporation, "the development of St. Louis—physical, economic, social—has been for the most part unanticipated and unguided" (Carpenter and Queen, 1954).

At the front end, jurisdictional divisions, parallel social and community organizations, rampant urban sprawl, and local communities that are often homogenous make it more difficult to be aware of the needs of other sectors of the community, let alone ascribe any legitimacy to them. These factors also inhibit the recognition of mutual interests and the points at which those interests intersect in the conduct of civic business. Robert Putnam cites a specific benefit of social capital as its ability to widen our awareness of the many ways in which our fates are linked (Putnam 2000).

Fragmented government, stratified civic institutions, and political exclusion do not provide effective structures for setting joint priorities and developing common plans and goals. In a related vein, mustering the political will and financial resources required for plan implementation is virtually impossible in a landscape of fragmented political power and isolated systems of financial resources. The authors of the 1997 "Pierce Report: A Call to Action" expressed this long-standing and often-cited St. Louis problem in their conclusion to the report as the fear that the St. Louis region "lacks a common vision; a shared focus" (*St. Louis Post-Dispatch* 1997).

As has been repeatedly noted and documented, fragmentation, stratification, and exclusion have undermined the well-being, growth, and quality of life of the entire metropolitan region. No one has been served well. From the perspective of social planning, however, these phenomena particularly exacerbate the problems of those who are disadvantaged and marginalized. It is harder for the needs of those in poverty, as well as children, racial and ethnic minorities, immigrants, and others, to be registered and recognized. Unrecognized, they will not be addressed.

In a reprint of the 1997 Peirce Report in the *St. Louis Post-Dispatch*, a business owner is quoted as saying, "The St. Louis culture is like many Clydesdale horses—strong and proud, but pulling in all sorts of directions at once" (*St. Louis Post-Dispatch* 1997). The quote is presented with an illustration of six large horses all in harness, hitched to a monolith representing St. Louis, each horse headed in its own, different direction. The simile is not at all a bad one. From the vantage point of social planning and development, however, in looking at the illustration one quickly recognizes that the analogy is flawed. In reality, all the civic "horses" are not of equal size and strength. While movement on civic issues in St. Louis is, indeed, usually slow, cumbersome, and proceeding at cross-purposes, it is eventually and ultimately in the direction of the interests of the more powerful civic stakeholders. That dynamic is, of course, true in virtually any community. It may, however, be fair to characterize as "truer" in St. Louis.

Aside from an inability to equitably develop common goals and joint plans, civic fragmentation, segmentation, and exclusion have additional repercussions for social planning and introduce complications at the operational level. A few examples follow.

Funding of initiatives to address social issues and community problems is complicated. Problems and needs tend to be concentrated in certain jurisdictions, and the resources that might be employed to address these issues are located elsewhere.

Amid the divisions that characterize St. Louis—and the resultant lack of coordination, competition, and sometimes outright conflict—funding to develop or implement plans to address critical issues is frequently lost. It has not been uncommon for federal agencies to get multiple competing proposals from within the St. Louis region. There have been instances in which the federal government had definitively pronounced in advance that it would only consider a single proposal for a metropolitan area; receipt of competing proposals will disqualify all applications from the community. In such circumstances the St. Louis region has, nonetheless, been known to submit multiple proposals.

National foundations in the arena of social development have, in large part, absented themselves from funding initiatives in the St. Louis region. They have become frustrated and disaffected by past experiences in which they invested in projects in the St. Louis area and then found that local stakeholders were unable to plan and work together in carrying out the initiatives. Some of these funders have been disappointed by the local byplay, taken their proverbial football and gone home, and returned at a later date to give the area a second chance—only to have the same experience again.

Curiously, in the St. Louis setting there have even been instances in which the same unit of government is operating, or funding, multiple initiatives focused on the same issues through undertakings that are not coordinated and, at some level, in competition. In the late 1990s, the State of Missouri had multiple agencies, projects, and initiatives working on the same essential set of social problems and issues. In the mix were the regular departments of state government (e.g., social services, education, health) conducting their ongoing operations, ARCHS (Area Resources for Community and Human Services), the local state Community Partnership Agency; the Family and Community Maintenance Organization; and a statewide resource agency, the Family Investment Trust. These organizations all had their own budget, collected their own data, developed their own plans, had relationships with other levels of government and nonprofit agencies, and sometimes competed for funds and clients. In the St. Louis area, even within the friendly confines of state government, common vision, shared values, and joint plans were not the order of the day. The trademarks of the region—fragmentation, lack of coordination, and competition—prevailed.

Another phenomenon that occurs as a result of the fallout of governmental fragmentation and civic segmentation might be characterized as "plan proliferation and fermentation." Because fragmentation and segmentation produce many different entities that engage in planning activities, many plans are produced. Implementation of these many plans is likely to proceed slowly—often it does not occur at all—because the plans are in competition for the political support and financial resources required to implement them.

Plans stack up; then they age. Eventually the plans become outdated and new data, analysis, and strategies are needed. New plans are produced, often on the same topic by multiple agencies, then the process repeats itself. Exacerbating this process is the fact that very frequently there are no resources to implement plans, in part because of the competition between plans. Since there often is ongoing pressure to address pressing social problems in some way, new plans are developed because it is cheaper and less politically complex than sorting out implementation of the old plans. In this cycle, plan development undermines plan implementation.

Finally, and most critical, the most significant way the phenomena of fragmentation, segmentation, and exclusion play out in terms of social planning relates to the political dynamics of planning and plan implementation. The ultimate political reality of any planning process is that the substance of the plan is determined by who is at the table when planning is carried out. If you are not represented in the process, it is extremely unlikely that your needs and interests will be addressed fairly and effectively by the plan. Inclusion of all community interests is extremely difficult to achieve in a setting where fragmentation and division are the norm.

By definition, governmental fragmentation greatly reduces the structures and processes through which there is an opportunity to address the misalignment of problems and resources. Local governments tend to be narrowly focused on the interests of largely homogenous populations. Structures for addressing issues on a regional basis either do not exist, or are likely to be narrow in focus and constantly under pressure from the jurisdictions and interests with the most political and financial clout.

In St. Louis, when regional mechanisms—usually special districts of some type—have been put in place to address community needs, they are usually "higher order" needs related to either the regional infrastructure (e.g., Metropolitan Sewer District) or the recreational and cultural interests of those for whom basic life needs are met (e.g., cultural and park districts). These extraordinary regional initiatives are rarely focused on the basic life needs (e.g., housing, health care, quality schools) of those segments of the population who are likely to find such needs unmet.

The St. Louis 2004 initiative may offer something of case in point. A major high-visibility, well-intentioned, and handsomely funded initiative launched in 1996, St. Louis 2004 set out with the express goal of transforming the St. Louis region by 2004. Its eleven primary initiatives ranged across downtown revitalization, neighborhood renewal, increasing health access for the medically indigent, and providing safe places for kids (Higgins 2001).

Although St. Louis 2004 unquestionably achieved some successes, there was a general sense in the community that it ultimately fell short of the high expectations it had raised. The primary critique of the initiative was that it failed to maintain its initial emphasis on community engagement and slowly became what the Pierce report characterized as an insider's game. A spokesperson for a grassroots community group observed that St. Louis 2004 was perhaps a think tank, but it was "not a real organization based in the community with the community's issues at hand." The leader of a high-visibility civic group raised related concerns about whether the initiative was sufficiently inclusive and collaborative. She specifically noted the St. Louis region's proclivity for top-down initiatives and its difficulty in meshing the "top-down" with the "bottom-up" (Higgins 2001).

St. Louis 2004 accomplished some good things. It did not achieve its goal of civic revival. A postmortem might suggest that its downfall was a long-standing St. Louis hurdle. The 2004 initiative targeted community problems that were large, complex, deeply rooted, and long standing. It did not, however, appear to have the will and expertise to effectively engage the members of the community who were most directly affected by the most challenging problems the St. Louis region faced.

2. Extreme Demographics

A second factor that has a strong and exacerbating impact on successful social and human service planning in St. Louis is what might be characterized in the vernacular of current popular culture as "extreme demographics." The St. Louis metropolitan region is about average on most standard measures of social and economic well-being. For a community with a staid and conservative reputation, however, St. Louis attains its average status through what is the equivalent of a statistical and demographic high-wire act. The region is not at all moderate in its socioeconomic makeup. Our "average" status is attained statistically by having large population groupings at both ends of the statistical spectrum. We have children, youth, and families in some locales who do exceptionally well in terms of the extent to which a broad range of life needs are met and how they stack up on the most frequently used measures of socioeconomic status. At the other end of the spectrum, we have large concentrations of the population who scramble daily, and often unsuccessfully, to get essential needs met. Compared to other metropolitan areas, St. Louis has a disproportionately large share of its population that is marginalized, living on the socioeconomic edge. This reality is reflected in the demographic statistics for the region's urban core and, for example, the area's perennially high ranking in the racial disparity index included in the East-West Gateway Council of Governments periodic reports, *Where We Stand* (East-West Gateway 2006).

There is a clear racial aspect to the socioeconomic disparities within the St. Louis region. As Joel Kotkin notes in *The Core of Rediscovery: St. Louis in the 21st Century*, "Indeed even today, St. Louis African-American communities lag behind their counterparts in most measurements of well-being, from business and homeownership to family income and education" (Kotkin 2004).

Almost certainly there is a close, and perhaps causal, relationship between the region's "extreme demographics" and the governmental fragmentation and civic stratification discussed above. A lengthy "chicken-and-egg" debate might be had about which came first: the demographic extremes or the fractured civic structures. From a social planning perspective, however, the most useful focus is on the insidious manner in which the two factors interact. The interaction is synergistic and negative, with the demographic extremes often reinforcing and fueling the fragmented and stratified civic landscape. In turn, the fractious civic culture exacerbates the factors that produced and maintain the demographic divide.

If, as suggested above, the focus of social and human services planning is for the community to address the problems of those segments of the population for whom basic needs are not met and opportunities to improve life circumstances are in short supply, then the St. Louis region starts the planning process from a significantly disadvantaged position. Our "extreme demographics" provide us with complex, monumental problems to be solved. Fragmented government and stratified civic structures (unless changed) necessitate that we undertake this difficult work with tools that are clumsy and ill suited to the task.

If the factors outlined above are viewed as structural—at least in the sense that they have been with us for so long that they might be regarded as "givens"—then the next issue is how, in conducting the business of social and human service planning, the St. Louis region has played the hand it was dealt. That brings the focus to the next two factors that affect local social planning and development efforts: resistance to the strategic use of data and an orientation to social planning as a charitable exercise, rather than a process of community development. Like the structural or historical factors discussed above, these more dynamic and elective issues are closely interrelated.

3. Lack of Data and Resistance to Its Strategic Use

The largest portion of the population in the St. Louis metropolitan area—and virtually all of its major institutions—is located in the state of Missouri, the "Show Me" state. Without the ability to marshal any empirical data on the topic, let's raise the question of what the Missouri state motto, "Show Me!" conjures up. Does it feel like a request to review the best-available information on the topic at hand for use in coming to a conclusion? Or is the message more of a petulant assertion that, "I know what I think, and I am not inclined to believe otherwise, regardless of the available evidence"?

In the tradition of the spirit reflected in the "Show Me" motto of Missouri, it often appears that the St. Louis region does not approach the function of social planning with the most sanguine orientation to the use of critical underlying data. There are indications that in St. Louis we may have our own—again borrowing from the current vernacular—"issues" with the use of data in conducting social planning and formulating public policy. There does not appear to be a general aversion to the idea of data and information in St. Louis. There are a multitude of organizations and agencies that compile and publish mountains of numbers and facts. Civic anxiety and resistance only seem to arise with the implication that data be actively employed to shape decision-making about civic goals or drive allocation of community resources.

A current-day example of civic resistance to the use of data to better understand and more effectively address critical socioeconomic issues facing the region is reflected in the reaction in some corners of the community to the report *Where We Stand*, published periodically by the East-West Gateway Council of Governments. Billed as a strategic assessment of the St. Louis region, *Where We Stand* provides data on more than eighty social, economic, fiscal, and physical variables examining how the St. Louis region ranks in relation to thirty-five other metropolitan areas with which St. Louis compares and competes. First published in 1992, the fifth edition of the report was published in 2006. In the report, data are provided in a straightforward series of charts and graphs with spare narrative copy directed to describing the significance of the variables and highlighting aspects of the data that are notable. Data are presented without recommendations or policy prescriptions.

Oddly, without the suggestion that the data are inaccurate or misleading, the report is regarded in some civic circles as controversial. East-West Gateway itself acknowledges this fact in the announcement of the release of its most recent edition of the report. What is hard to discern, however, is exactly what is controversial about unchallenged factual data that is presented in a straightforward fashion without commentary or prescription. There are other examples of this civic allergy to fecund data.

In conjunction with the St. Louis 2004 initiative, in the late 1990s a major project was initiated to develop the St. Louis Regional Report Card. The intent was "to create a process for annually reporting information on community quality of life." Three goals were identified: (1) identifying areas that need improvement; (2) assessing performance against goals; and (3) holding the community accountable for achieving progress (St. Louis Regional Report Card Steering Committee 1999). All of those exercises are standard, legitimate functions in a process of social planning directed to community development efforts and improvement of the quality of civic life. The study process for development of the report card involved a wide range of civic notables in conceptualizing the report card and the ways it might be used, as well as identifying specific indicators of community well-being that should be employed. The report from the steering committee for the initiative was published with the subtitle *Taking Stock. Taking Action.*

Apparently, however, it was determined in the wake of issuing the report that the community should not take stock and action, at least in so focused a way. Despite the high-level civic involvement in the planning process and the fact that financial resources were in hand, something different was done with the data-gathering initiative—something more diffuse, with a softer focus and fewer overt implications.

The United Way of Greater St. Louis is a tremendously effective and successful organization in generating resources to address the social and human services needs of the St. Louis region. While St. Louis ranks eighteenth in population among metropolitan areas with United Way campaigns, the local United Way regularly ranks in the top ten in terms of contributed funds (*St. Louis Commerce Magazine* 2002). Those funds are then allocated to community agencies through a carefully crafted, community-based allocation process. Frequently, however, there seems to be tension between United Way operations and broader community efforts to secure and employ data related to social planning and development.

The Health and Welfare Council of Metropolitan St. Louis (HWC) was founded in 1911 as the Central Council of Social Agencies employing a model used fairly widely throughout the country at the time. The council evolved through a variety of name changes and organizational structures until 1958, when it made its final name change. At that stage the HWC had a professional staff of 13 and member organizations totaling 197. In 1960 the council changed its structure and established project committees to address specific community needs. As is noted in the introduction to the archives for the HWC housed in the Western Historical Manuscript Collection at the University of Missouri–St. Louis, "The Council had expanded from its original purpose as an information and exchange network to one that included taking the initiative to define social problems and recommend effective action " (Western Historical Manuscript Collection 2007). In terms of breadth of focus and scope of operations, the HWC may well be as close as St. Louis has gotten to conducting broad-based, far-reaching social planning as it was understood in the context of its time.

The breadth of the HWC's reach and support is reflected in the materials from the Western Historical Manuscript Collection. The introduction to the collection notes that by 1960, funding for the HWC started with membership dues, grew to include funding from the Community Fund (later the United Way), and included funds from state and local government. By the mid-1960s, the Hospital Planning Commission merged its staff with that of the HWC, and a Joint Medicare Task Force was formed. In 1966 the council expanded its operations further when the Metropolitan Youth Commission contracted with the HWC for program and staff services.

By 1975, however, the HWC had disappeared, apparently around the issue of strategic use of data. The introduction to the collection of materials for the HWC in the Western Historical Manuscript Collection states that, "By 1975 major funding for HWC came from the United Way and its primary function was to provide service statistics for United Way member organizations." The introduction goes on to note, "In an effort to establish internal control of collecting service statistics, the United Way gradually withdrew its financial support from the Council." In July 1975, the HWC ceased operation (Western Historical Manuscript Collection 2007).

A few short years later, there was another cryptic and hard-to-decipher episode involving "service statistics" and the United Way. In the late 1970s and early 1980s, under United Way auspices, a community-based process was initiated to study the need for a comprehensive social service information and referral system (I&R) to be established in St. Louis, including the issue of who should operate such a system. Two uses for an I&R system were envisioned: connecting people to needed services and collecting data on community needs.

After months of deliberation, the study group concluded that there was a need for an I&R system and that the United Way would be the most appropriate organization to provide a home. After receiving the report, the United Way came back to the committee that conducted the study with the observation that the issue was complex and sensitive. The instruction was that the committee be expanded to represent more agencies and then reexamine the question. The committee was expanded, the issue reviewed again, and the same conclusion reached: the community needed an I & R system to connect people to services and provide information on social and human services needs. The response this time was to thank and dismiss the expanded committee. It was suggested that committee members had misunderstood the task with which they were charged and that their recommendations overstepped the scope of the issue they were supposed to address. Amid what was primarily befuddlement among the membership of what was now a quite large committee, one university policy analyst suggested that the likely issue was the implications that possession of far-reaching data on service needs produced by an I&R system would have for allocation of funds and program development.

In another arena of strategic data use, there seems to be an ongoing, low-level issue between United Way and other community organizations involved in research and social planning directed to program and policy development. The focus here is around community-asset data—specifically, information on community programs and services in the United Way's Community Service Directory. The directory provides an extensive listing of social services and programs in the St. Louis area, along with some details of their operations.

The United Way is a frequent partner, and not infrequent leader, in community efforts to address specific social problems and issues. A common pattern is that community partners come to the table to contribute their resources and work jointly to analyze and develop strategies to address critical issues facing the community. Often in this process, uses are identified for the information on community social service resources contained in the United Way Community Service Directory. Project partners frequently want to make use of the United Way information on community social service resources in addressing the issue at hand. In recent years, the data are usually sought in electronic form. The United Way regards the data as proprietary. Community partners are apt to see the data as something that should be contributed to the joint effort, as they are contributing the time and resources of their agencies. Usually, the initiative proceeds without benefit of the program information contained in the Community Service Directory.

The orientation of the local United Way to the strategic use of data has spilled over into its relationship with United Way of America. During a 2004 visit to St. Louis, Johnnetta Cole, chairwoman of the United Way of America's board of trustees, urged the local United Way agency to take a more active role with community partners in identifying community problems and helping to solve them. Cole is quoted in a *St. Louis Post-Dispatch* article as having said, "I think that St. Louis is not at this point among the local [United Way] organizations using this new impact model" (*St. Louis Post-Dispatch* 2004).

While the St. Louis region often appears resistant to strategically using—or sharing—data related to social planning and human services issues, there is another important aspect of the local data "issue." St. Louis usually lacks critical data on community assets—resources, services, and programs—that are available to address critical problems and needs facing the community.

Over the past three decades, there has been a major focus in social planning on use of models involving compilation of data on community problems and needs on one hand and information on the assets and resources required to address those issues on the other. In this research-based model, the data are employed strategically to address critical community issues.

The data can be used in two complementary ways. They can provide a tool to broadly assess the "balance" between community problems and needs and the resources available to address them. If the community has an elevated level of problems or needs related to a particular issue, does it have resources in place at a sufficient scale and of the proper type to effectively address the problem? In another variant of this approach, focus is on detailed assessment of "risk" and "protective" factors. Based on that data, policies and programs are strategically targeted to reduction of risk factors and promotion of protective factors.

A good example of this research-based approach to social planning and development is seen in the comprehensive strategy model based on risk and protective factors employed by the Office of Juvenile Justice and Delinquency Prevention of the U.S. Department of Justice. The model, developed by J. David Hawkins, Richard F. Catalano, and others at Developmental Research and Programs, was employed in the showcase SafeFutures initiative of the Justice Department that operated in St. Louis and a handful of other cities in the middle and late 1990s (U.S. Department of Justice 1995).

In both approaches outlined above, the underlying premise is to use data on problems and risks in combination with data on assets and protective factors with the intent of strategically developing and deploying the community resources required to effectively address problems and needs that have been identified. In this approach, possessing data on both sides of the "problem/risk" and "asset/protective factor" equation is essential.

With rare exception, St. Louis has lacked the data on community assets and resources that is now seen as a critical component of effective social planning. Strangely, there is constant interest, and occasional demand, for this type of information from planners, policymakers, program developers, and funding organizations in the local arena. The ability to answer a host of questions related to service gaps and duplication, use of effective best practice strategies, and the scope of community interventions related to particular problems and needs is dependent on possessing good data on the community's social development resources.

There have been occasional, sporadic efforts to assemble strategic information on community resources and assets in St. Louis. In the late 1970s, the Danforth Foundation provided funding to develop the Community Organization Inventory that was directed to comprehensively identify three types of community assets—churches, schools, and community organizations—in the city of St. Louis. In the late 1990s, Vision for Children at Risk developed resource inventories and maps for selected St. Louis neighborhoods, as well as a toolkit—the Community Resource Assessment Packet—to assist neighborhoods in conducting their own asset assessments. The work was carried out as part of the state-funded Family and Community Maintenance Organization Initiative.

In a similar vein, as part of its Consolidated Plan for the Department of Housing and Urban Development in 2000, the City of St. Louis Community Development Agency developed inventories and maps that identified a broad range of community assets and service resources for all seventy-nine neighborhoods that make up the city of St. Louis. About this same time, ARCHS developed asset maps for its neighborhood community clusters, as well as political jurisdictions and ZIP code areas. In 2006, the Incarnate Word Foundation underwrote a project to comprehensively inventory and map assets in the Benton Park West neighborhood in which some of the community initiatives it funded were concentrated. There have been a variety of other small, sometimes informal, efforts in neighborhoods and communities to get a handle on the resources, services, and programs in place to improve community life.

The aforementioned initiatives—big and small—have been limited in their ability to provide the type of community-asset data that are required in St. Louis for effective social planning. The focus of most of these efforts has been narrow, limited to a particular issue or small, localized geography. Asset inventorying and mapping projects that have been broader in scope, either covering a wide range of assets or larger geographic areas, have been one-time projects that provide only a point-in-time snapshot of community resources.

To be most useful, the data should be available on an ongoing basis. Without such data, interventions cannot be effectively targeted and resources will, inevitably, be wasted. The St. Louis region continues, however, to try to address large and complex social issues without the benefit of this critical information.

If, as suggested above, St. Louis has been resistant to the strategic use of data to conduct social planning, or failed to collect information critical to planning effectively, it is fair to ask why. Answering that question may provide the starting point for ameliorating the situation. Four possible explanations are suggested, as follows.

First, in a region with significant problems and stark demographic disparities, data that explicate those problems in detail are not likely to present the most flattering picture of the metropolitan region. This presents a problem, particularly for those community organizations whose efforts to improve the region entail civic promotion and presenting St. Louis in a favorable and competitive light. Civic promotion has won out over community assessment directed to better and more fully understanding of community problems so they can be more effectively addressed.

Second, data that are detailed and focused may have compelling implications for the civic strategies that should be pursued to address the problems documented. They may strongly suggest that a particular problem be addressed, or course of action be pursued. A data-driven civic agenda may be at odds with established community priorities or the strategies through which the community has traditionally addressed problems and needs.

Third, collecting and integrating comprehensive data related to the problems and needs the community faces, as well as the assets that are in place to address those issues, require drawing information from a variety of sources. In addition to assembling the data, making effective use of the information entails joint community efforts to analyze, understand, and employ data strategically to develop data-driven, research-based approaches to solving the problems and challenges faced by the St. Louis community. As already discussed, civic fragmentation, segmentation, and exclusion do not facilitate collaborative community activities, including the use of data.

Finally, collecting and synthesizing data—and particularly maintaining it in an accurate, current fashion on an ongoing basis—is a costly undertaking. In an environment where there are pressing problems, limited resources for social development initiatives, and strong competition for funds, strategies directed to assembling and analyzing data are likely to lack "curb appeal" and have trouble attracting the required resources.

4. Orientation to Social Issues as Charity, Rather Than Community Development

The traditional, historical orientation to social and human services planning was to approach the problems on which they focused as matters outside the mainstream of regular community business. Problems related to poverty, unmet material needs, crime, and other forms of social dysfunction were seen largely as the isolated needs of particular populations. They were addressed through charitable ventures and narrowly targeted government programs. These problems were perceived as existing apart from—and largely unrelated to—the mainstream functions of overall community and economic development. The conventional method for addressing social issues was almost exclusively through charitable giving by individuals and religious and civic institutions. Later, government began to address the needs of the marginalized and disadvantaged through programs that until very recently were characterized as "welfare."

The review of social planning in Toronto (cited earlier) describes these early efforts as "charitable services." The 1954 Carnegie Corporation–supported report on St. Louis, also cited earlier, makes it clear that social and human services problems were addressed locally almost exclusively through the efforts of charities and narrowly focused government programs. In a chapter titled "Getting Help—Social Welfare Agencies and Programs in St. Louis," in language that at the distance of half a century seems quaint, the report characterizes social service efforts as motivated "mainly by middle and upper class people whose consciences bother them in the face of the poverty, misery, and vice of city slums" (Carpenter and Queen 1954). In recent years, there has been a movement away from this perspective on social and human services problems, as well a major changes in the strategies regarded as successful in social planning and development efforts.

Efforts to address the problems of poverty, marginalization of particular populations, and reduction of social dysfunction are now frequently approached from the perspective of prevention, empowerment, and provision of opportunities linked to overall community and economic development efforts. There is an understanding of the link between the well-being of all community residents, including those who are disadvantaged or marginalized, and the overall health of the community and general quality of community life. As Gary S. Becker, the 1992 Nobel Laureate in Economics and professor of economics at the University of Chicago, has observed, "the primary determinant of a country's standard of living is how well it succeeds in developing and utilizing the skills, knowledge, health and habits of its population." He goes on to suggest that human capital can be neglected "only at a country's peril" (Becker 1998). There is nothing to suggest that these same dynamics do not apply to local communities and their economies.

Social planning increasingly looks beyond simply linking people to services or programs to address their immediate problems and needs, to strategies directed to prevention, asset development, and empowerment. The goal is to position individuals and communities to develop without external constraints, acquire needed skills and resources, pursue their aspirations, and realize their own potential. Development of human capital and strategic investment—along with promotion of social capital that was discussed earlier—are key concepts underlying this approach to social planning and development.

Many of the metropolitan areas with which St. Louis compares and competes appear to have made a faster transition to embracing this developmental and strategic investment approach to addressing the socioeconomic issues in their communities. They demonstrate a clearer grasp of the link between developing the full potential of all segments of the population, the success of broader community and economic development efforts, and the resultant quality of life. Efforts to address social and human services issues are being incorporated as vital components of broader community and economic development initiatives. There is a high degree of clarity about the returns on investments to be realized from broad-based social development.

Across the state in metropolitan Kansas City, for nearly two decades there has been top-level civic and business support for efforts to promote the well-being of children, youth, and families through such initiatives as the Partnership for Children. In a related vein, the Kansas City Civic Council has provided leadership in a far-reaching regional campaign to ensure that the critical early developmental needs of children are addressed. The goal is to promote the long-term well-being of children so the community can realize the resultant benefits in terms of community and economic development. The work in Kansas City reflects research-based, best practice approaches that draw on cutting-edge findings in the fields of both neuroscience and economics.

Similar civic initiatives focused on quality education, after-school programs, universal preschool, and youth employment are being carried out in metropolitan areas that include Minneapolis, Boston, Seattle, and Baltimore, to name a few. These are metropolitan areas that, perhaps not incidentally, usually rank better than St. Louis on the indicators in the East-West Gateway's *Where We Stand* report related to human capital development and the quality of community life.

St. Louis is not devoid of initiatives oriented to development of social and human capital and strategic community investment. Some of those efforts have been sustained over time, whereas others are more recent ventures.

For nearly two decades, the interrelated Vision for Children at Risk and St. Louis Metropolitan Children's Agenda initiatives (described earlier) have worked through a collaborative process to devise and implement data-driven, research-based plans to advance the well-being of children. The effort is focused on coordinated development and implementation of policy and program strategies across seven areas of fundamental childhood needs. In recent years, an additional component, the "Invest in Kids" campaign, has been added to the Children's Agenda initiative. The purpose of the campaign is to engage the community at all levels and in all sectors to make the type of strategic investments needed to promote the well-being of children and spur broader community and economic development.

In 2004, St. Louis Mayor Francis G. Slay initiated development and implementation of a Strategic Plan for Early Childhood Success, which is directed to ensuring that the full range of critical early developmental needs for children are addressed, so that children will be put on a positive life trajectory, avoid negative life outcomes, and contribute to the quality of community life. Now a Mayor's Commission on Children, Youth, and Families has been established to apply that approach more broadly to promoting the well-being of all children and families in the City of St. Louis.

Also in 2004, a coalition made up primarily of child- and family-serving agencies worked to establish a Children's Service Fund in the City of St. Louis under the aegis of the Mental Health Board. The fund is supported by a property tax that will provide dedicated revenues on an ongoing basis to address the needs of children, youth, and families. In administering the fund, the Mental Health Board has developed both a strategic planning framework and detailed outcome plans to direct allocation of funds and evaluate their use.

Other efforts to address social issues through efforts with a strategic focus on development of human capital include East-West Gateway (transportation, jobs, economic development), ARCHS (education and employment), Success by Six (early childhood development), Big Brothers and Big Sisters (mentoring and life skills), the Maternal, Child, and Family Health Coalition (health), St. Louis for Kids (youth development), the Healthy Youth Partnership (health and fitness), and the St. Louis Family and Community Partnership (child welfare). To varying degrees, all of these initiatives have been strategic—and at least to some extent, inclusive and collaborative—efforts driven by data and directed to implementation of best practice strategies.

Initiatives with the orientation of those outlined above—systemic in nature with a primary focus on development of social and human capital and strategic investment—are, however, still the exception rather than the rule in St. Louis. Social planning and development is more often pursued in the traditional vein, with a focus on raising funds to provide direct services and programs that can address problem behaviors.

The predominance of this charitable orientation has proved particularly difficult to overcome in efforts to dynamically engage the business and civic communities in the St. Louis region in social planning and development efforts. That more dynamic engagement is likely to remain elusive until more progress is made locally in establishing the now well-documented link between promotion of the well-being of those segments of the population that are disadvantaged and marginalized and overall community and economic development.

What is approached in many other metropolitan areas as a critical human development function—central to the success of overall community and economic development with a focus on strategic civic investment—is still often seen here as an optional, "charitable" nicety. The Kotkin report cited earlier quotes a local business executive as saying, "too many people would rather make philanthropic contributions. People have got to see the future is creating opportunities for the new generation" (Kotkin 2004).

The establishment of the Regional Business Council (RBC) in 2000 provides evidence of movement of the St. Louis business community toward an approach to addressing critical community issues through processes focused on social and human capital development. The founding assumptions for RBC assert, among other things, that the health of the region is a business issue and that business can be a catalyst for civic transformation. Departing from the frequent narrow organizational focus that has traditionally predominated in St. Louis, RBC's founding assumptions also identify partnerships as a key to successful civic ventures and call for relationships and linkages with a broad array of other community organizations. Specific RBC initiatives focus on aligning civic interests to work together on regional issues and targeting the economic advancement of ethnic minorities and quality education for minority youth (Regional Business Council 2006).

In a similar vein, at the turn of this century, Civic Progress identified the priority issues on which it would focus: regionalism, education, and racial and economic progress. There do appear to be some signs of change in the manner in which the St. Louis region is addressing social development and advancement of the quality of community life.

Conclusions

St. Louis is a metropolitan region possessed of many assets. Nonetheless, it has some serious—and to an extent unique—problems rooted in marked socioeconomic disparities among segments of the local population. Because of the peculiarities of local government structures and the manner in which civic business has traditionally been conducted, the negative impact of the area's socioeconomic disparities—and the resultant dysfunction that takes a variety of forms—is not isolated to the marginalized and disadvantaged individuals who are most directly affected. Problems have overwhelmed large population groups and entire jurisdictions, and now impede the overall growth, development, and well-being of the whole metropolitan region.

Strategic, effective community action is needed to address these problems. That action must be driven by comprehensive, coordinated plans that are developed through processes that involve representation of all segments of the community. Without broad-based involvement, strategic orientation, and community coordination, plans will miss their mark and be impossible to fund and implement.

In the face of this pressing need for effective social planning, St. Louis has a weak track record and continues to face some serious challenges to its ability to carry out successful planning. Those challenges include (1) fragmented, stratified, and exclusive civic structures; (2) extreme, geographically based socioeconomic disparities within the metropolitan area; (3) resistance to the strategic use of data for planning purposes, as well as a lack of critical information on community resources and assets; and (4) a predominant orientation to addressing social issues as a charitable exercise, rather than a process of social development and strategic investment closely linked to broader community and economic development functions and the overall quality of life in the St. Louis metropolitan area.

There are some signs of change in the approach that governmental, nonprofit, and business sector organizations in St. Louis are taking to address the critical socioeconomic and community development issues facing the St. Louis region. It is essential, however, that the St. Louis region continues to make changes in the way it addresses this range of concerns. Specifically, social planning and development efforts must be more inclusive, collaborative, data driven, and strategic, with a focus on development of human capital and improvement of the competitive capacity of the St. Louis region.

If such changes are not made, plans to address the region's socioeconomic problems and regional development challenges are likely to meet with limited success. The needs of disproportionately large sectors of the community will remain largely unmet, and the St. Louis region will continue to lose ground to the metropolitan areas with which it compares and competes.

References

Baughman, M. Eugene. *Metropolitan Metamorphosis: The Story of Change of St. Louis County, Missouri, from a Rural to an Urban Area*. St. Louis: County Planning Commission, 1954.

Becker, Gary S. "Human Capital and Poverty." *Religion and Liberty* 8, no.1 (January–February 1998).

Beem, C. *The Necessity of Politics: Reclaiming American Public Life*. Chicago: University of Chicago Press, 1999.

Carpenter, David B., and Stuart A. Queen. *St. Louis: The Social Life of a Modern Metropolis*. St. Louis: Department of Sociology and Anthropology, Washington University, 1954.

Chatterjee, Alina, et al. *Alternative Social Planning: A Paradigm Shift, Developing an Inclusive and Healthy Toronto*. 2004.

East-West Gateway Council of Governments. *Where We Stand: The Strategic Assessment of the St. Louis Region*. St. Louis: Author, 2006.

Ewalt, Patricia L., Edith Freeman, and Dennis L. Poole, eds. *Community Building: Renewal, Well-Being, and Shared Responsibility*. Washington, DC: NASW Press, 1998.

Facing Spokane Poverty: Social Capital and Poverty in Spokane County. Spokane, WA: Spokane Regional Health District, 2002.

Gateway to Giving Council. *Private Dollars for Public Good: A Report on Giving in the St. Louis Region*. St. Louis: Metropolitan Association for Philanthropy, 2004.

Heckman, James J. *Investing in Disadvantaged Young Children Is an Economically Efficient Policy*. 2006.

Higgins, Laura. "Bringing Home the Bacon." *Riverfront Times*, March 21, 2001.

"In Good Company." *St. Louis Commerce Magazine*, April 2002.

Infed. "Social Capital," www.infed.org/biblio/social_capital.htm.

Jencks, Christopher. *Rethinking Social Policy: Race, Poverty, and the Underclass*. Cambridge, MA: Harvard University Press, 1992.

Jones, Terrence. *Fragmented by Design*. St. Louis: Palmerston & Reed, 2000.

Judd, Dennis R. "The Several Faces of Civic Capacity." *City & Community* 5, no. 1 (March 2006): 43–46.

Kawachi, Ichiro, Bruce Kennedy, and Roberta Glass. "Social Capital and Self-Rated Health: A Contextual Analysis." *American Journal of Public Health* 89, no. 8 (August 1999): 1187–1193.

Kotkin, Joel. *The Core of Rediscovery: St. Louis in the 21st Century: Crafting a St. Louis Human Capital Strategy*. Regional Talent Project Report, 2004.

NSW Department of Local Government. *Social/Community Planning and Reporting Guidelines*, 1998.

"The Peirce Report: A Call to Action," reprinted in the *St. Louis Post-Dispatch*, March 9–16, 1997.

Planning & Urban Design Agency, City of St. Louis. *Consolidated Plan Strategy*. 2005.

Putnam, R. D. *Bowling Alone: The Collapse and Revival of American Community*. New York: Simon and Schuster, 2000.

Reavis, L. U. *St. Louis: The Future Great City of the World*. St. Louis: Gray, Baker & Co., 1875.

"Reinventing Planning: A New Governance Paradigm for Managing Human Settlements." World Planning Congress, Vancouver, BC, 2006.

Regional Business Council: Executives for Regional Growth and Civic Change. *Statement on Mission, Vision, Founding Assumptions, History and Initiatives.* 2006.

Schorr, Lisabeth B. *Within Our Reach: Breaking the Cycle of Disadvantage.* New York: Doubleday, 1989.

St. Louis City Plan Commission. *Comprehensive City Plan.* St. Louis: Author, 1947.

St. Louis City Plan Commission. *St. Louis Development Program.* St. Louis: Author, June 1973.

"St. Louis County Strategic Plan 2000–2004." Department of Planning, St. Louis County Government, 2000.

St. Louis Regional Report Card Steering Committee. "The St. Louis Regional Report Card: Taking Stock. Taking Action." 1999.

"United Way Must Go Beyond Fundraising, National Chair Says." *St. Louis Post-Dispatch,* June 16, 2004.

University of Missouri–St. Louis, Mercantile Library Collection. "Civic Progress." 2004. http://www.umsl.edu/~virtualstl/phase2/1950/events/civicprogress.html.

U.S. Department of Justice. *Guide to Implementing the Comprehensive Strategy for Serious, Violent, and Chronic Juvenile Offenders.* Washington: Office of Justice Programs. 1995.

Western Historical Manuscript Collection, University of Missouri–St. Louis. Introduction to the records of the Health and Welfare Council of Metropolitan St. Louis. www.umsl.edu/~whmc/guides/whm0434.htm.

Zizys, Tom, Mitchell Kosny, and Jennifer Bonnell. "A Review of Social Planning Activities in the City of Toronto." 2004.

Chapter 11
Pursuing an Elusive End: Highway and Transit Planning in St. Louis

Jerry Blair

On a typical day, residents of the St. Louis region make almost 10 million personal trips. Almost 88 percent of these trips use private vehicles (Nu-Stats 2003). Ninety years ago, people largely relied on streetcars, electric suburban and interurban rail, and horse-drawn vehicles for transport. The automobile was beginning to edge its way onto the urban stage, but it was still a minor actor.

It was, perhaps, inevitable that the automobile and its supporting infrastructure would come to dominate the urban landscape. Dispersed patterns of regional development enabled by the automobile ended up transforming the automobile into one of life's necessities. Planners inadvertently contributed to those patterns by arguing for the segregation of land uses.

The benefits of the automobile are profound and undeniable. It provided a level of mobility and flexibility unattainable with any other mode of transportation—at least for those capable of owning and operating a car. Those benefits, nevertheless, have come at a steep price. In one form or another, explicitly or implicitly, transportation planners have struggled to balance those costs and benefits over the last ninety years.

---

[1]This chapter uses City of St. Louis and regional plans as a lens for focusing on certain aspects of transportation planning in the region since 1917. There was no intent in this approach to neglect, or diminish, the importance of planning in other jurisdictions. The region referred to in the chapter consists of the City of St. Louis and Franklin, Jefferson, St. Charles, and St. Louis counties in Missouri, and Madison, Monroe, and St. Clair counties in Illinois.

A Planning Prelude

At the end of the First World War, the St. Louis City Plan Commission had existed for seven years. Established by ordinance in 1911, the Commission was a new government body created out of frustration with progress on the Civic League's *A City Plan for St. Louis* 1907 (Sandweiss 2001). While the Commission was active through its early years, it did not complete its first comprehensive plan until 1917, and a year later, as the war came to an end, it began considering how to prepare for the large number of residents (perhaps as many as 60,000) returning from government war service and possibly in need of jobs. That effort was a response to President Wilson's executive order directing the National Research Council to study postwar reconstruction problems. Effective reconstruction required, in the Council's words, "the intelligent planning and execution of plans for a better community" (City Plan Commission 1918). The Commission's response to the national imperative was *St. Louis After the War*, published in December 1918. The plan outlined a program of public works to help reinvigorate the city and offer meaningful employment to those returning home.

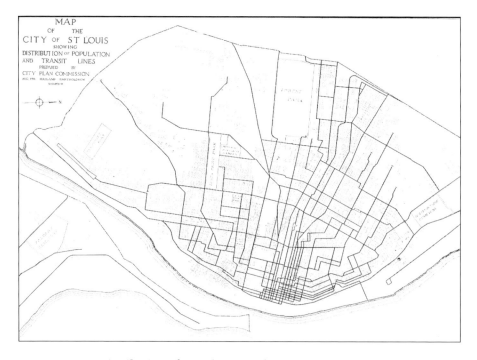

Distribution of Population and Transit Lines, 1917.

St. Louis After the War was largely a recap of a 1917 city plan with a few additions, including an assessment of St. Louis's financial standing compared to the nine other largest cities in the country. It showed that St. Louis was even then a low-tax, low-debt jurisdiction. It also included a suggestion that the city ultimately may have to take over and restructure the privately held transit system. Although much briefer than the 1917 plan, the report addressed a comparable set of issues: the riverfront, water and sewer systems, public buildings, streets and bridges, housing, parks and recreation, transit, and the persistent problem of the River Des Peres.

Perhaps the most notable aspect of the document was the introduction written by the St. Louis–born author Winston Churchill. In a rare intersection of planning and literary art, Churchill laid out a vision for city planning. He appealed to the civic leadership's better nature, calling for planning to focus on the broader community and its basic need for decent living standards and opportunities. In his opening paragraph, Churchill wrote:

> Before the war there is no gainsaying that our main civic ambition was a commercial one . . . our conception of a desirable city was chiefly utilitarian, in which the fine arts and the larger social good were sacrificed to a prosperity redounding largely in favor of the privileged and potentially privileged; a city which could give exceptional opportunities to the man born with the "business faculty." Not that the business faculty is by any means to be despised. But it is not the only quality needed in a rounded and happy community. And while commercial prosperity is essential, it can no longer have any permanence if other factors in a city's life and growth are slighted and neglected (City Plan Commission 1918).

A like spirit infused Harland Bartholomew, the man who would lead St. Louis into the era of progressive city planning and influence for decades the practice of transportation planning in the region.

Modern Transportation Planning Emerges

Harland Bartholomew took an unofficial advisory position with the City of St. Louis in 1915, and became engineer of the City Plan Commission in 1917.[2] As his plans for St. Louis and other cities indicate, all aspects of

---

[2]Although four years after arriving in St. Louis Bartholomew would establish the consulting firm Harland Bartholomew and Associates, Inc. one of the most prestigious planning firms of his time, he would retain his position with the city until the 1950s.

urban planning and development intrigued Bartholomew, but transportation in particular drew his attention. He saw transportation as having a key role in organizing space and creating the geographic linkages necessary for more productive land uses, thereby promoting economic and social growth.

Planning Process

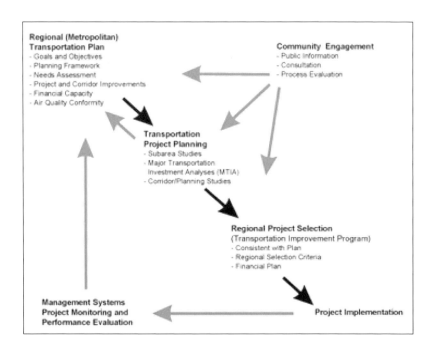

When Bartholomew arrived in St. Louis, he found a city spatially and socially fragmented. There was no strategic plan for city development. This especially was true in the area of transportation. Transportation decisions tended to be ad hoc and driven by residents' willingness or ability to pay for improvements through special assessments. There was no broad commitment by city government or residents to routinely fund public improvements for the greater civic good. Bartholomew's first major report would provide St. Louis with a systematic approach for confronting its problems, and it would encourage transferring the primary responsibility for planning public works from developers, individual residents, and neighborhoods to the local government. It would also attempt to rationalize the financing of infrastructure, differentiating between improvements that brought local versus citywide benefits. The report was a bold assertion of the necessity for comprehensive city planning.

With a title that would cause modern civic boosters to cringe, the Plan Commission (1917a) published *Problems of St. Louis* in 1917. The report was a compilation of plans completed or proposed. It embodied Bartholomew's "scientific"—later termed "society first"—approach to planning, emphasizing community (over individual) rights and focusing on the welfare of all citizens. The neglect of the general welfare, coupled with "selfish or unintelligent land subdivision," was the stated cause of the city's transportation problems. Overcoming these problems would require a strategy that linked transportation and land development, creating a cohesive, unified landscape (City Plan Commission 1918).

Despite the myriad issues discussed—including the pressing need for instituting districting or zoning—transportation was the centerpiece of the report—"streets are of first importance in a city plan" (City Plan Commission 1917b). The major street plan, along with additional but briefer chapters on transit and transportation issues related to industrial growth, dominate the text.[3] From a transportation perspective, the city's most pressing need was developing a structured approach for making transportation decisions that would address congestion issues related to the downtown business district and ensure appropriate connections to inaccessible land, primarily on the city's north and south sides.

In 1900, when St. Louis became the nation's fourth-largest city—a distinction it held for less than two decades—the city's population was 575,000. By 1920, the number of city residents climbed to 773,000, a 34 percent increase. Because the city's boundaries remained constant over that twenty-year period, population density increased from 9,373 to 12,590 persons per square mile. That rate of growth and densification produced its own set of problems, especially traffic congestion.

Among the prime concerns motivating the Commission was not, however, the city's growth, but migration out of the city. The movement of people and industries to East St. Louis and "attractive residential areas" in St. Louis County was resulting in the underutilization of land and the abandonment and deterioration of previously occupied properties within the city (City Plan Commission 1917b). While the city's growth remained strong, with the combined population increase in St. Louis and St. Clair

---

[3]*Problems of St. Louis* reproduces principal sections of *A Major Street Plan for the City of St. Louis,* also published by the Commission in 1917.

counties of 100,000 between 1900 and 1920 being just over half of the city's growth, the presence of so much undeveloped land in the city made the trend disturbing. Part of the solution was to create a balanced transportation system that would stabilize existing development and land values, especially in the business district, promote redevelopment of deteriorated sites, and increase the attractiveness of undeveloped land.

Table 1. Population of the St. Louis Region: 1900 and 1920

County	1900	1920	Change	Percent Change
Madison	64,694	106,895	42,201	65.2%
St. Clair	86,685	136,520	49,835	57.5%
St. Louis	50,040	100,737	50,697	101.3%
St. Louis City	575,238	772,897	197,659	34.4%
Outlying Counties	94,614	90,649	(3965)	(4.2%)
Region	871,271	1,207,698	336,427	38.6%

Source: Richard L Forstall, *Population of Counties by Decennial Census: 1900-1990*.
Note: Outlying counties include Franklin, Jefferson, and St. Charles in Missouri and Monroe in Illinois.

A balanced transportation system would require a citywide context, with improvements dictated by a comprehensive plan. What distinguished the 1917 plan from previous efforts was its intent to relate transportation decisions to the entire city rather than focusing simply on a particular location (City Plan Commission 1917b). Although critical that roads and transit lines reflect the built and planned environment directly served by the facilities, it was equally important that each facility fit within a systematic framework that served the needs of the broader community. Key to developing that framework was the concept of street differentiation.

Bartholomew would state elsewhere that traffic congestion was the result of poor street design, a declaration that would inform the city street plan (Bartholomew 1924). Improper street design led to underinvestment in some critical connections and overinvestment in less important ones, resulting in waste and inefficiency. Both problems plagued St. Louis. As put in *A Major Street Plan for St. Louis*, "To design a street according to its probable use is a reasonable but uncommon practice" (City Plan Commission 1917a).

Differentiation recognized that streets have varied roles, based on travel demand and land uses served, and that street design should account for the intended function of the facility and its location within the urban landscape. The plan identified three types of streets: large radial thoroughfares, cross town thoroughfares, and minor residential streets. Radial thoroughfares lead to the business district and serve as principal traffic arteries; cross-town thoroughfares connect the major radial arteries and serve some business development; and minor residential streets, with narrow widths and irregular alignments to discourage through-traffic, serve neighborhoods (City Plan Commission 1917b). These distinctions formed a classification system for effective street design.

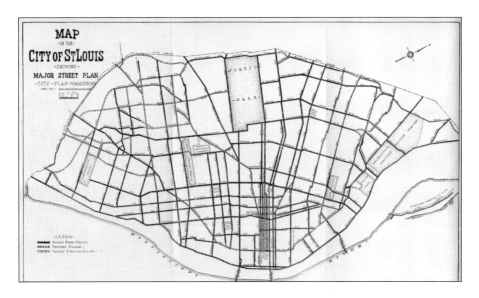

Major Street Plan, 1917.

Along with classifying streets, the report recommended width standards for principal roadways. Major streets without trolleys should be at minimum 60 feet and preferably 80 feet wide, providing 32 feet for sidewalks and 48 feet for six traffic lanes; streets with trolleys should be at minimum 80 feet and preferably 98 feet wide, providing 30 feet for sidewalks, 48 feet for six traffic lanes, and 20 feet for two trolley tracks (City Plan Commission 1917b).

Two fundamental problems emerged in viewing the city street system in light of these standards. First, although three-quarters of St. Louis's 940 miles of streets were 60 feet wide, there had been no discrimination in establishing those widths (City Plan Commission 1917b). Sixty feet was too wide for residential streets and too narrow for principal arteries. As a result, there was insufficient street capacity where needed and excessive capacity elsewhere. This problem could only be resolved over time through the application of differentiation. Second, in the downtown area, where additional width was vital to ease congestion, buildings were so close to many of the narrow, heavily traveled streets that there was little or no opportunity to expand capacity without disrupting surrounding properties. In response, the plan proposed a new Missouri law that would allow the city to establish building lines, or setbacks, along public streets.[4]

To evaluate the extent of transportation problems, the city conducted a traffic census over a two-month period in spring 1916. The census involved weekday traffic counts over an eleven-hour period at 245 sites along 84 streets. At a time when the city had fewer than 23,000 registered automobiles—approximately one auto for every 33 persons—the majority of vehicles counted were passenger autos. Auto ownership might not have been widespread, but the passenger car was fast becoming ubiquitous. The number of automobiles registered in the city had nearly tripled since 1911, and the number would grow sixfold over the next decade (St. Louis Regional Planning Association 1934). Despite the growth in auto traffic, nearly one-third of vehicles remained horse drawn. The competition between autos, trucks, horse-drawn vehicles, and streetcars for limited road space was creating unacceptable levels of congestion and delay, especially on streets leading into downtown.

Table 2. Traffic Census, 1916

Vehicle Type	Vehicle Count	Percent of Vehicles
Horse drawn	102,168	31.5%
Passenger auto	169,365	52.4%
Auto trucks	52,336	16.1%
Total	332,869	100.0%

Source: City Plan Commission of St. Louis, *Problems of St. Louis*.

A series of counts isolated traffic moving into and out of the business district, considered the principal destination of all trips, with the data cat-

---

[4]The plan also proposed a state law authorizing the city to approve land subdivision, giving the city some control over land use.

St. Louis Plans

egorized by direction of travel. Nearly 81 percent of the traffic consisted of autos, trucks, and horse-drawn vehicles, but streetcars clearly were the dominant mode of transportation. Having a seating capacity of up to 50 people, streetcars handled the vast majority of trips. A 1926 transit report noted that although only 8 percent of vehicles exiting the business district during rush hour were streetcars, those streetcars carried 73 percent of all passengers (Board of Public Service 1926). Annual transit ridership in 1915 approached 357 million, eight times the number of passengers using today's regional system (City Plan Commission 1920).

Directional data indicated that a disproportional number of vehicles were moving to and from the west when compared to the percent of population residing in western districts. Half of the vehicles and streetcars entering and leaving downtown traveled on east-west streets in the central corridor, while less than a third of the city's population lived west of downtown. In contrast, almost 38 percent of the city's residents lived south of downtown, but only 20 percent of the vehicles were on streets entering downtown from the south. The incongruity between directional traffic flows and population distribution, along with the high traffic loads on the east-west streets, led to two conclusions: the need for improved and widened east-west streets to distribute traffic more uniformly, and the need for better connections to the business district from the north and south (City Plan Commission 1917b). In lieu of these improvements, planners feared that the business district might shift west to Grand, creating a loss of investment value and severing the district's direct connection to Illinois (City Plan Commission 1917b).

Table 3. Traffic Entering and Leaving Business District

Direction	Vehicles	Percent	Streetcars	Percent	Percent Population Distribution
South	7,421	19.4%	1,676	18.5%	37.8%
West	19,578	51.1%	4,260	47.1%	31.6%
North	11,335	29.6%	3,105	34.3%	30.6%
Total	38,334	100.0%	9,041	100.0%	100.0%
Source: City Plan Commission of St. Louis, *Problems of St. Louis.*					

Sections of the major street plan not replicated in *Problems* provided a street-by-street assessment of needs throughout the city. The plan recommended widening most major radial streets on the city's north side and an extensive series of street widenings and extensions on the south side. Such changes would improve connections to underdeveloped parts of the city. *Problems*, however, focused on four immediate improvement needs, all enhancing access to the business district: widening Washington Avenue, which was becoming downtown's principal street, west to Grand; extending Twelfth Street south to Gravois, along with extending or widening Gravois from Twelfth to Grand; extending Twelfth Street north to Florissant; and widening Olive from Twelfth west to Channing. Consistent with Bartholomew's belief that "planning without mechanisms for achievement is worthless," the plan suggested a constitutional amendment enabling the city to double its debt limit, from 5 percent to 10 percent of assessed valuation, and legislation allowing bond financing of major public works apart from the debt limit (Lovelace 1993). The first suggestion bore fruit in the $88 million General Improvement Bond Issue approved by city voters in 1923.

Ultimately, the street plan proved conservative. Ostensibly intended to improve access to and from all reaches of the city, thereby encouraging responsible development and higher land values throughout, the plan's focus on downtown and the central east-west corridor tended to reinforce existing patterns. As suggested by Eric Sandweiss, the plan primarily confirmed what existed rather than created new possibilities for the city (Sandweiss 2001).

A follow-up report in 1919, *Twelfth Street: St. Louis' Most Needed Commercial Thoroughfare*, helped correct that central corridor bias. Recognizing that more than 450,000 people living north and south of downtown had no direct access to the business district, the plan identified Twelfth Street improvements as a priority. Once improved, the street would become the backbone of St. Louis, providing a broader series of street connections than any other contemplated improvement. Because growth further to the west of downtown would not benefit the city without an expansion of the city's boundary, future growth had to be to the north and south. Improving Twelfth would allow these areas "to be brought into more effective use" (City Plan Commission 1919).

Rapid Transit Considered

Problems of St. Louis considered transit indispensable to the healthy growth of St. Louis. In the preautomobile era, it essentially had governed the expansion of the city—its influence manifest in the correlation between unoccupied land and the availability of direct streetcar service. The increasing automobile presence did not diminish the perceived importance of transit to the city's future. Transit's capacity to move large numbers of people would continue to make it a critical component of an effective transportation network.

The city's ability to influence transit development was limited. Transit, although operating under public franchise, had always been a private enterprise. Since the 1899 consolidation of all streetcar properties under the United Railways Company, a single corporation owned the city's transit system. United Railways, a holding company, assigned operating responsibilities to the St. Louis Transit Company. Burdened by acquisition and start-up debt, both companies had limited resources to augment the system. That debt would drive the system into bankruptcy in 1919, where it would remain until 1927 when a new public utility, the St. Louis Public Service Company, formed to take over streetcar service in both the city and St. Louis County (Young 1996).

While the city could do little in 1917 to resolve transit's principal problems—a worsening financial situation, deteriorating physical assets, insufficient peak-hour capacity, and redundant, inefficient routing—it could ensure that the street system provided the connections and right-of-way required for more effective transit service. *Problems* emphasized the importance of considering transit and street plans simultaneously, and potential transit benefits informed many of the improvements proposed in the major street plan.

Along with improving streets to enhance the transit system, the city could also look to the future. Noting that St. Louis was the largest city in the country with a surface-only transit system, the plan suggested that the growing population of the city would soon require rapid transit. This could be in the form of rail operating in subways, on elevated structures, or in separate rights-of-way. Although the existing transit system could meet the city's immediate travel demands, planning for rapid transit well in advance of its need was essential. *Problems* called for a thorough study.

The St. Louis Transit System: Present and Future, published by the Commission in 1920, concluded an initial study of transit in the city. The most vexing problem, whether considering existing service or pursuing rapid transit, was financial. United Railways was in bankruptcy. The system's income, based on a fixed fare, was insufficient to cover operating costs, meet debt obligations, or attract private capital. Further, franchise requirements under which United Railways operated precluded the company from making changes that would improve the system's efficiency and economy.

To a degree, the system was stuck in place. The plan suggested that the future of transit "must become a matter of municipal credit and control, if not municipal operation" (City Plan Commission 1920).

Despite the financial problems, transit ridership was growing, nearly tripling since 1900 and increasing at double the rate of population growth. Adjustments were vital to ensure that the system was capable of meeting the city's immediate needs: congestion relief in the business district and more direct routings to all parts of the city. The former would strengthen the downtown area, always a major concern; the latter would improve citywide access and encourage land development. To meet those needs, the plan proposed a three-step program. The first two steps involved a series of streetcar reroutings, to either eliminate redundant transit lines or improve directness, and a number of extensions to expand the service area, especially to the north and south. Although the majority of people lived within a thirty-five minute transit trip from downtown, travel times from the northern and southern parts of the city could be well over an hour (City Plan Commission 1920). Proceeding with the first two steps was contingent on United Railways coming out of receivership as well as the implementation of a more flexible fare policy that would better align revenues with costs.

Table 4. Annual Transit Passengers (000s): 1900 to 1919

	1900	1905	1910	1915	1919
Passengers	141,951	263,114	335,596	356,815	409,010
Source: City Plan Commission, *The St. Louis Transit System: Present and Future.*					

The third step was implementing rapid transit. The plan saw no urgent need for rapid transit; in fact, it contended the city was not ready for it. It would become, nevertheless, a necessity within the next decade or two as the city continued to grow. Arguments against its near-term implementation were financial and practical. Neither the city nor United Railways had the resources to build such a system. There was insufficient demand from any one direction to warrant it. It would encourage population shifts to outlying areas of the city, negatively affecting land values in intermediate areas. This last argument presented a conundrum for the city. While the city desired to see those outlying areas develop, it was apprehensive that such development might come at the expense of development closer to the business district. "St. Louis," the report stated, "is a sprawling city and needs a greater intensity of development within the intermediate areas of the city before rapid transit facilities will be justified" (City Plan Commission 1920). That concern, however, related only to the provision of rapid transit, not the extension of streets.

It is difficult to overstate the importance early urban planners gave to the transit–land use linkage. Transit was almost deterministic in their thinking. The presence or absence of transit routes helped explain development patterns in the city. The westward movement of population through the central corridor was dependent on the profusion of direct streetcar routes. Correspondingly, lagging growth in the city's north side and south side reflected the lack of direct streetcar service. St. Louis County's 1930 highway plan, which devotes a considerable amount of space discussing transit needs, attributed unbalanced development patterns in the county to the absence of adequate transit services in its northern and southern reaches (Harland Bartholomew and Associates 1930). Planners did not neglect the symbiotic nature of the transit-land use relationship—transit pursued markets and markets followed transit—but they believed that transit had a distinct ability to encourage desirable land development.

Although the plan was wary about proceeding with rapid transit too soon, it did embrace one aspect of such a system—a downtown subway. Traffic congestion in the business district was among the city's most acute transportation problems. Removing streetcars from narrow downtown streets would provide significant relief, doubling street capacity and improving both auto and transit speeds. To accomplish this, the plan proposed two subway loops beneath the business district.[5] One would handle east-west streetcar traffic; the other would ultimately be for rapid transit. Streetcars would enter and exit the subway tunnels west of downtown. North-south streetcar lines passing through downtown would remain on the surface, rerouted onto streets with sufficient width to handle both automobile and transit traffic. Estimated cost of the two tunnels was $17 million (City Plan Commission 1920).

A Board of Public Service document presented to the Board of Aldermen six years later—*Report on Rapid Transit for St. Louis*—was less equivocal about prospects for rapid transit. The detailed report concluded that rapid transit was an immediate need and that St. Louis could afford it. Building on the 1920 plan, it proposed downtown subway loops for surface cars, along with a short tunnel on Grand Avenue. This was the first step. The

---

[5]A major obstacle to constructing the proposed loops was the 8th St./Washington Ave. tunnel, which would need to be abandoned if subways were to cut through it and reach the center of downtown. Seventy years later MetroLink would use that tunnel to traverse the central business district.

second step would construct six rapid transit lines, possibly in subways or surface rights-of-way separate from streets, halfway between downtown and the city's outer limits. These six routes would fan out from the business district to the north, northwest, west, southwest, and south. Those two steps could be completed within five or six years. The final step would extend the six lines to the city limits. Streetcars and buses, which were beginning to supplement and compete with trolley service on St. Louis streets, would feed the rapid transit lines. Total construction cost was between $128 million and $158 million (Board of Public Service 1926).

Conceived in optimism rather than realism, the financing plan proved unattainable. The proposed financing method grew out of two premises: Property owners contiguous to the lines would reap significant benefit from increased land values, and congestion relief and improved accessibility would lead to population and business growth, resulting in increased tax revenues and other tangible citywide benefits. Both the city and affected property owners, therefore, should share the cost burden. The plan called for meeting three-quarters of right-of-way and permanent construction costs through assessments on specially benefited properties, with the city supplying the remaining one-quarter by issuing public utility bonds. Nonpermanent items, such as track, electrical systems, and rolling stock, would be the responsibility of the operating company (City Plan Commission 1920). The plan constituted a serious effort to advance rapid transit in St. Louis, but it was simply too far ahead of public and political opinion to succeed. Nonetheless, the dream of rapid transit would persist, unfulfilled, through the next five decades.

Toward a Regional Perspective

In 1927, the Plan Commission published a ten-year retrospective on the city plan. Striking a self-congratulatory chord, the document reviewed accomplishments during the period, especially street and transit improvements: twenty-one major street projects completed with thirty-four in progress, and five transit projects completed with two in progress. The document also reflected on the future and the automobile's effect on cities and their structure. It is an "age of transformation," the document declared, stressing the corresponding necessity for planning beyond the city's boundaries. *Problems* had already identified the need for more expansive planning. That plan supported state legislation that would enable counties and small cities to create planning commissions. Planning commissions in jurisdictions bordering the city would provide for more harmonious development across the metropolitan district. It would also prevent those jurisdictions from committing the same costly mistakes the city had made during its development. But the document's aim was higher than just sound city or county planning; it proposed a comprehensive plan for the entire metropolitan district (City Plan Commission 1927).

Earlier in 1927, the Regional Planning Federation issued a prospectus for a regional plan. Bemoaning that St. Louis was lagging behind other major cities already engaged in such planning, the prospectus urged local governments to join in an effort to identify a logical system of public improvements for those areas of the region most suitable for development. The motivation was economic efficiency—"provision of adequate public improvements and coordination of development in the district means untold economies" (Regional Planning Federation 1927). Strategic investments would prevent redundant services and make the best use of the district's physical and fiscal resources. A lack of funding, typically betraying a lack of interest, stifled the Federation's efforts.

The first attempt at comprehensive regional planning occurred during the Great Depression, encouraged and partially funded by the federal government. To help implement New Deal initiatives, President Roosevelt created the National Planning Board in 1933 to support planning at all levels of government. In response, local leaders revived the Regional Planning Federation—renaming it the St. Louis Regional Planning Association and later the St. Louis Regional Plan Commission—and successfully applied for a federal grant to fund the plan. The Association's board of directors consisted of twenty-six officials and prominent citizens from the eight-county metropolitan district, with numerous other local representatives sitting on subject committees. Serving as principal consultant was Harland Bartholomew. With the goal of achieving unity and balance in regional development, the plan would take a comprehensive look at social, economic, and physical conditions in the region and prepare recommendations for improving highways, transit, other transportation facilities, sewers and water supply, recreation, and housing.

Fundamental changes were taking place in the urban landscape. Older areas were beginning to show signs of decline while previously undeveloped areas were experiencing rapid growth. Sprawling development patterns associated with increased auto use were the plan's prime concern. Because of the accessibility provided by the automobile, the region's population was spreading out faster than local jurisdictions could accommodate the growth. This created an imbalance between the supply of and demand for infrastructure, producing unbalanced, inefficient, and costly patterns of growth. A corresponding effect was the loss of population in older parts of the central city. The function of the plan was to establish a guide for directing future development. In a preliminary 1934 report, the Regional Planning Association characterized the essence of the plan in the following cautionary paragraph:

> The most desirable form or pattern of the future of the region should be clearly defined. It should be given some official status. Individual, cooperative and public activities can then be directed in harmony therewith. Any other policy of growth will ultimately lead to social and economic collapse (St. Louis Regional Planning Association 1934).

Planning had become serious business, at least to planners.

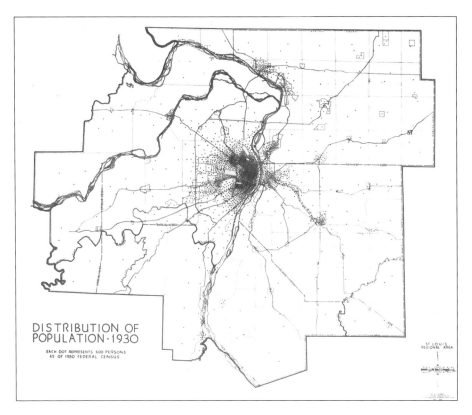

Population Distribution, 1930.

Although the population of the city would actually decline during the 1930s, its growth through 1930 remained robust. Between 1910 and 1930, however, combined population increases in St. Louis, Madison, and St.

Clair counties were 64 percent higher than the city's growth. During the 1920s, population growth in St. Louis County alone was twice the city's increase. St. Louis County increases were predominantly in the central corridor west of the city, while the most significant increases in Madison and St. Clair counties were in the industrial areas bordering the Mississippi River (e.g., Alton, Wood River, Granite City, East St. Louis).

Table 5. Population of the St. Louis Region: 1910 and 1930

County	1910	1930	Change	Percent Change
Madison	89,847	143,830	53,983	60.1%
St. Clair	119,870	157,775	37,905	31.6%
St. Louis	82,417	211,593	129,176	156.7%
St. Louis City	687,029	821,960	134,931	19.6%
Outlying Counties	95,911	94,805	(1,106)	(1.2%)
Region	1,075,074	1,429,963	354,889	33.0%

Source: Richard L Forstall, *Population of Counties by Decennial Census: 1900-1990.*

As notable as those population increases were, auto ownership had risen more dramatically. In 1911, there were under 7,800 automobiles registered in the city; by 1930, that number rose to nearly 169,000. The total number of automobiles registered in the region topped 305,000 in 1930, which equated to one car for every 4.5 persons (St. Louis Regional Planning Association 1934). Because of its development density, intensive transit service, and higher concentrations of low-income households, the city had the lowest ownership rate among the eight counties in the region (.205 autos per capita). Although auto ownership actually declined during the Depression, there was no doubt that the automobile was the mode of the future.

The plan projected population out to 1960. Its estimate of almost 2 million residents in the eight-county region by 1960 was slightly below the actual census count of 2.1 million. Planners anticipated that almost all the growth would occur within a ten-mile radius of downtown, principally within Lindbergh Boulevard in Missouri and in the American Bottoms in Illinois, with some strip growth along the radial highways leading to Belleville, Collinsville, and Edwardsville. Population within the outlying counties (Franklin, Jefferson, St. Charles, and Monroe) would either decline or remain static (National Resources Committee 1936). While the plan did a sound job of forecasting the regional total, it failed to foresee the declining position of the city, a more than tripling of population in St. Louis County, and significant percentage growth in the outlying Missouri counties.

Although planners did not anticipate the type of growth that would occur, they certainly were concerned about its possibilities. They saw many of the region's problems stemming from the inadequate control of and premature land subdivision. This had resulted in unwarranted public expenditures, improper development locations, inappropriate design, and inferior standards for improvements (St. Louis Regional Planning Association 1934). Premature land subdivision, in particular, had led to "abnormal" expenditures in some areas and the abandonment of land in older areas where adequate public investments existed (National Resources Committee 1936). These conditions had a profound effect on the adequacy of the transportation system. The plan's recommendations would emphasize the need for local planning commissions, master planning, and land use regulations and control.

Outside the City of St. Louis, development tended to concentrate around the radial highways extending from the Central Business District. Almost all these major routes were state highways. Because of population and industrial growth beyond the city's limits, congestion was becoming a problem, especially as travelers neared the center of the region. To evaluate this problem, planners conducted twelve-hour traffic counts on the region's principal highways. Traffic flows were highest in the areas of St. Louis County immediately west of the city and east of Lindbergh Boulevard, in the East St. Louis area and the East St. Louis–Belleville corridor, and in the industrial Alton–Wood River area. The only significant flow beyond the urban portion of the region (a twenty-mile circle around the Central Business District) was traffic crossing the Missouri River and continuing through St. Charles County on US 40 (today's I-70). Addressing congestion required widening and otherwise improving selected major radials extending from the Central Business District to outlying portions of the region. A minimum of four traffic lanes would be necessary within the urban district, with additional lanes required where on-street parking was present. The plan also proposed a number of new routes in the urban portion of the region to fill gaps in the existing system, and it encouraged grade separations at the intersections of some major radial highways and at railroad crossings along heavily traveled radials.

Then as now, crossing the Mississippi River was an important concern. During the twelve-hour traffic count, nearly twenty-five thousand vehicles crossed the five toll bridges spanning the Mississippi—Lewis and Clark, Chain of Rocks, McKinley, Eads, and Municipal (today's MacArthur). Over

90 percent of the traffic was on the three downtown bridges, and nearly two-thirds of that total was on the Municipal Bridge. Only the three-lane Municipal Bridge operated at capacity during the peak hour. Because of traffic conditions on the bridge, along with its importance in handling the most diverse array of intraregional trips, the plan recommended building a new downtown bridge north of the Municipal.

The lack of connector roadways in suburban areas also was a prime consideration. These principally were north-south routes providing access between the radial highways and between outlying communities. The lack of such connectors was especially acute in St. Louis County. Except for Lindbergh Boulevard, there were no continuous north-south highways traversing the County. The plan proposed a number of new or improved connector roadways throughout Madison, St. Clair, and St. Louis counties, but none of the recommended routes would bisect the central section of St. Louis County, where the issue was (and remains) most prominent. The priority recommendation was constructing a new route in Illinois extending south from Alton and crossing the Mississippi River, via a new bridge, to connect with Lindbergh Boulevard near Jefferson Barracks. This new route would not only facilitate traffic between major radial highways, it would also form, in conjunction with Lindbergh, an outer belt allowing travelers to bypass the more intensely developed, congested portions of the region.

Table 6. Mississippi River Bridge Crossings: 1935

Bridge	Traffic Volume	Percent of Total
Lewis and Clark	1,500	6.0%
Chain of Rocks	825	3.3%
McKinley	3,500	14.1%
Eads	2,750	11.1%
Municipal	16,354	65.9%
Total	24,829	100.0%
Source: National Resources Committee, *Regional Planning*, 31.		

Given the population growth assumptions informing the plan—that the city would continue growing, albeit at a more modest rate, and that nearly all population growth would occur within a reasonable distance from the Central Business District—the plan was sound. In retrospect, it is apparent that in the absence of comprehensive land use controls, the plan would not produce the preferred growth patterns. Widening radial highways would certainly improve access to and from downtown St. Louis, but it would also create development opportunities in suburban and outlying areas, encouraging more dispersed residential and business patterns and diminishing the regional draw of the city. Building more connecting roadways and a bypass would have similar effects. The planners were not blind to these potential outcomes, but their faith that unified and coordinated planning was a real, perhaps imminent, possibility quieted any concerns they might have otherwise expressed.

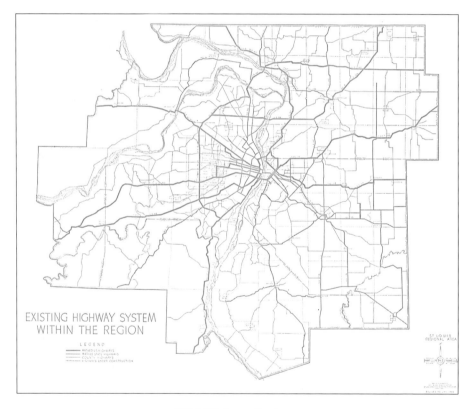

1934 Highway System.

The region's transit system was in flux during the mid-1930s. Transit was a mix of steam and electric interurban and suburban rail, streetcars, and buses. Since the creation of the People's Motor Bus Company in 1922, buses had competed with and replaced many streetcar lines in Missouri. Soon after buying out People's Motor Bus in 1934, the St. Louis Public Service Company, whose financial standing remained problematic, had four-hundred buses and nearly 1,500 streetcars operating in both St. Louis city and county (Young 1996). In Illinois, buses had replaced all streetcar lines and many electric interurban rail lines by 1935. Despite the significant levels of service provided by these systems, the plan concluded that the dispersal of population made it financially impractical to extend transit further, although the plan's objective was a transit system that would meet all needs. Developing an effective system would require, however, "a more evenly balanced distribution of population which in turn depends upon a sound urban land policy" (National Resources Committee 1936).

The plan produced no specific recommendations for transit beyond recognizing the need for improving existing routes and providing additional transit services to both supplement existing radial lines and provide cross-movements. The primary goal of any improvement was to expedite movements between outlying areas and the Central Business District. Rapid transit was an attractive option for these movements, but an extensive subway or elevated system was not essential. Concentrating rapid transit facilities in the congested portion of the region would be sufficient. Two basic options existed short of subway or elevated rail facilities: jointly using mainline railroads for commuter service, or constructing elevated or depressed highways with full grade separation for both automobile and transit use. The preliminary report had stressed the multimodal use of grade-separated thoroughfares, an emphasis missing from the final report. Whatever its form, rapid transit would require a feeder local bus system and a system of parking facilities at outlying stations.

The Regional Commission concluded its planning with a series of sixteen priority recommendations. In submitting the plan to President Roosevelt, the National Resources Committee combined three of the Regional Commission's recommendations into two of its own. First, there was a need for continuous and cooperative regional planning in St. Louis. Second, there was a need for a regional agency, authorized by interstate compact, to oversee planning and development in the region (St. Louis Regional Planning Association 1934). Those two recommendations would eventually lead to the creation, by interstate compact, of the Bi-State Development Agency in 1949. Unfortunately, the agency would receive neither the political nor the financial support needed to carry out its broad powers.

Expressways to Interstates

Optimism prevailed as the city emerged from the effects of the Great Depression and World War II. Most observers anticipated continued population growth, albeit at a much slower rate. Few imagined that the city would reach its population apex in 1950, followed by sharp declines through the rest of the century. In 1947, the Plan Commission drew up a new comprehensive plan for the city. Relative to transportation, planners boasted of having successfully transformed, through a series of bond issues, a horse-and-buggy street system to one meeting the demands of the automobile, and of having a transit system that directly served more than 99 percent of the city's residents (City Plan Commission 1947). Despite the rise in auto use, transit maintained a prominent role in moving people, especially in the downtown area. By 1946, streetcars and buses were transporting more people into the Central Business District than were automobiles. This was a reversal of trends through the 1930s and early 1940s. General satisfaction with the state of transit led to minimal recommendations for the system's improvement—extending a few bus lines and removing parking on some narrow downtown streets to facilitate traffic flow. The plan's highway recommendations were more ambitious.

Table 7. Persons Entering St. Louis Central Business District by Mode (000s), 7 a.m. to 7 p.m. Daily: 1916–1946

Year	Auto	Streetcar	Bus	Misc.	Total
1916	31	149	—	—	180
1926	71	158	18	28	275
1937	140	84	37	49	310
1941	150	90	45	50	335
1946	160	110	65	40	375

Source: City Plan Commission, *Comprehensive City Plan*, 59.

The focal point of the comprehensive plan was the Central Business District. Downtown, with its concentration of business and government facilities, was the heart of the city, and a prosperous city required a prospering downtown. Traffic congestion in downtown posed a threat to its continued prosperity. There was a fear that congestion would become so serious as to require the decentralization of the district, forcing businesses to move away from downtown and perhaps out of the city altogether. To address this issue, the plan made three recommendations: provide adequate parking facilities in downtown, make improvements to and better enforce traffic controls, and construct new expressways that would allow trucks and through traffic to bypass downtown congestion.

Expressways were not entirely new to St. Louis. The Red Feather Expressway—initially called the Oakland Avenue Expressway—opened in 1936 and eventually became part of US 40. Prior to 1947, however, there had not been a formally adopted plan that included an expressway component. Expressways would provide faster, uninterrupted traffic flow through grade separations accomplished by either elevating or depressing the roadways. A unique feature of the proposed system was the provision of parking facilities at exits near the Central Business District. These would allow travelers to park their cars on the perimeter of downtown and take transit to their final destinations, thereby reducing vehicle demand in the congested core.

Expressways would require a minimum two-hundred feet of right-of-way, with additional land needed for ramps. Acquiring and clearing that much right-of-way would have major impacts in densely developed cities. A later review of the expressway plan would stress that the system's development be closely coordinated with other city plans and initiatives. This was consistent with Harland Bartholomew's view that freeways, although potentially detrimental to city interests, could serve as a centerpiece for urban renewal efforts, providing a tool for reshaping and revitalizing cities. If freeways were to fulfill that role, it was essential that planning incorporate social and land use criteria, and that local governments, rather than the state highway departments, control planning and design decisions (Brown 2005).

Emerging federal policy provided the impetus and context for the city's expressway planning. Although the Federal-Aid Highway Act of 1956 initiated major construction of the Interstate Highway System, proposals for a national system of superhighways dated back to the early 1930s. As the Great Depression persisted, President Roosevelt began to consider construction of a national highway system as a way to put people to work. Enamored of the possibilities for a self-supporting but limited system of national toll roads—three north-south and three east-west highways—he called for a study. *Toll Roads and Free Roads*, completed in 1939, concluded that the toll proposal was not financially feasible, but it recommended a system of 26,700 miles of free highways. A follow-up study in 1944, *Interregional Highways*, proposed a national network of nearly forty-two thousand miles of rural and urban freeways (Weingroff 1993).

Authors of both studies were concerned with the system's potential impacts on metropolitan areas, a topic of spirited national debate in the planning and engineering communities. The authors believed that if planned in conjunction with other local initiatives, freeways could promote positive urban development. If not well planned, however, freeways could exacerbate and hasten deterioration of central cities. From their perspective, improperly located roads "will become more and more of an encumbrance to the city's functions and an all too durable reminder of planning that was bad" (Weingroff FHWA). To ensure that freeway development had a strong connection to urban planning, *Interregional Highways* recommended creation of regional authorities to cooperate with state officials in developing freeway routes.

Both studies proposed a hub/spokes/rim concept for developing urban freeways. The system would consist of freeways radiating from the central city (spokes), inner belts near and at intermediate distances from the central business district connecting radial freeways and bypassing downtown areas (hubs), and outer belts or circumferential freeways on the fringe of urban areas connecting radials and bypassing the interior parts of metropolitan regions (rims). That system of facilities, along with strict access limits, would discourage "ribbon development and the unwise subdivision of large tracts of suburban land," promoting instead orderly regional development (U.S. Department of Transportation 1943).

When Congress passed the Federal-Aid Highway Act of 1944 authorizing designation but not funding of a forty thousand-mile National System of Interstate Highways, the law did not commit to coordinated highway development planning or the creation of regional authorities. State highway officials, with the concurrence of the federal government, would designate the interstate routes. This essentially granted state and federal governments the ultimate decision-making power in the design and location of freeways. Although states would consult with cities to varying degrees, cities would not be in control of interstate routings within their jurisdictions.

Based on state recommendations, the federal Public Roads Administration identified the first 37,700 miles of interstate highways, including 2,700 miles of urban expressways, in August 1947. The agency reserved another 2,300 miles for additional urban circumferential and distributing routes (Weingroff 1996). The Missouri State Highway Department's recommended interstate/expressway plan for St. Louis differed from the city's comprehensive plan (Whitton 1958).

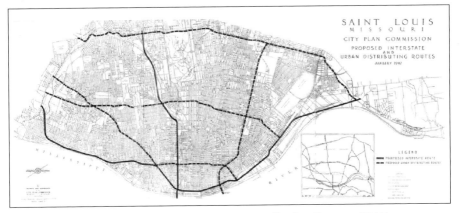

Proposed Interstate and Urban Distributing Routes, 1947.

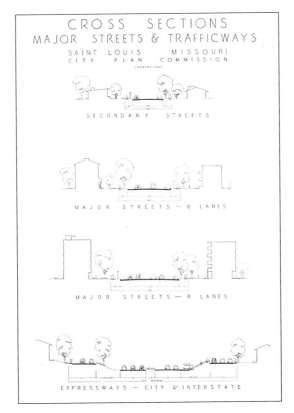

Cross Sections of Major Streets, 1947.

Working with the hub and spoke concept, the city plan envisioned three types of expressways: interstate expressway highways, urban distributing routes of the interstate system, and local expressways. The first two types would potentially involve federal funding, although Congress had not yet authorized specific funding for interstate construction. The plan identified four interstate routes, all radiating from the downtown area, along US 40 both east and west from the city, US 66 both northeast and southwest from the city, and US 50 east from the city. To complement these, the plan proposed three north-south and two east-west distributing routes. The north-south routes would connect the interstates; the east-west routes would connect the north-south distributing routes. Taken together, these routes would form an expressway grid. Finally, the plan proposed a local expressway from downtown to Forest Park Boulevard and then continuing west along Forest Park to Skinker.

Although the plan was the result of discussions with state and federal officials, there were two major differences between the state and city plan. First, Missouri did not recognize the distributing expressways proposed by the city. A further definition of urban routes by the Bureau of Public Roads could remedy this discrepancy. The second difference was more significant, if only because it illustrated the varied approaches of the two agencies. As proposed by the city, the northern interstate route would extend north from downtown to the Chain of Rocks Bridge, where it would connect with the region's circumferential interstate. The comparable route defined by the state ran north from downtown but then angled to the northwest, roughly along the alignment of today's I-70. City planners defined their route along a wedge of lower density properties to minimize disrupting existing land uses. This routing was consistent with the urban design principles articulated in *Interregional Highways*. State engineers located their route along the line of greatest travel desire, not heeding the admonition in *Interregional Highways* that in urban areas, "observations of the existing traffic flow may not be an infallible guide to the best locations" (Lovelace 1993). Neither agency ignored the other's concerns, but their priorities were fundamentally different.

As national momentum built for constructing an Interstate Highway System, the city, in 1951, completed a reexamination of expressway proposals. The study, funded by and conducted in cooperation with the state highway commission, focused on locations of the three major interstate-expressways, relegating the urban distributing routes (including the Innerbelt in St. Louis County) to local project status. Though conducted by the city, the study was not the responsibility of the Plan Commission, although the Commission would later review its findings.

Beyond the issue of land values, land use considerations were not central to the engineering study. Traffic considerations, population density, and minimizing the disruption of productive and high-value properties were the dominant principles. Property values were, perhaps, the most significant factor in determining expressway locations (St. Louis Urban Area Expressway Project Report 1951). Low-value properties became acquisition targets. There was little apparent consideration of the comprehensive plan's non-transportation objectives.

Final location recommendations differed to varying degrees from those identified in prior city and state plans. Pointing out that the city's proposed river route for the northern Mark Twain Expressway would require extensive viaduct construction and provide little traffic access because of the alignment's low population density, the study's recommendation conformed to the state's plan for a northwest routing. Similarly, the study proposed moving the alignment of the southern Ozark Expressway away from the river, a routing shared by both city and state plans, to improve access to the roadway. The recommended location for the east-west Daniel Boone Expressway was the most radical departure from prior plans. Rather than constructing the expressway in the Manchester Road. corridor well south of Forest Park, the route would begin with two branches leaving downtown along Clark and Franklin avenues. These branches would meet at Grand Avenue and then pass north of Forest Park to a junction with US 40 just west of Brentwood Boulevard in Richmond Heights. With the exception of the Clark Avenue branch, all routes would have six traffic lanes. Total cost was $163 million. Financing would come from federal, state, and local sources over a twenty-year period.

Anticipated benefits included shorter travel times and related increases in property values, congestion relief and mitigation of its blighting influence, fewer traffic accidents, improvements in transit efficiencies for buses using the expressway, and slum removal in areas affected by land takings. Perhaps the most curious benefit was "providing air and light space in congested districts," presumably related to the urban vistas opened up by demolishing buildings and replacing them with six lanes of pavement (St. Louis Urban Area Expressway Project Report 1951). A rudimentary benefit/cost analysis indicated that, based on travel time savings alone (valued at $1 per hour), annual benefits for all three expressways would exceed costs by 65 percent.

The study also itemized potential detrimental impacts. These included the loss of tax revenues associated with property acquisitions, possible "intolerable" congestion in the business district because of improved access, the blighting effects of elevated road structures, the expressways creating barriers between residences and community resources, and the out-migration of downtown residents leading to further blight. The report stated that the latter impact might actually prove beneficial if resettlement objectives were involved (St. Louis Urban Area Expressway Project Report 1951). Although listed, there was little apparent weight given to those impacts in locating expressway routes, nor was there any discussion of what actions might be required to mitigate them. Several of those potential impacts would have severe and long-lasting consequences for the city. Building the system, however, was the overriding concern.

Table 8. Expressway Costs and Direct User Benefits (000s)

Category	Ozark	Daniel Boone	Mark Twain
Capital Cost	$51,531	$60,486	$50,883
Annual Cost	$2,940	$3,332	$2,885
Annual vehicle-miles benefited	234,900	221,100	249,000
Annual travel time savings	5,034	4,738	5,336
Annual value of time saved	$5,034	$4,738	$5,336
Benefit/cost ratio	1.71	1.42	1.85

Source: City Plan Commission, *Expressway Plan for the St. Louis Urban Area*, 53–55.

That sense of urgency was evident in a review of the expressway plan conducted by the Street and Traffic Committee of the Plan Commission. Completed in 1952, the review concluded that the proposed expressway plan was generally sound, although it questioned some of the route deviations from the city's earlier plan and recommended further study of the Mark Twain Expressway's relocation. Despite those reservations, it emphasized that immediate action was imperative. St. Louis was lagging behind other major cities in developing an expressway system. The review requested that the Commission authorize staff to proceed with a study that would evaluate the route deviations in detail and examine the expressway plan within the context of land use plans, public housing and urban redevelopment initiatives, mass transportation, and off-street parking facilities (City Plan Commission 1952).

In the end, the state, not the city, would locate and design the interstate routes. Bartholomew's belief that local governments and their planning staffs should have the principal role in freeway development went unheeded. The state plan in the St. Louis area, as of 1958, consisted of three radial expressways that would become I-70, I-44, and I-55, along with the I-270 outer belt. Upgrading the Daniel Boone Expressway (today's US 40/I-64) to an interstate remained uncertain. Possible additions to the system included the Innerbelt in St. Louis County and the Eighteenth Street crosstown expressway in the city (Whitton 1958).

By the end of the 1950s, interstate and expressway construction in the city was progressing. Sections of I-70, US 40, and I-55 were completed or under way. During the decade, and before the interstate system could have much more than a construction impact, the city's population fell by over 100,000, declining from its high of nearly 857,000 residents in 1950. There were myriad reasons for that decline—income growth, postwar housing and mortgage policies, cheaper housing construction methods, zoning practices, rising auto ownership, arterial road construction, deteriorating conditions in the city, and so on, that pushed and pulled people and businesses into the suburbs—but interstate construction would accelerate and magnify the impact of those trends. Constructed according to uniform design standards and the need for speed, safety, and reliability, interstates did not fit comfortably within the urban landscape. Lacking integration with other plans and policies, they became a destructive rather than positive force for change in cities. Unguided by a thorough understanding of the nation's urban transportation problems, interstates exacerbated many of those problems. At a 1957 Urban Land Institute symposium, *The New Highways: Challenge to the Metropolitan Region*, Lewis Mumford exclaimed that the 1956 Highway Act "was based on a very insufficient study . . . a study of highways, not a study of the real problems, the study of transportation in our country" (Weingroff 2000).

Many voices raised related issues repeatedly during the two decades of discussion prior to the passage of the 1956 Act. The two major studies that birthed the interstate movement—*Toll Roads and Free Roads* and *Interregional Highways*—expressed concerns about the impact of interstates on cities and metropolitan areas. In the view of one scholar, "the modern urban freeway is a product of the contest of ideas over the freeway's role in the city" (Brown 2005). It was a contest between an engineering vision of what a freeway should be and a planning vision of what the freeway should accomplish in the urban context. The engineering vision prevailed.

In the two decades following the 1956 Act, backlash over the interstate program and its impact on urban areas caused the U.S. Congress to establish planning and process requirements that would give local officials a formal role in approving transportation projects using federal funds (Deakin 2006). Through a series of laws, the federal government required the establishment of a continuing, comprehensive, and cooperative (3-C) transportation planning process in all urban areas with populations of 50,000 or greater (1962); encouraged the formation of regional planning organizations controlled by local elected officials (1965); required the preparation of environmental impact statements to analyze the social, economic, and environmental effects of proposed federal actions and to give the community a larger voice in decision-making (1969); and mandated creation of metropolitan planning organizations to carry out the regional 3-C planning process (1973).[6] Responding to changes in federal requirements, local officials created the East-West Gateway Coordinating Council as a not-for-profit, voluntary association of governments in 1965. The Council was later designated the Metropolitan Planning Organization (MPO) for the bi-state, eight-county St. Louis region.

Rapid Transit Reconsidered

At a special election on January 25, 1955, St. Louis City and County residents voted on a proposal by the Transit Board of Freeholders to create a Metropolitan Transit District. The District would be governed by a seven-person commission responsible for taking over from the Missouri Public Service Commission the authority to regulate transit fares, schedules, and routings; conduct a comprehensive survey of transit needs; and determine whether public ownership of the transit system would best meet the needs of the district (St. Louis and St. Louis County Transit Board of Free-holders 1955). Future ownership arrangements would be the subject of a subsequent ballot measure. Mayor Raymond Tucker and County Supervisor Luman Matthews opposed the proposal, believing that a transit study should precede any other action. Voters rejected the proposition. After the measure's defeat, the city and county commissioned a comprehensive transit survey.

Impetus for the transit district proposal was the faltering state of the transit system. Ridership on Public Service Company routes had declined by almost two-thirds during the preceding decade, and ridership for all transit companies operating in the region had fallen by 46 percent since 1950.[7] Auto ownership and the "explosion" of the urban area were the

---

[6]The major pieces of legislation were the Federal-Aid Highway Acts of 1962 and 1973, the Housing and Urban Development Act of 1965, and the National Environmental Policy Act of 1969.

[7]The Public Service Company provided nearly 80 percent of all transit services in the region, operating buses and the five remaining streetcar lines. There were ten other bus operators in the region (three in Missouri and seven in Illinois) and two companies providing jitney service.

major factors in transit's decline. Those two factors had resulted in population densities that were insufficient to support existing transit services. While 50 percent of trips to downtown used transit, only 11 percent of trips within St. Louis city and county began or ended in the central business district. Transit handled only 15 percent of trips that had both an origin and destination within the city and county (W. C. Gilman and Co. 1959). Declining patronage and the associated loss of fare revenue were putting severe financial strains on the system.

Table 9. Public Service Company Transit Revenue Passengers and Passenger Car Registrations, St. Louis City and County: 1945–1957

Year	Transit Passengers	Car Registrations
1945	334,753,358	206,346
1950	215,915,978	307,482
1955	136,095,511	388,016
1957	114,891,943	422,024
Percent Change 1945–1957	(65.7%)	104.5%

Source: Wilbur Smith and Associates, *A Highway Planning Study for the St. Louis Metropolitan Area*, 9, 11.

Table 10: Total Transit Revenue Passengers, Missouri and Illinois (000s): 1950 and 1957

State	1950	1957	Change
Missouri	228,208	123,274	(104,934)
Illinois	21,879	11,828	(10,051)
Total	250,087	135,102	(114,985)

Source: W. C. Gilman, *St. Louis Metropolitan Area Transportation Study*, 79.

From a transit service perspective, regional growth patterns were unsettling. After only modest growth during the 1930s—a decade that saw a small decline in the city's population—the region's population grew by 40 percent between 1940 and 1960. St. Louis City shared in that growth during the 1940s before experiencing a significant decline during the 1950s. St. Louis County was the main benefactor of the region's population growth. In 1940, the city's population was nearly three times as large as the county's. By 1960, the number of county residents fell only 46,500 short of equaling the number living in the city. Population growth rates over the twenty-year period in the six other counties ranged from a low of 22 percent for Monroe County to 107 percent for both Jefferson and St. Charles counties.

Table 11. Population of the St. Louis Region: 1940 and 1960

County	1940	1960	Change	Percent Change
Madison	149,349	224,689	75,340	50.4%
St. Clair	166,899	262,509	95,610	57.3%
St. Louis	274,230	703,532	429,302	156.5%
St. Louis City	816,048	750,026	(66,022)	(8.1%)
Outlying Counties	104,207	179,420	75,213	72.2%
Region	1,510,733	2,120,176	609,443	40.3%

Source: Richard L Forstall, *Population of Counties by Decennial Census: 1900-1990.*

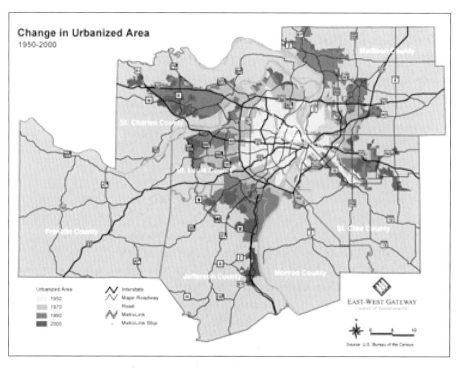

Change in Urbanized Area, 1950–2000.

According to the comprehensive transit survey, published in 1959, dispersed development patterns necessitated consolidating and reconfiguring existing transit services and implementing some form of rapid transit. Consolidation would eliminate competition for the most productive transit markets, which produced service redundancies, and would allow for implementation of a single fare structure with transfer privileges. Reconfiguration after consolidation, preferably under a public authority, would enable development of a coordinated system. A public authority was preferred because it would have a higher probability of generating the revenue needed to carry out the study's recommendations. Changes required to reconfigure existing services involved removing duplicative routes, creating more direct routings, and moving bus lines to major arterials with good traffic controls to attain higher speeds. If the system was to compete with the automobile in suburban areas, however, rapid transit was a necessity.

The study screened five types of rapid transit: airborne facilities —helicopters with heliports; carveyors—a moving belt or sidewalks; pavement-borne transit—electric buses or trolleys; monorails; and standard rapid rail on surface tracks. It screened out the first as impractical, the second and third as good for short distances but inadequate for longer suburban services, and the fourth as too expensive. Surface rail along existing railroads received more consideration, but the study concluded that following existing rail rights-of-way would make the system inflexible and expensive. Much of the existing rail right-of-way was too narrow to accommodate separate tracks for rapid rail, and jointly using tracks with freight trains created operational and safety issues. Additionally, the tracks were not located within walking distance of dense population concentrations, and there were no good sites for a downtown terminal. Using existing rail lines would require some type of supplementary circulation system in the downtown area, possibly subways. Potential patronage simply did not justify the expenses involved.

Instead of rapid rail, the study concluded that rapid bus transit was most appropriate for St. Louis. Buses would operate on exclusive highways (busways) in the urban core and mix with other traffic on expressways in outer suburban areas. The study recommended seven routes. Four routes would be alongside expressways radiating from the Central Business District; two would follow Gravois and the combination of Franklin, Easton, and Page, in anticipation of a future Page Expressway; and one would be a crosstown route paralleling Kingshighway. Alleys could provide much of the right-of-way for constructing the exclusive busway sections, minimizing disruption and acquisition costs. A typical section would be forty-two feet wide and carry three lanes. Stations would be one mile apart. When completed, there would be eighty-six miles of rapid bus transit, forty-two miles on exclusive grade-separated busways, and forty-four miles on expressways (W. C. Gilman and Company 1959).

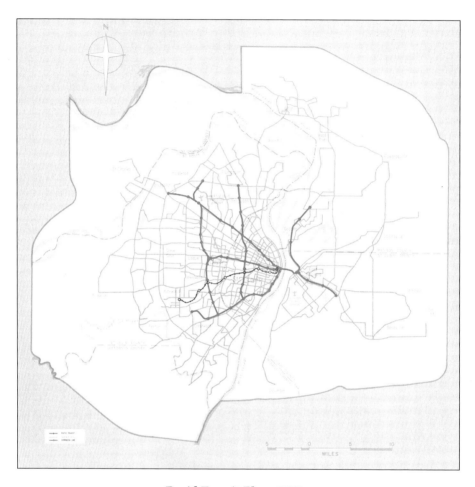

Rapid Transit Plan, 1971.

An essential element of the plan was a downtown loop. This would be a separate bus facility, either elevated over or alongside existing streets, routed along Eleventh, Lucas, Sixth, and Chestnut. If elevated, the structure would be eighteen feet high and sixty feet wide. The study also recommended construction of a suburban and intercity bus terminal in the three blocks bordered by Washington, Broadway, Franklin, and Sixth. This would directly connect with the bus loop and enable intercity buses to access the terminal without using congested downtown streets (W. C. Gilman and Company 1959).

Total cost to construct the system was $175 million, not including the downtown terminal. Estimates of annual operating costs through 1980 for the entire transit system ranged from $19 million to $21 million, compared to annual revenues of $30 million to $32 million. After depreciation, and depending on whether the system was under public or private ownership, the annual balance would range from $6 million to $9 million, leaving sufficient funds under public ownership to finance the capital cost (W. C. Gilman and Company 1959).

The study's recommendations, however, went beyond infrastructure improvements. It proposed that the bi-state area create a regional authority with expansive jurisdiction over transportation planning. Commensurate with that jurisdiction, the authority should have a reliable annual source of public funds, whether through taxing powers or other mechanisms, to plan and finance transportation projects (W. C. Gilman and Company 1959).

There was subsequent little progress made on constructing a rapid bus transit system or creating a regional authority, but discussions about what to do with the transit system continued. Those discussions culminated in the Bi-State Development Agency's acquisition and consolidation of fifteen privately owned transit firms in 1963. A $26.5 million revenue bond issue financed the acquisition.

Two years later, Bi-State decided to proceed with an updated feasibility study for rapid transit. Conducted in cooperation with the newly formed East-West Gateway Coordinating Council (now the East-West Gateway Council of Governments), the study examined the potential role of rapid transit in creating a more balanced transportation system. Regional growth patterns were of major concern. While rapid transit could not reverse the dispersal of population and employment, it could moderate the spread and alleviate some of the negative effects of decentralization. Rapid transit had potential for promoting more orderly and desirable land use development, as well as increasing accessibility and real estate values, enhancing mobility for those without cars, and providing a viable option to the automobile (Parsons Brinckerhoff et al. 1971). The key was building a system extensive enough to make a difference.

The regional transit system, while stabilizing under Bi-State's management, continued to lose riders. In 1967, the year the study began, annual transit ridership dropped below 79 million. This was the lowest ridership figure since Bi-State took control of the system, and the second-lowest during the twentieth century. It represented a 68 percent decline in transit passengers since 1957. Accompanying the decline in transit ridership was a 50 percent increase in automobile registrations. By 1966, there were 845,000 autos registered in the region, or roughly one car for every 2.7 residents (Parsons Brinckerhoff et al. 1968).

The first two phases of the three-phase study examined existing conditions and screened a range of rapid transit alternatives to identify those most appropriate for the region. Phase III, not completed until 1971, presented a detailed evaluation of two alternatives: bus operations on public highways and rail rapid transit. A key assumption influencing the technical analysis was the projected level of population growth through 1990. Population estimates used in the study put the region's 1990 population at almost 3.2 million people. Forecasts for the city's population indicated a decline into the 1970s before stabilizing at 600,000 by 1990 (Parsons Brinckerhoff et al. 1971). Unfortunately, the region's population increased by less than 8,000 between 1970 and 1990, not quite reaching 2.4 million people by 1990, and the city's population fell to under 400,000. Optimistic population forecasts led to an overestimation of transit's future market potential.

The Phase III report concluded that buses operating on existing and planned highways could provide an interim solution to St. Louis's transit needs, but substantially improving transit service and ridership would require a grade-separated system operating in exclusive rights-of-way. It recommended eighty-six miles of "rail-like" rapid transit: five radial routes, two crosstown routes, a short Missouri-Illinois Connector, a possible line to Kirkwood contingent on negotiations with the affected railroads for joint use of their rights-of-way, and a restructuring of the bus system. Routes would combine at-grade, aerial, and subway sections. Proposed routes were the following:

- Northwest: downtown to I-270/St. Charles Rock Rd. along the Natural Bridge corridor

- West: downtown to Clayton along the Olive-Lindell corridor

- Southwest: downtown to Crestwood along the Gravois corridor

- Missouri-Illinois Connector: downtown to East St. Louis via the Eads Bridge

- Southeast: East St. Louis to Edgemont along the IL 15 corridor

- Northeast: East St. Louis to Granite City along the IL 3 corridor

- Kingshighway: I-270/W. Florissant to Gravois/Morganford along the Kingshighway corridor

- Innerbelt: Hazelwood to Affton along the Innerbelt corridor

- Kirkwood: downtown to Kirkwood along Terminal Railroad Association and Missouri Pacific Railroad rights-of-way (Parsons Brinckerhoff et al. 1971).

Capital cost for the entire eighty-six mile system was nearly $1.5 billion, in 1970 dollars. Estimated 1990 patronage was 600,000 riders a day, producing $76 million a year in fare revenue, more than sufficient to cover the estimated $71 million in annual operating costs (Parsons Brinckerhoff et al. 1971). With the Urban Mass Transportation Assistance Act of 1970 authorizing substantial increases in federal expenditures for transit capital programs, the report suggested that federal funds could cover two-thirds of proposed capital costs. The remaining one-third would rely on undefined state and local sources.

The report proposed an implementation strategy that would begin with adopting the eighty-six mile system as the region's long-range transit strategy and then selecting an initial priority plan. As recommended by the report, the initial plan would consist of the Northwest route to I-270/Lindbergh, the West route through Clayton to the first stop on the north Innerbelt line, the Southwest route to Broadway/Chippewa, and the Missouri-Illinois Connector. Cost of these initial segments was $633 million (Parsons Brinckerhoff et al. 1971). Because a source of local funding was required, a public referendum on the plan and its financing was necessary. Prior to submitting the issue to voters, the report recommended preliminary engineering to establish detailed construction requirements and costs, preparation of a financial plan, and a prereferendum public information campaign.

East-West Gateway conducted a series of follow-up studies to examine the social and economic impacts, public perceptions, and costs associated with long-range transit strategy. The impact study estimated the benefit/cost ratio at 1.14, based on a wide array of user benefits, and indicated that areas along the proposed transit routes would experience significant redevelopment, increases in land values, and population and employment growth (Consad Research Corporation 1972). Most of these benefits would accrue to the city. A survey of 200 community leaders and 843 registered voters found general agreement on the desirability of rapid transit, but less consensus regarding financing and construction priorities and the role that transit should play in the region (Consad Research Corporation 1972). The re-examination of costs, requested by the Urban Mass Transportation Administration, revised the capital cost of the long-range transit program to $1.9 billion, in 1973 dollars (East-West Gateway Coordinating Council 1973).

Ultimately, this proved too ambitious a program for the region. There was neither the public nor the political will to take on a project of this scale and cost. During the late 1970s and early 1980s, however, discussions began to coalesce around possibilities for light rail transit. Light rail was less expensive, less disruptive, and more flexible in implementation, being appropriate for both grade-separated and street applications.

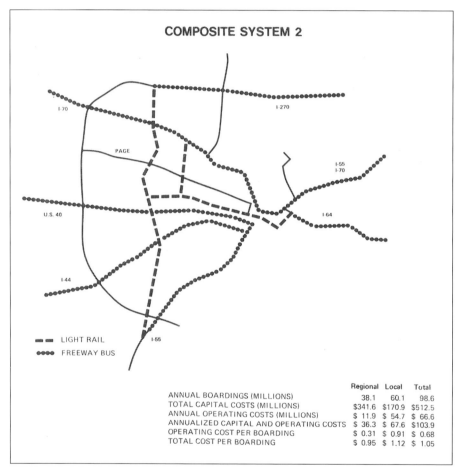

COMPOSITE SYSTEM 2

	Regional	Local	Total
ANNUAL BOARDINGS (MILLIONS)	38.1	60.1	98.6
TOTAL CAPITAL COSTS (MILLIONS)	$341.6	$170.9	$512.5
ANNUAL OPERATING COSTS (MILLIONS)	$ 11.9	$ 54.7	$ 66.6
ANNUALIZED CAPITAL AND OPERATING COSTS	$ 36.3	$ 67.6	$103.9
OPERATING COST PER BOARDING	$ 0.31	$ 0.91	$ 0.68
TOTAL COST PER BOARDING	$ 0.95	$ 1.12	$ 1.05

Bus–Light Rail Plan, 1978.

In 1978, East-West Gateway completed a mass transit study examining both bus and light rail systems. The Council's original recommendation proposed a composite freeway bus-light rail system for the region, with forty miles of light rail extending from East St. Louis to Clayton and from I-270 on the north to Lemay Ferry on the south, with a spur from the East St. Louis/Clayton route to I-70. Upon review, the Urban Mass Transportation Administration (UMTA) questioned the ridership potential for light rail in St. Louis and gave no assurances that the agency would participate in its funding. It did agree, nevertheless, to allow St. Louis to further study light rail prospects. In response to UMTA's position, the Council's Board of Directors reconsidered its original recommendation and voted to proceed with an all-bus plan (East-West Gateway Coordinating Council 1978).

Despite UMTA's reservations, some elected officials and community leaders continued to advocate for light rail. Notable among them were Congressman Robert Young and Mayor Vince Schoemehl. At their urging, East-West Gateway completed a systems analysis for light rail in 1982, and the Council's Board of Directors authorized an application for federal funds to conduct an alternatives analysis and prepare a draft environmental impact statement for light rail in the East St. Louis/Clayton/Lambert Airport corridor in 1983. These actions conformed to the project development process required to qualify transit new starts projects for federal funding.

The planning was contentious. There was strong public opposition in University City, Clayton, and Normandy to the preferred route. Residents of University City and Clayton simply opposed light rail going through their cities; Normandy residents were concerned about proposed mixed-traffic operations on Natural Bridge. The adopted alignment avoided these issues by locating the light rail route along Norfolk and Western right-of-way, which was acquired for the project, and by using elevated structures to reach Lambert Airport. In 1988, East-West Gateway completed preliminary engineering and a final environmental impact statement, and subsequently turned the project over to Bi-State for final design, construction, and operation.

A year later, the Council published a systems analysis that examined the potential of light rail in nine other corridors throughout the region. Most of the nine were roughly equivalent to, although more expansive than, the rapid transit corridors identified in the 1971 plan. Essentially constituting a long-range plan for light rail transit, the systems analysis established priorities that have guided subsequent rail planning. The St. Clair County and Cross County light rail extensions emerged from the systems analysis, and five other corridor have been subjects of additional planning studies, ranging from a feasibility study to major investment studies to alternatives analyses with the preparation of draft environmental impact statements.

After a decade of planning, engineering, and construction, MetroLink opened in July 1993. Many who had been involved with its development held their breath, not knowing how the community would respond, but the route immediately exceeded ridership expectations. Nearly seventy years after the city's confident 1926 report, rapid transit in St. Louis was a reality.

Regional Planning Arrives

Since its inception, the East-West Gateway Council of Governments (renamed in 2005) has been the agency responsible for the regional 3-C transportation planning process. In 1973, its responsibilities were expanded and codified in federal law when it became the federally designated metropolitan planning organization (MPO) for the St. Louis region. As the MPO, East-West Gateway was required to prepare regional long-range transportation plans, develop a short-range Transportation Improvement Program (TIP) that allocated federal funds to specific projects over a three- to five-year period, and prepare a Unified Planning Work Program that theoretically organized all transportation planning occurring in the region. MPOs were supposedly a mechanism for ensuring comprehensive and coordinated planning and decision-making in urban areas. The requirement may have existed, but the requisite authority did not. Although the Council assumed the decision-making mantle in some niches, such as rail transit planning, its long-range plan and TIP generally were compilations of transportation decisions made by others, especially the state highway departments.

The *Intermodal Surface Transportation Efficiency Act of 1991* (ISTEA) changed that. ISTEA shifted away from the single mode focus of earlier federal legislation, promoting planning for an integrated transportation system encompassing highways, transit, freight, bicyclists, and pedestrians. The law increased the flexible use of federal funds, allowing most categories of funding to be used for either highways or transit purposes, with some qualification. It required explicit consideration of specific social, economic, environmental, and land use factors in planning and project development. As part of plan and project development, it mandated major investment studies to examine multimodal solutions in corridors or sub-areas where transportation problems were likely to warrant the use of federal funds, and it increased the emphasis on involving the public in all aspects of planning and programming. Although most of these issues, along with increased planning funds, empowered MPOs, two items were most critical to enhancing their role. First, except for projects using National Highway System Bridge and Interstate Maintenance program funds, the law gave MPOs the authority to select, in consultation with the states, the projects that would receive federal funds. The states would be responsible for selecting projects for the exempt funding categories, but those decisions would require cooperation with the MPO. Second, the law mandated that plans and TIPs be fiscally constrained. Projects could not move into the long-range plan or TIP unless it was demonstrated that anticipated revenues were sufficient to pay for them. This shifted the plan and program from being a wish list of projects to an investment strategy. In other words, it required establishment of clear priorities among competing projects. Although subsequent federal transportation bills modified a number of these provisions, ISTEA gave local officials, working through the MPO, new authority to influence and decide how federal transportation funds are spent in metropolitan areas.

Lacking a comprehensive regional plan to provide a context for transportation decisions, East-West Gateway's first long-range plan after the enactment of ISTEA, *Transportation Redefined*, engaged local officials, community leaders, and citizens in a process to create a set of regional goals and objectives. From these goals and objectives, the Council established seven focus areas to guide decision-making: preservation of the existing infrastructure, safety and security in travel, congestion management, access to opportunity, sustainable development, efficient movement of goods, and resource conservation. Given the state of the region's infrastructure, the top priority was maintaining highways, bridges, and transit assets. These focus areas were translated into measures for evaluating plan priorities, projects proposed for TIP inclusion, and alternative transportation solutions in corridor studies.

The regional planning and decision-making process established in *Transportation Redefined* incorporated four principal elements. The long-range plan establishes policies and principles for transportation planning and investment, and it identifies a plan of priority investments. Corridor, subarea, or issue studies serve as a mechanism for evaluating system deficiencies identified in the plan and for developing projects for plan inclusion. The Transportation Improvement Program translates the plan's priorities into investment decisions, allocating federal funds to specific projects. Finally, involving the public through informational materials and presentations, interviews and focus groups, public meetings, workshops, and other forms of community outreach permeates the entire process. With some modifications, the focus areas and these four elements continue to guide the Council's planning efforts.

Patterns of regional growth remain a vexing challenge for transportation planners. St. Louis is still a relatively slow-growth metropolitan area.

After losing nearly one-quarter of a million residents in the 1970s, the region's population increased almost7 percent between 1980 and 2000. During this period, population in the city fell to under 350,000, while the outlying Missouri counties experienced brisk growth. St. Charles County's population nearly doubled over those two decades, and it became the third most populous county in the region. Obviously, growth in formerly undeveloped areas creates a demand for new transportation infrastructure. While pressure to meet those needs builds, the extensive infrastructure investment in previously developed areas requires constant attention. Building the new while maintaining and enhancing existing infrastructure is straining the resources available to the region.

Table 12. Population of the St. Louis Region: 1980 and 2000

County	1980	2000	Change	Percent Change
Madison	247,691	258,941	11,250	4.5%
Monroe	20,117	27,619	7,502	37.3%
St. Clair	267,531	256,082	(11,449)	(4.3%)
Franklin	71,233	93,807	22,574	31.7%
Jefferson	146,183	198,099	51,916	35.5%
St. Charles	144,107	283,883	139,776	97.0%
St. Louis	973,896	1,016,315	42,419	4.4%
St. Louis City	453,085	348,189	(104,896)	(23.2)
Region	2,323,843	2,482,935	159,092	6.8%

Source: Richard L Forstall, *Population of Counties by Decennial Census: 1900-1990.*

In *Legacy 2030*, the region's long-range plan adopted by the Council in 2005, the financial plan indicated that $13.5 billion would be available to fund transportation needs over the following two decades. Simply keeping the highway system in good condition through 2030 would require two-thirds of anticipated highway funding, leaving a $2.8 billion balance for major projects. The picture was very different for transit. Maintaining existing transit assets and service levels would require $1 billion more than anticipated revenues. This shortfall would mean that the region could not afford any MetroLink extensions beyond the Cross County corridor through the term of the long-range plan. It also would require reductions in transit service, unless additional revenues became available.

Legacy 2030 considered sixty highway and transit projects with a total cost of $8.2 billion for inclusion in the priority investment plan, including five MetroLink extensions. Most projects had emerged from corridor planning studies. In addition, the long-range plan identified another twenty-seven corridors where transportation problems warranted planning studies. Potential cost of projects in these corridors was another $2.1 billion. These $10.3 billion in projects balanced against the $1 billion shortfall for transit and the $2.8 billion available for highways. The result was a modest investment plan, including twenty-eight projects costing $2.3 billion, mostly dedicated to upgrading interstate highways. The investment plan falls far short of what is required to meet the region's congestion, safety, and mobility needs.

Table 13. Long-Range Plan Financial Capacity Analysis ($ millions): 2007–2030

Revenue/Expense	Highways	Transit	Total
Revenue available	$8,302	$5,162	$13,464
Preservation & operation cost	$5,531	$6,187	$11,718
Balance for major projects	$2.771	($1,026)	$1,746
Major project cost	$5,256	$2,940	$8,196
Total Balance	($2,485)	($3,966)	($6,450)

Source: East-West Gateway Coordinating Council, *Legacy 2030*, 87–89.

Conclusion

It is a curious thing. After ninety years of transportation planning and billions of dollars invested, the region still contends with many of the same issues that planners confronted in the early twentieth century. Congestion persists. Transit perseveres in a financial twilight zone. Concerns about urban sprawl abide as a topic for intellectual debate, not action. Needs and desires continue to dwarf resources. And the critical linkage between transportation and land use decisions remains a weak link.

That these issues remain does not imply that transportation planning has been a futile endeavor. It does imply, perhaps, that some variable is missing from the formula. Planning works within a constrained environment. There are regulatory boundaries, political realities, competing interests, public perceptions, agency turfs, resource limitations, and imperfect tools and knowledge. One constraint absent from that list is a regional development plan.

Transportation planning essentially is a problem-solving exercise. Effective solutions require sound problem definitions. The necessity of defining transportation problems before proposing solutions is so axiomatic that it seems almost absurd to make the statement. Recall, however, the passage from the city's 1917 major street plan (1917a): "To design a street according to its probable use is a reasonable but uncommon practice." Purpose and need statements too often define problems as if transportation were an end unto itself. The focus on facilities and service levels neglects the larger purpose of transportation, which ultimately is to improve the lives of people. Starting from that premise—defining problems in that context—typically leads to different types of solutions. This was the point of Lewis Mumford's charge that the Interstate Highway System stemmed from a study of highways, not a study of the nation's transportation problems.

One of the challenges to developing insightful problem statements is the lack of a regional framework within which to fit the evaluation of transportation needs and solutions. In one form or another, the call for a comprehensive regional plan weaves its way through the last ninety years of transportation planning. Whether in the form of a regional land use plan, growth plan, metropolitan development guide, or agreed-upon urban design principles, the absence of a comprehensive plan is the missing variable in the transportation planning formula.

Joel Stone, director of transportation planning at the Atlanta Regional Council, was an invited speaker at a transportation seminar held in St. Louis during October 1973. His topic was the transportation–land use dilemma facing metropolitan areas: land use creates the need for transportation while transportation acts as a catalyst for land use development, producing a never-ending, uncontrolled cycle. During his comments, he cited Wilfred Owen's *The Metropolitan Transportation Problem*, stating that the solution to this socially and economically inefficient cycle will be "the ability to develop urban communities in which satisfactory transportation is possible." "We wonder," Mr. Stone continued, "whether we should continue to develop more sophisticated and highly efficient transportation systems to serve an ever-changing land use pattern or whether our emphasis should be on controlling our land use pattern for the future and then providing the transportation facility that would meet a controlled plan (Southern Illinois University at Edwardsville 1974).

If and how St. Louis chooses to confront that dilemma will determine the future effectiveness of regional transportation planning.

References

Bartholomew, Harland. "Reduction of Street Traffic Congestion by Proper Street Design." *Annals of the American Academy of Political and Social Science* 166 (November 1924): 244–246.

Board of Public Service. *Report on Rapid Transit for St. Louis.* St. Louis: Author, 1926.

Brown, Jeffrey. "A Tale of Two Visions: Harland Bartholomew, Robert Moses, and the Development of the American Freeway." *Journal of Planning History* 4, no. 1 (February 2005): 3–32.

City Plan Commission of St. Louis. *Comprehensive City Plan.* St. Louis: Author, 1947.

———. *Expressway Plan for the St. Louis Urban Area: Statement and Review.* St. Louis: Author, 1952.

———. *A Major Street Plan for St. Louis.* St. Louis: Author, 1917a.

———. *Problems of St. Louis.* St. Louis: Author, 1917b.

———. *St. Louis After the War.* St. Louis: Author, 1918.

———. *The St. Louis Transit System: Present and Future.* St. Louis: Author, 1920.

———. *Ten Years' Progress on the City Plan of St. Louis: 1916–1926.* St. Louis: Author, 1927.

———. *Twelfth Street: St. Louis' Most Needed Commercial Thoroughfare.* St. Louis: Von Hoffman Press, 1919.

Consad Research Corporation. *Socioeconomic Study of a Proposed Rail-Like Rapid Transit System for the St. Louis Metropolitan Area.* Vol. II, *Impacts and Public Perceptions.* Pittsburgh, PA: Author, 1972.

Deakin, Elizabeth A. "The Social Impacts of the Interstate Highway System." *TR News* 244 (May–June 2006): 16–17.

East-West Gateway Coordinating Council. *Cost Estimate Review and Update for the St. Louis Area Rapid Transit System.* St. Louis: Author, 1973.

———. *Legacy 2030: The Transportation Plan for the Gateway Region.* St. Louis: Author, 2005.

———. *Mass Transit Program for the Saint Louis Metropolitan Area.* St. Louis: Author, 1978.

Forstall, Richard L., comp. and ed. "Population of Counties by Decennial Census: 1900–1990." 1995. Report by the U.S. Bureau of the Census—Population Division, March 27, 1995. http://www.census.gov/population/cencounts/il190090.txt and mo190090.txt.and mo190090.txt.

Harland, Bartholomew, & Associates. *A Preliminary Report on a System of Major Highways for St. Louis County, Missouri.* St. Louis: Wellington, 1930.

Lovelace, Eldridge. *Harland Bartholomew: His Contributions to American Urban Planning.* Urbana: University of Illinois, 1993.

Missouri State Highway Department. *A Traffic Survey of St. Louis Metropolitan Area.* Prepared in cooperation with Public Roads Administration and Federal Works Agency. Jefferson City, MO?: 1947.

National Resources Committee. *Regional Planning, Part II—St. Louis Region: Report of the St. Louis Regional Planning Commission.* Washington, DC: Government Printing Office, 1936.

NuStats. *Household Travel Survey: Final Report of Survey Results.* Prepared for the East-West Gateway Coordinating Council. Austin, TX: Author, 2003.

Parsons Brinckerhoff et al. *St. Louis Metropolitan Area Mass Transportation Study, Phase I Report: Analysis of Existing Transit System.* St. Louis: Author, 1968.

———. *St. Louis Metropolitan Area Rapid Transit Feasibility Study: Long-Range Program.* St. Louis: Author, 1971.

Regional Planning Federation. *A Regional Plan for the St. Louis District.* St. Louis: Author, 1927.

Sandweiss, Eric. *St. Louis: The Evolution of An American Urban Landscape.* Philadelphia: Temple University Press, 2001.

Southern Illinois University at Edwardsville. *Proceedings of the Greater St. Louis Transportation Seminar, October 11 and 12, 1973.* Edwardsville, IL: Department of Engineering and Technology, Southern Illinois University at Edwardsville, 1974.

St. Louis and St. Louis County Transit Board of Freeholders. *Proposed Plan of the Metropolitan St. Louis Transit District.* St. Louis: Author, 1955.

St. Louis Regional Planning Association. *A Preliminary Report on a Regional Survey and Plan: St. Louis Regional Area.* Prepared for the National Planning Board. St. Louis: Author, 1934.

St. Louis Urban Area Expressway Project Report. *Expressway Plan for the St. Louis Urban Area in Missouri, 1951*. Cooperating agencies: U.S. Bureau of Public Roads, U.S. Department of Commerce, Missouri State Highway Commission, City of St. Louis. St. Louis: Author, 1951.

U.S. Department of Transportation—Federal Highway Administration. "Urban Design Principles." *Interregional Highways* (January 1943). www.fhwa.gov.

W. C. Gilman and Company. *St. Louis Metropolitan Area Transportation Study, 1957–'70–'80*. New York: Author, 1959.

Weingroff, Richard F. "Federal-Aid Highway Act of 1956: Creating the Interstate System." *Public Roads On-Line* 60, no. 1 (Summer 1996). http://tfhrc.gov/pubrds/summer96/p96su10.htm.

_____. "The Genie in the Bottle: The Interstate System and Urban Problems, 1939–1957." Report by the U.S. Department of Transportation-Federal Highway Administration. Public Roads On-Line 64, no. 2 (September/October 2000). http://www.tfhrc.gov/pubrds/septoct00/urban.htm.

_____. "A Peaceful Campaign of Progress and Reform: The Federal Highway Administration at 100." *Public Roads On-Line* 57, no. 2 (Autumn 1993). http://tfhrc.gov/pubrds/fall93/P93au1.htm.

Whitton, Rex M., "The Interstate System in Missouri." Paper presented to the Advertising Club of St. Louis, St. Louis, July 29, 1958.

Wilbur Smith and Associates. *A Highway Planning Study for the St. Louis Metropolitan Area*. Vol. 1, *Highway and Travel Facts*. Prepared for the Missouri State Highway Commission. New Haven, CT: Author, 1959.

Young, Andrew D. *St. Louis and Its Streetcars: The Way It Was*. St. Louis: Archway Publishing, 1996.

Chapter 12

The Challenges to Workforce Development Planning in Postwar St. Louis

David Laslo

Since the end of World War II, workforce development planning in the St. Louis region has been confined to efforts that have been motivated and underwritten by external resources that have come in response to economic and employment crises associated with specific local firms and industries. These planning efforts have been largely short-term in tenure and have lacked an institutional infrastructure of organizations and funding that could ensure greater gains in the general level of employment and skills in the St. Louis workforce over a longer period of time. And while the outcomes of these local planning efforts have been mixed in terms of labor market outcomes, they suggest that similar, more coordinated, and longer-term efforts are needed to raise the skill level and productivity of the St. Louis workforce. In order to make local companies more globally competitive, successful workforce planning will require overcoming a number of significant obstacles that have stifled attempts in the postwar period in St. Louis and gradual and continual integration of private and public interests and organizations. Success of any future workforce development planning effort must be organized around a consensus of workforce issues, with an agreed-upon priority and strategies for how they will be addressed.

In St. Louis, as elsewhere in the United States, workforce development planning has largely been left to a federally mandated and funded "second chance" system of workforce intermediaries (Giloth 2004, 1). A system ostensibly created to assist those of workforce age to acquire the skills necessary to find and retain family-supporting employment. Historically, it has been aimed at those who have failed or dropped out of the first chance system[1] of formal education and training institutions. This second chance system has often been criticized for its lack of coordination and focus, but most likely its performance is a product of its changing policy context and legislative mandates that often work against large-scale efforts at better performance and reform. But in St. Louis, as the economy and workforce continues to evolve in the twenty-first century, there is an increasing need for greater flexibility in the use of federal funds and more long-term collaborative efforts among business, education institutions, and workforce intermediaries that will create a better-prepared workforce.

This chapter begins by defining workforce development and workforce planning as it is used in this discussion and includes a description of what constitutes the "second chance system" of workforce intermediaries and the role they play in effecting labor market outcomes in the workforce development planning efforts of the postwar period. The chapter then examines the history of workforce development policy and planning in the United States, tracing its roots in the public works projects of the Great Depression and the 1960s War on Poverty through the current Workforce Investment Act of 1998, noting the key legislation that has attempted to alter its focus and improve its ability to meet the workforce needs of specific workforce populations. This section includes a discussion of the five most salient features of postwar workforce development policy as a context in which the efforts at workforce planning in the St. Louis region can be examined. The chapter continues with an examination of how St. Louis workforce development planning has mirrored national policy and economic events. It will then look at a number of recent attempts at workforce planning in the St. Louis region that will provide insight into the continued need for workforce planning and the obstacles that often challenge their ability to enjoy greater success. These recent examples of workforce planning efforts include the Regional Jobs Initiative, Bridges-to-Work, Defense Adjustment Project, and the Workforce Development Policy Group. The chapter then discusses the obstacles and challenges to long-term success in the St. Louis region that includes a wide and complex set of variables such as the targeting of specific populations, limited and restrictive funding mandates, political and governance fragmentation, the spatial distribution of jobs and population, and the lack of integration between the first and second chance systems of workforce and workforce-

---

[1]The first chance system is the constellation of institutions that includes the K–12 system, technical and vocational schools, two-year and community colleges, four-year postsecondary colleges, and private sector training institutions.

related systems. The chapter concludes with a discussion on the prospects for future workforce development planning in the St. Louis region.

Defining Workforce Development Planning

Every year, in regions across the United States, millions of Americans face a wide range of challenges to full and gainful employment. In some instances, potential workers have not taken full advantage of their educational opportunities and struggle mightily to find work that pays a family-supporting wage and has prospects for advancement. In other instances, incumbent workers find that their jobs have moved or have been eliminated and are left with obsolete skills and experience. And this combines with growing evidence that the number of well-paying, family-supporting jobs with career potential are shrinking relative to jobs that are low-wage and have no prospect for career advancement (Harrison and Weiss 1998, 10). With the wealth and prosperity of a region often very dependent on the quality and supply of its labor force, adequately addressing these challenges becomes a serious social and economic issue and points toward the need for improved planning of workforce development. So what is workforce development and planning and what role can it play in the regional labor market?

For purposes of this discussion, workforce development is defined as the constellation of activities related to the work world, from recruiting, placement, and mentoring to follow-up counseling and crisis intervention. Training is but one component of this greater set of activities aimed at assisting those who populate the second chance system either through failure in the primary education and training system, job dislocation, or the need for skill upgrade or change for incumbent workers. Typically, the second chance system includes an array of organizations and institutions that provide services such as GED high school equivalency programs, basic skills remediation, English as a Second Language, short-term training, long term training, on-the-job training, dislocated worker and reemployment programs, and upgrade training for incumbent workers. In this context, workforce development is essentially the set of activities often described as "a fragmented hodgepodge of programs" (Giloth 2004, 1). The target population of workforce development has consistently been minority, disadvantaged, and dislocated workers, but more recently, it has come to include the training needs of incumbent workers, that is, currently employed persons. Coordinating and improving the performance of these activities has been the focus of workforce planning.

Workforce development planning is considered the efforts to overcome the fragmentation of the workforce development system and the introduction of coordination and efficiency to program and service delivery. Workforce planning is also considered to have a regional or multijurisdictional scope whereby the necessary training needs of resident workers or a local industry or firm can be acquired without regard for jurisdictional boundaries. Regional development workforce planning needs reflect the spatial distribution of jobs and people in a particular region brought about by the ongoing decentralization of jobs and people. This has been a salient feature of the St. Louis region and most regions across the United States, and it is the premise from which many workforce planning efforts have stemmed. Workforce development planning has also focused on efforts to overcome the training and skills mismatch of jobs and target populations that occur as a result of economic events such as industry economic restructuring and firm specific acquisition, buyout, or merger. Workforce development planning in the St. Louis region has reflected the general focus of these planning efforts and has paralleled the changes in national legislative mandates that have occurred in response to crises. The story of St. Louis workforce development planning begins with national policy.

Rooted in Crisis and Ideology: The History of Workforce Development Planning

The history of workforce development planning at the national, state, and local level is generally a story that traces changes in economic and social conditions and the gradually lower priority it has been given at the national policy level (Giloth 2004, 11). Beginning with the public works projects of the Work Projects Administration (WPA), Civilian Conservation Corps (CCC), and the Unemployment Insurance program (UI) motivated by the widespread misery brought on by the Great Depression in the 1930s, public workforce development and planning involved public job creation in the context of national economic planning. But by the end of World War II and with the flood of ex-servicemen returning to the U.S. labor market, the Full Employment Bill of 1946 had created the general tenor of workforce development planning for the next fifty years that would emphasize small-scale, directed human capital investment rather than the pursuit of active labor market policies. This is in direct contrast to other developed countries that have engaged in active labor force development policies

(Giloth 2004, 3; O'Leary et al. 2004, 5–6). The impact of this legislation shaped U.S. workforce policy and its attendant legislation in five key ways over the subsequent fifty years:

1. It separated workforce training activities from national economic planning. This meant that workforce development and planning took a backseat to economic growth management and policy development at the national level. As a result, workforce development and planning have been confined to addressing specific segments of the labor force with little connection to business demand or changes to economic structure.

2. The limiting of workforce development resources to low-income and minority populations has been a key feature of postwar workforce development planning and policy. Because of its separation from national economic planning, the responses to the social unrest of the 1960s targeted the poor and minority populations within the labor force as an antipoverty program. The emphasis on specialized workforce investment of low-income workers and welfare recipients had the effect of forever casting the image and perception of national and local workforce development planning efforts as limiting public training efforts. This has had the added effect of restricting the constituency for workforce planning policies and therefore lowered the prospects for changing the emphasis and direction of such policies (Giloth 2004, 11).

3. A continued emphasis on human capital and supply-side strategies rather than public job creation or sector strategies that "sought to affect employer or industry decisions and behaviors" (Giloth 2004, 11). Although the Comprehensive Employment and Training Act (CETA) of 1973 continued to target the disadvantaged (low income, welfare recipients and disadvantaged youth), it reintroduced public service employment as a workforce development strategy. This legislation created local advisory boards, called Private Industry Councils (PIC), as it sought to decentralize control from national and state authority. CETA attempted to guarantee input from a broader range of interests, including education, labor, and business, through mandated local representation. However, this strategy of public service employment proved to be rife with mismanagement and corruption and was abandoned under controversy as new legislation in the early 1980s continued attempts to consolidate and coordinate the workforce planning efforts of locales.

4. There have been inadequate resources provided by federal legislation and budget allocations. The Job Training Partnership Act (JTPA) of 1982 was designed to reach only about 5 percent of the of the population in need of and eligible for workforce services (Lafer 1994, 2002). As a result of the dismal performance of the local CETA efforts, the JTPA reduced the "largesse and public service employment of CETA" while introducing mandates to increase performance measures and to increase the amount of business representation on the PICs (Giloth 2004, 13). Widespread layoffs during the 1980s lead to the additional eligibility of dislocated workers in workforce budget allocations, and, often, they became the focus of workforce planning efforts due to the local impact of economic events such as plant closings and industry restructuring. While these efforts were essentially rooted in the economic crises of the time, a general restructuring of the economy away from heavy manufacturing to services, they reflected the reactive and underfunded state of workforce development in the United States. Compounding this paucity of funding was the rapid growth and fragmented state of workforce development programs.

5. Myriad restrictive funding sources for addressing workforce development and planning issues were created. Reacting quickly to the social unrest of the 1960s, employment and training policies and their attendant programs and funding grew rapidly into a fragmented and complex system. Through the adoption of small-scale, decentralized efforts and policies that targeted specific populations with employment and training needs over more universal workforce policies, this complex web of programs created what has been called funding "silos" (Giloth 2004, 12). These silos have frustrated workforce planning efforts by tightly defining and targeting program funds. Often, fund use is restricted to specific populations and types of training. The Workforce Investment Act (WIA) of 1998 is the most recent attempt to bring more coordination to disparate programs and funding sources within a framework of "work first" ideology and a broadening of program eligibility. It also attempted to expand business involvement on its governing boards (Workforce Investment Boards) in order to emphasize more local control over meeting local labor demand.

The 1990s were a time of general prosperity and by some measures a time of full employment that had the effect of shifting the focus of antipoverty-based employment policies. By this time, the over-thirty year search for how to reduce poverty through employment policies became defined as a "work first" philosophy. It shifted responsibility from the state to individuals and exchanged skill training job placement and reduced dependency on public assistance as paths to self-sufficient employment (O'Leary, et al. 2004, 10). This shift in general philosophy and the legislation that accompanied it, the Personal Responsibility and Work Opportunity Reconciliation Act (PRWORA) of 1996 combined with the WIA to create a national human resources policy that emphasized self-sufficiency and local control. The WIA attempts to reform the second chance system of workforce development and planning into "a new comprehensive workforce investment system . . . that is intended to be customer focused, to help individuals access the tools they need to manage their careers through information and high-quality services and to help employers find skilled workers" (O'Leary et al., 2004, 11). The most significant feature of WIA has been the creation of one-stop career centers where all employment and training programs are assembled in one physical location with universal access to core employment services and with some restrictive access to more intensive training.

In general, the history of workforce development and planning reflects a "deep confusion in America regarding how to best help people obtain the jobs that lead to family-self-sufficiency" (Giloth 2004, 2). The politics behind the policies that evolved over this period ranged from conflicts over ideas and ideologies to distribution of resources, from to how best to calm civil unrest to the devolution of authority and resources to states and localities (Giloth 20004, 12). It has also been marked by its policy isolation from other important economic (national economic management) and social (education and universal training) policies and its general state of chronic underfunding relative to actual need. It has also been noted for its emphasis on human capital investment versus policies that would impact the nature of firm behavior and industry decisions. It also has reflected the sporadic and limited amount of business involvement in shaping workforce development policies; this inconsistency has limited its constituency and its prospects for achieving greater national policy priority. These features of postwar workforce development are evident in a brief history of workforce development planning in the St. Louis region, and they provide a backdrop for identifying the challenges and obstacles that have and continue to constrain successful workforce planning.

Workforce Development Planning in the St. Louis Region: A Mirror of National Policy and Local Crisis

Postwar workforce development planning in the St. Louis region mirrors the pattern of national policy and the features that have marked its implementation. It has been often characterized locally by its lack of connection and coordination from other key policy systems, such as the formal education system and economic development strategies, and the limiting of its constituencies to groups within the lowest socioeconomic segments of the population. This has contributed to low-priority status on the local policy agenda and a level of funding that meets only a small fraction of the need relative to local demand for job readiness and skills training. Local workforce development planning has also been characterized by the legislatively restricted nature of the available funding. Collectively, these features appear to have constrained workforce development planning to such a degree that little or no workforce development planning has occurred in St. Louis that has not been motivated and underwritten by national legislation or foundations or otherwise prompted by "emergency" financial support from the national government in response to industry or firm-specific crises. This reactive state of workforce development planning reflects the realities of "local political arrangements [that] largely shape and constrain the way in which national policy is implemented in St. Louis" (Cummings et al. 2004, 182). Attempts at regional workforce planning have generally been prompted by a local economic event or crisis, such as the "peace dividend" downsizing of the McDonnell Douglas Corporation in the early 1990s after the end of the cold war. Another prompt was the injection of significant foundation resources, such as the Regional Job Initiative of the Annie E. Casey Foundation in the mid-1990s; this was aimed at prompting reform in order to improve the performance of the local second chance system of workforce development. Without such financial externalities, there have been no significant attempts at regional workforce development planning that would have expanded the scope of training and skills beyond those that addressed the populations mandated by federal legislation or effected by economic events, such as downsizing, mergers, or restructuring.

Ideally, workforce development planning would be part of a greater system of labor market components that included the K–12 education system, the private training system, transportation, related support social services, and business through sector or industry-wide initiatives. Instead, workforce development planning operates in a virtual policy or systems vacuum with only episodic and limited connection with other workforce and workforce-related systems. The limited history of such initiatives in the St. Louis region reveals that attempts have been made to connect the existing second chance system and the population it serves with other labor market-related systems. These have included the Bridges-to-Work Initiative of the 1990s that attempted to "bridge" the spatial mismatch between jobs in the region's core with available jobs in outlying suburbs through specific transportation strategies and social support services, or the Defense Adjustment Project of the early and mid-1990s that sought to help transition former defense industry workers at the downsizing McDonnell Douglas Corporation into new occupations and careers. They also have included the six city Regional Jobs Initiatives of Baltimore's Annie E. Casey Foundation. The initiative sought to reform the coordination and performance of the second chance system in St. Louis through an injection of new and less restrictive use of job training funding and the Workforce Development Planning Policy Group that attempted to create a greater policy system through dialogue aimed at reaching a consensus on labor market policy priorities. With mixed results, these attempts at workforce development planning show how isolated it has been, and much of it remains today due to the legislation that created it and to the local demographic, economic, and governance context.

Governance fragmentation. Many local observers and professionals working within the second chance system have cited local political arrangements and the complex system of governance as responsible for the lack of cohesive local workforce development planning and the limited success of what has been attempted. The policy preference for local, parochial interests over greater regional initiatives has typically derailed regional attempts at workforce development planning (Cummings et al. 2004, 182). Recent research indicates that besides six Workforce Investment Areas, there are two state governments, nine community colleges and two-year institutions, nine major technical and vocational schools, fifty school districts, and three public colleges and universities in the St. Louis region. Reaching consensus on priority labor force needs and a means of cooperation across an increasing number of interests has proven to be a daunting task given the complexity and number of interests that could potentially be involved. Achieving both a consensus of labor force need and the creation of the necessary institutional structure for long-term cooperation has heretofore proven to be difficult within the current governance and economic context.

Business involvement. According to many local observers of and professionals in second chance workforce intermediaries, business in general does not consider the clientele of the second chance system as a potential source of skilled and available labor. These perceptions were undoubtedly formed in the early days of the War on Poverty and may have been reinforced by the controversies surrounding earlier programs such as those implemented in St. Louis under the CETA with its emphasis on public employment and placement over job readiness and sustainable employment (Cummings et al. 2004, 191–193). But the succession of subsequent legislation (JTPA and WIA) has now sufficiently expanded the eligibility for services so that these past perceptions are now entirely outdated. And although there have been numerous examples of businesses that have engaged the system and have expressed satisfaction with the workers they have received from it, they remain a relative few compared to the potential labor and skills demand that has existed in the St. Louis region over the past several decades. This lack of positive perception and limited business involvement within a highly fragmented governance structure has severely limited the prospects for significant workforce development planning. With greater direct business involvement, workforce development planning could achieve a higher profile and potentially a higher priority on the regional development agenda.

Marginal focus. Limiting the scope of workforce development planning to subsets of the potential labor force such as minorities and low-income welfare recipients at the local level has also been viewed as reinforcing the economic and social divides within the St. Louis region and has constrained its ability to achieve significant long-term planning for workforce development (Cummings et al. 2004, 181–189). The CETA and JTPA programs of the 1970s and 1980s in St. Louis and the controversies and political divisions that characterized their implementation did little to reverse or ease these challenges. Because they were legislatively mandated to address low-income workers, minorities, and welfare recipients, the second chance system for workforce development planning became perceived as an antipoverty program and a solution to a "black" problem (Cummings et al. 2004, 189). With the population and jobs within the St. Louis region decentralizing away from the core of the region, it became increasingly challenging to match and place workers who possess limited resources for transportation and other support services such as childcare. In a region of approximately 2.6 million people and a labor force of approximately 1.4 million in 2005 that now spreads across sixteen counties in Missouri and Illinois, the majority of low-income persons and persons of poverty remains concentrated in the core counties of the region, namely St. Clair

County in Illinois and the City of St. Louis and northeastern portions of St. Louis County. As a result, workforce development planning, which has been almost universally tied to addressing the needs of the lowest economic and educated segments of the regional workforce, has been restricted to attempts at overcoming the spatial mismatch between these workers and the location of jobs. It is an indication of the lack of consensus about which segments of the labor force, beyond those eligible for federal support, should and could be addressed (Cummings et al. 2004, 177).

Inadequate and restricted funds. In 1995, there were 163 workforce programs administered by a wide range of federal agencies, each with their own set of guidelines and targeted populations (Grubb 1996). These funding "silos" have had the effect locally of constraining use of funding to specific populations and training that often has not captured regionwide public attention or been of broad interest to commercial enterprise. This targeting of specific populations has translated locally into a directing of resources toward geographically concentrated populations within an ever-expanding regional land area that has typically included an increasing number of parochial interests. This growing number of regional demographic differences and local perceptions of priority workforce needs have often worked against finding common ground for workforce development planning (Cummings et al. 2004, 181–189). In light of local degrees of indifference toward specific, targeted populations and a lack of consensus around more universal labor force needs, the introduction of external funding from the national government and foundations has been the sole source of motivation for local workforce development planning.

Generally, St. Louis workforce development planning parallels the national pattern of operating in general isolation from larger economic development management and planning and instead focusing on segments or subsets of the regional labor force rather than crafting more universal training and skills development policies. This is a direct consequence of national policy that has defined workforce development planning as essentially an antipoverty program that has limited its constituencies and therefore its ability to attract more resources and the necessary interests, namely greater business involvement and public attention. At the local level, this has translated into efforts aimed at utilizing funding as it came available in response to new legislation, responses to economic events and crises and philanthropic attempts to underwrite reform in workforce development practices and planning. The low frequency of workforce development planning can be attributed to a lack of involvement and connection with other important labor force–related systems and private sectors of the economy. This has limited its ability to capture sufficient public attention, more direct business involvement, and the minimum of political support and cooperation it would need to gain a higher priority on the regional development agenda. Recent examples in St. Louis illustrate how limited and targeted funding has constrained workforce development planning to those efforts that have provided external funding specifically for regional planning efforts.

Recent Attempts at Workforce Development Planning in St. Louis

Since the late 1980s, the most prominent attempts at workforce development planning efforts in the St. Louis region have been tied to local economic restructuring, economic events, and job and population decentralization. They have also been directly shaped by legislative mandates that are attached to available dollars from the federal government and the needs they were designed to address. The results of these efforts have been mixed as the examples that follow will illustrate. They will also provide a basis for discussing the salient challenges to workforce development planning and the prospects for future workforce development planning.

Defense Adjustment Project

Developed in response to the downsizing of the McDonnell Douglas Corporation in the early 1990s, due to defense spending cuts following the end of the cold war, the Defense Adjustment Project (DAP) was perhaps St. Louis's most successful postwar workforce-related planning effort. Largely underwritten by $23.7 million in funding from the Economic Development Administration (EDA) of the U.S. Department of Commerce over an eight-year period, the DAP sought to smooth the transition of dislocated defense contract and defense supplier workers to other careers and jobs. Between July 1990 and January 1991, McDonnell Douglas announced initial layoffs totaling 9,500, but would continue to downsize through much of the 1990s, reducing its total employment to 21,800 by 1997. This 47 percent decrease in direct employment was a significant blow to the local economy that rippled across jurisdictional boundaries throughout the region. Subsequent military base retrenchments and closings affected another 3,600 workers in July 1995. In general, the end of the cold war created an economic crisis of such magnitude and shared pain that it would provide more than sufficient motivation for regional workforce development planning.

In terms of longevity and breadth of participation, the DAP enjoyed a relatively high rate of success among the brief history of workforce development planning initiatives in the St. Louis region. The impact of the defense downsizing was felt by workers and communities across the region and the recognition of a common and shared problem brought important and significant interjurisdictional and multiinstitutional cooperation. A list of participants would grow to include several regional chambers of commerce; numerous state and local economic development organizations; state, county, and local job training departments; labor, and defense contractors. Although not without its conflicts and controversies, the twenty-two-member DAP Task Force was able to create a wide range of workforce development initiatives that were tied to regional economic development. These included entrepreneurial training, small business incubators, and an international business center that ostensibly was designed to assist the companies created by dislocated workers reach new markets globally. However, these efforts were considered secondary to the re-employment efforts of the laid-off defense workers and included a research component that conducted an assessment of the needs and capacities of the laid-off workers. This research was used to enhance existing employment services, identify gaps in services, and design the programs to fill them. The DAP thus was designed to address the immediate employment needs of the laid-off defense workers and to address the needs of businesses affected by defense spending cuts.

Workforce development planning within the context of the DAP took advantage of many nascent initiatives and was successful in bridging and coordinating resources across the wide array of services within the second chance system. The DAP successfully lobbied the Department of Labor to win greater flexibility in the use of available training resources for laid-off defense workers entering similar occupations, and it supported the concept of a job resource clearinghouse through the creation of one-stop career centers. These centers were in multiple regional locations that sought to consolidate and coordinate local and federally supported employment services. It also created a business incubator and entrepreneurial training program for affected defense workers who sought to create their own enterprises. The DAP created a regional manufacturing training initiative called the Cornerstone Partnership that sought to upgrade the education and skills of manufacturing workers The DAP further sought to meet labor needs of business through the targeting of high-growth industries and the Regional Jobs Initiative funded by the Annie E. Casey Foundation (described in more detail below).

The DAP lasted over eight years and was able to overcome many traditional obstacles related to parochial interests and funding legislative mandates. It also was able to attach to or help facilitate concepts and initiatives such as the one-stop career centers and business incubators. Similarly, it was able to hold together sufficient regional cooperation that allowed it to attract additional funding for projects such as the manufacturing training center (the Cornerstone Partnership) and to have conducted enough research regarding labor demand and worker trainer needs that it was able to attract sufficient common ground for some consensus on need among a relatively large number of interests over an extended period of time. In terms of the amount and length of cooperation that it achieved, the DAP enjoyed perhaps the most success of any local workforce development initiative.

Bridges-to-Work

The Bridges-to-Work Program (BTW) was motivated by what was called the "suburban-urban employment divide" and the availability of Department of Transportation funding to address that issue in the early 1990s. The BTW program identified areas of "origin" from which persons of working age who met program eligibility standards could receive a series of employment, support, and transportation services. These areas were generally found in high unemployment and poverty sections in the north, central, and southeastern portions of the City of St. Louis and the near northeastern portions of St. Louis County. The "destination" for the program participants was employers in a quadrant of west St. Louis County bounded by the major interstates, I-270 on the east, I-64 on the north, I-44 on the south, and the St. Louis County boundary on the west. After meeting job readiness criteria and deemed qualified for job placement by the second chance system of job training partners, program participants would receive support services and transportation in order to find employment in the designated area. This bridging of the job spatial mismatch was believed to be an important antipoverty and workforce development planning effort within the context of a tightening labor market and expanding regional employment landscape.

The capacity to implement the BTW program was built around a "core governing group" of key economic development, transportation, social service, and employment and training organizations. This core governing group included the JTPAs of the City of St. Louis and St. Louis County, the East-West Gateway Coordinating Council (the regional transportation planning agency), the Bi-State Development Agency (EWGCC, the regional public transportation agency, now the East-West Gateway Council of Governments), the Missouri Department of Social Services, the Urban League of Metropolitan St. Louis, and the Economic Council of St. Louis County. An additional Advisory Council that included participating employers and the offices of the elected officials of the City of St. Louis and St. Louis County provided oversight to program implementation and was charged with "developing an implementable funding strategy to continue operation of the program" (East-West Gateway Coordinating Council 1995, 62). With a staff of five and an annual budget of approximately $750,000 the BTW program hoped to place and maintain employment for approximately 800 persons annually from the urban areas of origin to companies in the suburban areas of destination. During its more than seven-year run, the BTW program had approximately sixty companies in various parts of the destination area participate in the program.

Eventually, the BTW program had difficulty maintaining itself when funding from governmental and nonprofit sources dried up under mixed reviews of success. While there were many individual successes documented in journalistic accounts of the program, the cost and effort of transporting workers to and from core urban areas to entry-level suburban jobs proved too expensive to maintain. Likewise, the recruitment of eligible workers to fill the suburban jobs became a continuing challenge. According to observers and participants involved in the implementation of the program, it is believed to have achieved a large proportion of its stated goal for job placements, but was unable to retain but a small proportion of those placements over time. The several additional hours necessary to hold an entry-level paying job in a suburban location because of the lack of available transportation often proved to be too taxing relative to any incremental pay that was achieved by working in a particular suburban location or company.

Ultimately, the BTW program demonstrated that a pressing need for entry-level workers in the St. Louis region was exacerbated by a tightening labor market and the decentralization of jobs and people. In creating the justification for the program, it identified the fact that workforce development issues had skill and training components, as well as other social and transportation issues all within a spatial context. To address this combination of issues meant bringing together a wide range of organizations and institutions with separate missions and resource capacities that proved challenging to maintain. It also highlighted the integration of these organizations and institutions that would be necessary to make significant workforce development impacts on labor supply and demand. It did, however, demonstrate again that a specific and directed funding source could provide the necessary means for collaboration and cooperation across multiple jurisdictions and service delivery organizations. And while many individual workers and companies benefited from the program, the numbers were only a very small fraction of what would be necessary to make a significant impact on labor force supply and demand in the "origin" and "destination" areas and at a regional level.

Regional Jobs Initiative

The Regional Jobs Initiative (RJI) found its genesis in 1996 when the Annie E. Casey Foundation chose the St. Louis region as one of six sites for experimental second-chance system reform. By helping to underwrite this experiment at system reform for a seven-year period, the foundation hoped to promote and motivate greater intrasystem and inter-system integration in order to improve the labor market outcomes of the second chance system and the long-term employment prospects of "young job seekers in the urban core" (EWGCC 1996, 1). With an annual Strategic Investment Plan budget of approximately $3 million ($700,000 from the Casey Foundation), the RJI was organized around seven "doors of innovation," or programs that would achieve reform by testing and institutionalizing new labor market connections. These programs included creating a community center for health careers, a construction recruiting program focused on mentoring, and a clerical job placement program for welfare recipients. The Strategic Investment Plan identified projects and prototypes that were to be used to test the new relationships, practices, protocols, and policies that would lead directly to long-term "systems reform." The Strategic Investment Plan identified the many discrete elements and systems in what was called the regional labor market infrastructure.

Improvements in the performance outcomes of the regional labor market infrastructure were said to require a number of system connections both within it and with other workforce-related systems. According to planning documents, this included "improved connections between jurisdictions within the same 'system,' stronger linkages between systems themselves and customer-focused programs that focus systems on the needs of employers and the capacities of job-seekers more precisely" (EWGCC 1996, 1). It was believed that "between 1997 and 2004, as the plan is implemented, amended, and evolves, the learnings from the ambitious program it sets forth will frame the first integrated, inter-jurisdictional Job Policy Agenda that post-world War II St. Louis has ever had" (EWGCC 1996, 1). Considering the dearth of workforce development planning that had occurred in the St. Louis region in the postwar period, this was not an entirely untrue statement. In large part because of its status as the regional Metropolitan Planning Organization (MPO) for transportation and its concurrent experience with the BTW program, the Casey Foundation chose the East-West Gateway Coordinating Council as the oversight agency.

As required by the reform agenda of the Casey Foundation, the RJI targeted its resources on low-income and poverty populations in a portion of the northwest section of the City of St. Louis and many of the adjacent municipalities of St. Louis County similar to one of the areas of "origin" under the BTW program. In doing so, the RJI reflected a targeted population and prescriptive approach that was consistent with the programs and organizations that had considerable experience in addressing these issues. And while much of the rhetoric associated with the RJI struck a familiar and worthy antipoverty refrain, the framing of the Initiative around these issues restricted the interest and participation to the stakeholders previously involved with workforce development or those in the second chance system. As a result, the choice of workforce development newcomer EWGCC to oversee the initiative was a source of local animosity and contention and doomed the RJI to limited, incremental successes (Cummings et al. 2004, 204–205). Like most similar programs and initiatives, there were successes on an individual level, as there were many successful transitions to the workforce from the welfare rolls given the concurrent Welfare-to-Work legislation of the late 1990s. And on a programmatic scale, the creation of numerous programs (notably construction and life skills) in the Met Center (previously the Cornerstone Partnership) in the inner ring suburb of Wellston were considered relative successes and were welcome additions to the greater menu of job training and skills-related programs provided in the region. Still, given the resources devoted to it and the large challenges posed by the employment prospects of many in poverty populations, the impact of the RJI was relatively insignificant given the size of the target population and its persistent poverty status.

At the same time, attempts to reform the second chance system failed completely as no consensus on a unifying idea or shared beliefs about system reform was reached. Without such a common belief system, the ambitious reform agenda ostensibly to be generated by the RJI's seven "doors of innovation" remained just an ambitious agenda. However, increasingly these initiatives and an additional funding source did give organizations and institutions in the second chance system experience in how to collaborate and cooperate across previously rigid and often contentious political, jurisdictional, and legislative boundaries and, as one workforce development professional observed, "We need each other." Many have noted that the political fragmentation and diffusion of power in the St. Louis region are major constraints to reform in the St. Louis region, and it could be concluded that the scale of the reform agenda of the RJI doomed it from its outset (Jones 2000; Cummings et al. 2004, 199). In the final analysis the RJI did contribute to the identification of many useful components of the employment needs associated with addressing low-income and poverty populations and it did expand and give experience to the region's second chance system on the means of cooperation and collaboration while acknowledging that workforce development poses regional challenges. Ultimately, the RJI taught the St. Louis region that it will require a broad consensus on common ideas in order to shape the necessary reform agenda and the building of the necessary capacity to carry it forth. The RJI may have achieved greater success had it attempted smaller, incremental reforms built upon shared ideas on how best to institutionalize collaboration across numerous political and jurisdictional boundaries. It also demonstrated that reforms may be better received and supported if they are developed from within the region rather than imposed by external sources.

St. Louis Regional Workforce Development Policy Group

The St. Louis Regional Workforce Development Policy Group (WDPG) was formed in late 1999 as an attempt by regional planning and economic development institutions to address the broader workforce development issues that faced the region beyond those associated with the workforce needs of the low-income and poverty populations. The region's experience with the DAP, BTW, and RJI highlighted the many challenges to expanding workforce development planning beyond its legislative mandates and identified the broader training, skills, and spatial issues at a regional level. Underwritten by funding for planning called Community Audit made available through the new Workforce Investment Act of 1998, the WDPG attempted to find a consensus of priority workforce development needs through the convening of workforce-related stakeholders. Through a guided process of cogitation, the EWGCC and the St. Louis Regional Chamber of Commerce sought to produce a "coherent workforce development strategy that would develop a unified labor market in which it could attract and retain both firms and talented young people to work in them" (EWGCC 1999, 1).

According to its mission statement, the St. Louis Regional Workforce Development Plan was "to build a strategy for the efficient and effective investment of public and private resources in a coordinated system that develops and continuously improves the region's human capital, anticipating and responding to the changing demands of our dynamic regional economy" (EWGCC 1999, 1). This strategy was to be developed through a thirty-eight-member policy group that included a wide range of workforce stakeholders from both Missouri and Illinois in the St. Louis region. The list of participants included many of those that had been active members of the DAP and RJI, the eight elected officials of the counties that were under the planning auspices of the EWGCC, and twelve representatives from the large postsecondary education institutions in the St. Louis region. Against the backdrop of national legislation (WIA) that sought to further reform the second chance system of workforce development and a "full employment" economy, there was a belief among the conveners of the WDPG that it could develop such a strategy while developing support for the consolidation of workforce development resources in fewer institutions and organizations. This reform and consolidation strategy was to prove to be anathema to the entire strategy process.

Although the premise and goals of the WDPG were consistent with the lessons learned from the previous workforce development planning efforts (DAP, BTW, and RJI), this effort never got past the initial discussion stages. Early in the process, the issue of reform and consolidation came to the forefront and it quickly became the issue that dominated the agenda. Once the agenda moved away from addressing workforce development planning issues on a regional basis, including reaching a consensus around ideas for priority needs and the strategies to address them, the process was doomed. This turn rekindled long-standing political rivalries, and significant change became a highly unlikely outcome. The more politically charged attempt at creating larger, regional workforce development institutions changed dramatically the stated intent of the initiative. This produced waning participation by business and the education institutions, and the chances for developing a meaningful regional workforce development plan melted away quickly. Consolidation and reform efforts failed and, ultimately, there was little to show for the region's efforts except that it served as a reminder of how essential it was to find unifying ideas as a common ground for participation and collaboration. The WDPG was full of the proper rhetoric and well-meaning stated intentions, but fell victim to personal and political ambitions and a major drift away from its intended purpose.

The Challenges to Workforce Development Planning

Many factors work against effective and long-term local workforce development planning in the St. Louis region. At the broadest level, the second-class status of workforce development policy at the national level restricts the effective planning of broader workforce development policies to specific, targeted populations and, by most estimations, severely under-funds the training and skill development needed under rapidly changing and evolving labor markets (Lynch 1994, 1–2; Giloth 2004, 17). The lack of funding support generally and the continued defining of workforce development as policies aimed at the lowest socioeconomic segments of the labor force translates into workforce development planning that addresses only a fraction of labor demand and its skill requirements. The wide array of economic and demographic factors that have impacted how work is organized and undertaken and the emergence of global labor markets have created rapidly changing demand for new skill sets and job requirements. Workers today must be multiskilled and equipped to handle cross-functional competencies. Under current policies, these skill and training needs are addressed only on a limited and small scale and often in haphazard fashion. Over time, this policy configuration is believed to contribute to an accumulating training and skill deficit (National Research Council 1999, 30–105). This skill and training deficit is exacerbated by the "work first" philosophy of current welfare and antipoverty policies that are favored over training and family-supporting career development. This provides a monumental challenge as it is a direct contradiction to a more universal approach that would provide skill development and training as part of policies aimed at meeting large-scale labor demand while also managing the national economy.

As the recent cases of workforce development planning in St. Louis illustrated, the common ground for greater collective action was generally found in the shared impacts of economic crises and the availability of additional federal funding to address the workforce issues associated with it. Similarly, the introduction of significant external funding for reforming the performance of the second chance system was sufficient motivation for some cooperation and collective action. Without such events and external funding, workforce development planning is reduced to small-scale cooperative efforts among local workforce investment boards and their contractors such as the community colleges, other training and employment service providers, and State agencies. And while these organizations recognize that the spatial dimensions of workforce development preclude a strict adherence to parochial interests, the limited resources available limit the ability to meet local needs and participate in greater cooperative arrangements. Ultimately, because the responsibility for the measurement of funding performance is at subregional and county levels, the measurement of the benefits of regional or other cooperative initiatives is often problematic and a major impediment and challenge to workforce development planning.

The challenges presented by national workforce development policy and its historical political context and the local economic, social, and geographic dimensions that have constrained workforce development planning make it apparent that the incentives for participation and investment in it are not particularly strong. Because the benefits of workforce development planning accrue over extended periods of time and to individual workers and firms, measuring benefits to the region or across multiple jurisdictions proves difficult to do. This is in contrast to economic development policies and projects, such as physical infrastructure, that have an accepted and established range of tools and measures that portray the benefits of each project. These types of benefits, such as increased tax revenues and job creation, are generally wider in impact than those associated with workforce development and provide greater justification and incentive for cooperation. And compounding this benefit mismatch is the ability of individuals to move to and from each region that, in effect, transfers skills and training to regions that have not invested in workforce development. This has often provided a disincentive to invest in human capital strategies and training and is cited as a main reason that private investment in training is well below that of other developed nations (Lynch 1994, 4). So until workforce development planning can provide an accepted wider and more diverse range of benefits, the limited benefits it offers today will continue to be a challenge of significant dimension to overcome. As the skills of the St. Louis workforce continue to evolve in the twenty-first century, the necessity of finding a common definition of workforce issues and problems is an essential first step to overcoming the considerable challenges to workforce development planning.

Looking Ahead to Twenty-first Century Workforce Planning in St. Louis

In order to move beyond the small-scale human capital and antipoverty strategies that define workforce development planning in the early twenty-first century, workforce development must redefine itself more broadly around shared priorities for workforce development needs. For example, the prioritization of workforce development needs could stem from a goal of making St. Louis enterprises more globally competitive through the identification of the skills, training, and education necessary to do so. By establishing global competitiveness as the priority for workforce development, workforce development planning could achieve a higher priority among competing regional development issues and would allow it to move beyond its current isolation from other workforce-related systems and in more frequent and direct participation with business. Understanding the labor issues involved in increasing the competitiveness of St. Louis through improvements in human capital investment would require extensive research, but ultimately would offer a much wider range of benefits to the region and to regional participants. By framing workforce development as a means to greater global competitiveness, the prospects for deeper integration of the second chance system into regional growth policies would increase significantly.

A consensus on priority workforce development issues and shared ideas about how to plan should stem from a fuller and better understanding of both the supply and demand for labor within the St. Louis region. This understanding will only come from extensive ongoing research that involves the direct participation of business. This research will allow for the formulation of reforms and strategies that will become the basis of how workforce development planning will be defined and as a blueprint for assembling the resources and civic capacity to carry out specific plans. This research should focus on particular problem definitions as it relates to education, skills, and training required to meet demand and to provide a measurement of the dimensions of those problems. The resulting basic strategies for workforce development plans will be related to necessary funding resources, the participation of essential education and training institutions, and business. Strategies might include a prioritization of regional sectors and addressing them through an incremental approach.

A greater integration of the first and second chance systems of workforce development should be an essential feature of any redefinition of workforce development planning. Achieving greater global competitiveness should begin with the K–12 system and an integration of job readiness and labor force participation skills into its curriculum. It may also be necessary to change the emphasis of the first chance system on college preparation to a more broad-based emphasis on skills and workforce readiness. With only about one in three workers in the United States with college degrees, it is increasingly evident that not everyone has an interest or the motivation to attend and complete college degrees and therefore it is not a reasonable expectation for many workforce participants. While it remains evident that postsecondary education is crucial to supplying a large proportion of the skills necessary for a growing and productive economy, there is also a greater need to have institutions and entities that can provide workforce training and job readiness skills for those that are not on track to attend institutions of higher education. There is a significant portion of the school-age population that would benefit from more job readiness skills and non-college career planning.

The integration of the second chance system into a greater workforce development system would include collaboration with vocational and technical schools, two-year and community colleges, four-year colleges and universities, proprietary training schools, nonprofit training organizations and private sector training institutions. This integration of first and second chance systems should begin incrementally through the expansion of partnerships and collaborations centered on the workforce issues identified as essential to the region's vitality. The lessons of previous workforce development planning efforts that have attempted sweeping reforms in the absence of consensus of workforce development issues should preclude quixotic attempts at integrating fully the first and second chance systems. Rather, fuller integration should build through a series of smaller, incremental partnerships that encourage future and larger collaboration through experience and the creation of mutual trust. Once these collaborations have been established and have demonstrated a positive track record of producing labor outcomes, their future will hinge on the institutionalization of a mutual funding source. This funding might come from newly created sources or from existing sources that have been given revised legislative mandates or flexible spending guidelines. In either case, integration of workforce development organizations and systems will depend on long-term funding support.

The prospects for future workforce development planning that transcends past efforts and addresses a broader range of pressing workforce issues may be prompted by an increasing tightening of the labor market brought about by changing demographics and a continued decentralization of jobs and people within the region. An aging population and declining fertility rates will combine to produce an ever-tightening labor market as supply will decline relative to demand (Harris 2006, 122–146; Karoly and Panis 2004, 15–32). At the same time, the St. Louis region continues to experience minimal population growth while continuing to expand its land area, continuing a pattern of uneven development and distribution of jobs and workers (Laslo 2004, 4–5). These developments have prompted efforts in the past, such as the BTW and RJI, but were undone by missteps in the framing and organization of the efforts as noted previously. However, this pending tightening of the labor market may be more universal than the conditions that prompted previous efforts, and thus may provide the region with the common ground for addressing workforce development in a much more proactive and coordinated fashion. As changing demographics and the spatial distribution of people and jobs continues to transform the regional match of labor supply and demand, the region's economic future may hinge on its ability to develop a regional workforce development infrastructure that can respond more quickly and precisely to changing labor demand. Providing the regional labor force with the skills necessary to keep St. Louis companies competitive in a global context will begin with greater and fuller cooperation across the first and second chance systems and a consensus on who will need skills and training and how those critical skills will be provided.

References

Cummings, Scott, Allan Tomey, and Robert Flack. "Workforce Development Policy in the St. Louis Metropolitan Region: A Critical Overview and Assessment." In *Workforce Development Politics: Civic Capacity and Performance*, edited by Robert P. Giloth. Philadelphia: Temple University Press, 2004.

East-West Gateway Coordinating Council. Bridges-To-Work: Connecting Jobs and People. Annual report. St. Louis: Author, February 1995.

———. The St. Louis Regional Jobs Initiative: Strategic Investment Plan. St. Louis: Author, January 1996.

———. The St. Louis Regional Workforce Development Policy Planning: Mission Statement and Organizational Goals. St. Louis: Author, 1999.

Giloth, Robert P., ed. *Workforce Development Politics: Civic Capacity and Performance*. Philadelphia: Temple University Press, 2004.

Grubb, W. Norton. *Learning to Work: The Case for Reintegrating Job Training and Education*. New York: Russell Sage, 1996.

Harrison, Bennett, and Margaret Weiss. *Workforce Development Networks: Community-based Organizations and Regional Alliances*. Thousand Oaks, CA: Sage, 1998.

Jones, E. Terrence. *Fragmented by Design: Why St. Louis Has So Many Governments*. St. Louis: Palmerston & Reed, 2000.

Karoly, Lynn A., and Constantijn W. A. Panis. *The 21st Century at Work: Forces Shaping the Future Workforce and Workplace in the United States*. Santa Monica, CA: RAND Corporation, 2004.

Klein, Herbert S. "The U.S. Baby Bust in Historical Perspective." In *The Baby Bust: Who Will Do the Work? Who Will Pay the Taxes?* edited by Fred R. Harris. Lanham, MD: Rowman & Littlefield, 2006.

Lafer, Gordon. "The Politics of Job Training: Urban Poverty and the False Promise of JTPA." *Politics and Society* 22, no. 3 (September 1994): 349–388.

Laslo, David. "The St. Louis Region, 1950–2000: How We Have Changed." In *St. Louis Metromorphosis: Past Trends and Future Directions*, edited by Brady Baybeck and E. Terence Jones, 1–23. St. Louis: Missouri Historical Society Press, 2004.

Lynch, Lisa M., ed. *Training and the Private Sector.* Chicago: University of Chicago Press, 1994.

National Research Council. *The Changing Nature of Work: Implications for Occupational Analysis.* Washington, DC: National Academy, 1999.

O'Leary, Christopher J., Robert A. Straits, and Stephen A. Wandner. "U.S. Job Training: Types, Participants and History." In *Job Training Policy in the United States.* Kalamazoo, MI: W. E. Upjohn Institute for Employment Research, 2004.

St. Louis Economic Adjustment and Diversification Task Force. Comprehensive Economic Development Strategy. St. Louis Economic Adjustment and Diversification Program, 1991–1999. St. Louis: Author, August 1999.

Index

parking, 168

parks, 40, 139

population, 2, 10, 21, 36, 40, 44, 50, 58, 62, 64, 69, 86, 95, 105, 112, 114, 117–121, 132, 139, 143, 147, 151, 185, 187, 191, 193, 196, 201, 208, 217, 233, 239, 245, 277, 293, 299, 302, 305, 310–314, 320, 323, 331, 335, 337–348, 353, 355, 357, 359, 361, 368, 371, 374, 378, 380, 389, 395

Problems of St. Louis, 331

Professional Development School (PDS) project, 271

Quinn et al. v. Millsap et al., 73

rapid transit, 336–340, 347, 356–366

Regional Business Council (RBC), 323

Regional Commerce and Growth Association, 156, 248

Regional Housing and Community Development Alliance (RHCDA), 214

Regional Jobs Initiative, 388–390

Regional Parks Initiative, 216

RegionWise, 244

riverfront, 1–15, 21–26, 43, 46–51, 100, 173–174

roads, 90, 136–145, 148, 174, 344, 348–356

roads plan, 40–51

Roos, Lawrence K., 191

Saarinen, Eero, 12

Schoemehl, Mayor Vincent, 157, 176, 180

separation of St. Louis City and County, 55, 61

Slay, Mayor Francis, 163, 177, 322

Smith, Luther Ely, 3, 7–9, 12, 16, 19, 86, 92

social planning, 297–397

Soulard, 39, 92, 130, 131, 148

St. Louis, city planning, 17–53

St. Louis, county planning, 185–203

St. Louis 2004, 205–225, 310–311

St. Louis Civic League, 18

St. Louis Community Development Agency, 151

St. Louis Community Partnership. *See* Area Resources for Community and Human Services (ARCHS)

St. Louis Regional Planning Association, 341

St. Louis Regional Report Card, 314

St. Louis Regional Workforce Development Policy Group, 390–391

Standard Act, 146

Sustainable Neighborhoods Initiative, 213

About the Editor

Mark Tranel is the Director of the University of Missouri–St. Louis's Public Policy Research Center, as well as the Director for PPRC's Applied Research Division and Research Associate Professor of Public Policy Administration at UM–St. Louis. Over the past seventeen years, Dr. Tranel has been the principal investigator or research project manager on more than sixty applied research projects in the metropolitan St. Louis area. He has taught public administration in the UM–St. Louis Department of Political Science, as well as economic development at the Southern Illinois University–Edwardsville Department of Public Administration and Policy Analysis. He is an active participant in a number of housing and community development organizations, including the Board of Directors of North County, Inc., and the Missouri Budget Project. Prior to joining the staff at UM–St. Louis his experience included Director of Real Estate Development, Economic Council of St. Louis County, where he was responsible for industrial development sites and the small business incubator program, and Manager of Neighborhood Preservation and Community Planner, Normandy Municipal Council. He has contributed to such books as *Hidden Assets: Connecting the Past to the Future of St. Louis*, *Revitalizing the City: Strategies to Contain Sprawl and Revive the Core*, and *St. Louis Metromorphosis: Past Trends and Future Directions*.